John Elliott Cairnes

Essays in Political Economy

Theoretical and Applied

John Elliott Cairnes

Essays in Political Economy
Theoretical and Applied

ISBN/EAN: 9783337134082

Printed in Europe, USA, Canada, Australia, Japan

Cover: Foto ©Suzi / pixelio.de

More available books at **www.hansebooks.com**

ESSAYS.

ESSAYS

IN

POLITICAL ECONOMY

THEORETICAL AND APPLIED.

BY

J. E. CAIRNES, M.A.

Emeritus Professor of Political Economy in University College, London.

London:

MACMILLAN AND CO.

1873.

PREFACE.

THE following Essays have appeared in various periodicals at intervals in the course of the last fourteen years. They consist in part of attempts to apply the principles of economic science, as that science has been understood by the ablest writers in this country and in France, to the solution of actual problems, of which those presented by the Californian and Australian gold discoveries, and by the state of land tenure in Ireland, are the most important. So much of the volume may not improperly be described as Essays in Applied Political Economy. The remaining Essays deal mostly with topics of a theoretical kind; one—Political Economy and *Laissez-faire* — is expository of the character of economic science, and two—those on Comte and Bastiat—are critical and to some extent controversial. To two of the Essays relating to the Gold Question I have appended postscripts, in which the principal facts involved in the particular aspect of the movement treated in each are traced down to the present time. I have also in some instances subjoined notes, where later events have served to throw light on the questions discussed.

These remarks will sufficiently indicate the general character of the present volume. On one portion of its contents, however,—that which relates to the gold discoveries and their effects,—it has seemed to me that something further in the way of comment and elucidation would be desirable. The problem there discussed is one of which the practical solution is still in process of being worked out ; and since the papers which attempt to deal with it were written, a considerable period of time has elapsed, in which the movement forming the object of the inquiry has continued to unfold itself. Such an experience offers an opportunity of bringing the views therein advanced to the test of experiment. I venture to think that, fairly judged, they will be found capable of standing this test, and that in the main the anticipations formed respecting the course of wages and prices under the action of the new gold have been sustained by the event. But in order to apply the criterion fairly, the conditions under which the experiment has proceeded ought to be taken account of. I have therefore thought it well to prefix to this portion of the volume an introductory chapter, in which the subject is discussed from the advanced standpoint we have now attained, and the reader is furnished with the data requisite for a just estimate of the speculation.

I take this opportunity of acknowledging with thanks the courtesy of the proprietors of the several periodicals in which these Essays originally appeared in consenting to their re-appearance in the present form ; and, at the same time, I am anxious to express my deep obligations to my valued friend Professor Fawcett, at whose suggestion it was that they were collected, and by whose kind encouragement and effective aid I have profited largely in preparing them for the press.

J. E. C.

KIDBROOK PARK ROAD, S.E.

CONTENTS.

APPENDICES.

ESSAYS.

ESSAYS.

ESSAYS ON THE GOLD QUESTION.

INTRODUCTORY.

In submitting to the judgment of the public that portion of the present volume which relates to the economic aspects of the Gold Question, I am desirous at the outset to guard myself against two possible misapprehensions. In the first place I desire it to be understood that the question discussed in the Essays on that subject is, not the gold discoveries and their consequences, but the much narrower one involved in the economical effects of the increased supplies of gold. The two problems, though to some extent mutually implicated, are substantially distinct. To the one belongs the impulse given to the movement of population, which has resulted in the rapid peopling and definitive settlement of districts that without this stimulus might long have continued the slow and chequered career which up to that time had characterized their march, together with all the social and political consequences which have flowed from that

B

movement both in Europe and in the scenes of the discoveries; to the other, the effects resulting from the increased abundance of money on the industry and trade of nations and the fortunes of individuals : and it is to the solution of this latter problem alone that the Essays on the Gold Question are addressed. And, secondly, the reader will do me the favour to remember that the views expressed on the subject of the future of trade and price are to be understood, not as predictions of the actual course which events would take, but only as an attempt to forecast the directions in which that course would be modified by the increased supplies of gold; in other words, to trace the consequences which would result from this cause, supposing all other things to remain the same. The conditions of productive industry and the needs of human beings are constantly undergoing change, and, wholly irrespective of the increased supplies of money, a variety of powerful agencies have during the period under consideration been acting upon trade and prices. The actual course which the phenomena have taken, therefore, has not been the consequence of any single influence, such as that proceeding from the increased production of gold, but the composite result of the combined action of many; so that to judge of the operations of any particular cause it becomes necessary, as far as possible, to eliminate, and, in mercantile phrase, discount what is due to the action of other contemporaneous causes. These points being premised, I proceed to consider how far the views advanced in the Essays on the Gold Question have been

borne out by the test which an experience of some
fourteen years since they were written has furnished.

On one point the opinion alike of economists and
of the public seems now to be at one. It is now
generally agreed that within twenty years a substantial advance in general prices has taken place.
But beyond this general conviction there is little
accord. People differ as to the extent of the advance,
and as to its cause. The former point is one on
which the opinion of even the best informed statis-
tician cannot be regarded as more than conjecture.
The data for anything approaching to exactness in
such an estimate do not exist; and I shall certainly
not attempt now, as I have not attempted in what
I have formerly written, to offer any estimate pretending to exactness. I content myself with the
general admission that a substantial advance has
occurred, and that so far my anticipations have been
borne out by events. But prices having risen, to
what is the rise to be attributed? Here too, as I
have said, there is a divergence of opinion. Amongst
economists I think it is pretty well agreed that the
advance is, at least in large measure, due to the effects
of the gold discoveries. But, on the other hand, there
is, on the part of commercial writers, and in general
of all who view the question from the standpoint of
practical business, a strong disposition to ignore, or
altogether to deny, the influence of this cause in
determining the results. The enhanced scale of
wages and prices is not disputed, but it is referred
to such causes as "the recent great development of
trade," "changes in supply and demand," or "the

effect of strikes ;" and the facts seeming in each given
instance to be traceable to one or more of such influences, the incident of an increased abundance of gold
is regarded as something superfluous and irrelevant, and which need not be taken account of in
seeking their explanation.   Such a mode of argument,
however, I do not hesitate to say, implies a fundamental misconception as to the nature of the problem
to be solved.   For to show that an advance of prices
is connected with a development of trade,* with
changes in supply and demand, or with the action of
strikes, is not to prove that it is *not* due to the gold
discoveries.   An increased supply of money does not,
and cannot, act upon prices, or upon the value of the
metal composing it, in any other way than by being
made the instrument of trade, by affecting demand
and supply, or by furnishing employers with the
means and the motives for advancing the wages of
their workmen ; and, consequently, however clearly
the advance may be traceable in each given case to
an occurrence of this nature, the problem still lies
open : nothing has been done towards determining the
question whether the increased monetary supplies may
not have been an indispensable condition to the

---

* I may here remark that " a development of trade," which is so frequently assigned in explanation of a high *régime* of prices, not only is
inadequate in itself to explain this result, but, so far as it operates at all
upon general prices, tends to lower them, partly by cheapening the cost
of commodities, and partly by increasing their quantity ; for the effect of
having more commodities to exchange is to create an increased need
for circulating medium, which must, in the absence of an increased
supply, tend to raise its value—*i.e.* to lower prices.   In point of fact, the
increased development of trade since 1850 has been one of the causes
which has helped to neutralize to some extent the effects of the increased
supplies of gold.

realization of the advance. I have said the problem
still lies open; but in saying this I have conceded too
much. It sometimes happens that the proximate
occurrence to which the rise in price is referred is of
a kind which necessarily implies an increased supply
of money as the remote cause. I will illustrate my
meaning by an example. In the sixth volume of
the " History of Prices," * Mr. Newmarch had shown
that an advance of prices on an extensive scale had
taken place between 1851 and '56; and the question
arose, whether this was to be referred to the action
of the new supplies of gold. Mr. Newmarch decides
in the negative, on the ground that the results were
traceable to an increase in the demand for commodities
relatively to the supply; to an increase, that is to say,
in the demand for commodities in general, for nothing
less than this would suffice to explain the facts. Now
I maintain that, had Mr. Newmarch's object been to
establish the contradictory of the conclusion he had
in view, had he aimed to show that the high prices
then prevailing were the result of the increased money
supplies, no more effectual line of argument could
have been taken for this purpose than the one he has
adopted; for, putting aside the case of an increased
demand resting on an undue inflation of credit (undoubtedly one of the causes in operation in 1856,
though it is not referred to in Mr. Newmarch's explanation), an increase in the demand for commodities
relatively to the supply can mean nothing else than an
increase of *money* demand in relation to commodities;
and to show that prices generally have risen from this

* Pp. 224, 225.

cause is simply to show that money has become depreciated. Mr. Newmarch's argument, so far as he made his position good, was thus a complete demonstration of the monetary depreciation which it was his purpose to disprove.

And a nearly similar criticism may be made on that explanation which refers the high scale of prices to the effects of strikes. The argument commonly takes this form. The men, it is said, having enforced their demands for increased wages, their employers are obliged to raise the prices of their commodities in order to secure their profits. But this being equivalent to a withdrawal of a portion of the advance — since the same money no longer purchases the same goods—the workmen, to make good their position, strike again, and obtain a further advance, which is followed on the employer's part by a further rise in prices, and so the cycle is repeated. Such was the explanation offered a little time since in the leading columns of an influential journal. It did not occur to the writer, that, if the principle of his argument was sound, there is no reason why the upward movement in prices should ever stop. It is, however, beyond question that an advance in price has in some instances been established in the way described, that is to say through a successful strike issuing in a higher price for the commodity ; but those who have perceived this much, have failed to perceive what rendered this consummation possible. How has it happened that the capitalist producer has been enabled to maintain the advance in price urged on him by the action of his workmen ? In many instances the commodities so

raised in price are produced for foreign markets.
How comes it that our foreign customers acquiesce
in the demand ?   In the energetic competition which
English products have now to encounter on all sides,
why do they not rather turn to other markets, or
become producers of the commodity themselves ?
There are but two possible modes of explaining the
result : either prices in other markets have risen
proportionally with prices in our own, in which case
we have to consider whence comes the money which
supports those prices ; or money has become a cheaper
commodity with our foreign customers, so that they
find it more profitable to pay the increased price
demanded by the English producer, than to divert
their capital from its actual investment—an investment
which enables them, directly or indirectly, to procure
gold on those cheaper terms.   Adopt which hypothesis you please, and the same fact will in the end
confront you—an increased supply of money rendering
possible an advance in general prices, which, but for
this condition, could never have occurred.

I venture to lay down broadly this proposition, that,
when an advance in the price of any of the great staples of industry becomes definitive (monopoly apart),
there are two, and only two, adequate explanations
of the fact : either the cost of producing the article
(understanding by cost, not the money outlay, but
the real difficulties of production) has increased ; or
the cost of producing or obtaining money has diminished.   A change in supply and demand will indeed
produce temporary effects on prices, but apart from the
conditions just stated it is incapable of permanently

altering them. For example, the present high price
of coal is certainly due to an increased demand for
the commodity as its proximate cause;* but will this
high price become definitive? Only on one or other
or both of the conditions I have stated being satisfied.
If the increased demand can only be met by incurring
increased physical difficulties of production so great
as to need the present high rates to compensate them,
then the present rates will become the normal rates
for coal. Or again, the cost of producing coal remaining the same, if the present prices, in consequence
of the increased abundance of money, do not represent
a greater real cost than the lower prices of former
years, in this case too the present scale of prices will
be maintained. Or once more, if both these conditions
are partially satisfied,—if the real cost of producing
coal be raised in some degree, and the real cost of
obtaining money reduced in some degree,—on this
assumption also, the alterations in cost being sufficiently great, we should be justified in expecting a
continuance of present rates. It thus appears that
the question of an advance in price, where the advance becomes established and normal, is in all cases
(monopoly apart) a question of cost of production : it
is due either to an increased cost of producing the
commodities, or to a diminished cost of producing or
obtaining money, or to a combination of both these
conditions. All explanations which fail to trace the

---

* The two latest returns of the quantity raised, Professor Jevons informs
me, are as follows :—

1870.   110,430,000 tons.

1871.   117,439,000   „

phenomenon to one or other, or to some combination of
these, are of the kind which would place the earth upon
an elephant, and the elephant on a tortoise, leaving
the tortoise to find his footing as best he may.

The doctrine advanced in the following Essays not
merely asserts a prospective depreciation of gold as a
consequence of the gold discoveries, but attempts to
state the *modus operandi* of depreciation ; in other
words, the order of advance by which the ultimate
higher level of prices would be reached. At the time
the Essays were written, the opinion was nearly
universal, and indeed it would seem still to be far
from extinct, that a depreciation of money could only
show itself in a uniform action upon all prices—not,
I presume, that it was supposed that the prices of all
commodities would necessarily advance *pari passu*, but
that, in so far as they were affected by the increase
of money, this would be the nature of their progress ;
and, accordingly, no such uniform movement being discoverable in the actual phenomena, it was invariably
concluded that such enhancement of price as was
found to exist must be due to some other cause than
the increased supplies of gold. This view I ventured
to combat ; and, as just intimated, not content with
recording a mere general denial of the current doctrine,
and with asserting a definitive depreciation of gold as
even then accomplished, I attempted further to state
the mode and order in which the monetary movement,
as it proceeded, would be developed. As regards
the first portion of my thesis, I need not hesitate now
to say that it has been fully verified by events. A

general rise of prices has admittedly occurred; but in this general advance there are no traces of that uniformity in the march which the prevailing view anticipated. What has happened has been a great rise in the prices of some commodities, a more moderate rise in those of others, in the case of some a very slight rise or none at all. Further, up to a certain point, I am entitled to claim a substantial verification of the views I put forward as to the order of the advance of prices. For example, I had said that, resolving commodities in general into the two grand classes of crude products and manufactured goods, the rise in price would be more rapid in the former than in the latter class; while, as amongst commodities of the former class, I asserted that animal products would advance more rapidly than those of vegetable growth. Now I think I shall not need to go into details to prove that, speaking broadly, this has in fact been the course which prices have followed. The articles of which the advance in price has been most marked have been such as butcher's meat, butter, bacon, and other provisions of the animal kind. Mineral products and agricultural products of the vegetable kind have come next in order; while manufactured goods, unless where, as in the case of cotton, the raw material has been affected by causes of a very exceptional nature, have shared but slightly in the upward movement, or not at all. So far, I say, I can claim for the views advanced a substantial verification from the course of events. With regard, however, to that part of my speculation which attempted

to describe the order of the movement in prices
as it would be felt in different countries, only a
more qualified claim to verification can be advanced.
Not that I am disposed to make any retractation as
regards the economic principles on which the speculation rests : so far as I am aware, the tenor of events
has only tended to corroborate and fortify these ; but
in some instances, the action of the cause I was in-
vestigating has been overborne by influences of a
violently disturbing kind, not foreseen at the time the
Essays were written, and of course, therefore, not
taken account of in my speculation. This has been
especially the case with what I have said respecting
the probable course of prices in the United States
and in India. The civil war in the former country
causing a sudden cessation in the supply of cotton,
and leading to a large increase of taxation and to
the issue of an inconvertible paper currency, operated
powerfully upon the whole course of commercial and
monetary affairs ; nor was its influence by any means
confined to the immediate scene of its occurrence.
Its effect in the United States was to accelerate
powerfully the upward movement of prices, already
sufficiently marked,* not merely as measured in the
depreciated paper currency, but as measured in gold ;
for the enlarged issue of paper currency had the
effect of setting free a large quantity of gold formerly
required for the maintenance of cash payments ; and
the increased taxation, so far as it fell upon commodities, acted on prices directly in proportion to its
amount. The result has been that prices in the

* See Appendix G.

United States, instead of advancing, as I expected would happen, nearly *pari passu* with prices in England, have progressed with much greater rapidity.* On the other hand, the civil war in the United States caused a large diversion of the demand for cotton from that country to India. This would of course lead to an increase of specie remittances to the latter country; and other causes, more particularly a sudden development of railway enterprise, resulting in an investment of upwards of 60,000,000*l.* sterling, acted powerfully in the same direction. At the same time, while gold and silver were thus pouring into India in an exceptionally large stream, the credit system of the country was, by the establishment of numerous banks of issue and deposit, undergoing rapid extension. All these occurrences have conspired to give an impulse to the movement of prices in India, far beyond what it was possible to anticipate fourteen years ago. Accordingly, the exceptional slowness, which I was led to expect would characterize the advance of prices in Asiatic countries, has certainly, so far as India is concerned, not been realized. At the same time I am not prepared to admit, even as regards India, that the deviation from the course I had ventured to trace is by any means as great as the round assertions frequently made about Indian prices would seem to imply. These assertions may be true, so far as they go; but India, it must be remembered, is a country of vast extent; the means of communication over the greater part of it are still very imperfect; and, consequently, the

* See Mr. Wells' Reports.

widest discrepancies in the scale of prices prevail in different districts. Some interesting evidence of this will be found in Mr. Ollerenshaw's paper on "The Export Trade in Cotton to India" (Manchester Statistical Society, April 1870), in which he remarks that, "even in the same presidencies, prices have been in one place double those in another, and that this is not exceptional, but constant." And I find in Mr. Brassey's recent work the following striking differences in the rates of wages recorded as prevailing in Bombay and Bengal :*—

	In Bengal per month. Rupees.				In Bombay per month. Rupees.
Carpenters . . .	9	.	.	.	25
Masons . . .	$5\frac{5}{16}$	.	.	.	21
Labouring Coolies .	6	.	.	.	$9\frac{10}{18}$
Horse-keepers . .	5	.	.	.	$8\frac{9}{16}$

I believe the truth to be that a great advance in wages and prices has taken place in and around particular localities; for example, the cotton districts north and east of Bombay, and in general wherever railway or public works are being carried on. The reports which come to us in this country respecting Indian prices are derived mostly, if not entirely, from observation of what is taking place in those districts; but that the state of things in those favoured centres of activity is no safe criterion of the general condition of prices throughout India, we need only refer to the prices of her leading staples in the great commercial markets to satisfy ourselves. Of these a considerable number, including Rice, Sugar, Tea, Rum, and Sago,

* " Work and Wages," p. 60.

have positively fallen since 1850; while of the rest, though a few, such as cotton and hemp, that have been subject to exceptional influences, have risen very greatly, the larger portion show but a moderate advance.* I may here add that I have been not a little fortified in my conviction of the essential soundness of the view which I took as to the bearing of the increased money supplies upon the relation of prices in Europe and in the East, by the remarkable corroboration which that view has since received from the independent investigations of my friend Professor Jevons. In a paper read before the London Statistical Society in 1865,† Professor Jevons showed, in an elaborate series of tables, not only that the course of Oriental and European prices down to that year had in the main been coincident with the course foreshadowed in my essay, but that a similar phenomenon—namely, a divergence of prices as between Europe and tropical countries—had manifested itself in the early part of the present century, when various causes—partly economical and partly political—had led to a temporary redundancy of the precious metals in Europe. In a word, it appears from Professor Jevons' investigations that, on two distinct occasion within the present century, an exceptional abundance of the precious metals was followed by the same results—those results being what theory applied to the facts had led me to anticipate.

Another incident which I was led to expect would

* I am indebted for these facts to information kindly furnished me by Professor Jevons.

† See London Statistical Society's Journal for 1865.

accompany the course of monetary depreciation was a
more rapid advance of prices and rates of wages in
England than on the Continent of Europe.   In effect
I had placed the Continent, as regards the order of
advance in prices, in an intermediate position between
England and the United States on the one hand, and
Asiatic countries on the other.   In the main I believe
the results have been in accordance with my forecast ;
though it would seem that the general coincidence has
not been without some serious exceptions.   As I
learn from Mr. Brassey's work, just referred to, the
rates of wages in the engineering trades and other
branches of industry which minister to railway construction have, within twenty years, risen much more
rapidly in France and Germany than with us ; and,
what is a noteworthy feature of the phenomenon,
while these particular industries are those in which the
rise in wages has been greatest on the Continent, they
are those in which it has been least in this country ;
indeed, it appears from Mr. Brassey's tables that in
some of those trades no sensible advance at all had
been established in England up to 1869,* though I
apprehend the case would be different if the figures
were carried on to the present year.   Both facts—
the exceptional rapidity of the rise in engineering
and other ancillary trades on the Continent, and
the exceptional slowness of their advance here—are,

---

* "Work and Wages," p. 157.   It is pertinent to my purpose to
observe that Mr. Brassey's tables commence with 1854—three years,
that is to say, after the occurrence of the gold discoveries, and when that
ascending movement in wages and prices which culminated in 1857 had
already made considerable progress.

I have no doubt, mainly due to the cause to which
Mr. Brassey assigns them. " The real explanation is
to be found in the circumstance that, as the railway
system was first established in this country, so we
were the first in the field as locomotive engine
builders " (p. 192) ;—that is to say, in the period
between 1840 and '50 England had a practical
monopoly of the engineering business of the world.
" The science of building locomotives was an occult
science on the Continent ;" and during the period of
Continental apprenticeship which followed, the rates of
pay in that calling would naturally be low.   But as
skill and knowledge were acquired with experience, a
portion of the world's demand was naturally transferred from us to them.   It necessarily followed that
engineering wages suffered abatement here just as
they were beginning to advance abroad, and the
impulse then given has not yet spent itself.   I may
add to Mr. Brassey's explanation, that a succession of
great wars on the Continent during the period under
review must have brought into special and exceptional requisition the products of engineering skill ;
and this, I have no doubt, has also contributed to the
result we are considering.   It has thus happened,
comparing the Continent with England, that the movement in wages in the callings in question has been in
opposite directions in relation to the general movement
of prices.   It has shot in advance there while here it
has lagged behind.   If, however, we have regard, not
to particular employments, but to the general progress
of industry here and abroad, I think it will be found
that the evidence goes on the whole to support the

view which I had advanced. I rest this opinion chiefly on the general tenor of the reports from our agents in foreign countries, published in the early part of this year. Taking these reports as a whole, they seem to me to speak in that sense. But I think the same conclusion may be deduced from facts furnished by Mr. Brassey, though it would seem that his own opinion favours the opposite view. For example, I find it stated (pp. 18, 19) that "inquiries in Spain and France, Belgium and Prussia, show that pro-visions in those countries are from 20 to 30 per cent. dearer than twenty years ago." Now, though I do not pretend to have gone of late minutely into the question, I will venture to assert that the advance in the prices of provisions in England during the same time has been very considerably greater than this. To take a few important items, I find that, comparing 1851 with the present year, the advance in the price of mutton has been 58 per cent.; of beef, 68 per cent.; of butter, 42 per cent.; of bacon, 60 per cent.* And I have little doubt that, omitting the article of flour (the movements in which since 1851 have been substantially uniform over Western Europe), the less important articles of provisions, such as potatoes, poultry, cheese, fresh vegetables, &c., have experienced a rise little, if at all, short of that shown by these figures. Accepting then Mr. Brassey's state-ment as to the advance in the prices of this class of articles in the leading Continental countries, I am justified in saying that the rise has been considerably greater here than there. But this fact, duly weighed,

---

* See *Economist.* Prices current for those years.

will be found to go far to decide the whole question;
for, if we consider what the commodities are in which
a serious deviation of local prices from the common
standard is possible, we shall find that, with the exception of houses, they consist mainly of provisions.
Of dry goods and articles of general manufacture—of
all commodities, in a word, not quickly perishable
and easily portable—the prices in different European
countries, allowance being made for the effect of tariffs,
will, as a rule, not differ by more than the cost of
carriage between the compared localities. A more
rapid advance, therefore, in the price of provisions
in England than on the Continent, means a more
rapid advance of local prices here than there. And
it means more than this. The great consumers of
provisions are the masses, whose expenditure it is
that must in the main determine for this class of goods
the fluctuations of price. Where, therefore, the prices
of provisions have in a given period advanced more
rapidly in one country than in another, the reasonable
inference is that the movement in prices has been
preceded by a parallel or nearly parallel movement in
wages.

On no other hypothesis, so far as I can see, is the
phenomenon explicable. I am inclined, therefore, notwithstanding the evidence Mr. Brassey has brought
forward of a more rapid rise of wages in engineering
and kindred trades abroad than with us, to abide by
the view taken in the Essays. Comparing prices and
wages here and on the Continent of Europe, and
making allowance for disturbing causes, they appear,
on the whole, to have progressed, under the influence

of the increased supplies of money, much as I
ventured to predict they would progress; that is
to say, they have advanced more rapidly here than
there. Such at least seems to me to be the tenor
of the evidence down to the present time.

With these remarks I now submit these speculations to the judgment of the reader.

ESSAY TOWARDS A SOLUTION OF THE GOLD QUESTION.

*THE AUSTRALIAN EPISODE.**

In the discussions which have taken place respecting the probable consequences of the Californian and Australian gold discoveries, there is a branch of the general question which has not yet received from economists that degree of attention, to which from its scientific importance it seems to be entitled. I allude to the effects produced by those events in the countries which have been the scene of their occurrence. In the great world of commerce, the action of the new money for the most part escapes notice amid the variety and complexity of the phenomena in which it is involved. The area over which the increasing supplies have to act is immense, the extraneous incidents affecting the course of their diffusion are numerous, and the real tendency of the movement is thus in these cosmopolitan transactions not easily discoverable. But within the more limited sphere of the auriferous countries this is not the case. The gold

* *Frazer's Magazine*, September 1859.

discoveries have there been the predominant influence, and being less controlled by circumstances, the real character of the new agencies and the results to which they are leading come distinctly and prominently into view. California and Australia, during the period of their auriferous history, furnish us with what Bacon would call "an ostensive or predominant instance" of the action of such agencies, showing their nature (to borrow his language) "naked and palpable, and even in its exaltation, or in the highest degree of its power—that is to say, emancipated or freed from impediments, or at least, by force of its native energy, dominating over these, suppressing and coercing them." * Hence, by studying the effects of the gold discoveries in these countries, we may gain a clearer and steadier view of the real nature of the causes which are at work than we are likely to obtain from the more extended and complicated transactions of general commerce. By tracing the events which are there presented, we may be guided to conclusions which (if the illustration be allowed) may serve as a sort of economic chart of the new monetary influences—a chart which, though it may be drawn upon an exaggerated scale, will all the more clearly indicate the true direction of the currents, and the ultimate goal whither they are bearing us.

With this view, I propose in the following paper to examine the effects of the gold discoveries in Australia on its trade, industry, and pecuniary relations. The course of events in California during its auriferous history has been extremely similar, and the

* " Novum Organon," Lib. ii. Aph. 24.

description of the movement in the former country will in its main features be found applicable to the latter.

Regarded in its economic aspects, the discovery of gold in Australia may be thus briefly described : It was an occurrence by which a common labourer was enabled, by means of a simple process requiring for its performance little capital or skill, to obtain about a quarter of an ounce of gold—in value about £1 sterling—on an average in the day.* This is the fundamental fact from which the remarkable series of events which we have lately been contemplating took its rise, and to which the whole movement following upon the gold discoveries is ultimately traceable. The immediate effect was a general disorganization of industry throughout the Australian colonies. The ordinary pursuits of the place were for a time entirely suspended ; and the imaginations and hopes of the community outstripping even the marvellous realities of the case, the whole industrial population rushed as by a single impulse to the gold-fields. The gold fever, however, in this its first and full intensity, was not of long duration. Actual trial soon reduced the extravagant expectations raised by the first announcements to a more sober and correct appreciation of the true conditions of the discovery. Those who had overrated the gain, as well as those whose constitution and habits unfitted them for the toils and exposure of gold-digging, and who did not fall victims to their mistake, returned after a short trial to their former occupations. The extraordinary excitement subsided ;

* "Correspondence relative to the late Discoveries of Gold in Australia." Presented to Parliament, February 1852. Pages 32, 51.

but in the meantime a change had taken place in the
conditions of Australian industry, a new and vigorous
branch of production had struck root, overshadowing
all the old occupations of the country and entirely
superseding many of them, and a new monetary
régime had been inaugurated.

The immediate result of the change was a general
rise of money wages throughout the country. Formerly the wages of common labour in Australia had
ranged from 3s. to 5s. a day. The same labour was
now, by washing the auriferous sand, capable of
producing gold worth 20s. a day. It followed as a
necessary consequence that, other things being equal,
hired labourers would not work for less. Other things
indeed were not equal. The toil of gold-digging was
severe, its results were precarious, and the further the
removal from the coast the higher was the price of
provisions. All these circumstances influenced wages
in different occupations and in different localities;
but, making allowance for these, the standard of
pecuniary remuneration in Australia was henceforth
the rate of earnings on the gold-fields.

During the two years immediately following the
first discoveries, this standard continued at the high
point above indicated—namely, about a quarter of
an ounce of gold per man each day, equal to about
£1 sterling; but towards the close of 1853 a great
decline in the proceeds of gold-digging took place.
The cream of the richest auriferous deposits had by
this time been skimmed away; and it was henceforth
necessary to dig deeper for materials which, when
reached, proved of inferior quality. The Commis-

sioners appointed in the following year to report on
the gold-fields accordingly describe a great falling off at
this time from the richness of the early returns; * and
although many new gold-fields have since been opened
the high average standard of the early discoveries has
not again been reached.† During the two years just
passed (1857 and 1858), the rate of gold earnings per
man has not exceeded on an average ten shillings
a day—a decline of one-half from the early returns.
On the whole, we may say that during the first and
most productive period of gold-digging, the standard
of money wages in Australia rose in rather more than
a fourfold proportion as compared with the pre-gold
times, and that during the last five years this proportion has been reduced by one-half; so that money
wages in Australia are at the present time (1859) rather
more than double those which formerly prevailed.‡

But this rise in the pecuniary remuneration of the
labourer involved further consequences. The Australian employer could not continue to pay quadruple
or double rates to his workmen while the commodities
which he sold remained at their former price. In
order to the maintenance of his profit, it was necessary that the price of Australian productions should
rise in proportion as wages had risen; and this
result accordingly followed in due course.§

---

* "Further Papers relative to the Discovery of Gold in Australia."
Presented to Parliament, February 1856. Page 55.

† Westgarth's "Victoria" (1857), p. 171.

‡ Ibid. p. 150. [Since 1859 the rates, with occasional variations, have
on the whole slightly declined, following the course of gold production
(1872).]

§ As to the connection between wages and prices when money is
falling in value, see *post*, pp. 58–60, and note * to latter.

The advance, however, in money wages and prices which these circumstances necessitated, though rapid, was not instantaneous.* For more than a year after the gold discoveries had occurred, it was held sensibly in check by the peculiar state of the local currencies. For there was at this time no mint in Australia; the increased requirements for coin could only be met by a transmission of bullion to London, there to be coined, and afterwards re-imported; and this process required from six to eight months at the least for its accomplishment. Pending the arrival of the new coins, prices were not indeed prevented absolutely from rising; for numerous expedients were in their absence freely resorted to for supplying the place of the ordinary currency; † but nevertheless prices were, by the straitness of the circulation, kept very considerably under their natural level, as determined by the cost of gold,—a fact which was sufficiently proved by a remarkable fall in the price of gold throughout the whole of this period.‡ The arrival, however, of sovereigns in large quantities from England, in the winter of 1852–53, quickly put an end to this exceptional state of the markets. The price of gold, and with it the prices of other things, rose to their natural level; and pecuniary rates generally throughout the country were brought permanently

---

* See the Table of Prices contained in Mr. Westgarth's "Address to the Melbourne Chambers of Council," given in the Appendix to his "Victoria, or Australia Felix." 1853.

† Of which expedients the passing of the Bullion Act by the Government of South Australia was the most important.

‡ A fall from £3 17s. 10½d. per ounce, the London Mint price, to 60s., 50s., and, it is stated, in some instances to 40s. per ounce. See the Appendix to Westgarth's "Victoria, or Australia Felix." 1853.

into conformity with the new conditions of producing gold.

But the advance in general prices, which was thus easily and rapidly effected within the limited area of the gold districts, could by no means be accomplished with the same facility amongst the great commercial populations of the world. The disturbance of industrial pursuits in the larger theatre, though resulting in an extensive emigration, was yet, in comparison with the general business of the world, inconsiderable, while the supply of gold required, in order to render possible a fall in its value over so large an area of transactions, was immense. The necessary conditions, therefore, to a rise in general prices not being susceptible of speedy fulfilment, money rates throughout the world at large did not, and could not, advance with the same rapidity with which they advanced in the gold countries. A divergence of local prices and rates in Australia from the general level of commercial countries has been the necessary consequence,— a divergence which has altered fundamentally her commercial position in relation to the rest of the world, and has been followed by a series of changes in her domestic industry and foreign trade which I shall now attempt to describe.

The great staple industry of Australia has, from an early period in the history of the colony, been her cattle-farming; the advantages which the country possesses for this pursuit in her extensive open plains, covered with rich natural grass, being unsurpassed in any part of the world. The fruits of this industry are the usual pastoral products, of which butcher's meat,

wool, and tallow are the principal. Until the occurrence of the remarkable events we are considering,
the two latter of these constituted the leading commodities of the foreign trade of the country. For the
former—butcher's meat—as it was unfit for a distant
traffic, she was compelled to trust for a market to the
local population, which being extremely limited, the
supply of meat was with difficulty disposed of, and
the article was consequently often a drug in the
colonial markets. The difficulty, however, thence
arising to the pastoral interest, was met by the conversion of a large portion of their meat into tallow,
and by the starting of an export trade in this commodity. By this means the several branches of trade
connected with pastoral farming in Australia were
placed upon a sound foundation, and by the beginning
of 1851 they were in a highly flourishing condition.
But in the summer of that year the gold discoveries
occurred, and the consequences which have ensued
in this leading department of her industry have been
not a little remarkable.

On the first outbreak of the gold mania in 1851,
the pastoral interest was subjected to the same inconvenience which was felt by all other occupations in
Australia. The minds of shepherds and shearers were
not proof to the attractions which had acted so powerfully on workmen in every other walk of industry, and
the " squatting " stations were for a time abandoned for
the more enticing pursuits of the gold-fields. As the
only means of obtaining the requisite supply of labour,
the squatters were obliged to submit to the same
advance in wages which at this time took place in all

other occupations. But, as has been pointed out, a rise in money wages requires (if profits are to be maintained) a corresponding rise in the price of the commodities which the more highly-priced labour produces. This necessary rise was effected without difficulty in articles produced in Australia for domestic consumption; but the chief product of the pastoral industry was wool, and the chief market for wool was Europe, in which a fourfold or a twofold rise in price—such a rise, that is to say, as would have indemnified the Australian farmer for the advance in his labour rates—was simply impossible, or at the least could only have been obtained by a curtailment of supply, which, as Europe had other resources for this material besides the Australian sheep farms, it was not in the power of Australia to effect. On the news, therefore, of the gold discoveries reaching this country, great alarm was felt for the stability of this trade. Mr. Lalor, in his work on "Money and Morals," strongly urged upon Government the duty of assisting the emigration of shepherds, with a view to supply the necessary labour. But supposing this were done, what security was there that the emigrating shepherds would not follow their predecessors to the gold-fields? In truth the wool trade was at this time in serious jeopardy. It has been saved from the danger that was impending through a circumstance which, in the first excitement of the movement, escaped the attention of observers—through the influence, namely, which the same event that endangered the supply of wool has exercised on other branches of the industry to which wool belongs. The immense

immigration which followed the gold discoveries created a sudden demand for butcher's meat; a more
than quadruple rise in the price of meat in Australia
has been the consequence,—a rise which has covered
the increased outlay on sheep-farming, thus providing
the necessary inducement for the continuance of the
supply of sheep, and therefore of wool. The wool
trade of Australia has thus been preserved from
extinction; but it is important to observe that it
is now upon a different footing from that on which
it formerly stood. Previous to the gold discoveries,
while wool formed the leading product of pastoral
industry, the extension of sheep-farming depended
principally on the extension of the demand, chiefly
in Europe, for this article. But since that event,
wool has, in the calculation of the farmer's profits,
become subordinate to meat, which is now the
great support and mainstay of his trade. The progress of pastoral farming will therefore in future be
governed, not by the requirements of Europe for wool,
but by those of Australia for meat,—in other words,
by the increase of the colonial population; and as this
cannot be expected to keep pace with the general
demand for wool, a falling off in the rate of increase
at which this branch of industry was formerly pro-
gressing may accordingly be looked for; indeed, the
decline has already become very apparent.*

So far as to the pastoral industry of Australia.
Let us now trace the influence of the gold discoveries

* See Westgarth's "Victoria" (1857), p. 118; and "Statistical Abstract
of the United Kingdom" (1858), p. 17. [Since this was written, the trade
in preserved meats has sprung up, and this will of course enlarge, and
already has perceptibly enlarged, the limits of the wool production (1872).]

upon the occupation which, along with pastoral pursuits, forms in general the principal resource of young communities—agriculture.

If we are to accept the very high authority of Humboldt, the discovery of the Australian gold-fields should rather assist than hinder the progress of its agriculture. In his " Political Essay upon the Kingdom of New Spain," that eminent writer thus observes :—

" It cannot be doubted that, under improved social institutions, the countries which most abound with mineral productions will be as well if not better cultivated than those in which no such productions are to be found. But the desire natural to man of simplifying the causes of everything has introduced into works on political economy a species of reasoning which is perpetuated because it flatters the mental indolence of the multitude. The depopulation of Spanish America, the state of neglect in which the most fertile lands are found, and the want of manufacturing industry, are attributed to the metallic wealth, to the abundance of gold and silver ; as, according to the same logic, all the evils of Spain are attributed to the discovery of America, or the wandering race of the Merinos, or the religious intolerance of the clergy !

" We do not observe that agriculture is more neglected in Peru than in the province of Cumana or Gugana, in which, however, there are no mines worked. In Mexico the best cultivated fields, those which recall to the mind of the traveller the beautiful plains of France, are those which extend from Salamanca towards Silao, Guanaxuato, and the Villa de Leon, and which surround the richest mines of the known world. Wherever metallic seams have been discovered in the most uncultivated parts of the Cordilleras, on the isolated and desert table lands, the working of mines, far from impeding the cultivation of the soil, has been singularly favourable to it. Travelling along the ridge of the Andes, or the mountainous parts of Mexico, we everywhere

see the most striking examples of the beneficial influence
of the mines on agriculture. Were it not for the establishments formed for the working of the mines, how many places
would have remained desert? how many districts uncultivated
in the four intendancies of Guanaxuato, Zacatecas, San Luis
Potosi, and Durango, between the parallels of 21° and 25°,
where the most considerable metallic wealth of New Spain
is to be found? If the town is placed on the arid side or
the crest of the Cordilleras, the new colonists can only draw
from a distance the means of their subsistence and the maintenance of the great number of cattle employed in drawing
off the water, and raising and amalgamating the mineral
produce. Want soon wakens industry. The soil begins to
be cultivated in the various ravines and declivities of the
neighbouring mountains wherever the rock is covered with
earth. Farms are established in the neighbourhood of the
mine. The high price of provisions, from the competition
of the purchasers, indemnifies the cultivator for the privations
to which he is exposed from the hard life of the mountains.
Thus from the hope of gain alone, and the motives of mutual
interest, which are the most powerful bonds of society, and
without any interference on the part of the Government in
colonization, a mine, which at first appeared insulated in
the midst of wild and desert mountains, becomes in a short
time connected with the lands which have long been under
cultivation." *

It seems unquestionable that, in the manner described by Humboldt in the above passage, a discovery of the precious metals, by attracting people
to a locality otherwise undesirable, or of which the
other recommendations were previously unknown, may
hasten the progress of agriculture over the earth, or
may lead to the cultivation of districts which, but for
such discoveries, might for ever have remained barren ;

* Vol. ii. pp. 405-8.

nor will anyone dispute the opinion of so competent a witness that the neglect of agriculture in some of the States of Spanish America was due in a large degree to defects in their social institutions ; but, accepting thus far the opinion of Humboldt, I yet venture to question the doctrine (for to this length does the passage I have quoted seem to go) that, speaking with reference to a country *in which occupation has been effected and society established*, the possession of mineral treasures is favourable, or can be otherwise than un-favourable, to the cultivation of the soil.   It is one of the best established principles of economic science— the principle on which the whole theory of foreign trade is based—that the possession by a country of any extraordinary advantage in production operates, in proportion to the extent of the advantage, as a premium against all other industrial pursuits.   And the grounds of the principle are sufficiently obvious ; for the possession of exceptional facilities in production makes it clearly the interest of the country which enjoys them to satisfy its wants for other things, rather through the medium of an exchange with other nations of the article to which such special facilities apply, than by the direct production of commodities in raising which the country has no special advantage.   And this being the general principle which regulates foreign exchange, it is one which, from their portability and the universality of the demand for them, applies to the precious metals in an especial degree.   I therefore find it impossible to believe that the mineral resources of the Spanish American States did not exercise on these countries an influence prejudicial to the progress of their agriculture, and that these were not among the causes which contributed to that backward state of cultivation which Humboldt notices and describes.

And this conclusion is entirely confirmed by the recent experience of Australia. It is not indeed contended that the discovery of mineral treasures in that country has not given an impulse to cultivation by hastening its general settlement, in the same manner as in the metalliferous districts of America. What I contend for is, that, the country being once occupied and settled, the presence of rich gold-fields must operate unfavourably upon its agriculture, or, to put the same point differently, that the area of cultivation, under the influence of this cause, will be confined within limits short of those which it would have attained, had the community reached the same stage of advance under different economic conditions; and this, I think, is sufficiently proved by the recent history of Australia,—a history which exhibits the strange, and I believe unprecedented, spectacle of a country, possessing an immense unoccupied territory, and a soil of more than average fertility, importing more than one-half its food.*

I am quite aware, indeed, that other causes besides the gold discoveries are responsible for the past history of agriculture in Australia—more particularly a land system contrived with singular ingenuity to cramp and pervert the natural development of the country. But injurious in many respects as may have been, and may still be, the operation of this system,—amongst others, in excluding from the possession of land, and in fact

* The *Times* (Melbourne Correspondent), February 3rd, 1858.

driving from the colony, a class of small proprietors whom on social grounds it would be most desirable to retain,—it can scarcely be maintained that this is at present the principal cause of the failure of Australian agriculture, when we find that of the land which has been sold only a small portion has been brought under actual cultivation.* If the quantity offered in the market is insufficient for the agricultural wants of the country, this circumstance would only give an increased value for this purpose to the land which *has* been sold ; and yet the greater portion of this remains as yet untilled. It appears to me that this state of things can only be explained by reference to other causes than the restraints of the land system ; and what these causes are our former reasonings sufficiently indicate. Obviously they are to be found in the new money *régime* introduced by the gold discoveries. The high rate of wages thus established, being peculiar to the gold countries, places the Australian farmer, in common with other employers of Australian labour, under an exceptional disadvantage in competing in the markets of the world, and compels him, therefore, to confine cultivation to soils in which the superior richness of the natural agent compensates the cultivator for the high pecuniary charges with which he has to contend. It is thus that the gold-fields of Australia present a barrier to the development of its agricultural resources —a barrier which, after all the restrictions of the land system are removed, must continue to operate, and

---

* Westgarth's "Victoria" (1857), p. 81. Further Papers, &c., February 1856, p. 33. *Australian and New Zealand Gazette*, December 11th, 1858, p. 568.

which will probably for many years to come render its richest provinces a drain upon the subsistence of over-peopled Europe, instead of what under happier conditions they might become,—liberal contributors towards our already heavily-tasked resources.

Against this reasoning it will perhaps be urged that agriculture has made considerable progress in California, which has already become an exporter of food. This is true, and is a striking proof of the fact to which every traveller in that country has borne testimony, the extraordinary fertility of the Californian soils,—a fertility which enables agriculture to hold its own even against the competition of the gold mines. The fact, however, in no degree invalidates the principle above stated; it only proves that California enjoys over other countries an advantage in raising food, up to a certain point, *as great as she enjoys in obtaining gold.*

The extension of agriculture in Australia has thus, though stimulated for the moment, suffered a real check from the gold discoveries ; and the same influence has been felt throughout every branch of industry in that country, gold mining alone excepted. The premium which has operated against sheep-farming and tillage has operated against all other industrial pursuits. Many districts in the northern portion of New South Wales are represented as favourable to the growth of cotton. " In Moreton Bay," says a colonial writer, " the cotton-tree grows most luxuriantly, and appears more inclined to assume a perennial form than in even the most favoured districts of America. But," he adds, " up to the present time the cost [price] of cultivation has been found too high to make the business of cotton-growing profitable." Tin and antimony, we are told by another authority, abound in many parts of Victoria. Some of the richest tin ores in the Ovens districts have, it seems, been worked to some profit; but although antimony ore "appears to be unlimited in quantity," "the value in the home market [more properly the price of raising it in Australia] will not admit of its being touched as yet by the eager fingers of com- merce." * Such has been the effect on the industry of raw produce; and in manufacturing industry the influence of the gold discoveries has been still more complete and sweeping, nothing in the nature of a manufactured product, even of the coarsest kind, being now made in the colony, which can by any possibility be imported.†

As a proof of the soundness of our economic know- ledge, it is interesting to observe that all this has happened in strict conformity with the established principles of economic science. According to these principles, the exchange of commodities among differ- ent nations is regulated, not by the absolute, but by the comparative, cost of the commodities exchanged‡— not by the circumstance that the commodity imported

---

* Westgarth's "Victoria" (1857), pp. 112-13.

† "We all wear imported boots and shoes," says the *Times'* Corres- pondent, "and it is cheaper to buy new than to get the old mended."

‡ See chapter on "Foreign Trade," Ricardo's Works, pp. 76-7; also Mill's "Principles of Political Economy," Book III. chap. xvii. The reader must observe that by "cost" is meant the *real difficulty* involved in the production of a commodity, *not the amount of money* necessary to remunerate the labour by which this difficulty is overcome. The only commodity of which the *cost* was affected by the gold discoveries was gold; but the *price* of producing everything was altered.

from a foreign country may be produced with less labour in the country from which it is obtained than in the country which imports it, but by this, that it may be produced by *comparatively* less labour than some *other* commodity, which is also made the subject of exchange.   Thus the essence of the gold discoveries, regarded economically, consisted, as has been said, in the reduction in the cost of raising gold which was thereby effected,—a reduction which, not being shared by other countries, involved a change in the comparative costs of Australian and foreign productions. The consequence of this change has been a corresponding change in the character of her foreign trade, brought about, as we have seen, through an action on money wages.   Thus Australia, instead of raising her own corn, as under ordinary circumstances she would do, imports the greater portion of it.   If we ask why is this ? we shall be told that the price of labour is there so high that she cannot afford to compete with foreign countries.   This is true ; but why is the price of labour so high in Australia ?   The answer is, because the cost of gold is so low ; the rate of money wages, as we have seen, always rising and falling as the facilities of producing gold increase or diminish.*   The true explanation, therefore, of the importation of corn into a country possessing abundant resources for

---

* Which shows, by the way, the absurdity of attempting to measure the cost of gold, as some writers have done (see Tooke's " History of Prices," vol. vi. p. 226), by the *pecuniary* outlay necessary to its production.   The fact is that *this* (so far as *gold* is the money employed) scarcely ever varies ; the gold price of producing gold representing merely the ratio of the outlay to the return, or the rate of profit, so that if *price* be taken as the criterion of *cost*, the cost of gold would never vary unless so far as the rate of profit varies.

agriculture is, that she possesses *comparatively* still greater resources for the production of gold; so that she finds it profitable to obtain her corn rather through the medium of her cheap gold, than by its direct production. And the same explanation applies to every circumstance of her recent trade : *e.g.*, previous to the gold discoveries Australia produced her own cheese and butter; she now largely imports these articles.* To what is this change due ? The pastures of New South Wales and Victoria offer unusual facilities for dairy-farming, and these facilities have not deteriorated since 1851 : the cost of butter now is the same as then ; † and yet, with these resources at her disposal, Australia draws her chief supplies of butter from Ireland,—an old and densely peopled country. The explanation of this singular commerce is that which has just been given. The natural facilities possessed by Australia for raising butter, superior though they are to those which we in this country possess, are yet not so much superior as her facilities of raising gold are superior to our means of commanding it. It therefore manifestly becomes her interest to turn her capital and labour to gold-mining, rather than to dairy-farming, and to satisfy her requirements for butter through the medium of that commodity in which her advantage is pre-eminent. By following this course she enjoys the same, or nearly the same, advantage over other countries, in obtaining her butter,

---

* The sum paid by the colony of Victoria alone to Great Britain on this account in the last year reached the large amount of £800,000.— *Australian and New Zealand Gazette.*

† The reader will bear in mind the distinction between the *cost* and the *price* of production. See *ante*, p. 36, note ‡.

which she enjoys in obtaining her gold, and, strange as
it may seem, secures this commodity at less cost—at
a smaller sacrifice of ease and leisure—than its production exacts from the Irish farmer who raises it.*

The importance of thus conceiving the commercial
effects of the gold discoveries is, that it enables us at
once to perceive the precise nature and bounds of the
advantage which Australia and California reap from
their gold-fields. By means of them they are enabled
to obtain their gold at rather less than one-half the
sacrifice formerly necessary ; and, therefore, unless so
far as the purchasing power of the metal has since
declined, they can, through the medium of it, obtain all
their other commodities on terms proportionally easier.
We have seen that, as regards domestic productions,
these have all risen in price in the same proportion as
gold has fallen in cost, whence it follows that, so far as
this portion of their consumption is concerned, the gold
countries derive no advantage from their cheap gold.
They obtain in return for a given sacrifice, twice as
much gold as formerly, but they also pay twice as
much for every domestic production. With their
foreign trade, however, it is otherwise. Prices throughout the world have not risen in the same degree as the
cost of gold has been reduced ; and consequently upon
this portion of their dealings Australia and California
are gainers,—gainers directly in proportion to the
reduced cost of their gold, modified by the rise, so far
as it has taken place, in foreign prices. A given
exertion of labour enables them to command, not only

---

* A possibility which was foreseen and pointed out by Ricardo. See
his Works, p. 77.

more gold, but more of every other thing which foreign countries can supply. It is thus exclusively in the foreign branch of their trade that the advantage of their cheap gold resides : it is only *in so far as they part with their money* that they derive from it any benefit; and yet, so completely in Political Economy is the ostensible at variance with the real, and so inveterate, consequently, are the prejudices of mere experience, that the cry of ' Protection' has been heard even in Victoria. It might, perhaps, shake the Victorian protectionist's faith in his doctrine, if he would reflect that his most effectual protection against the foreigner would be the exhaustion of his own gold-fields.

Such have been the results of the discovery of gold on the industry, trade, and general interests of Australia. Let us now observe the light which these conclusions throw on the more general questions connected with this occurrence. And, in the first place, as to the extent of the prospective depreciation. We have seen that, in the disturbance in the value of gold, or, what comes to the same thing, in the gold prices of commodities, which followed the discoveries, there was a point about which the fluctuations moved, and beyond which the advance or decline did not permanently pass. Prices were in the first instance forced upwards through an increased demand for commodities; the increase of demand led to an increase of supply, and this to a reaction in prices towards their former level. In the case of imported commodities this reaction was carried to the full extent of the previous rise, but in domestic products the decline was arrested at a higher point, the further fall being prevented by the check

given to production through the high rate of money
wages. The natural level of Australian prices, and
therefore the value of gold in Australia, was thus
determined by the rate of wages measured in gold,
and this, as we have seen, was regulated by average
earnings on the gold-fields. The rate of gold earnings, or, as this is in technical language expressed, "the
cost of gold," is therefore the circumstance which, in
the final resort, regulates the value of the metal, and
sets the limit beyond which depreciation cannot permanently pass. Now we have seen that in Australia
gold wages have, in consequence of the gold discoveries, risen in rather more than a twofold proportion; and since, whether gold is raised from mines
or imported in exchange for commodities, gold wages,
or the return to labour in gold, will always represent
the cost of the metal,* it follows that the cost of gold
has been reduced in Australia by the gold discoveries
to the extent of about fifty per cent. Fifty per
cent., therefore,—equivalent to a twofold advance in
prices,—gives the maximum beyond which (on the
supposition that no more productive mines are discovered) the general value of gold cannot permanently
fall. Further, it has appeared that, although a reduction in the cost of gold tends to cause a corresponding
fall in its value, the actual realization of this result
depends upon the possibility of so enlarging the circulation as to render this fall possible. Thus we have
seen that the price of gold in Australia fell, pending
the enlargement of the currency, by the importation of
sovereigns from England, which is, in other words, to

* See on this point Senior's Essay "On the Cost of obtaining Money."

say that the value of the currency was, during this
period, maintained above its natural cost level. This
severance of value from cost was indeed in Australia
of brief continuance, because, the local circulation
being small, it required but a short time to double,
quadruple, or otherwise augment it as the occasion
might render necessary. But throughout the world at
large, the process of augmentation, owing to the vast
dimensions of its currencies, is one necessarily of slow
accomplishment, and, pending its fulfilment, the value
of gold is of necessity maintained above the level
prescribed by its cost. It is this which at present
sustains the value of gold in the general markets of
commerce, notwithstanding the cheapening of its production effected by the gold discoveries. Whether
that value will ever be lowered in the same proportion,
whether gold will ever fall throughout the world at
large as it has fallen in Australia and California,
depends upon whether the conditions which have
lowered its value in them can be generally satisfied—
that is to say, depends upon *whether the increased
supply which such a fall would render necessary can be
obtained at the present cost.* Into the further discussion
of this question I do not now enter,* the object of this
paper being to point out the principal issues which the
general problem involves, not to attempt their solution.
But from the facts which have been stated, we are
justified in concluding that, so long as the present
want of conformity between the cost and the value of
gold continues, so long a constant premium will exist

* The reader will find some remarks on this aspect of the question in
the Fourth Essay, *post*, p. 109 *et seq.*

on its production, and so long our supply of gold
will continue to increase.

But, secondly, let us consider what light our conclusions respecting the gold countries throw upon
a question which has been much discussed,—I mean
the effect of this movement on the real wealth, the
substantial well-being, of the world. That the gold
discoveries have added to the real wealth of the
inhabitants of Australia and California is indeed
exceedingly apparent; but what has been their effect
upon the interests of other nations? Has the cheapness of Australian or Californian gold added equally
to the effectiveness of *their* industry, and extended
their command over the comforts and enjoyments of
life? The answer of some writers to this question
has been very strongly in the affirmative; but, with
the light derived from the previous discussion, we may
perhaps see grounds for arriving at a different conclusion. We have seen that the gain of Australia and
California from their gold-fields is confined to that
portion of their trade which they carry on with foreign
countries; that it is only *in so far as they part with
their gold* that they derive from it any benefit. Now
the world, as a whole, has no *foreign* trade; it has
no means of exchanging for the productions of other
planets the gold which it produces; from which it
seems to follow that, regarded as a single community,
the world is incapable of realizing those conditions on
which the benefit to be derived from cheap money
depends. The conclusion to which this consideration points is, that the operation of the new
gold will be confined to causing a new distribution of

real wealth in the world without affecting its aggregate amount; and that, consequently, the gain of the gold countries must be reaped at the expense of other nations.

This conclusion is no doubt much at variance with prevailing notions, and with the deep-seated prejudices of the "mercantile system;" and will not, therefore, be easily admitted. Nevertheless, if we reflect on the character of the commerce which has arisen out of these discoveries, we may see reason for accepting its truth. The trade between the gold countries and the rest of the world is one in which consumable commodities on one side are exchanged against money, or the materials of money, on the other. A large portion of the industry of the world is, through the medium of this trade, employed in ministering to the real wants —the appetites, tastes, and other human needs—of Australia and California. Let us inquire what is the want to which these countries minister in return. It will be said to the want of more gold—the want of an enlarged circulating medium. True ; but what is the foundation of this want ? and in what way does its satisfaction promote human happiness ? Human industry is not rendered more efficient, nor human happiness more full, by the use of two coins instead of one. Why, therefore, may not the business of production and exchange be carried on upon the former terms ? I apprehend that the correct answer to this question is that gold—the great medium of exchange and universal equivalent—having been cheapened in Australia and California, these countries of necessity possess an exceptional advantage in their commercial dealings with the rest of the world, until the gold prices of commodities in other countries are proportionally raised, and that to effect this object—to raise the prices of their productions in proportion to the diminished cost of gold—the quantity of their gold circulation must be increased. The nations of the world have thus by the gold discoveries been placed under the necessity of enlarging their currencies ; and this can only be accomplished by parting with their productions in exchange for the required supply. Hence the character of the traffic which we are now witnessing,—a traffic in which consumable goods are exchanged for money, and real for nominal wealth. It is therefore no natural want to which this one-sided trade is subservient, no desire, the satisfaction of which adds an iota to human enjoyment : it is merely an artificial requirement, a disagreeable and unprofitable necessity, originating in the gold discoveries, and satisfied at the expense of commercial nations.

I am aware indeed that there are writers who regard gold not simply as a convenient medium for the exchange of commodities independently produced, but as in itself a source of productive energy, as "the motive power of all industry and commerce," * and who accordingly consider "an addition to the quantity of money to be the same thing as an addition to the fixed capital of a country"†—as equivalent in its effects upon industry to "improved harbours, roads, and manufactories." ‡ According to such views the influence of the gold discoveries must be universally

---

* Seyd's " California and its Resources," p. 5.
† Tooke's " History of Prices," vol. vi. p. 46.　　　‡ Ibid.

beneficial,—beneficial, not merely in relation to the
countries which produce the cheap money, but in a
still more eminent degree in relation to those which
permanently retain it. But in spite of the plausibilities
of the mercantile theory, common sense, no less than
economic science, will continue to ask how the world
is enriched by parting with its real wealth ?—how the
well-being of Europe and Asia is promoted by parting
with the materials of well-being, receiving in return
not materials of well-being, not augmented supplies of
wool and tallow, corn and provisions, not those commodities which new countries are specially fitted to
produce, and of which old countries are pressingly in
need, but what ?—increased supplies of the precious
metals, a more cumbrous medium of exchange !

So singular and abnormal indeed has been the
course of industrial affairs hitherto in the gold countries,—so strange has been the spectacle of a country
abounding in resources which she dares not touch, and
drawing from other countries commodities which she is
specially fitted to produce,—that it has not failed to
attract the attention of thoughtful observers, and to
suggest the pertinent inquiry, how long is this state of
things to continue ?   Is the development of the great
and varied resources of Australia and California to be
perpetually subordinated, if not indefinitely postponed,
to the single pursuit of gold-mining ?   Are the other
nations of the world destined to continue for ever
labouring in the service of the gold countries, for no
other than the barren reward of an addition to their
circulation ?   These questions have been frequently put,
but I am not aware that they have as yet been satis-

factorily answered. The writers who have started them have indeed, correctly enough, connected the present condition of Australian industry with the high price of labour in that country, but they do not seem to perceive very clearly upon what the maintenance of this high price of labour depends. It is commonly spoken of as resulting from the scarcity of workmen, and the inference appears to be made that it will gradually disappear as population increases ; but this mode of reasoning arises from confounding the temporary with the permanent causes which regulate wages. India is a less densely peopled country than Great Britain, but the rate of wages in India is many times less than the rate of wages in Great Britain. The fact is, the average rate of money wages in a country is regulated, not by the movements of population, but by the causes which determine for it the cost of its money.* In the gold countries, as we have seen, these causes are the productiveness of industry in raising gold : and, therefore, so long as the present productiveness of the gold-fields is maintained, the rate of money wages in Australia and California cannot fall permanently below its present level. How long this rate of productiveness is likely to last, is a question the discussion of which would carry me entirely beyond the necessary limits of this paper; but on the supposition of its being maintained, we can have no difficulty in discovering the condition on which the industrial development of the gold countries depends.

That condition is briefly this—that prices throughout the world should rise in proportion as the cost of gold

* See Senior's Essay " On the Cost of obtaining Money."

in the gold countries has fallen. So long as the present pecuniary rates of the gold countries are *exceptional*, so long Australian and Californian producers of other commodities than gold will labour under a disadvantage in their competition with gold miners ; and so long the non-monetary exports of those countries will be limited to that small class of commodities, in which their advantage over other countries is as great as it is in their command of gold. But with the advance of gold-prices in foreign markets, this class of commodities will be extended. With the fall in the value of money, it will become less profitable to raise and export money; with the rise in the price of other things, it will become more profitable to raise and export them ; and a larger share of the whole labour and capital of the country will consequently be turned to the latter purposes. We may illustrate the principle by an actual case. For several years subsequent to the gold discoveries timber was largely imported into Australia from the Baltic; and I perceive that it is still upon the list of her imports. But during all this time there have been within a few miles of the localities where this Baltic timber has been used, extensive forests of gum-trees, inviting the axe of the pioneer, capable of affording timber perfectly suited to the purposes for which timber in the mining districts is principally required. Indeed this gum-tree timber has been freely employed where it could be obtained close to the spot where it was wanted, but rather than go fifty miles to cut it, the Australian workman prefers to import it from the other side of the globe. The explanation of this conduct is the low comparative cost of Australian gold. A day's labour employed in crushing quartz or in digging auriferous clay, enables the Australian to obtain more timber than the same labour employed in felling trees. Every rise in prices, however, in foreign markets, will diminish the cost of gold to the foreigner, and thus lessen the comparative advantage of gold digging : the domestic production will gradually gain upon the foreign trade, and the area over which timber-cutting is profitable will be extended. This process has already taken place to some extent, partly through the rise in the cost of gold, with the exhaustion of some of the richer deposits, partly through the advance in the price of timber in foreign markets ; and it will doubtless continue. It is obvious that the same principle will operate equally in the case of every commodity which the gold countries are capable of producing. With every rise in gold prices throughout the world, gold will become a less profitable remittance ; other commodities will become more profitable ; and this will continue, until either prices throughout the world rise in proportion to the reduction in the cost of gold —that is to say, to double their present amount— or until through the exhaustion of the present gold-fields, gold can no longer be produced at its present cost.[*]

It will not be till one or other of these contingencies happens, that the industrial development of the gold countries can be fully accomplished, or that the world can derive from their commerce that contribution to its real well-being and happiness, which their great and varied resources render them so competent to yield.

* See Postscript, p. 50.

POSTSCRIPT.

The history of the Australian trade since this essay was written furnishes so striking an illustration of the views put forward in this paragraph, that perhaps I may be pardoned for referring to it. During the whole of this time, the double process referred to—the gradual exhaustion of the richer gold-fields, and the simultaneous rise in prices throughout the world external to the gold countries—has been in operation; and every step in the movement has witnessed some new development of Australian industry. Thus, while between 1856 * and 1870 the production of gold in Victoria had fallen from 11,943,000l. to 6,119,000l., or to a little more than one-half of its former amount, the non-monetary exports of the colony had increased from 3,546,000l. in 1856 to 6,351,000l. in 1870; the increase taking place chiefly in wool, tallow, and preserved meats. But the effect of the double process of failing gold mines and rising prices in foreign countries has been felt, up to the present, far less in increasing the number and the amount of exports than in curtailing those of imports, and in developing domestic production. The foreign trade of Victoria presents the singular and almost unique spectacle of a steady decline in its amount over a period marked by an extraordinarily rapid growth of population and general wealth. I have no returns of the population of that colony for 1856 (the date at which the commercial statistics begin),

---

* I commence with 1856, this being the first year of the publication of "The Statistical Abstract for the Colonies," from the last number of which (1872) the figures in the text are taken.

but it was probably between 300,000 and 400,000;
in 1861, it was 541,000, and in 1870, 729,000; in
other words the population must have nearly doubled
itself in these sixteen years; the general prosperity
of the country during the same time being almost unexampled.   But the noteworthy circumstance is, that
while the country was thus prospering, its external
trade was undergoing constant contraction, falling
from a total of 15,489,000*l.* in 1856, to 12,470,000*l.*
in 1870.   The fact, I may mention in passing, shows
how little the foreign trade of a country, as measured
by its exports and imports, furnishes a correct criterion
of its industrial progress or growth in real wealth.   The
explanation of the phenomenon is that which I have
given in the foregoing essay : with every decline in the
productiveness of the mines, and with every advance
in foreign prices, the gain on importation decreased and
home production became relatively more profitable.
The result has been that, from being a large importer
of breadstuffs, butter, beer, boots and shoes, provisions, spirits, &c., Victoria has either discontinued
altogether or greatly curtailed her importation of all
these commodities, which she now produces from her
own internal resources.   Is this course of development
for the advantage of Victoria ?   Plainly, I think, if we
have regard to her general interests, social and political
as well as pecuniary, we must answer in the affirmative;
though, as economists, we must also recognize that,
looking at the question from a purely material standpoint, this affirmation cannot be made good; since it
is certainly a fact that the diminishing returns of her
gold-mines have deprived her of that command of

foreign markets which she formerly possessed; while the resort to her own fields of production in lieu of foreign markets, being as it is a *dernier ressort*, cannot but indicate a diminishing productiveness of her general industry. But whatever may be the interests of Victoria herself in this matter, as regards the interests of other countries the case is clear. Had her gold-mines continued as rich and productive as they were during the first few years following the discoveries, and had gold prices through the world remained at the then level, Victoria would have continued to export gold in quantities ever increasing as her population and capital increased, for which the world would have had to pay in the commodities of real wealth. In return for the products of their labour in the form of the conveniences and comforts of life, foreign countries would have gained an addition to their circulation. Instead of this, their industry is now being gradually relieved from this task of adding to their currencies, while the returns on their trade, no longer consisting of barren metal, take the form of increasing supplies of wool, tallow, and meat.

ESSAY TOWARDS A SOLUTION OF THE GOLD QUESTION.*

THE COURSE OF DEPRECIATION.

No one, I think, who has attended to the discussions occasioned by the recent gold discoveries, can have failed to observe, on the part of a large number of those who engage in them, a strange unwillingness to recognize, amongst the inevitable consequences of those events, a fall in the value of money. I say, a strange unwillingness, because we do not find similar doubts to exist in any corresponding case. With respect to all other commodities, it is not denied that whatever facilitates production promotes cheapness—that less will be given for objects when they can be attained with less trouble and sacrifice : it is not denied, *e.g.*, that the steam-engine, the spinning-jenny, and the mule have lowered the value of our manufactures ; that railways and steamships have lessened the expense of travelling : or that the superior agricultural resources of foreign countries, made available through free-trade, keep down the price of our agricultural

* Read before the British Association, September 1858.

products. It is only in the case of the precious
metals that it is supposed that a diminution of cost
has no tendency to lower value, and that, however
rapidly supply may be increased, a given quantity
will continue to command the same quantity of other
things as before.

Amongst persons unacquainted with economic
science, the prevalence of this opinion is doubtless
principally due to those ambiguities of language, and
consequent confusion of ideas, with which our monetary phraseology unfortunately abounds, many of which
tend to encourage the notion of some peculiar and
constant stability in the value of the precious metals.
Thus, the expression "a fixed price of gold" has led
some people to imagine that the possibility of a
depreciation of this metal is precluded by our Mint
regulations. The double sense, again, of the phrase,
"value of money," has countenanced the same error;
for people, perceiving the rate of interest (which is the
measure of the value of money in one sense of the
phrase) remaining high, while the supply of gold was
rapidly increasing—perceiving money still scarce according to this criterion, notwithstanding the increase
in its production—have asked whether this did not
afford a presumption that its value would be permanently preserved from depreciation; a bank rate of
discount at 6, 8, or 10 per cent., as they remarked,
affording small indication of money becoming too
abundant.

It appears to me, however, that misconceptions
respecting the influence of an increased supply of gold
upon its value and upon general prices are by no means

confined to the class who could be misled by such
fallacies, but that even among economists (at least
among economists in this country) we may observe the
same indisposition to believe in an actual and progressive depreciation of this metal.   It is not indeed
denied—at least, I presume it is not denied—by anyone pretending to economic knowledge, that the
enlarged production of gold now taking place has a
tendency to lower its value; but it seems to be very
generally supposed that the same cause—the increased
gold production—has the effect, through its influence
on trade, of calling into operation so many tendencies
of a contrary nature, that, on the whole, the depreciation must proceed with extreme slowness, the
results being dispersed over a period so great as to
take from them any practical importance, and that, at
all events, up to the present time no sensible effect
upon prices proceeding from this cause has become
perceptible.

The existence of this opinion amongst economists
is, I apprehend, to be attributed in some degree to
the circumstance that so few have taken the pains to
compare the actual prices of the present time with
those of the period previous to the gold discoveries,
but much more to the fact, that the character of the
new agency and the mode of its operation are not in
general correctly conceived. I believe the most general
opinion with reference to the action of an increased
supply of money upon its value is, that it is uniform—
takes place, that is to say, in the same degree in
relation to all commodities and services, and that
therefore prices, so far as they are influenced by an

increase of money, must exhibit a uniform advance; *
and, no such uniformity being observed in the actual
movements of prices, the inference has not unnaturally
been drawn, that such enhancement as has taken
place is not due to this cause; that it is not money
which has fallen, but commodities which have risen
in value.

Now I am quite prepared to admit that an increase
of money tends ultimately, where the conditions of
production remain in other respects the same, to affect
the prices of all commodities and services in an equal
degree; but before this result is attained a period of
time, longer or shorter according to the amount of the
augmentation and the general circumstances of commerce, must elapse. In the present instance the additions which are being made to the monetary systems
of the world are upon an enormous scale, and the disturbance effected in the relation of prices is proportionally great. Under such circumstances it is very
possible that the inequalities resulting may not find
their correction throughout the whole period of progressive depreciation; a period which, even with our
present facilities of production and distribution, may
easily extend over some thirty or forty years. During
this transitionary term the action of the new gold on
prices will not be uniform, but partial. Certain classes

---

* "In relation to the influence of the gold discoveries on the prices of
agricultural produce, it is plain that it could be only the same upon them
as upon those of any other class of commodities. *If it has caused a rise
of* 20 *per cent. in their favour, it must have caused a rise of* 20 *per cent.
in everything else."—Times*, City article, August 6, 1852. And the same
assumption, either expressed or implied, runs through most of the reasoning which I have seen on this question.

of commodities and services will be affected much more powerfully than others. Prices generally will rise, but with unequal steps. Nevertheless there will be in these apparent irregularities nothing either capricious or abnormal. The movement will be governed throughout its course by economic laws; and it is the purpose of the present inquiry to ascertain the nature of these laws and the mode of their operation.

The process by which an increased production of gold operates in depreciating the value of the metal and raising general prices appears to be twofold : it acts, first, *directly* through the medium of an enlarged money demand, and, secondly, *indirectly* through a contraction of supply.*

When an increased amount of money comes into existence, there is, of course, an increased expenditure on the part of those into whose possession it comes, the immediate effect of which is to raise the prices of all commodities which fall under its influence. It is obvious, however, that the advance in price which thus occurs will be, in its full extent, temporary only ; since it is immediately followed by an extension of production to meet the increased demand, and this must again lead to a fall in price. Some writers who have treated this question, observing this effect, have somewhat hastily concluded that under the operation of this

---

* According to Mr. Newmarch ("History of Prices," vol. vi. pp. 224-25) the depreciation of money may occur by a process which is neither of these, when money operates upon prices neither through demand nor yet through supply, but " by reason of augmented quantity." I must confess myself wholly unable to conceive the process here indicated.

principle the level of prices would never permanently
be altered, since, as they have urged, each addition to
the circulating medium, forming the basis of a corresponding increase of demand, gives a corresponding
impetus to production; every increase of money thus
calls into existence an equivalent augmentation in the
quantity of things to be circulated; and the proportion
between the two not being ultimately disturbed, prices,
it may be presumed, will return to their original level.*
The least reflection, however, will show that this
doctrine has been suggested by a very superficial view
of the phenomena.

For—not to press the obvious *reductio ad absurdum*
to which this argument is liable—how is this extension
of production to be carried out? In the last resort
it is only possible through a more extended employment of labour. But, when once all the hands in a
community are employed, the effect of a further
competition for labour can only be to raise wages;
and, wages once being generally raised, it is plain
(supposing all other things to remain the same) that
profits can only be maintained by a corresponding
elevation of prices. When, therefore, the influence

* [It may be worth while to preserve a specimen of the sort of Political
Economy that was talked and written on this subject some fifteen years
ago. A leading article in the *Examiner* (December 13, 1856) contains
the following : " The additional supply of the precious metals has stimulated the industry of the world, and in fact produced an amount of wealth
in representing which they have been themselves, as it were, absorbed."
. . . . "But the produce of the Australian and Californian gold, as well
as that of silver which has accompanied it, is likely to go on ; and it may
be asked if this must not in course of time produce depreciation. We
think it certainly is not likely to do so ; . . . . on the contrary, it will
surely be absorbed by increasing wealth and population as fast as it is
produced."]

of the new money has once reached wages, it is evident that there will be no motive to continue production to that point which would bring prices to their former level, and that consequently an elevation of price must, at this stage of the proceeding, be permanently established.

So far as regards articles which fall *directly* under the action of the new money. With respect to those which do not happen to come within the range of the new demand, price is, I conceive, in their case raised by an indirect action of the new money in curtailing supply.

We have seen that the effect of the efforts to extend production in the directions indicated by the new expenditure must be to raise wages; but it is plainly impossible that wages should continue to advance in any of the principal departments of industry without affecting their rates in the rest; whence it will happen that, under the operation of the new monetary influence, some departments of industry will experience a rise of wages before any advance takes place in the prices of the commodities produced by the labourers whose wages have risen. It is evident that in all departments of industry which may be thus affected—in which prices will not have shared the advance which has affected wages—profits will fall below the general average; the effect of which must be to discourage production until, by a contraction in the supply of the articles thus furnished, the price shall be raised up to that point which will place the producers on the same footing of advantage as those in other walks of industry.

An increased supply of money thus tends, by one mode of its operation, to raise prices in advance of wages, and thus to stimulate production; by another, to raise wages in advance of prices, and thus to check it; in both, however, to raise wages, and thus ultimately to render necessary, in order to the maintenance of profits, a general and permanent elevation of price.*

This being the process by which increased supplies of money operate in raising prices, in order to ascertain the laws of their advance we must attend, first, to the direction of the new expenditure; secondly, to the facilities for extending the supply of different kinds of commodities; and, thirdly, to the facilities for contracting it.

With regard to the first point—the direction of the new expenditure—this will naturally be determined by the habits and tastes of the persons into whose possession the new money comes. These persons are the inhabitants of the gold countries, and, after them, those in other countries who can best supply their wants. Speaking broadly, we may say that the persons who will chiefly benefit by the gold

---

* It must not be supposed that this is inconsistent with the fundamental doctrine maintained by Ricardo, that "high wages do not make high prices." That doctrine assumes the value of money to be constant. Ricardo was quite aware of the exception to the general principle, and points it out in the following passage :—

"Money, being a variable commodity, the rise of money-wages will be frequently occasioned by a fail in the value of money. A rise of wages *from this cause* will, indeed, be invariably accompanied by a rise in the price of commodities ; but in such cases it will be found that labour and all commodities have not varied in regard to each other, and that the variation has been confined to money."—RICARDO'S *Works* (Second Edition), p. 31.'

discoveries belong to the middle and lower ranks of society; in a large degree to the lowest rank, the class of unskilled labourers. The direction of the new expenditure will consequently be that indicated by the habits and tastes of these classes, and the commodities which will be most affected by it will be those which fall most largely within their consumption.

With respect, secondly, to facilities for extending supply, these will be found to depend principally upon two circumstances: first, on the extent to which machinery is employed in production; and, secondly, on the degree in which the process of production is independent of natural agencies which require time for accomplishing their ends. The distinction marked by these two conditions, it will be found, corresponds pretty accurately with two other distinctions—with the distinction, namely, between raw and manufactured products; and, amongst raw products, with that between those derived from the animal and those derived from the vegetable kingdom. An article of finished manufacture, in the production of which machinery bears a principal part, and which is independent, or nearly so, of natural processes, may after a short notice be rapidly multiplied to meet any probable extension of demand. An article of raw produce, being in a less degree under the dominion of machinery, and depending more upon natural processes which require time for their accomplishment, cannot be increased with the same facility; and production will consequently, in this case, be comparatively slow in overtaking an extension of demand. But of raw products, those derived from the animal are still less under the dominion of machinery than those derived from the vegetable kingdom, and still more dependent on the slow processes of nature, and, consequently, production must in their case be still more tardy in overtaking demand. Supposing, then, the extension of demand to be in all three cases the same, the immediate rise of price will, *cæteris paribus*, be in all the same; but in the case of articles of finished manufacture, this rise will be quickly corrected by the facilities available for increased production, while in raw vegetable products the correction will take place more slowly, and in raw animal products more slowly still.*

But, thirdly, I said that the progress of prices under

---

* The following passage occurs in the "History of Prices," vol. vi. p. 170:—"The groups of commodities which exhibit the most important instances of a rise of price are the raw materials most extensively used in manufactures, and the production of which does not admit of rapid extension; and, second, the groups of commodities in which there is little, if any, rise of price in 1857, as compared with 1851, are articles of colonial and tropical produce, the supply of which drawn from a variety of sources does admit of being considerably and expeditiously enlarged." The *fact* of the rise of price in raw materials is here admitted, though, in ascribing that rise, as by implication the passage does, to the paucity of the sources of supply, the explanation is, as I conceive, erroneous. The sources, *e.g.*, from which tea and sugar are drawn are not more various than, nor indeed so various as, those from which beef and mutton, butter and provisions, timber, tallow, and leather are drawn; yet all these latter articles have very considerably advanced in price. Again, amongst colonial and tropical produce Mr. Newmarch includes rum and tobacco, and he might also have included cotton; yet these articles, though falling within the class which he says admits of being expeditiously enlarged, and which therefore, according to his theory, should *not* have risen in price, *have in fact risen* in a very marked manner. It appears to me that these phenomena can only be understood by reference to the principle which I have endeavoured to explain further on——namely, the efficacy of the currency of different countries in determining local prices.

the influence of the gold supplies would be governed
by the facility with which supply can be contracted.
Everyone who has practical experience of manufacturing operations is aware that, when capital has
once been embarked in any branch of production,
it cannot at once be removed to a different one the
moment the needs of society may require a change ;
whence it happens that, on any sudden change taking
place in the direction of a nation's expenditure, or
when from miscalculation production has been extended
beyond existing wants, producers frequently choose
to continue their business at diminished profits, or
even at a positive loss, rather than incur still greater
damage by suffering their capital to lie idle, or by
attempting to transfer it suddenly into some new
branch of production.   The supply of a commodity is
not therefore always, or generally, at once contracted
on the demand for it falling off, or on its production
becoming less profitable, and, where this is so, it is
evident that prices must at times continue depressed
below the normal level ; the duration of the depression
depending on the length of time required to effect
a transference of the unproductive capital to some
more lucrative investment.   Now the difficulty of
accomplishing this will generally be in direct proportion to the amount of fixed capital employed ; and
the principal form in which fixed capital exists is that
of machinery.   It is, therefore, in articles in the production of which machinery is extensively employed—
that is to say, in the more highly finished manufactures—that the contraction of supply will be most
difficult ; and this, it will be observed, is also the kind

of commodities for extending the supply of which the facilities are greatest. While, therefore, manufactured articles can never be very long in advance of the general movement of prices, they may, of all commodities, be the longest in arrear of it.

The operation of this principle will be shown chiefly in that class of articles which feels the effect of the new gold only through its indirect action—that is to say, through its action upon wages. With respect to such articles there is no extension of demand, and the price consequently can only be raised through a contraction of supply. It is evident that of all commodities this is the class in which the rise of price must proceed most slowly.

From the foregoing considerations, then, I arrive at the following general conclusions :—

First.—That the commodities, the price of which may be expected first to rise under the influence of the new money, are those which fall most extensively within the consumption of the productive classes, but more particularly within the consumption of the labouring and artisan section of these.

Secondly.—That of such commodities, that portion which consists of finished manufactures, though their price may in the first instance be rapidly raised, cannot continue long in advance of the general movement, owing to the facilities available for rapidly extending the supply ; whereas, should the production, from over-estimation of the increasing requirements, be once carried to excess, their prices, in consequence of the difficulty of contracting supply, may be kept for some considerable time below the normal level.

Thirdly.—That such raw products as fall within the consumption of the classes indicated, not being susceptible of the same rapid extension as manufactures, may continue for some time in advance of the general movement, and that, among raw products, the effects will be more marked in those derived from the animal than in those derived from the vegetable kingdom.

Fourthly.—That the commodities last to feel the effects of the new money, and which may be expected to rise most slowly under its influence, are those articles of finished manufacture which do not happen to fall within the range of the new expenditure ; such articles being affected only by its indirect action, and this action being in their case obstructed by impediments to the contraction of supply.

This is one class of laws by which I conceive the ascending movement in prices will be governed ; and up to this point I have the satisfaction of finding my conclusions very fully corroborated by the independent investigations of a French economist, M. Levasseur, who, in some articles lately contributed by him to the *Journal des Économistes*, has, by an entirely different line of investigation from that which I have followed— namely, by generalizing on the statistics of prices in France during the period of 1847 to 1856—arrived at conclusions in the main points identical with those which I have now advanced.*

There is, however, another principle to which I venture to call attention, which has not, so far as I know, been noticed by any of the economists who have

* See Appendix, for a summary of M. Levasseur's conclusions.

treated this question, but which, it appears to me, must exercise a powerful influence on the course of the movement. The principle to which I refer is that efficacy which resides in the currency of each country, into which any portion of the new money may be received, for determining the effect of this infusion on the range of local prices.

It is evident that the quantity of metallic money necessary to support any required advance of prices throughout a given range of business will vary with the character of the currency into which it is received ; that the quantity required will be greater in proportion as the metallic element of the currency is greater ; and, on the other hand, less in proportion as the credit element prevails. If the currency of a country be purely metallic, a given addition of coin will increase the aggregate medium of exchange in that country only by the same amount ; if, on the other hand, the currency consist largely of credit contrivances, each addition to its coin becomes the basis of a new superstructure of credit in the form of bank-notes and credits, bills of exchange, cheques, &c., and the aggregate circulation is increased not simply by the amount of the added coin, but by the extent of the new fabric of credit of which this coin is made the foundation. Applying this principle to the different countries of the world, it follows that a given addition to the metallic stock of Great Britain or the United States, in whose monetary systems credit is very efficacious, will cause a greater expansion of the total circulation, and therefore will support a greater advance in general prices, than the same addition to the currency of countries like France, in which credit is less active; and that, again, the effect in countries like France will be greater than in countries like India or China, in which the currencies are almost purely metallic, and where credit is comparatively little used.

Now, this being so, if we consider further that the countries which receive in the first instance the largest share of the new money—namely, England and the United States—are also those in which from the character of their currencies a given amount of coin will produce the greatest effect; and, on the other hand, that Asiatic communities, in which from the weakness of the credit element the currencies are least expansible, receive but a small portion of their share of the new money direct from the gold countries; * being compelled to wait for the remainder till it has flowed through the principal markets of Europe and America, affecting prices in its transit;—if, I say, we consider these facts in connection with the principle to which I have adverted, I think we must recognize in that principle—in the influence of the currency of

---

* [From statistics recently furnished by the *Economist*, I learn that the facts have not been as I here assumed, at least since 1858 (the date from which full returns of specie imports have been published by the Board of Trade); and it is probable I was mistaken in my supposition with regard to what had occurred before that time. Since 1858, of 90,000,000*l.* of gold received and retained by India and the East, some 49,000,000*l.*, more than a half of the whole, appear to have gone there *directly* from Australia, the remainder only having come through Europe. This error as to matter of fact will, no doubt, affect to some extent the conclusion contended for. The causes tending to a divergence of European from Asiatic prices have not been, it seems, as powerful as I had supposed; and, in point of fact, this feature in the movement has been less marked than I sketched it; but for this, other causes besides that noticed here have been responsible (1872). See Introductory Chapter, p. 12.]

each country on the range of its local prices—an agency which must modify in no small degree the general character of the movement which is now in progress.

In speaking of the influence of the currency of a country on the range of its local prices, I should explain that I use the words "local prices" in a somewhat restricted sense—namely, with reference to the locality in which commodities are *produced*, not to that in which they are sold, their price in the latter place being always determined by their price in the former. Thus, when I speak of Australian, English, or Indian prices, I shall be understood to mean the prices of their several products in Australia, England, or India.

Understanding the words, then, in this sense, let us see how far local prices are likely to be affected by the cause to which I have adverted.

In the first place, then, let it be observed that a very remarkable divergence of local prices from the range previously obtaining in the international scale has already taken place.* The prices of all articles *produced* in Australia and California are at present on an average from two to three times higher than those which prevailed previous to the gold discoveries; these rates have now been maintained for several years, and are likely to continue : but, while this advance has taken place in the gold countries, in no part of the world external to those regions have prices advanced by so much as one-third. The possibility of a divergence of local prices is thus, as a matter of fact, established ; and the explanation of the phenomenon I take to be

* See *ante*, pp. 24, 25.

this. The sudden cheapening of gold in Australia and California quickly led, through the action of competition amongst the different departments of industry, to a corresponding advance in the prices of everything produced in those countries ; *this advance being in their case possible*, because, from the limited extent of the transactions, the local circulation was quickly raised to the point sufficient to sustain a double or triple elevation ; but it was impossible that the currencies of all countries should be expanded in the same proportions in the same time ; and, consequently, prices in other countries have not risen with the same rapidity. The cause, therefore, of this divergence of local prices —the circumstance which keeps general prices in arrear of that elevation which they have attained in Australia and California—is the difficulty of expanding the currencies of the world to those dimensions which such an advance would require. This expansion, however, is being gradually effected by the process we are now witnessing,—the increased production of the precious metals, and their diffusion throughout the world. But, as I have said, the diffusion is not uniform over the various currencies, nor are the currencies receiving the new supplies of uniform susceptibility ; and the inequalities are such as to aggravate each other ; the currencies which are the most sensitive to an increase of the precious metals receiving in the first instance nearly the whole of the new gold ; while the least sensitive currencies are the last to receive their share. And these, it appears to me, are grounds for expecting amongst other countries further examples of that phenomenon of local diver-

gence, of which one has already been afforded by the
gold countries.

To judge, however, of the extent to which such local
variations of price can be carried, we must advert to
the corrective influences which the play of international
dealings calls into action ; and these appear to me to
resolve themselves into the two following :—namely,
first, the corrective which is supplied by the competition
of different nations, producers of the same commodities,
in neutral markets ; and, secondly, that which exists
in the reciprocal demand of the different commercial
countries for each other's productions.

The first form of the corrective is obviously the
most powerful, and must, so far as its operation
extends, at once impose a check upon any serious
divergence. Thus it is evident that prices in England and the United States could not proceed very
much in advance of prices on the continent of Europe,
since the certain effect of such an occurrence would
be to send consumers from the dearer to the cheaper
markets, and thus to divert the tide of gold from
the currencies of England and America to the currencies of France, Germany, and other continental
states,—a process which would be continued until
prices were restored to nearly the same relative level
as before. But it is only amongst nations which are
competitors in the same description of commodities
that this equalizing process comes into operation : as
between countries like England and America on the
one hand, and India and China on the other—in which
the climate, soil, and general physical conditions differ
widely, in which consequently the staple industries

are different, and whose productions do not, therefore, come into competition in the markets of the world—this corrective influence would be felt slightly or not at all. The only check which could be counted on in this case would be that far weaker one which is furnished by the action of reciprocal demand in international dealings. Thus, supposing prices to rise more rapidly in England than in India, this must lead, on the one hand, to an increased expenditure in England on Indian commodities, and, on the other, to a diminished expenditure in India on English commodities, with this result—a steady efflux of the precious metals from the former to the latter country. Such an efflux, as commercial men are well aware, has long been a normal phenomenon in our Eastern trade, but it has lately assumed dimensions which constitute it a new fact needing a special explanation. I believe that explanation is to be found in the circumstances to which I am calling attention.

English and American prices, and with them money incomes in England and America, have, under the action of the new gold, been advancing more rapidly than prices and incomes in Oriental countries; and the result has been a change in the relative indebtedness of those two parts of the world, leading to a transfer to the creditor country of corresponding amounts of that material which forms the universal equivalent of commerce. It is true, indeed, that other causes have also contributed to this result, and in particular I may mention the failure of the silk crop in Europe, which has largely thrown us upon China, as a means of supplementing our deficient supplies. But the main cause

of the phenomenon in its present proportions is, I
conceive, to be found, not in any such mere temporary
disturbances, but in the natural overflowing (consequent
upon the increase of the precious metals) of the redun-
dant currencies of Europe and America into the more
absorbent and impassive systems of Asia.* This, then,
I say, is the only substantial corrective afforded to the
advance of prices in Europe and America beyond
their former and normal level in relation to prices in
the East ; and the question is, will this corrective be
sufficient to neutralize the tendency to a divergence ?
Will the flow of the precious metals from West to East
suffice to keep prices in England and America within
the range prescribed by the inelastic metallic systems
of Asia ? I do not conceive that the corrective will
be adequate to this end, and I rest this conclusion
upon the facts and principles which I have stated—the
vast proportion of the whole gold production which
finds its way in the first instance into the markets of
England and America, the comparatively small portion
which goes direct to the markets of Asia,† the highly
elastic and expansible currencies of the former coun-

---

* Accordingly we find that the drain which, during the revulsion of
trade following on the commercial crisis of 1857, had for a while ceased,
has, with the revival of trade, recommenced. As a proof how little mere
practical sagacity is to be trusted in a question of this kind, it may be
worth while to mention that, only three months since, mercantile writers
were confidently predicting *the turning of the tide of silver from the East
to England.* The following is from a circular of Messrs. Ellisen & Co.,
quoted in the *Times'* City article, July 28th, 1858, apparently with the
editor's approval :—" The time is rapidly approaching when silver will
also be shipped from here (China) to England." So far from this being
the case, the drain to the East has again set in, and gives every indication
of assuming its former dimensions. Every mail to India during the
present month (November 1858) has taken out large amounts of silver.

† See *ante*, p. 67, note *.

tries, and the extremely impassive and inexpansible currencies of the latter.

We find, therefore, two sets of laws by which the progress of prices, or (which comes to the same thing) the depreciation of gold under the action of an increased supply, is regulated : first, those which I explained in the earlier portion of this paper, which depend chiefly on the facility with which the supply of commodities can be adjusted to such changes in demand as the new money expenditure may occasion ; and, secondly, those which result from the action of the new money on the currencies into which it is received. According to the former principle, the rise in price follows the nature of the commodity affected ; thus it will in general be greater in animal than in vegetable productions—in raw produce than in finished manufactures. According to the latter principle, the advance follows the economic conditions of the locality in which the commodity is produced. Thus the rise in price has been most rapid in commodities produced in the gold countries ; having in these at a single bound reached its utmost limit—the limit set by the cost of procuring gold. After commodities produced in the gold regions, the advance I conceive will proceed most rapidly in the productions of England and the United States ; after these, at no great interval, in the productions of the continent of Europe, while the commodities the last to feel the effects of the new money, and which will advance most slowly under its influence, are the productions of India and China, and, I may add, of tropical countries generally, so far as these share, as regards their economic conditions, the general character of the former countries.

Such appear to be the general principles according to which a depreciation of the precious metals, under the action of an increased supply, tends to establish itself. With a view to ascertain how far, in the progress of prices up to the present time (1858), any trace of their operation can be discerned, I have drawn up some statistical tables;* and, although from the imperfect nature of the materials which I have been able to collect, I cannot claim for the result a complete verification of the theoretic conclusions which I have ventured to advance, I think they are such as to justify me in placing some confidence in the general soundness of those views. Before, however, stating the results of the tables, two or three remarks must be premised.

First, I would crave attention to this fact, that the present time [1858] is one singularly free from disturbing influences, and that such as do exist are of a kind rather to conceal than to exaggerate the effects of depreciation. Thus, we have had three harvests in succession, of, I believe, more than average productiveness (the last year of deficiency being 1855); and this cause of abundance has been assisted by free trade, which has opened our ports to the produce of all quarters of the world. Again, although in the period under review we have passed through a European war, yet we have now enjoyed two years and a half of peace, during which, I think, the economic influences of the war may be taken to have exhausted themselves.

* See Appendix.

It is true, indeed, that we have an Indian revolt still on hands, besides having but just concluded some hostile operations in China. But these disturbances have not been of a kind to interfere seriously with the general course of trade, except in some few Oriental commodities in which their effects are slightly apparent.

But what renders the present time peculiarly important as a point of comparison with former periods, is its being in immediate sequence to a severe commercial crisis. The effect of the crisis of last winter has been effectually to eliminate one great disturbing element from those causes to which a rise of price might be attributed—the element of credit. Trade is now suffering depression in almost all its branches; and prices, after a period of undue inflation, have, through an ordeal of bankruptcy, been brought to the test of real value. In the fluctuations of commerce we have reached the lowest point of the wave; whatever, therefore, be the range of prices at the present time, we may at least be sure that no commercial convulsion is likely to lower it.

We have further to remember that in an age like the present, in which science and its applications to the arts are in all civilized countries making rapid strides, there exists in most articles of general consumption (but more particularly in the more finished manufactures) a constant tendency to a decline of price, through the employment of more efficient machinery and improved processes of production. Now, taking all these circumstances together,—the propitiousness of the seasons, the action of free-trade, the absence

of war, the contraction of credit, and the general
tendency to a reduction of cost proceeding from
the progress of knowledge,—it appears to me that,
were there no other cause in operation, we should
have reason to look for a very considerable fall of
prices at the present time, as compared with (say) eight
or ten years ago. Prices, however, as the following
tables will show, have not fallen; they have on the
contrary very decidedly risen, and the advance has
moreover, as the same tables will also show, on the
whole proceeded in conformity with the principles
which i have in this paper endeavoured to establish.
And this is my ground for asserting that the depreciation of our standard money is already, under the
action of the new gold, an accomplished fact.

ESSAY TOWARDS A SOLUTION OF THE GOLD QUESTION.

INTERNATIONAL RESULTS.[*]

In a former essay[†] it was attempted, from a review of the industrial history of Australia since the late discovery of gold, to make some general deductions respecting the character of that event, and of its influence upon national interests. Among other conclusions it was maintained that the tendency of the gold discoveries, or, to speak with more precision, the tendency of the increased production of gold, was rather to alter the distribution of real wealth in the world than to increase its amount; the benefit derived by some countries and classes from the event being for the most part obtained at the expense of others. It was shown, for example, that the gain to Australia and California from their gold-fields accrued to them exclusively through their foreign trade—their cheap gold enabling them to command on easier terms than formerly all foreign productions; while, on the other hand, the only result to foreign nations of the traffic

---

[*] *Fraser's Magazine*, January 1860.
[†] Essay I. of this Series.

thence arising was an increase in their stock of money
—a result rendered necessary indeed by the new
conditions of raising gold introduced by the gold
discoveries, but in itself destitute of any real utility.
It was shown, in short, that, as regards commercial
nations, the effect of the gold discoveries was to place
them under the necessity of enlarging their currencies,
compelling them to pay for the requisite increase by
an increased export of their productions.

To this conclusion I was led by direct inference
from the facts presented in the gold countries. In the
present paper it is proposed to follow up the inquiry,
with a view to a more particular ascertainment of the
consequences formerly described ; the object being to
discover in what manner the loss arising from the gold
movement is likely to be distributed among commercial nations, and how far this loss may in particular
cases be neutralized or compensated by other influences which the same movement may develop.

In the discussions which have hitherto taken place
upon this question, the inquiry into the consequences
of the gold discoveries has been confined almost exclusively to that aspect of the event in which it is
regarded as affecting fixed contracts through a depreciation of the monetary standard.* As soon as the
probability of depreciation is settled, and the effects of

---

* See Stirling's "Gold Discoveries and their probable Consequences ;"
Chevalier "On the probable Fall in the Value of Gold ;" Levasseur's
contributions to the *Journal des Economistes*, 1858 ; M'Culloch's article
'Precious Metals,' in the "Encyclopædia Britannica." In all these,
and in many other minor productions on the same subject, almost the
only consequences of the gold discoveries which are taken account of
are those which occur in fixed contracts through a depreciation of the
standard.

this upon the different classes of society, according as
they happen to be debtors or creditors under fixed
contracts, explained, the subject for the most part is
considered as exhausted. I venture, however, to think
that this mode of treatment is very far from exhausting the question. It seems to me that, independently
altogether of the existence of fixed contracts, independently even of gold being a standard of value,
the increased production of this metal which is now
taking place will be attended—indeed has already been
attended—with very important results. Let us observe
for a moment the movement which is now in progress.
Australia and California have during the last eight
or ten years sent into general circulation some two
hundred millions sterling of gold. Of this vast sum
portions have penetrated to the most remote quarters
of the world; but the bulk of it has been received
into the currencies of Europe and the United States,
from which it has largely displaced the silver formerly
circulating; the latter metal, as it has become free,
flowing off into Asia, where it is permanently absorbed.
Viewing the effect as it occurs in the mass of the
two metals combined, it may be said that the stream
which rises in the gold regions of Australia and California flows through the currencies of the United
States and Europe, and, after saturating the trade of
these countries, finally loses itself in the hoards of
China and Hindostan. The tide which comes to
light in the sands and rocks of the auriferous regions,
disappears in the accumulations of the East. In
conjunction, however, with this movement there has
been a counter one. With every advance in the

metallic tide, a stream of commodities has set in
in the opposite direction along the same course,—
a stream which, issuing from the ports of Europe,
America, and Asia, and depositing as it proceeds a
portion of the wealth with which it is charged, finds
its termination in the markets of the gold countries.
Here, then, we find a vast disturbance in the conditions of national wealth,—a disturbance originating
in the gold discoveries, and resulting in a transfer,
on an enormous scale, of consumable goods—the
means of well-being—from one side of the globe to
the other. This disturbance, it is evident, is entirely
independent of the accident that gold happens to be
in some countries a standard of value, as well as of
the existence of fixed money-contracts ; for it includes
within the range of its influence countries in which
gold is not, no less than those in which it is, the
monetary standard ; and it affects alike persons
whose bargains are made from day to day, and those
who engage in contracts extending over centuries.
The fact is, the movement in question is the result,
not of gold's being a standard of value, but of its
being a source of purchasing power ; and the influence
of the gold discoveries having been hitherto regarded
almost exclusively with reference to the former function, the vast effects which they are producing through
the action of the latter—that is to say, by altering the
distribution of purchasing power in the world—have
been almost wholly overlooked. It has indeed been
perceived that a great influx of the precious metals
is taking place, accompanied with certain consequences on the trade of the world ; but so far

as I know, beyond some general phrases respecting the stimulus given to production by an increase of money, and the great development of commerce which it is causing, no attempt has yet been made to state the principles by which the movement is governed, or the effects which may flow from it. It is to these questions, then, that I would now solicit the reader's attention, and towards their solution the following remarks are offered as a contribution.

Those who have followed the course of this controversy are aware that, by most persons who have taken part in it, it has been assumed, almost as an axiom, that no depreciation of gold in consequence of the gold discoveries has, up to the present time, taken place.* As a matter of fact, however, we know that the gold prices of all commodities produced in Australia and California have risen in at least a twofold proportion; † while we have seen that (so long as the conditions of producing gold remain as at present) this rise must be permanent. To express the same thing differently :— in the purchase of every commodity raised in the gold countries two sovereigns are now required, and (the above conditions being fulfilled) will continue to be required, where one was formerly sufficient; and if this does not amount to a fall in the

---

* The principal exceptions to this statement are M. Levasseur (who, in an article in the *Journal des Économistes*, March 1858, estimates the rise of prices in France since 1847 at 20 per cent. on all commodities), and Dr. Soetbeer of Hamburg, who, in his table of prices given in his "Contributions to the Statistics of Prices in Hamburg," arrives at a similar result (see Appendix). Many other writers, indeed, acknowledge that prices have risen, but the rise is always attributed to causes distinc from the increased production of gold.

† See *ante*, p. 24.

value of gold, I must confess myself unable to understand the meaning of that expression. It is not to be
supposed that so remarkable a fact as this should have
escaped the attention of those who have written on
this question : it seems to me rather that the ignoring
of it in the discussion is to be attributed to a want of
definite ideas respecting value in the precious metals,
as well as respecting the mode in which changes in
their value are accomplished. The language which is
commonly used on the subject would seem to imply
that gold and silver possess throughout the world a
uniform value, and that all changes therein proceed in
a uniform manner, showing themselves at the same
time in all countries, and in respect to all commodities.
But nothing can be further from the truth than such a
notion. Gold and silver, like all other things which
are the subjects of international exchange, possess local
values ;* and it is by a succession of operations on the
local values of gold of an unequal and fluctuating
character, that its depreciation is being effected, and
that (the conditions of production remaining as at
present) its value will continue to decline. The twofold rise of prices in the gold countries forms the first
step in this progress ; and it will be through a series
of similar partial advances in other countries, and not
by any general movement, that the depreciation of the
metal throughout the world will be accomplished, if
that consummation is indeed to take place. With the
question of depreciation, however, I am at present no

---

* See on the subject of the local values of the precious metals,
Ricardo's "Works," pp. 77—86, and Mill's "Principles of Political
Economy," Book iii., chaps. xix. and xxi.

further concerned than may be necessary to show the bearing of these changes in the local values of gold upon the movements of trade, and, through these, upon national interests.

There is no need here to resort to argument to prove that a general rise or a general fall of prices, provided it be simultaneous and uniform, can be attended—always excluding the case of fixed incomes and contracts already entered into—with no important consequences either to nations or to individuals. It is evident that such a change would merely alter the terms in which transactions are carried on, not the transactions themselves. But when the rise or fall of prices is not general—in other words, when the change in the values of the precious metals is merely local— it will be seen that important consequences must result. Supposing, *e.g.*, the prices of all commodities produced in England to be doubled, while prices throughout the rest of the world remained unchanged, it is evident that half the commodities exported from England would, under these circumstances, be sufficient to discharge our foreign debts. With half the capital and labour now employed in producing goods for the foreign markets, we should attain the same result as at present—the procuring of our imports; while the remaining half would be set free to be applied to other purposes—to the further augmentation of our wealth and well-being. England would, therefore, in the case we have supposed, be benefited in all her foreign dealings to the full extent of the rise in price. On the other hand, foreign countries would, in exchange for the commodities which they send us, receive in return

of our commodities but half their present supply.
Their labour and capital would go but half as far as
at present in commanding our productions, and they
would be losers in proportion. It is evident, therefore,
that while nations have not, any more than individuals,
any interest in the positive height which prices may
attain, every nation, as well as every individual trader,
is interested in raising, *in relation to others*, the price
of its own productions. The lower the local value,
therefore, of the precious metals in any country, the
greater will be the advantage to that country in
foreign markets.

This being the manner in which nations are interested in changes in the value of gold, let us now
observe the effect which the gold discoveries are producing in this respect. As has been already stated,
the local value of gold in Australia and California has
fallen to one-half,—the prices of their productions
having risen in a twofold proportion;* and prices in
other parts of the world having undergone no corresponding change, these countries realize the position
which we have just been considering in our hypothetical case. A given quantity of their capital and
labour goes twice as far as formerly in commanding
foreign productions, while a given quantity of foreign
labour and capital goes only one-half as far in com-

* This statement is not given as strictly accurate. On the whole, the
advance of local prices in the gold countries is at present (1859) considerably more than this, some leading articles, as house-rent, meat, &c.,
having risen in a fourfold proportion and upwards. I adopt the proportion of two to one, because money wages have risen in about this
ratio, and money wages, under a depreciation of the precious metals,
ultimately govern money prices.

manding theirs. The world has thus, through the gold discoveries, been placed in its dealings with California and Australia at a commercial disadvantage ; and from this disadvantage it can only escape (always supposing the present conditions of producing gold to continue) by raising the prices of its productions in a corresponding degree. Every country, therefore, is interested in raising as rapidly as possible the prices of its productions,—in other words, in the most rapid possible depreciation in the local value of its gold.* The sooner this is effected, the sooner will the country be restored to its natural commercial footing in relation to Australia and California ; while in relation to countries where prices do not rise with the same rapidity, it will possess the same kind of advantage which is now enjoyed by the gold countries.

This conclusion, I find, is directly at variance with the opinion of some economists of eminence. Mr. M'Culloch, for example, in his recent contribution to the " Encyclopædia Britannica," † maintains " that the mischievous influence resulting from a fall in the value of the precious metals depends in a great measure on the rapidity with which it is brought about." But I apprehend the difference between Mr. M'Culloch and myself arises from his attending exclusively to a single class of consequences,—those, namely, which result, in the case of fixed contracts, from a depreciation of the standard. With respect to this

---

* For the general ground of this assertion the reader is referred to Mr. Mill's chapters on ' International [Values,' and on ' Money as an imported Commodity,' in his " Principles of Political Economy ;" also to Mr. Senior's Essay " On the Cost of obtaining Money."

† Article ' Precious Metals.'

class of effects, it is quite true that the evils which
they involve will be increased by the rapidity of the
depreciation; but as I have shown, the new gold is
producing effects quite independently of its operation
upon fixed contracts; and it is to those other effects
that the statement I have just made is intended to
apply. The distinction which I have in view will be
best exemplified by recurring to the experience of the
gold countries. In these the value of gold fell by more
than 50 per cent. in a single year, the depreciation
involving a proportional loss to creditors with a corresponding gain to debtors, and entailing in addition those
numerous incidental evils which always result from a
sudden disturbance of social relations. No one, however,
on this account, will say that the sudden depreciation
of gold in Australia and California was not for these
countries a great gain. The nature and extent of that
gain I endeavoured on a former occasion to estimate.*
It consisted, as I showed, in the increased command
conferred by the cheapness of their gold over markets
in which gold prices had not proportionally risen. With
every rise in the price of Australian and Californian
products, or, what comes to the same thing, with every
fall in the local value of their gold, their power of
purchase in foreign markets increased,—an increase
of purchasing power which, as we know, was immediately followed by a sudden and extraordinary influx
of foreign goods. Now, precisely the same principle
applies in the case of other countries. A fall in the
value of gold will, where gold is the standard, lead to
a disturbance in fixed contracts, with the concomitant

* See *ante*, p. 39.

evils; but it will at the same time, as in the case just
considered, place the countries in which it occurs in a
better position commercially in the markets of the
world.   Supposing, *e.g.*, a rise in prices to take place
in all commercial countries equivalent to that which
has occurred in California and Australia, the consequence would be what I endeavoured to explain in the
paper just referred to : the export of gold from California and Australia, at least on its present scale, would
at once cease, and the world would receive instead an
increased supply of agricultural and pastoral products,
and of other commodities which those countries are
fitted to produce,—a result which, I venture to think,
would be a gain for the world.   On the other hand,
supposing the rise in price to be confined to a single
country—say to England—then England would at once
be placed on a footing of commercial equality with
California and Australia, while as regards other countries she would occupy the same vantage-ground which
California and Australia now possess.   She would, in
short, obtain her gold at half its present cost (for she
would receive twice as much as at present in return
for the same expenditure of labour and capital), while
the gold thus obtained would be expended on foreign
commodities of which, according to the hypothesis,
the prices had not risen.   Notwithstanding, therefore,
the evils which undoubtedly attend variations in the
standard of value, more especially in an old and
highly artificial community like ours, it is nevertheless,
I maintain, for the interest of every country, that, a
fall in the cost of gold having been effected, the progress of depreciation should *in it* be as rapid as pos-

sible. Until, by a depreciation of gold corresponding to that which has occurred in California and Australia, the value of that metal is brought into harmony with its cost, we must continue to receive from those countries little more than a barren addition to our stock of money. But with each successive step in the progress of depreciation, there will be for the nation in which it occurs a nearer approach to the footing of commercial equality with the gold countries from which it has been temporarily displaced ; while in its dealings with other places where the decline has been less rapid, the nation so circumstanced will, during the period of transition, enjoy a commercial superiority. As a general conclusion, therefore, we may say, that in proportion as in any country the local depreciation of gold is more or less rapid than the average rate elsewhere, the effect of the monetary disturbance will be for that country beneficial or injurious.

This conclusion, I may in passing remark, throws light upon a practical question of some interest at the present time,—I mean the question of introducing a gold currency into India. The measure has been advocated by Mr. M'Culloch, on the ground that, by providing a new market for the increased supplies of gold, its effect would be to "counteract that fall in its value which is so generally apprehended." * There can be no doubt that the effect of the measure would be what Mr. M'Culloch describes ; but, if the above reasoning be sound, this circumstance, instead of being a reason for introducing gold into the currency of India, affords (*so far as the interests of India are con-*

* "Encyclopædia Britannica ;" article ‘Precious Metals.’ p. 473.

cerned) a strong reason against the adoption of this course. Mr. M'Culloch does not state whether the effect which he anticipates upon the value of gold would be general or local; whether extending over the whole commercial world, or confined to the markets of India,—a point of vital importance in determining the character of the result. If the effect were general—if, while counteracting depreciation in India, it influenced the value of gold *proportionately* in other parts of the world—then it must be conceded that the result would be entirely beneficial. The evils incident to a disturbance of fixed contracts would be avoided, and no others would be incurred. But this is just the point which I venture to deny. The adoption of gold as the monetary standard of India would certainly not affect the local value of gold in Australia and California; for, as I proved on a former occasion, the value of gold in these countries is determined by its cost, and its cost depends on the productiveness of the gold-fields. Nor, for reasons which will be hereafter stated, would it influence more than in a slight degree the range of gold-prices in England and the United States. The operation, therefore, of the measure would be to depress gold-prices in India, or at least to prevent them from rising in that quarter as rapidly as they otherwise would; while in California and Australia, in England and the United States, it left their course substantially unaffected. Now this result would tend undoubtedly to the advantage of California and Australia, of England and the United States, but, as it seems to me, would as clearly be injurious to India. The purchasing power of the former countries over the markets of India would, through the relative superiority of their prices, be increased, but the purchasing power of India over _their_ markets would, for the opposite reason, be diminished. An English or American merchant, instead of discharging his debts as at present through the medium of silver which he has to purchase with gold at 62_d._ per ounce (and may soon have to purchase at a higher rate), might discharge the same debts with gold directly; and gold being by hypothesis more valuable in India than before, the same amount would of course go further. But an Indian purchaser of English or American commodities would have the same sum in gold to pay as if no change had taken place in the currency of India; while the gold prices of his native productions being lower, his ability to pay would of course be less. It seems to me, therefore (and the considerations here adduced are entirely independent of the reasons which exist on the score of good faith—the Indian debt having been contracted in a silver currency), that, viewing the matter from the side of Indian interests, the introduction of a gold currency into India must be regarded as a measure decidedly detrimental.*

---

* Referring to the adoption of a silver standard by Holland in 1851, Mr. M'Culloch characterizes it as a measure "in opposition to all sound principles." I confess I am at a loss to conjecture what sound principle was violated in preferring as the standard of value that metal, the value of which there was every reason to believe would be the steadier of the two. [I may say now (1872) that I am disposed to assign much less importance to this question of a change in the monetary standard of India than I did when the above passage was written. The reasoning assumes the possibility of a serious divergence in the relative values of gold and silver; but I now believe that such a divergence is practically out of the question.

Returning once more to the general question, we may consider the following conclusions as established : —1st, that the effect of the cheapening of gold upon commercial countries being to compel them to enlarge their metallic currencies, for which enlargement they must pay by an export of their productions, each country will endure a loss upon this head to the extent of the additional sum which may be requisite for each : and 2ndly, that while there will be a general loss from this cause, yet the progress of depreciation over the world not being uniform or simultaneous, the primary loss may, through the disturbance in international values thence arising, in particular cases, be compensated, or even converted into a positive gain ; the loss or gain upon the disturbance being determined according as the rise of prices in any country is in advance or in arrear of the general average. To ascertain, therefore, the effect of the movement upon any particular nation, we must consider the manner in which, in its case, these two principles will operate.

With respect to the first, I am aware that, in speaking of the loss imposed on a country by the necessity of enlarging its currency—by the necessity of receiving and keeping increased supplies of gold

the grounds for which opinion will be found further on (*post*, p. 141). This circumstance, however, does not affect the theoretic point argued with Mr. M'Culloch. *If* the exchange of the existing silver for a gold standard in India were calculated to produce the effects Mr. M'Culloch expected from it, the measure, it still seems to me, would be open to the objections I have urged against it. But I do not believe that the effects in question would result; and I can well conceive that, having regard to the general convenience of commerce, the change might on the whole be advantageous.]

and silver—I am using language which, notwithstanding what was said on a former occasion in its
justification, and notwithstanding that it is merely in
strict conformity with the most elementary principles
of economic science, will still appear paradoxical to
many.   I would therefore, before proceeding further
with this branch of the argument, ask the reader to
consider the case of a private merchant who is compelled to increase the stock of cash with which he
carries on his business.   The metallic circulation of a
country performs in relation to the community functions precisely analogous to those which are discharged
for a merchant by his cash reserve.   If a merchant
can safely dispense with a portion of his ready cash,
he is enabled, with the money thus liberated, either
to add to his productive capital, or to increase his
private expenditure.   On the other hand, if he finds
it necessary to increase his reserve of cash, his productive capital must be proportionally encroached
upon, or his private expenditure proportionally curtailed.   And precisely the same may be said of the
currency of a nation.   Where a country does not itself
yield gold or silver,* every increase of its metallic
circulation must be obtained—can only be obtained—
by parting with certain elements of real wealth—elements which, but for this necessity, might be made
conducive to its well-being.   It is in enabling a nation

---

* Even where it does yield these metals, the necessity of augmenting
the currency is not the less an evil, since the operation will occupy, with
no result but that of avoiding an inconvenience, a portion of the labour
and capital of the country, which, but for this, might have contributed to
its positive welfare.

to reduce within the narrowest limits this unproductive portion of its stock, that the chief advantage of a good banking system consists; and if the augmentation of the metallic currency of a country be not an evil, then it is difficult to see in what way the institution of banks is a good. In regarding, therefore, the necessity imposed upon commercial countries of enlarging their metallic currencies as injurious to their interests, I make no assumption which is not in perfect keeping with the best known and most generally recognized facts of commercial experience.

An increase in the metallic currency of a country, then, being an evil, let us consider what the circumstances are by which the augmentation rendered necessary by the gold discoveries will be determined. This, it is evident, will principally depend—the amount of business to be carried on being given—on the extent to which substitutes for metallic money are in use; in other words, on the degree of perfection which the banking system of each country has attained. To illustrate this, let us suppose a given sum of metallic money—say a million sterling—to be introduced into two countries in which the currencies are differently constituted—*e.g.*, into England and India. In India coin is the principal medium of circulation*—in many

---

* [The reader will bear in mind that this was written in 1859. The state of the Indian currency at that time may be gathered from the following extracts from a paper on "The Trade and Commerce of India," read before the British Association in 1859.] "Intimately connected with Indian trade and commerce is a sound system of banking. At present there are only three banks of importance in India—the banks of Bengal, Bombay, and Madras. These have no branches, the absence of which constitutes one of the main defects of the system. The few other banks in India do not issue notes, and employ their capital in making advances

parts the only one, and consequently a million sterling
introduced into the currency of India would represent
only an equal, or little more than an equal, addition to
its total medium of circulation—to the whole monetary
machinery by which the exchange of commodities is
effected and prices maintained. But in England,
where the currency is differently constituted, the result
would be different. The great bulk of the circulating
medium of this country consists of certain forms of
credit; and the amount of these credit media standing
in a certain large proportion to the coin in the country,

on bills of lading, in exchange operations, and in some instances in
loans to members of the Service, at high rates of interest ; but afford
no banking facilities for conducting the internal trade of the country."
The writer then refers to a table, showing the state of the three leading
banks (Bengal, Bombay, and Madras) in the preceding June, from
which it appears that the bullion at that time in the coffers of the
banks was *in excess* of the notes in circulation, the amount of these
latter being, for the whole of India, 2,241,471*l.*, or about one-tenth of
the amount issued by the Bank of England alone ; while the total
amount of "accounts current" was only 1,855,000*l.*—about one-sixth
of those held by some of the private banks of London, and not one-
fifteenth of those of the Bank of England. The total amount of commercial bills discounted in these three leading banks of India is set down at
278,906*l.*! "And this," it is observed, "in a country where the gross
annual revenue is 34,000,000*l.* ; the export trade, on an average of
the last five years, 24,000,000*l.*; the import trade, on the same average,
23,000,000*l.*, with an internal trade to an extent almost impossible to
estimate." ("The Trade and Commerce of India," by J. T. Mackenzie,
read before the British Association, 1859, pp. 15, 16.)   In the evidence
taken before the late Committee "On Colonization and Settlement in
India," Mr. Alexander Forbes, when questioned with reference to the large
absorption of silver in India, expressed his opinion that the silver was all
required for current coin.   "It has often been said that the natives hoard
silver : now my experience is that they do not hoard silver; they hoard
gold ; and that the silver is actually required for the commerce of the
country."   And this he traces (Answers 2,222, 2,223, 2,372–80) to the want
of banking accommodation and the imperfect means of communication
generally in the country. See also the evidence of Mr. Mangles (Answers
1,625 - 1,633).

the effect of introducing a million sterling into our currency would be to increase the medium of circulation by an amount very much greater than that of the added coin. Let us consider for a moment what becomes of a sum of coin or bullion received into England. I do not now speak of that moving mass of metal which passes (so to speak) *through* the currency of the country—which, received to-day into the vaults of the Bank of England, is withdrawn to-morrow for foreign remittance—but of gold which is permanently retained to meet our genuine monetary requirements. Of such gold a portion—greater or less, according to circumstances—will always find its way into the channels of retail trade ; and so far as it follows this course, its effect in augmenting the circulation will be, as in India, only to the extent of its actual amount. But a portion will also be received into the banks of the country, where, either in the form of coin, or of notes issued against coin, it will constitute an addition to their cash reserves. The disposable cash of the banks being thus increased, an increase of credit operations throughout the country would in due time follow. The new coin would become the foundation of new credit advances, against which new cheques would be drawn, and new bills of exchange put in circulation, and the result would be an expansion of the whole circulating medium greatly in excess of the sum of coin by which the new media were supported. Now credit, whatever be the form which it assumes, so long as it is *credit*, will operate in purchases, and affect prices in precisely the same way as if it were actually the coin which it represents. So far forth, therefore, as the new money enables the country to support an increase of such credit media—to support them, I mean, by cash payments—so far it extends the means of sustaining gold-prices in the country; and this extension of the circulating medium being much greater than in proportion to the amount of added coin, the means of sustaining gold-prices will be in the same degree increased. Thus, supposing the ratio of the credit to the coin circulation of the country to be as four to one (and the proportion is greatly in excess of this), the addition of one million sterling of coin would be equivalent to an increase in the aggregate circulation of four millions sterling,* and one million sterling of gold would consequently, in England, for a given extent of business, support the same advance in gold-prices as four times that amount in India. It follows from these considerations, that, in order to raise prices throughout a given range of transactions to any required level, the quantity of metallic money which will be necessary will vary in different countries, according to the constitution of their currencies; the requirements of each increasing generally in an inverse ratio with the efficiency of its banking institutions.

---

* Strictly speaking, this conclusion would not follow on the above supposition, the efficiency of different forms of credit in performing the work of circulation being (as pointed out by Mr. Mill, " Principles of Political Economy," vol. ii., pp. 58—61) different, and only some of them being in this respect equal to coin. But such distinctions do not affect the general truth of the principle contended for in the text, that the necessity for coin varies inversely with the use of credit. Besides, as I intimated, the proportion of credit to coin in our circulation is much greater than I have assumed; and a million of coin taken into our currency would really be equivalent to more than four millions added to a purely metallic one.

We may thus see how very unequal will be the operation of the gold discoveries with respect to commercial communities. The reduction in the cost of gold to which they have led has, as we have seen, produced in the gold countries a twofold rise of gold-prices; and supposing the present conditions of raising gold to continue, the same cause must ultimately lead to the same result throughout the world; imposing upon each country the necessity of so enlarging its currency as to admit of this advance. But we have seen that the quantity requisite for this purpose varies according to the monetary status of the country for which it is required; and inasmuch as the new money must be paid for by commodities, the abstraction of commodities, and therefore the loss of the means of well-being, to which each country must submit, will vary with the same circumstance. On the supposi-tion, therefore, on which we are arguing, the quantity of new money which England would require would be, when compared with the extent of her business, ex-tremely small, and her loss of real wealth small pro-portionally. The same would be true of the United States, where credit institutions have also attained a high degree of efficiency, and whose paper conse-quently forms a large proportion of the whole circu-lation. In France, the use of credit being more restricted, the requirements for coin would be greater, and consequently also the loss of consumable com-modities; while in India and China, and indeed in Asiatic communities generally, the circulating medium being almost purely metallic, the requirements for coin would, in proportion to the business in which it was employed, attain their maximum, with a corresponding maximum of loss in the elements of well-being.*

The operation of this principle is indeed, in the actual circumstances of the world, in some degree concealed by the complex conditions under which it comes into play. Thus Great Britain and the United States, instead of obtaining the smallest shares, receive in the first instance nearly the whole of the new gold. On the other hand, the quantity which goes to India and China from the gold countries is comparatively trifling;† and although a large drain of treasure has set in thither from Europe, yet this consists chiefly of silver. If, however, passing by the accidents of the movement, we attend to its essentials, we shall find that the results are entirely conformable to the principle I have endeavoured to describe. For though the bulk of the new gold comes in the first instance to England and the United States—determined thither by the course of international demand—yet England

---

* It is curious to observe the contradictions in which persons are involved who, still under the influence of the mercantile theory of wealth (and there are few even among professed economists who are free from its influence), are nevertheless sensible from experience of the advantages of a system with which it is incompatible. Thus several witnesses before the late Committee on Indian Colonization refer to the large influx of silver into India in recent years as a sure indication of the increasing prosperity of that country ; yet, almost in the same breath, they speak of the deficiency of banking accommodation as among its most pressing wants. Now it is certain that, just in proportion as banking accommodation is extended, the absorption of silver by India will decline ; whence it would follow, if the reasoning of the witnesses be sound, that the effect of the extension of banks would be to check the growing prosperity of the country. See "Minutes of Evidence," Questions 1,625–1,633, 2,221–2,223.

† This order in the diffusion of the new gold has not been sustained See *ante*, p. 67, note.

and the United States do not form its ultimate destination. The monetary requirements of these countries being easily satisfied, the mass of the metal, on
reaching these markets, becomes immediately disposable for foreign purchases; by which means the
United States and England are enabled to transfer to
other countries this unprofitable stock, the commodities
with which in the first instance they parted being
replaced by others which they more require. So also,
although the metallic drain to the East is composed
principally of silver, the efflux—at least in its present
proportions—is not the less certainly the consequence
of the increased production of gold; for the silver
of which it consists has been displaced from the
currencies of Europe and America by the gold of
Australia and California; and the drain to the East is
only not a golden one, because silver alone is in that
region the recognized standard. As the final result of
the whole movement, we find that, while the metallic
systems of England and the United States are
receiving but small permanent accessions, those of
India and China are absorbing enormous supplies.
The former countries, though the first recipients of the
treasure, yet, not requiring it for domestic purposes,
are enabled to shift the burden to others, whose real
wealth they command in exchange; while the latter,
requiring what they receive, are compelled to retain it.
Having parted with their commodities for the new
money, they are unable afterwards to replace them.
As their stock of coin increases, their means of well-
being decline, and they become the permanent victims
of the monetary disturbance.

But, secondly, we concluded that the loss of real
wealth resulting from the augmentation of their currencies would in particular countries be compensated,
and might in some be even converted into positive
gain, by the disturbance which, during the period of
transition, would take place in international values.
As has been already remarked, a general rise of
prices in all countries, if simultaneous and uniform—
since it leaves the proportions in which commodities
are exchanged undisturbed—leads to no change in
international values, and produces no effect upon
national interests.   But where prices rise unequally,
international values, and through these, national interests, are affected.   We have therefore to consider
how far, in the actual circumstances of the world, a
rise of prices in particular countries, unaccompanied
by a corresponding advance in others, is possible, and,
in so far as it is possible, in what order the several
changes may be expected to occur.

As regards the question of possibility, this is placed
beyond controversy by the example of California and
Australia.   It is a matter of fact that prices in those
regions have advanced in a twofold proportion, while
no corresponding rise of prices has occurred throughout the world.   The circumstances, however, of the
gold countries will probably be thought of too exceptional a character to form the basis of any general
conclusion ; and it will therefore be desirable to advert
for a moment to the causes which produced in California and Australia that local elevation of price, with
a view to consider how far the same conditions are
capable of being realized elsewhere.

These causes, as was formerly shown,[*] were the special facilities for producing gold enjoyed by California and Australia, combined with the limited range of their domestic transactions. The sudden cheapening of gold, involving a corresponding increase in money earnings, placed an extraordinary premium on the production of the metal, while the limited range of their domestic trade rendered the necessary enlargement of their monetary systems an easy task. On the other hand, the immense extent of the aggregate commerce of the world required, in order to secure a similar advance, a proportional increase in its aggregate stock of money, an augmentation which could only be accomplished after the lapse of a considerable time. Prices therefore rose rapidly in the gold countries, while over the area of general commerce the rise has been but slow.

Such being the circumstances which produced the local divergence of prices to which I have called attention, it will at once be seen that of the two conditions which I have stated, the latter—the necessary enlargement of the local currency—may in most countries, though not in all at the same time, be fulfilled, if not with the same rapidity as in Australia and California, still after no very long delay. It has been computed,[†] for example, that the total quantity of gold coin circulating in Great Britain amounts to 75,000,000l. sterling. Assuming this to be correct, it would follow (all other conditions being supposed

---

[*] See *ante*, pp. 25, 26.

[†] "History of Prices," vol. vi. app. xxii. This also is Mr. M'Culloch's estimate: "Encyclopædia Britannica," article 'Precious Metals,' p. 465. [It will be borne in mind that these estimates apply to the period immediately preceding the first publication of these Essays (1859-60).]

identical) that an addition of 75,000,000*l.* would be
sufficient to effect an elevation of our local prices
equivalent to that which has occurred in Australia.
Now at the present rate of production, the quantity
of gold which arrives annually in Great Britain cannot
fall much short of 30,000,000*l.* sterling; * so that
were we merely to retain all that we receive, we
should at the end of two years and a half be in a
position, so far as the augmentation of our currency
is concerned, to maintain the same advance in price
as has occurred in the gold countries.   If, then, prices
in Great Britain have not risen in the same degree,
the result, it is evident, cannot be due to the difficulty
of procuring the supply of gold necessary for the
enlargement of our currency.   It remains, therefore, to
be considered how far those special facilities for procuring gold which have operated in the gold countries
may come into play in other parts of the world.

The extraordinary facilities for procuring gold
enjoyed by Australia and California depend, of course,
on the possession of their gold mines ; and this being
so, it might seem as if all countries, not being like
them auriferous, were by the nature of the case precluded from fulfilling this condition of the problem ;
but this by no means necessarily follows, as will be
evident if we reflect that there are other modes of
obtaining gold than by direct production, of which
modes the efficiency enjoyed by different countries
differs almost as much as the degrees of fertility in

* [20,000,000*l.* would have been nearer the mark, but, at the time
this paper was written, no trustworthy statistics of gold imports existed.
Either amount, however, answers equally well the purpose of the
argument (1872).]

different gold mines. Where countries do not themselves produce gold, the mode by which they obtain
it is through their foreign trade. Now it is a fact
well known to economists * that, with reference to
the cost of commodities, the terms on which foreign
trade is carried on differ greatly in different countries,
the labour of some going much further in commanding
foreign productions than that of others. According,
however, to the conditions on which foreign productions generally are obtainable, will be those on which
gold may be obtained. If a country possess special
facilities for supplying markets where gold can be
given in exchange, it will obtain its gold more
cheaply—at a less sacrifice of labour and capital—
than countries which do not share these facilities, and
amongst such countries it will therefore occupy precisely the same position as an auriferous country whose
mines are of more than the usual richness among
the countries which yield gold. It is thus possible
for a non-auriferous, no less than for an auriferous,
country to possess exceptional facilities in the means
of procuring gold, and therefore to fulfil the second of
the conditions by which a divergence of local prices
from the ordinary level of the world may be effected.

Now, it appears to me there are two countries
which possess in an eminent degree the qualifications
requisite for attaining this result—I mean Great
Britain and the United States : the former, as being
par excellence the great manufacturer among civilized

---

* See Ricardo's "Works"—chap. vii., on Foreign Trade. Mill's
"Principles of Political Economy," chaps. xvii., xix. Also Senior's Essay,
"On the Cost of obtaining Money."

nations—the manufacturer more particularly of descriptions of goods—as cotton, woollen, linen, and
iron—which enter largely into the consumption of
the classes by whom chiefly the gold countries are
peopled ; and the latter, as the principal producer of
raw material, as well as of certain commodities—as
grain, tobacco, sugar, and rice—which are also largely
consumed by the same classes. In these circumstances, Great Britain and the United States enjoy
peculiar advantages in the markets of the gold-
countries, and these advantages are extended and
confirmed by other important incidents of their position. Thus they possess the greatest mercantile
marine in the world, by which they are enabled to
give the fullest scope to their manufacturing and
agricultural superiority, while by race, language, and
religion they are intimately connected with the producers of the new gold,—a connection from which
spring ties, moral, social, and political, to strengthen
and secure those which commerce creates. Great
Britain and the United States thus possess in their
foreign trade a rich mine,* worked by their manu-
facturers, planters, and farmers, tended by their
mercantile marine, and protected by their naval
power,—a mine by means of which they are enabled
to obtain their gold on terms more favourable than
other nations. The effect of this, in ordinary times,
is shown by a scale of money rates, wages, salaries,
and incomes, permanently higher than that which

* "The mine worked by England is the general market of the world :
the miners are those who produce those commodities by the exportation
of which the precious metals are obtained."—SENIOR's *Essay* "*On the
Cost of obtaining Money,*" p. 15.

elsewhere prevails; but, in times of monetary disturbance like the present, when the cost of gold having been reduced its value is falling, these advantages, it seems to me, must tell, as analogous advantages have told in the gold countries, in a more rapid realization of the results which are in store—in a quicker ascent towards that higher level of prices and incomes, which the cheapened cost of gold is destined ultimately to produce.

There is reason, therefore, on considerations of theory, to expect a repetition in England and America of that phenomenon which has been already exhibited in Australia and California,—a divergence of local money-rates from the average level of surrounding countries. On a future occasion I shall endeavour to ascertain how far, in the case of Great Britain, these *à priori* conclusions are supported by facts—how far prices and incomes have here, under the influence of the gold discoveries, outstripped the corresponding movement in other countries.* Having settled this point, we shall be in a position to form a general estimate of the benefit which may thence accrue to us. Meanwhile, however, I may, in conclusion, point out the mode in which the advantages incident to the monetary position we shall occupy are likely to be realized.

And here it may be well to call the reader's attention

---

* [Some evidence on the point will be found in the Appendix; but the inquiry here contemplated was never carried into effect. A very interesting and carefully prepared paper on the subject, however, was read some years later by my friend Professor Jevons before the London Statistical Society, when I had the satisfaction to find that the results of his entirely independent investigations to a very large extent corroborated the conclusions at which I had arrived, mainly by way of deduction from the general principles of the science.]

to the distinction, sometimes overlooked, between a fall
in the value of gold and a rise in the price of commodities. A rise in the price of commodities, if general,
implies commonly a fall in the value of money; but,
according to the ordinary use of language, alike by
economists and in common speech, money would, I
apprehend, in certain circumstances be said to have
fallen in value, even though the prices of large classes
of commodities remained unaffected. For example,
supposing improvements to have been effected in some
branch of production resulting in a diminished cost of
the commodity, the value of money remaining the same,
prices would fall : if under such circumstances prices
did not fall, that could only be because money had not
remained the same, but had fallen in value. The continuance of prices unaltered would, therefore, under
such circumstances amount to proof of a fall in the
value of gold. Now when, in connection with this
consideration, we take account of the fact that over the
greater portion of the field of British industry improvement is constantly taking place, it is obvious that the
mere movements of prices here, taken without reference
to the conditions of production, are no sure criterion
of changes in the value of gold.

The truth is, in a large class of commodities—in
all those to which mechanical or chemical inventions
are extensively applicable—even on the supposition of
a very great depreciation of gold, no considerable
advance in price is probable. Gold, for example,
might have fallen since the beginning of the present
century to the extent of 75 per cent.—that is to say,
four sovereigns now might be equal to no more than

one sovereign at the commencement of the period—and
yet in a large class of manufactured goods no advance
in price would be apparent, the reduction in the cost of
production being in more than an equal proportion.
In ordinary times, agricultural operations escape in a
great degree the influence of industrial progress ; but
within the last ten years—that is to say, since the
repeal of the Corn Laws, which nearly synchronized
with the gold discoveries—the spirit of improvement
has been as busy in agriculture as in any other department of industry, and, in conjunction with importations
from foreign countries, has acted, and must for some
time at least continue to act, powerfully upon the price
of raw products in this country.

The depreciation of gold, therefore, may be realized
either in a corresponding advance of prices, or in the
neutralization of a fall which in the absence of depreciation would have occurred ; but in whatever form it
may come to us, our gain or loss as a nation will be
the same, and will depend upon the condition I have
stated—the more or less rapid depreciation of our currency as compared with the currencies (convertible,
like ours, into gold) of other countries. Whether,
the conditions of production remaining unaltered, the
depreciation be indicated by a corresponding advance
of prices, or, those conditions undergoing improvement,
the fall in the value of gold merely operates in neutra-
lizing, as regards price, the effects of the cheapened
cost of commodities—in either case *the gold price of the
products of English labour and abstinence will rise.* A
given exertion of English industry will reap a larger
gold reward than before ; and foreign commodities not

rising in price in the same degree, the larger gold
reward will indicate, *over so much of our expenditure as
is directed to foreign productions*, a real augmentation of
well-being. As regards that portion of our expenditure which falls upon the products of our own industry,
individuals and classes will, according to circumstances,*
be benefited or injured by the change ; but as a nation,
we shall neither gain nor lose, since here the increased
cheapness of gold will be exactly neutralized either by
a corresponding advance in price, or by the prevention in
the same degree of a fall which would otherwise have
taken place. It is in this way—by the increased command which she obtains over foreign markets by her
cheap gold—and not, as is commonly supposed, by
finding an outlet for her wares in California and
Australia, that England will benefit by the gold discoveries. That outlet for her productions—were the
movement to stop here—however it might benefit
individuals, would for the country at large be an injury
and not a boon ; it would deprive her of that which
might conduce to her comfort and happiness, and
would give her "a breed of barren metal" in exchange.
But the movement does not stop here. The money
which she obtains from the gold countries, instead of
absorbing, like India or China, she employs in purchasing the goods of other nations. It is in the enlarged
command which she acquires over such goods that her
gain consists, and it is thus that she indemnifies herself,
though at the expense of the nations who ultimately
retain the new gold, for the loss—the indubitable loss
—which she is called on in the first instance to sustain.

* On this point see *post*, p. 147 *et seq.*

ESSAY TOWARDS A SOLUTION OF THE GOLD QUESTION.

It is now rather more than three centuries since the conquest of Mexico and Peru by the Spaniards, and the discovery of rich mines of the precious metals in those regions, excited the cupidity of Europe and opened a new epoch in human affairs. Of the numerous occurrences which conspired about that time to break the spell of old ideas, and to carry the world rapidly over the border line of mediævalism into the full movement of modern civilization, this was certainly not the least powerful. The subsequent depreciation of gold and silver, and the revolutions in private property, though the most conspicuous, were by no means the sole, nor even the most important, consequences of that event. The rage for gain — the *auri sacra fames*—awakened by the golden visions of the new Eldorado, hurried across the Atlantic those numerous and daring adventurers who laid the foundation of the Transatlantic states. The vast sums of gold and silver liberated

* *The Edinburgh Review*, July 1860.

by their exertions supplied, and rendered possible, the remarkable expansion of Oriental trade which forms the most striking commercial fact of the age that followed. Less directly, but still intimately, connected with the same event, were the sudden growth and temporary splendour of the Spanish monarchy, as well as its rapid decline; the establishment of the Poor Laws in England; the financial embarrassments of Charles I., which resulted in the Long Parliament and the Revolution; and the rise and progress of British maritime power.

Once more after the lapse of three centuries, the world has witnessed another great discovery of the precious metals. The auriferous sands and rocks of California and Australia are as much superior, in richness and abundance, to those which rewarded the industry of the Spanish adventurers, as these latter were superior to all which had been previously known; and gold has now for eight years been pouring into Europe in an exuberant tide of wealth beyond all former experience. What, then, will be the result of these Californian and Australian discoveries? and how far will they resemble in their scope and influence their prototypes of the sixteenth century? These are questions which, in the presence of such facts, cannot but force themselves upon every thoughtful mind.

But since the epoch of which we have spoken— since the day when the sparkling veins on the sides of Potosi attracted the eye of the Indian shepherd—a mighty change has come upon the world. Society in all its constituents has been profoundly modified. Commerce has grown to dimensions of which the merchants of the sixteenth century could have formed no conception. The entire foreign trade of the greatest commercial nation then in existence probably did not much exceed that which is now carried on in a single English or American port. The total tonnage of the united galleons which constituted the Spanish mercantile marine only amounted a century later, as we are informed by Robertson, to 27,500 tons—little more than the tonnage of the *Great Eastern* steam-ship. Some of the most populous and wealthy communities of the present day had not yet begun to exist; and the whole quantity of the precious metals then in use was probably less than that which now circulates in some second-rate European kingdoms. The conditions under which the experiment of the sixteenth century was tried are no longer those with which we have now to deal, and the precedents of that period may therefore be thought to have little application to the present time.

But, on the other hand, if we examine the details of this change, we shall find that the facts of which it consists are of a nature, in relation to the influence of the gold discoveries, in a great degree to counteract and neutralize each other; some of them tending not less powerfully to enhance, and give increased efficacy to that influence, than others tend to impair it. The stability of trade has increased with the increase of its mass ; but, on the other hand, the agencies at our disposal for acting upon trade have increased in a still greater proportion. The quantity of the precious metals now in existence may be twenty or thirty times greater than when Columbus made his memorable

voyage, and the difficulty of affecting their value may
be proportionably greater; but against this we have to
consider, that for one Spaniard who in the sixteenth
century engaged in mining, twenty or thirty English
or Americans are now thus employed, and that these
latter are equipped with means and appliances of production far superior to any which their predecessors
could command. The area of commercial intercourse
has been greatly enlarged, and commercial relations
indefinitely multiplied : but not more so than the
means of locomotion and the facilities of postal communication; while we have further to note, that
commerce possesses now, in the agency of credit, an
auxiliary to metallic money of wondrous potency,
which in the earlier period was entirely unknown.
Notwithstanding, therefore, the changes which have
taken place in the trade and wealth of the world, the
circumstances of the present time are not such as to
preclude the possibility of a recurrence of events
similar or analogous to those which the first American
discoveries drew after them. Those events were, as
we have said, of the greatest moment to mankind :
they included the rapid colonization of America by
European races; great and lasting changes in the
channels of trade; striking vicissitudes in the fortunes
of nations; and a monetary revolution the effects of
which have been felt in every quarter of the globe.

The precedents of history, then, no less than the
character of the facts, give to the Californian and
Australian gold discoveries an interest of no ordinary
kind, and we have therefore to tender our thanks to
M. Michel Chevalier and his translator, for having

brought to the notice of the public the momentous questions which those discoveries involve. The subject indeed has not been entirely overlooked in this country, but it has not yet 'been treated, either here or elsewhere, by any writer whose opinions command the same respect as those of M. Chevalier; and we therefore welcome the appearance of his volume as undoubtedly the most important contribution which has yet been made to this discussion.

But, while we gladly bear testimony to the ability and learning with which M. Chevalier has treated this subject, and to the logical acuteness with which he has dissected and expounded many of its problems, it certainly seems to us that he has failed to seize fully the nature and the extent of the principles which the increased production of gold has brought into play. In the work before us, the discussion is confined to a single aspect of the gold question—"the probable fall in the value of gold," and the effects of this on our pecuniary relations : to another, and not less important view of the movement—the changes which the new gold, by altering the distribution of purchasing power in the world, may produce in the movements of trade and the fortunes of nations, changes of which some striking illustrations have already been afforded,—to this aspect of the case M. Chevalier scarcely alludes.

And yet the distinction on which it rests is real.* If, to borrow the illustration of Hume, the world should awake some morning, every one finding in his pocket an additional sovereign, or (modifying slightly

* As has been shown in the preceding essays.

the supposition) every one finding his money income
increased in some certain proportion,—such an occurrence would tend to lower the value of money, but
(unless so far as it affected fixed contracts) would not
alter the relative purchasing power of individuals, nor
therefore the distribution of commodities, nor the interests of mankind.   But if, instead of being dispensed
with this impartiality, the entire addition of new sovereigns should fall to the lot of a few persons, the
money incomes of the rest remaining as before, this
—supposing the amount of the addition to be in each
case the same—would tend, equally as in the former
case, to lower the value of money ; but its effects
would not end here : while increasing the total
quantity of money, it would at the same time alter
the relative purchasing power of individuals—a result
which would be followed by a corresponding change in
the distribution of real wealth amongst them, and consequently of general well-being.   This view of the
case M. Chevalier has neglected to expound.   He has
discussed with considerable fulness the effects of a
depreciation of money ; but he has altogether overlooked the results which may follow from a redistri-
bution of purchasing power over the world.   We
have in the outset called attention to this incom-
pleteness (as we deem it) in his mode of treating the
gold question, because we think he has thus been led,
not only to omit from his consideration an interesting
range of topics, but to attribute to a depreciation
of money results which are due to a different cause.
The justification and pertinence of this criticism will
appear in the course of the following observations.

The facts which form the ground for expecting
a fall in the value of gold are thus stated by M.
Chevalier. At the beginning of the present century
the quantity of gold which arrived every year to augment the metallic wealth of Christendom amounted, in
round numbers, to about 2,500,000*l.* sterling. By
the year 1848 this supply had increased to upwards
of 8,000,000*l.*; the field of production having been
in the meantime extended by the opening of new
mines in the Ural Mountains, and the discovery of
auriferous sands in Siberia. In 1848 the Californian
discoveries occurred, which were followed in 1851 by
those in Australia. The result of the whole has been
to raise the rate of production from 2,500,000*l.*, the
annual yield at the commencement of the century, to
38,000,000*l.* sterling, the present annual yield; being
an increase, as compared with that time, in the proportion of 15 to 1, or, as compared with the period
immediately preceding 1848, of 5 to 1.

Or the facts of the case may be thus represented.
The region which, until the discovery of the mines
of Siberia, was the chief seat of gold production for
European nations, was America. Now the total quantity of gold raised throughout the whole continent of
America during the interval from the first voyage of
Columbus to the discovery of the mines of California
—that is to say, during a period of 356 years—
amounted in round numbers to about 400,000,000*l.*
sterling. At the present time (as has been stated
above) the *annual* supply has reached 38,000,000*l.*
sterling. It thus appears that the civilized world
receives now in a single year nearly one-tenth of all

the gold obtained in the principal field of supply throughout the whole period from the discovery of America down to the year 1848.

Or, once more, the altered conditions of producing gold may be presented through the medium of the average produce of a day's work. M. Chevalier has not furnished us with any standard with which to compare the present rate of gold earnings, except the returns of the gold-washers of the Rhine, which scarcely afford a fair basis of comparison. We learn, however, from Humboldt that, at the commencement of the century, when he visited New Spain, the Mexican miner, "who was the best paid of all miners," "gained at least from twenty-five to thirty francs per week of six days."* This would be equivalent to from 3s. 6d. to 4s. 2d. a day of our money, which amount, since the rate of wages in mining always follows the average returns to mining labour,† we may take as representing the average earnings of miners at the commencement of the century. Now, according to some authorities quoted by M. Chevalier, and which are fully confirmed by statements which we have seen, as well as by the current rate of wages in the country, the average earnings of gold miners in California at present are at the rate of nineteen francs per man daily, equal to about 15s. 2d. The earnings in Australia he sets down at the same amount; but we are convinced that this is an over-estimate. From official accounts, confirmed by private information, we have no hesitation in saying

* "Political Essay on New Spain," vol. iii. pp. 237—240.
† See ante, p. 23.

that gold earnings in Australia at present do not exceed on an average 10s. a day per man. Even, however, reducing to this amount M. Chevalier's estimate, we have still an average produce for the two countries of 13s. per man daily, a rate of return nearly four times greater than that which was obtained from the best mines of Mexico half a century since. When, in connection with this fact, we consider the greater accessibility — arising partly from political causes, partly from the progress of the art of navigation—of the present gold countries, the superior enterprise and skill of the miners, and the larger capital at their disposal, we may form some conception of the immense increase which has taken place in the world's means of obtaining gold.

Such is the present state of gold production. But before these facts can be made the data for conclusions respecting the future, it is important to ascertain the extent of our existing resources. What are the auriferous capabilities of California and Australia, and of those other regions from which gold is now derived ? Will the golden tide now pouring in continue with perennial flow ? or will it, after inundating us for a while, suddenly disappear, like the Australian streams whence it is extracted ? These are questions on which geology should be able to enlighten us, and some eminent authorities in that science are of opinion that the present extraordinary production cannot long continue. We are reminded, that auriferous formations are for the most part superficial ; that the richest deposits are those which lie nearest the surface ; that the countries which were once the chief seats of supply,

as Spain and Lusitania, are auriferous no longer ; and
that, consequently, in proportion to the energy and
skill with which the new gold fields are worked, will
be the rapidity of their exhaustion.

"Judging from experience," says Sir Roderick Murchison,
"all gold veins in the solid crust of the earth diminish and
deteriorate downwards, and can rarely be followed to any
great depth except at a loss in working them. Again, as
the richest portions of the gold ore have been aggregated
near the upper part of the original veinstones, so the heaps
of gravel or detritus resulting either from former powerful
abrasion, or from the diurnal wear and tear of ages, and
derived from the *surface* of such gold-bearing rocks, are, with
rare exceptions, the only materials from which gold has been,
or can be, extracted to *great* profit. These postulates, on
which I have long insisted, in spite of the opposition of
theorists and schemers, have every year received further con-
firmation, and seem on the whole to be so well sustained as
matters of fact, that the real problem we have now to solve is,
how much time will elapse before the gold of Australia is
finally riddled out of these heaps or basins, or extracted from
a few superficial veinstones ?" *

And with respect to the prospects of quartz mining,
Sir Roderick adds :—

"So long as the miner is near the surface, these veinstones
will unquestionably repay the cost of working them. When,

* "Address to the Geographical Society, 1857," pp. 453–455.   In
referring to Sir Roderick Murchison's opinion, it is proper to add that his
views respecting the practical results of gold mining have reference to the
state of mechanical science, as applied to mining operations, *at the time
when he wrote*. In a note to the first edition of his "Siluria" (p. 436), he
expressly guards himself on this point : " I would further guard any
nferences I have drawn from our previous state of knowledge, by saying
that my opinions were formed irrespective of the new discoveries in
mechanical science, crushing machines, &c. The improved application
of mercury may indeed liberate a notable quantity of ore from a matrix of
apparently slight value, and thus set at nought the experience of ages."
And see also the recent edition of the same work, pp. 489 *et seq.*

however, they are followed downwards into the body of the rock, they have usually been found impoverished, either thinning out into slender filaments, or graduating into silver or other ores; so that these insulated thin courses of auriferous quartz—mere threads in the mountain masses—will soon be exhausted for all profitable purposes, when the upper portions shall have been quarried out." *

To this view of the case M. Chevalier opposes the consideration of the vast extent of California and Australia, and the great richness of the alluvium which has been hitherto worked.

" The conditions in which deposits are found in California and Australia are such, that it is not a very sanguine view to suppose that in each of these countries alluvial ground will be found equal to 60,000 hectares of deposits of a metre in thickness, and of the richness of 1 to 100,000 " (P. 65):

conditions which, he says, would give an annual yield for each country of 16,000,000*l.* sterling for a hundred years. We think it, however, more to the purpose to quote the following passage from the report of Mr. Selwyn, who lately conducted the geological survey of Victoria, and who is referred to by Sir Roderick Murchison as a competent witness. " The trap-plains," says Mr. Selwyn, "to the westward are very extensive; and there is every probability of gold deposits existing underneath the trap over the greater portion of them. The limit, therefore, to the period during which these tertiary gold deposits of Victoria may be profitably worked, may be regarded as indefinitely remote."* We may add, that the accounts received from practical

* " Address to the Geographical Society, 1857."
† " Quarterly Journal of the Geological Society," p. 534.

persons in the gold countries are far from supporting
the opinion that the gold formations are extremely
superficial. On the contrary, we hear on all hands
of digging being carried on with profit at a very
considerable depth, ranging frequently from 100 to 300
feet below the surface, and of quartz veins improving
as they descend.* But, besides such statements,
which may not be free from exaggeration, there are
undisputed facts which it seems difficult to reconcile
with the theory of speedy exhaustion. For example,
the most extensive gold fields in Victoria are those of
Ballarat and Mount Alexander; they were amongst
the earliest discovered; they have been worked without intermission for eight years; and it is from them
that the principal portion of the Australian supply is
still derived.† Nor ought we, in estimating the prospects of the future, to overlook the probability of
improvements in the means of production. The
modes of extraction at present in use are generally of
a very crude description. Frequent interruptions of
work occur from want of water; and, though this
obstacle has been overcome in California by the
erection of extensive water-works, this obvious remedy
has still to be applied in Australia. There is thus
great room for improvement in the business of producing gold, and, with Anglo-Saxon enterprise and

* See "Further Papers relative to the Gold Discoveries," presented
to Parliament, February 1856, pp. 47, 48, 56. See also Westgarth's
Victoria," pp. 178, 185; Seyd's "California," pp. 30—44; and Times,
February 16, 1858, San Francisco Correspondence.

† The Brazils also furnish instances of gold fields which have maintained their productiveness for a long period, as well as (as Sir Roderick
Murchison admits) of "successful subterraneous mining."

intelligence directed to the task, we cannot doubt that
improvement will be effected.   On the whole, if we
might venture an opinion respecting a matter on which
we make no pretension to practical knowledge, we
should say that, in speculating upon the auriferous
resources of the new gold countries, too implicit a
reliance has been placed on mere experience.   It is
admitted that the detritus of California and Australia
greatly exceeds in richness any auriferous material
hitherto known : why then may it not exceed any
former material in extent as well as in quality ?   The
history of gold digging in those countries up to the
present time, and the accounts we continue to receive
from a succession of travellers of the great auriferous
tracts which are still untouched, certainly afford ground
for this presumption ; and we are therefore disposed
to concur with M. Chevalier in the opinion, that the
present extraordinary supply of gold is likely to be
continued for, at least, some considerable period.

We assume, then, that the present production of
gold will continue ; and what we have now to consider is the probable effect of this upon the value of
the metal.   The tendency of an increased production
of any commodity is to lower its value, and this
tendency will be realized in fact, unless the demand
for the commodity at the original value increase in a
corresponding degree.   On the supposition, therefore,
that the production of gold continues at its present
rate, the maintenance or decline of its value will
depend upon the extension which may contemporaneously take place in the means of employing it.
This is the position of M. Chevalier, and it is one

which will, we believe, be accepted by all competent
reasoners as the true ground on which the question
should be argued.

By those who deny the probability of an impending
fall in the value of gold we are reminded of the
numerous circumstances which are likely to occur to
occasion an increased demand for it. We are told of
the extraordinary rapidity with which cosmopolitan
commerce is now expanding; of the increased requirements for money incident to an increase of population;
of enlarged consumption of gold in plate, jewelry, and
decoration; of countries now circulating inconvertible
paper which will soon adopt a metallic standard; of
the loss from hoarding and shipwrecks; of the loss
from " wear and tear ; " and of other possible purposes
and occasions which may create a need for an increased
supply of gold. These various requirements, it is
maintained, will generate a demand for the new metal
as fast as it is sent forth from the mines, and will
thus prevent any fall in its value. This argument
M. Chevalier has met by a comprehensive review
of the various incidents here enumerated, in which
he endeavours, by a careful analysis of the facts
of each, to estimate the probable amount which it
may be able to absorb. The result of this investigation is the conclusion, that the utmost quantity
which can be disposed of in the modes suggested,
after allowing in the most liberal manner for every
contingency that may arise, will not at the end of
ten years exceed 1,275,000 kilogrammes of gold, or
about 178,000,000l. sterling. On the other hand, on
the supposition of the present rate of production

continuing, the increase of supply at the end of ten
years will not be less than 2,500,000 kilogrammes,
or 350,000,000*l.* sterling. The result of the comparison carried over a period of ten years is thus
to show an increase in the supply of gold greatly in
excess of the probable requirements of the world
at its present value; the inevitable consequence of
which, as M. Chevalier contends, must be a general
fall in the value of the metal. Such is the conclusion
of this eminent economist—a conclusion full of warning
to this and every other civilized community, and which
has been adopted certainly on no slight or unconsidered
grounds. For the extensive and interesting array of
facts and reasonings by which this opinion is supported,
we must refer our readers to M. Chevalier's volume.
We shall confine ourselves here to some remarks on
those branches of the argument which appear to us
of most importance.

And here, before engaging in the discussion, it may
be well to enter a *caveat* against an ambiguity of
language which has introduced much confusion into
popular reasonings upon this subject. We allude to
the expression so frequently used in the controversy—
"a demand for gold." With reference to this phrase,
it must always be understood that the demand spoken
of is a demand *at some given value of the metal;* since,
without this qualification, an inquiry into the probable
extension of the demand for gold would be an inquiry
without an object, and indeed destitute of all significance. There can be no doubt that the increased
supplies, however great, will find a market somehow,
and be absorbed in the commerce and consumption

of the world ; but the question is, *upon what conditions?* upon the condition of retaining its value as at present, or of submitting to a reduction ? 1600 millions sterling of gold and silver have been supplied to the world by America since the time of Columbus, and this vast amount has been absorbed ; but observe upon what terms. On the terms of a fall in the value of silver in the proportion of 6 to 1, and in that of gold of 4 to 1.* " The present essay," therefore, says M. Chevalier, "is not written to prove that this extraordinary production of the precious metals cannot be employed on any terms, which would be absurd," but to prove that it cannot be absorbed consistently with maintaining its present value in relation to other commodities. " Mankind is not rich enough, nor will it soon be, to pay at so dear a rate for so large a mass." Such is the question to be solved ; let us now consider some of the facts on which the solution depends.

Of the numerous causes which have been suggested as likely to afford a vent for the new gold, none seems at first sight to present so large a field for absorption as the expanding dimensions of commerce ; and yet there is none on which so little expectation in this respect can be legitimately founded. The expansion of general commerce in the last half-century has indeed been enormous. In the United Kingdom, in the United States, throughout the continent of Europe, in California and Australia, even in India and China, the progress has been rapid beyond all precedent.

---

* These are M. Chevalier's estimates. We are inclined to think they are excessive, but they are used here merely in illustration of the principle in question.

This rapid expansion, moreover, has been more especially remarkable during the last ten years, and the
causes of it (among which the adoption of a free-trade
policy by this country must be considered the principal), so far from having exhausted themselves, are
not considered as having yet yielded more than their
first-fruits. Instead, therefore, of any slackening of
commercial progress, we have rather to look for an
acceleration of its pace. The wealth of the world is
thus rapidly increasing, and the augmented wealth, it
is urged, will require for its circulation a medium of
exchange proportionately large. Here, then, is a field
for the new gold of almost boundless extent. Here
is an outlet into which the rising tide may flow off
without any danger of surcharging those channels of
circulation which are already full.

To this argument we might object, that the increase
of international transactions (by which it is customary
to estimate the progress of trade), although it always
indicates an increase in the elements of real wealth,
by no means indicates a corresponding increase, still
less a corresponding increase in the *value* of such
elements, or therefore in the need for a circulating
medium. But, without entering into the somewhat
complicated considerations connected with this point,
and admitting, as we do, the probability of a considerable increase in the requirements of the world for a
circulating medium, the question remains, Is gold the
material by which such requirements will be met?
M. Chevalier contends, and we think with good reason,
that it is not. The proportion of the trade of the
world which is carried on with metallic money is daily

diminishing, and constantly tends to diminish ; and the probability is, that the future expansions of trade will be chiefly supported, not with coin, but with those contrivances of credit and of paper currency, the immense advantages of which over metallic money we have already learned to appreciate.

Few persons, who are not practically engaged in business on a large scale, have an adequate conception of the extent to which credit expedients of one kind or another are now employed in the conduct of commercial affairs. In the principal commercial countries it may with little exaggeration be said, that the great wholesale transactions of trade are effected exclusively through this medium. Perhaps the most striking example of what can be accomplished by this means is afforded by the London Clearing House—the institution in which the accounts of the London bankers are daily settled.

"In 1839 this establishment had already attained such efficiency that for the annual liquidation of 950,000,000l. sterling, or 3,000,000l. daily, it only required, on an average each day, 200,000l. in sovereigns, or rather in bank-notes. At present, with a mass of transactions amounting to 1,500,000,000l. or 2,000,000,000l. sterling annually, instead of a proportionate addition to the 200,000l. required for the daily balance being necessary, not a shilling is wanted ; the Clearing House now dispenses completely with the use of bank-notes; all is settled by the transfer of sums from one account to another in the books of the Bank of England." (P. 84.)

To such perfection has the system of credit been brought in this country. But, to appreciate the full force of the argument founded on the resources of credit, we should consider that, besides the field opened for its employment in the future expansions of trade, a large one exists in much of that which is now carried on. In Great Britain and the United States, the use of credit may indeed be thought to have reached its maximum; but this cannot be supposed of other portions of Europe and America, and still less of the vast communities of Asia. In India, though more than a century under British rule, the advantages of credit, as a medium of exchange, are only beginning to be understood. The circulation of bank-notes is exceedingly limited, and is still confined to some of the Presidency towns; cheques, by which so large a portion of the business of this country is carried on, are but slightly used; and the great mass of transactions is effected by a transfer of rupees bodily in every sale. The magnitude of the transactions conducted in this manner may be estimated by the fact stated by Sir Charles Napier, that the escort of treasure constituted one of the severest duties of the late Bengal army; from 20,000 to 30,000 men being constantly occupied in this manner. The quantity of the precious metals employed in thus carrying on the internal traffic of India has been variously estimated between 150,000,000*l.* and 300,000,000*l.* sterling. But this state of things is evidently not destined to be of long continuance. Mr. Wilson's recent minute gives grounds for believing that the Indian Government are alive to this subject, and that India will soon enjoy the advantages of an effective paper system. Such an event cannot fail to be attended with important consequences on the trade and industry of

that country; and among these consequences we may
expect this, that, instead of requiring, as now, continuous large additions to her present enormous stock
of metallic money, she will not only be enabled to
dispense with these, but will find it for her interest to
part with a large portion of what she now employs :
the coin thus liberated will form a new tributary to
swell the increasing supplies, and the influences tending to depress the value of gold will be increased.

These observations apply to the wholesale transactions of commerce : they are not, in the same degree,
applicable to the retail dealings of individuals. We
say, not in the same degree, because they are applicable
to a certain extent even to them. Amongst the upper
and middle classes, at least in this country, the practice
is becoming every day more general of paying private
accounts through the medium of bankers' cheques, in
which way retail transactions, in the aggregate of very
large amount, are settled without the employment
either of bank-notes or of metallic money. This practice, however, is confined to that comparatively limited
portion of society whose private dealings assume
dimensions sufficiently large to render the employment
of credit convenient. For the mass of the population,
who live mostly from hand to mouth, and whose
dealings are on a very small scale, credit accounts are
obviously unsuitable, and their purchases are accordingly effected almost wholly with coin. In this department of business, therefore, we find a field for the
employment of gold which credit cannot well occupy,
and which will increase with the increase of population.
It becomes, therefore, important to ascertain the extent

of the outlet which may be afforded in this direction
for the increasing supplies.

With a view to this, M. Chevalier has instituted a
comparison between the rate at which population is
now advancing and that at which gold is increasing ;
the result of which is to show that, while population
in civilized countries is advancing at the rate of one
and a half per cent. per annum, gold—at least that
portion which goes into general circulation—is increasing by more than 10 per cent. per annum.*   Or, to
put the same point differently, that while to satisfy
the requirements of population an annual production
of 3,000,000*l.* would be sufficient, the amount actually
applicable to this purpose will, supposing the present
scale of production to continue, not fall short of
20,000,000*l.* annually.   It would seem, therefore, that
the mere growth of population promises but an inadequate market for the new gold.   And this conclusion
is further confirmed by the fact, of which M. Chevalier
reminds us, that in the dealings of the masses the metal
which is principally employed is not gold, but silver or
copper.   The lowest gold piece in this country is
worth ten shillings, the lowest in France is worth four
shillings, and the inconvenience which would result
from a smaller coin sets a limit to further reduction.
It is, therefore, among a portion only of the working
classes—those whose purchases are sufficiently large
to make the use of such coin possible—that gold
circulates at all, or can be expected to circulate ; and
this circumstance, he argues, must reduce within very

---

* This proportion is not given by M. Chevalier, but may be deduced
from his statements.

narrow limits the field for its employment in this
direction.

These considerations would seem to settle the
question, so far as the requirements of the masses are
concerned. Nevertheless there is an element of the
case, not included in M. Chevalier's reasonings, which
leads us to assign greater importance to this application of the new gold than the facts which he has
stated would seem to warrant. The industrial history
of Great Britain since the gold discoveries supplies us
with a fact but little in accordance with the above cal-
culations; the fact, namely, that since the year 1851
the population of this country, which at the utmost
has not increased in the interval by more than 10 per
cent., has absorbed into its retail circulation (according
to the best estimate which we have been able to form)
an addition to its gold currency of not less than 40
per cent.*—an addition which, though not wholly
unaccompanied by an advance of prices, has not been
productive of any effect in this respect commensurate
with its amount. Now to what are we to attribute this
anomalous circumstance? How are we to explain the
fact that the gold currency of this kingdom has increased in a degree entirely out of proportion to
the apparent requirements of its population, *without
undergoing any corresponding depreciation in its value?*
It appears to us that the explanation is to be found
in the operation of a principle to which we adverted
in the opening of this article, and to which we shall

---

* See on this point the facts and estimates given in Appendix xxii. to
the sixth volume of the "History of Prices;" also the statistics of gold
coinage given in the same volume, p. 154.

have occasion again to advert,—the tendency of the increased production of gold to alter the distribution of wealth throughout society. This principle, operating through our trade with the gold countries, has for the last eight years been acting upon the pecuniary relations of different classes in this country; and the result has been a change in the distribution of our national wealth sensibly in favour of the industrial portion of the social body. We do not here enter into the grounds of this opinion, which would involve us in economic discussions of an inconvenient length. But, in illustration of the general tendency of the gold discoveries to favour the industrial classes, we may refer to the triple and quadruple wages now enjoyed by those amongst them who have emigrated to California and Australia, and to the remarkable advance which during the last eight years has taken place in the wages of almost every class of labourers at home,*— an advance which has been accompanied by no corresponding movement in the incomes of other classes. A large increase has thus taken place in that portion of the general wealth which circulates among the industrial population; and this is just the portion in which the circulation of coin is most extensive. It is evident therefore (assuming, as we do, this fact to represent a general tendency) that, under the influences engendered by the new discovery, the demand of the population for gold coin may augment much more rapidly than a mere regard to the increase of its numbers would lead us to suppose. As the produc-

* See Dr. Strang's "Papers on Wages," published in the London Statistical Journal.

tion of gold continues, the proportion of the aggregate
wealth of the world which goes to the industrial
classes will increase; and, the field for credit contracting as we descend in the scale of society, the
necessity for coin will increase also.   In this way, it
seems to us, a market may be opened for the new
gold greatly more extensive than the considerations
adduced by M. Chevalier would lead us to suppose;
and a large amount of the new supplies may be thus
disposed of, without involving the necessity of a fall,
or at least of a corresponding fall, in their value.   At
the same time we are far from thinking that the
demand thence arising will be sufficient to prevent the
ultimate depreciation of the metal; though, as the
example of this country proves, it may sensibly retard
this result.   At all events, the principle is one which
should not be overlooked in an examination of the
causes which may neutralize the direct tendencies of
the gold movement.

So far as to the demand afforded to the gold supplies by the progress of trade and population.   Let us
now consider briefly another mode of disposing of the
new gold, on which some writers have laid much
stress : we mean the employment of it in the arts, in
plate, and for decorative purposes.   And here, as in
the case we have just been considering, an examination of the facts shows upon what slight grounds
they proceed who anticipate a large absorption of
gold by these uses.   The desire for display, at least
in that gross form of the propensity which finds
satisfaction in the possession of gold plate or in
the **wearing of** massive ornaments, is an attribute

of semi-barbarous life, which, instead of increasing, declines with the advance of society.

"The display of gold in utensils more or less massive is the luxury of the less refined part of the community, whose eye is instinctively attracted by the glare of a dazzling metal, and whose desire is excited for an object to which there is vulgarly attached the idea of great riches. It is a species of magnificence which was reserved for the sovereigns of primitive nations; it constituted the splendour of the Incas, and that of Attila and of Genseric; it was the pride of the savage races whom the Europeans discovered in America." (P. 98.)

The same passion for ornaments is a powerful instinct amongst the native races of Hindostan, with whom they serve at once as a mode of investment and a means of decoration. But, as civilization makes progress, tastes of a different order are developed. Vanity perhaps loses nothing of its power, but it exhibits itself under a different guise, and is directed to different objects. Luxury, in its modes of display, as in other respects, undergoes refinement, and mankind seek enjoyment, less in the gratification of external sense, and more in the cultivation of the higher faculties. The superfluous expenditure of a nation advancing in civilization is accordingly devoted less and less to objects which absorb mere masses of gold and silver, and more and more to purposes of a higher order—to the beautifying of its domains, the embellishing of its houses, the general cultivation of its tastes; and parks and mansions, pictures, sculpture, and books, take the place of accumulations of plate and collections of jewelry.

This tendency of civilization to check the consump-

tion of the precious metals is very strikingly shown by
some figures quoted by M. Chevalier. From returns
given in Porter's " Progress of the Nation," it appears
that the consumption of gold plate in England during
the first half of the present century has not kept pace
even with the progress of population. Notwithstanding the great increase which has taken place in the
means of all classes during the interval, the average
Englishman of the present day consumes less gold
than the Englishman of fifty years back.

"From the first quinquennial period of the century to
that which closed in 1850, the increase in the quantity
of gold which paid duty was 50 per cent.; during the
same time the increase of population was much greater: it
doubled. Then if we take into account the quantity of gold
required for this manufacture, we are amazed at its small-
ness. It is an atom in comparison with the total production.
During the last quinquennial period of the half-century, the
annual average has only been 7,636 ounces." (Pp. 92, 93.)

For the two years 1855 and 1856 the average
consumption in this form was ten thousand ounces.
For the same years the total production was nearly
ten millions—that is to say, nearly a thousand times
greater! In France a similar state of things is exhibited. There also the consumption of the precious
metals proceeds more slowly than the increase of
population.

But it will be said, if the fashion of using gold in
plate and ornaments is declining, other forms of this
kind of expenditure have amazingly increased.

" Paris gilds itself not a little, and is surprisingly addicted
to gold lace. Is there not in these two employments a

consumption large enough to enable the producers of gold
to dispose of their precious commodity, almost indefinitely,
without any reduction in its value ?   To reply to this question, let us calculate the quantity of metal which is required
to gild a given surface.   Gold, as is known, is the most malle-
able of metals ; it is so to a degree of which it would be
difficult, without ocular illustration, to form an idea.   The
goldbeater makes it into leaves which, thanks to the progress
of his art, are now so thin that 14,000 form only the thickness
of a millimetre, and, consequently, 14,000,000 of leaves laid
one upon another would make a thickness of only a metre
(about 39 inches).   A cubic metre of solid gold, which would
not weigh less than 680,440 ounces, would suffice to gild a
surface of 3,450 acres, and 35,300 ounces would cover with
gold 179 acres.   It is a result which quite confounds the
imagination.   And yet the metal used in the manufacture of
gold lace is spread over a much larger surface.   The substance of the threads of which this lace is made consists of
silver, the surface alone being gold, and one gramme of gold,
worth 2*s*. 10*d*., suffices to gild a thread 120 miles in length.
In a piece of 20 francs (16*s*.), there is gold enough to
cover a thread which would extend from Calais to Marseilles.
. . . . . Let us now suppose that a room, suitably gilded,
consumes five square metres of gold leaf, which is, I believe,
sufficient.   At this rate 35,300 ounces would gild 144,000
saloons or apartments ; that is to say, at least twenty times
the number which are thus embellished in one year in all
those cities where the houses are of a character to require
their interiors to be gilded.   With the remainder, what a
multitude of picture-frames, books, kettle-drums, cloths, epau-
lettes, and all kinds of objects, might be clothed in a dazzling
covering of gold !   Let the number of gold leaves required
for each apartment be multiplied, let the number of books
and picture-frames be augmented, and still we shall arrive at
no result which deserves a moment's consideration.   At Paris,
where nearly all the gold leaf is beaten which is consumed in
France and a part of Europe, the quantity of gold operated
upon does not exceed 40,650 to 42,400 ounces." (Pp
95—97.)

It would therefore seem that not much is to be expected from the extending use of gold in manufactures
as a means of disposing of the new supplies. No
doubt, as depreciation sets in, the fall in the value of
the metal will, as in the case of other commodities,
have some effect in inducing a larger consumption;
but, with the facts before us which have just been
cited, this can scarcely be expected to occur to an
extent which would materially retard the fall.

And here we may mention an incident of the
decline in the value of gold, which is strangely at
variance with popular anticipations, and will probably
be cited as a proof that no depreciation has taken
place. People generally imagine that as gold declines
in value gold manufactures of all kinds will become
cheaper. In one sense they will; they will be obtainable at a less outlay of labour; but they will not
become cheaper in the sense in which the word is
commonly understood—that is to say, they will not be
obtainable *at a lower price.* On the contrary, in all
countries where, as in this, gold is the standard metal,
as its value declines *the price of gold manufactures will
rise.* A little reflection will make this plain. Suppose
the exchange-value of gold to fall, let us consider what
will be the effect of this upon the price of a gold snuff-
box. So far as the *material* of the article is concerned,
it is evident that the fall in the value of gold will have
no effect, will be simply nugatory, since the same cause
which will reduce the value of the material will reduce
also the value of the coin (or notes convertible into
coin) with which it is procured; the relation between
money and raw gold will continue the same as before,

and the price of the material of the box will therefore continue unaltered. But the material is only one element of the cost ; there is, besides this, the labour expended in the making, and this also must be included in the price of the snuff-box. Now the effect of a fall in the exchange-value of gold will be to raise the money-price of labour in common with other things ; whence it is plain that, with the progress of this fall, the price of the snuff-box, which must cover the cost of labour as well as that of raw material, must constantly rise. The effect may not be very perceptible in gold articles of much solidity ; but in such manufactures as gold lace, in which the value of the workmanship greatly exceeds the value of the material, the rise in price will be nearly as remarkable as if gold did not enter into their composition.

Such are the two principal outlets which have been suggested as likely to create a market for the new gold ; and, considerable as they at first sight appear, this examination of them has shown how entirely inadequate they must prove to sustain its value, supposing the production of the metal to continue at its present rate. The facts of the case thus distinctly point to a general depreciation of gold as the inevitable result of the causes now in action.

Against this conclusion, however, will be urged our experience of the movement up to the present time. Already, it will be said, for eight years the golden stream has been flowing : not less than 200,000,000*l.* sterling of metal have already been added to the common stock ; and yet we look in vain for those signs of depreciation which, if there be any foundation for the apprehensions which have been expressed, should surely by this time have displayed themselves. No perceptible change, it is asserted, has yet taken place in the general level of prices, no disturbance has been experienced in our pecuniary relations. If, then, under the weight of this large augmentation, the value of the metal has been sustained, there is clearly some fact or principle at work which has been overlooked in the reasonings on the subject ; and if this fact or principle (whatever it may be) has been hitherto efficacious in preventing a fall, may we not expect that it will continue to be so ? If no sensible effect has up to the present been produced, why, with only the same influences to contend against, need we be apprehensive for the future ?

This argument is to be met by a twofold answer : first, by a denial of the fact which is assumed, that no change has taken place in the value of gold; and secondly, by pointing to a circumstance which has hitherto retarded its decline, but the influence of which must soon diminish.

With respect to the first point it should be observed, that it must always be a matter of considerable difficulty to ascertain whether, in point of fact, gold has during a given time fallen in value or not, unless the fall happens to be of a very marked and unequivocal kind. This must be so from the absence of any independent standard of value by which its variations can be measured, as well as from the variety of causes which, besides the value of money, affect the prices of commodities, and thus complicate the problem. There is, moreover, a principle in constant operation which,

in a large class of cases, tends to conceal any fall
which may occur in the value of the precious metals—
we mean, the progress of the industrial arts. Every
improvement in productive industry tends to promote
cheapness and to lower price ; and, as such improvements are constantly occurring, a fall in the value of
gold will be as often shown in preventing a fall in the
price of other things as in causing a rise. To ascertain, therefore, whether a change in the value of gold
has really occurred must always be a difficult problem,
requiring for its solution not only an extensive collection and accurate analysis of prices, but also a careful
examination of the various causes affecting production
on the one hand and consumption on the other : and
it is a problem which, applied to the last ten years,
presents, owing to the numerous causes of powerful
disturbance which have been in action during that
time, even more than the usual difficulty. We do not,
therefore, propose to enter into this question here, but
shall content ourselves with referring in a note * to
some publications, in which it has been discussed with
considerable fulness. By reference to these the reader
will find that the facts of the case, far from being
favourable to the assumption that the value of gold
has been unaffected by the increased supply, lead
rather to the conclusion, that there are grounds for
believing that a definitive depreciation of the metal
has already taken place.

* See tables of prices from 1851 to 1857 (" History of Prices," vol. vi.
pp. 160—167) ; also an article by M. Levasseur in the *Journal des
Economistes*, March 1858 ; also tables published by Dr. Soetbeer of
Hamburg, giving returns of prices from 1831 to 1857 ; also the Appendix
to this volume.

But, secondly, the above reasoning is to be answered
by pointing to a circumstance which has undoubtedly
acted up to the present time in counteraction of the
causes tending to depress the value of gold, but the
efficacy of which is diminishing, and may soon be
entirely exhausted.   This circumstance is the displace-
ment of silver by gold in some currencies, and more
particularly in that of France—a circumstance to which
M. Chevalier very forcibly directs our attention, and
which ranks unquestionably as of primary importance
amongst the causes which have modified the gold
movement up to the present time.

In the controversies which have taken place on this
question, it has been almost uniformly assumed on the
one side and conceded on the other, that, for the purpose of detecting variations in the value of gold, no
better test can be selected than the price—that is, the
gold-price — of silver;* and the price of silver not
having risen more than 3 or 4 per cent. in the last ten
years, it is argued that this ratio represents the utmost
extent of the depreciation which can have taken place
in gold.   Indeed some writers have pressed this argument so far, as to maintain that gold has not fallen
even to this extent; the rise in the price of silver, as
they allege, being due rather to the increase in the
demand for it than to the fall in the value of gold.

* Strange to say, even M. Chevalier makes this concession, although
the facts which he adduces effectually expose its fallaciousness.   "The
only good measure of the rise or fall occurring in the value of gold, is
that which takes place in its price in silver money." He adds: "Then
it must be premised that no disturbance shall have arisen to cause a
sudden change in the value of silver." But such a disturbance is produced *ipso facto* by a change in the value of gold.

But surely nothing can be more fallacious than the test
of value which is thus set up. If anything unfits one
commodity for measuring the value of another, it is the
circumstance that they may both be applied to common
purposes. No one would think of measuring the
fluctuations in wheat by comparing it with oats,
because, both grains being employed for the same or
similar purposes, any change in the value of one is
sure to extend to the other. When, *e.g.*, the wheat
crop is in excess while the oat crop is an average one,
it always happens that a portion of the consumption,
which in ordinary years falls upon oats, is thrown upon
wheat ; the effect of which is at once to check the fall
in the price of the more abundant grain, while, by
diminishing the need for the other, it causes it to parti-
cipate in the decline. The influence of the increased
abundance of one commodity is thus distributed over
both ; the fall in price being less intense in degree in
proportion as it is wider in extent. Now this is
precisely what is happening in the relations of gold and
silver. The crop of gold has been unusually large ;
the increase in the supply has caused a fall in its
value ; the fall in its value has led to its being substituted for silver ; a mass of silver has thus been
disengaged from purposes which it was formerly
employed to serve, and the result has been that
both metals have fallen in value together ; the
depth of the fall being diminished as the surface
over which it has taken place has been enlarged.
The scene on which this interchange of gold and
silver has hitherto been exhibited on the largest scale
is the currency of France, in which, owing to the

existence of a double standard,—or (if M. Chevalier
prefers the phrase) a double legal tender,—one or the
other metal is employed according as its worth in the
markets of the world happens to vary in relation to its
valuation at the French Mint. Until a recent period,
the metal which formed the staple of the French
currency was silver, but, owing to the fall in the value
of gold consequent upon the discoveries, gold is now
rapidly taking its place, and becoming the principal
medium of circulation. Up to the year 1852 the
importation of silver into France was always largely
in excess of its exportation ; but in that year the tide
turned, and has since continued flowing outward with
increasing volume. M. Chevalier states that by the
end of 1857 France had parted with 45,000,000l.
sterling of silver. On the other hand, during this
time she had coined more than 100,000,000l. sterling
of gold. The currency of France has thus, to borrow
the curious but not unapt figure of our author, played
towards gold the part of a parachute to moderate its
descent. But in proportion as gold has thus found a
market, silver has been deprived of one ; and the
45,000,000l. of silver liberated from the currency of
France is as much an addition to the disposable supply
in the world, and tends as effectually to lower its value,
as if it had been raised immediately from the mines.
The fall in the value of gold has thus, up to the
present time, been at once checked and concealed,—
checked by being substituted for silver, and concealed
by being compared with it.*

* We are aware it has been maintained that the value of silver, so far
from having fallen, has really risen during the last few years ; in proof of

This substitution, however, of gold for silver in French circulation is not a process which can be carried on indefinitely, and M. Chevalier shows that it has already nearly reached its natural termination. When this has happened, the new gold will be deprived of that which has hitherto constituted its best market, the parachute which has moderated its descent will no longer be available; and what will be the consequence?

"From that moment," says M. Chevalier, "the fall in gold will be rapid. In a word, if, down to the present time, the immense production, of which Australia and California have been the theatre, has not produced a greater fall in gold, it is France which is the cause." (P. 62.)

which we are referred to the increased demand for it for Oriental remittance. That silver has risen in its *gold*-price owing to this circumstance, we admit, but we deny that this is a proof of a rise in its *value*, any more than a rise in the gold-price of any other commodity would prove a rise in its value at a time when the supply of gold was rapidly increasing. During the last two years (1858 and 1859) the demand for silver for the East has been affected a good deal by requirements connected with the Indian Mutiny; but if we investigate the causes of the extraordinary demand which has characterized the last four or five years, we shall find that they are in a principal degree traceable to the increased production of gold, operating through the expenditure of enlarged money incomes in England and the United States on Oriental productions; and that thus the increased demand for silver, which is alleged as a proof that silver has risen in value, *is in reality a consequence of the large amount of gold available for its purchase.* Now if a disturbance in the relative values of the precious metals, arising from *this* cause, is to be taken as a proof, not that gold has fallen, but that silver has risen in value, then it would be quite impossible ever to prove a depreciation of gold. The same argument might be applied to all other commodities; in each case it could be shown that the rise in price was the result of an increased demand for the article, and every advance in general prices would be attributed, not to the depreciation of money, but to the enhancement of commodities. In short, since money can only fall in value by being made the instrument of demand, the value of money could, according to this mode of reasoning, never fall.

We are disposed to qualify in some degree our
assent to this opinion. We think that, on the occurrence of the contingency in question—the exhaustion
of silver from the French currency—the depreciation
of gold will be more rapid, but we question if the
acceleration of the decline will be as great as the
words we have quoted seem to imply. M. Chevalier
appears to assume that, when the process now going on
in France is completed, all further substitution of one
metal for the other will be at an end, and that the
action of future supplies, concentrated on gold alone,
will tell in the depreciation of this metal with proportionate effect. But we question the correctness of
this assumption. We are inclined to think that the
substitution of gold for silver in France is only a very
striking example of a process which has been in unob-
served operation over a much wider area, and which
will continue after the French movement has ceased.
In India, where there is an immense silver currency,
the process has already begun, and signs are not wanting that it will soon assume more important dimensions.
The Indian Government, for reasons set forth in Mr.
Wilson's Minute on the introduction of a gold currency,
have indeed refused to establish a double standard in
that country ; and we cannot, therefore, count upon a
contingency of this kind as likely to carry on in the
East the process which must ere long be complete in
France : still, considering the great suitability of gold
for the purposes of ornamental manufacture, and of
hoarding—purposes which prevail so extensively in
India, and for which gold is much better adapted than
silver—we cannot doubt but that, as, in the course of

depreciation, the metal becomes obtainable on more favourable terms, it will gradually find its way, if not into the circulation, at least into the ornaments and hoards, and eventually displace silver to a considerable extent. These considerations do not apply to India alone : they are applicable more or less extensively to other countries where silver is the currency, and more particularly to China, where there is a large silver circulation, and where the habits of the people are in many respects similar to those of the people of Hindostan. For these reasons, we cannot concur in the assumption, that, when the movement in the French currency is concluded, the future action of the new gold must be concentrated upon the gold currencies of the world. We think that its effect will still continue to be shared, though probably in a less degree than heretofore, by the other precious metal ; and that consequently the fall in gold, though accelerated, will not proceed with that rapidity which M. Chevalier seems to anticipate.*

* [The writer can now (1872) claim the verdict of events in favour of the view which he here ventured to maintain against that taken by M. Chevalier. Indeed, the course of depreciation has been even less affected by the completion of the process of substituting gold for silver in the currency of France than he anticipated. That process would seem to have been completed about the year 1861, when the coinage of gold in France fell from 27,000,000*l.* and 18,000,000*l.*—the amounts which it had reached in the years 1859 and 1860—to less than 4,000,000*l.* (See *Economist*, 29th June, 1872, article " On the Coinage of Gold.") But he is not aware that any sensible change in the rapidity of the depreciation of gold can be traced to that period. It would be difficult indeed to determine this question by reference to general prices ; but if any effect, such as M. Chevalier anticipated, occurred, it would have shown itself in a rise in the price of silver. In point of fact, the price of silver has undergone little change over the whole of this period, and is now rather lower than when M. Chevalier wrote. This may be partly due to the increased production of silver in recent years, which would more or less counteract any tendency to an advance in its price ; but I have no doubt the principal cause is that

But, although for these reasons we do not anticipate that rapid and sudden fall in the value of gold which M. Chevalier regards as the sure result of the exhaustion of silver from France (or more correctly, of the repletion of the French currency with gold), we nevertheless fully admit, supposing the present production to continue, that the contingencies to which we have adverted can at the utmost delay, they cannot prevent, this catastrophe. Regarding therefore, with him, an extensive depreciation of gold as probable, we shall conclude this article by adverting to some of the consequences which this result is likely to entail.

These consequences are at once so numerous and so complicated, they will be felt in such large and in such minute transactions in life, that to develop them fully would require a volume instead of a few pages. As we have already intimated, there is a wide department of this question on which M. Chevalier does not enter at all *—of the existence of which indeed he scarcely seems to be aware ; but even within the range to which he has confined himself, the questions which arise are both numerous and important.

One of the most important aspects of every social change is its effect on the working classes—those who

assigned in the text—the extensive substitution of gold for silver, not only in various currencies in different countries, but in all those uses in which the two metals may be indifferently employed. In truth, so completely are gold and silver identified as economic agencies by this capacity for mutual substitution, that in judging of the probable effect of increased supplies of either metal, the safest course would probably be to consider them as one commodity, and to compare, not gold with gold and silver with silver, but the aggregate additions made to both metals with the aggregate quantities of both previously existing.]

* That discussed in Essay III. of this volume.

live by the sweat of their brow, and who in every
country form the bulk of the population.   Let us then
inquire, What will be the effect of the gold discoveries
on the interests of this large section of mankind?
Will the event tend on the whole to improve or to
deteriorate, to raise or to depress, their condition?
The opinion of M. Chevalier is that, during the period
while depreciation is in progress—a period which may
extend over ten or twenty, or possibly over thirty or
forty years—the effect may be prejudicial.   As soon
indeed as the movement shall have reached its lowest
point, and gold shall have found its natural level, then
he conceives the wages of the workman will rise in
the same proportion as the price of his food, so that,
while paying and receiving larger sums of money, he
will be placed substantially in the same position as at
present; but, pending the attainment of this result, the
ordeal of depreciation will, as he thinks, be for the
working classes a disastrous one.

" Experience shows that, when provisions rise, wages are
not necessarily raised in the same proportion.   Not that an
upward movement of wages does not follow a continued dearness of provisions, but in the majority of employments it
follows far behind.   The working population are of all classes
of society the most dependent, because they are the most
necessitous.   Being the least able to wait, owing to the
pressure of want, they are the more apt to resign themselves
to the terms offered them.   Hence it is that the benefits
which they expect to derive from a rise of wages are only
yielded to them after many delays.   It were easy to cite
examples in proof of this assertion.   It has been the subject
of remark by Mr. Tooke in his important work on the
' History of Prices.'   In his historical inquiry respecting
the precious metals, Mr. Jacob has several remarks in

the same sense, and among others he states his opinion that the institution of the Poor Law, which it is known dates from the reign of Elizabeth, was in England the effect of the changes caused by the fall in the precious metals." (Pp. 117, 118.)

From this opinion of M. Chevalier (which is endorsed by Mr. Cobden in his preface) we venture to dissent. We do not believe that the working classes, *as a body*—whatever may be the case with particular sections of them or in particular countries—will be injured by the depreciation of gold. We hold, on the contrary, that the general effect of the gold discoveries will be to alter the distribution of wealth in their favour, and on the whole to benefit them.

According to M. Chevalier, the industrial classes will suffer during the progress of the depreciation of gold, because the prices of the commodities they consume will constantly rise in advance of the rise in their wages. Now this we conceive to be, as a general proposition, essentially impossible. If the prices of the labourer's provisions and clothing rise, this result can only happen (assuming that the rise proceeds from an abundance of money) because more money is spent on those commodities ; and, inasmuch as the labouring classes themselves immensely outnumber all classes who consume the same commodities, it is plain that it is *their* expenditure, and consequently *their* wages, which must substantially regulate the rise. The rise in wages, in short, is (where it proceeds from an abundance of money) the cause of the rise in the price of commodities, and consequently cannot be preceded by its own effect.

The circumstance which misled M. Chevalier appears from his reference to the remark of Mr. Tooke; for the case which Mr. Tooke had in view was the rise in the prices of corn and provisions which occurred during the last French wars—a rise due indeed in some slight degree to the depreciation then existing in the English currency, but, according to the opinion of Mr. Tooke, and we believe of all persons who have examined the facts of that time, due principally to the unusual number of deficient harvests which then occurred, aggravated as this circumstance was by the interruption of supplies from abroad during the war. The rise in prices at that time proceeded, in short, from a dearth of commodities, not from an abundance of money; and the rise in wages which followed, as a matter of necessity, fell short of the advance in provisions, since it was only thus that consumption could be kept within the limits of supply. It is by confounding the effects of these two very different cases that M. Chevalier has fallen into the error of supposing that the labouring classes, as a body, must suffer from the depreciation of gold.

But the view thus suggested has probably been confirmed by another circumstance. It would seem, as a matter of fact, that prices *in France* have up to the present time advanced more rapidly than wages.*

---

* See the articles by M. Levasseur, published in the *Journal des Économistes*, February and March 1858. [Since 1858 the relative advance in wages and prices, at least in some important trades, would seem to be in an opposite sense. The following I quote from Mr. Brassey's recent work (pp. 158, 159):—"Mr. Fane says, in his report to Lord Stanley, that 'the general rate of money wages in France has increased about 40 per cent. in the last fifteen years, in those industries which

This, however, is not a necessary or general consequence of the depreciation of gold, but, like the case
of England in the sixteenth century to which Jacob
refers, is to be attributed to that other operation of the
gold movement, of which we have more than once
spoken—the change it is causing in the distribution of
national wealth. In the sixteenth century this disturbance was in favour of the Spanish, the Portuguese,
and the Dutch ; while the English, further removed
from the spring-head of the new metal, received their
supplies more slowly and in scantier streams. Money
incomes in England therefore rose less rapidly than
prices in common markets, and the population of England suffered accordingly. We have no doubt that
this was a leading cause of the industrial distress
which prevailed throughout a portion of the reign of
Queen Elizabeth,* and which led to the introduction
of the Poor Law. In the present gold movement,
however, the tables have been turned, and the monetary disturbance is now in favour of the Anglo-Saxon.
It is now England and the United States that have
their hands in the till, and the money which they
extract is employed in raising prices against the nations

compete with foreigners in the neutral markets. This rise in the money
wages has been accompanied by a considerable rise in the price of food
and clothing; still, the relative proportions in which money wages and
the prices of commodities have risen, leave a margin in favour of the
former.' "]

* See on this point a curious work, entitled "A Briefe Conceipte touch-
ng the Common Weale of this Realme of England," published in 1581
and attributed to William Stafford. Of this work Anderson, in his
"Annals," conjectures that it was written by direction of the Queen's
ministers, "since scar. cly any ordinary person in those early days could
be furnished with so copious a fund of excellent matter."

which in the sixteenth century were gainers at their
expense.   It is to this cause—the disturbance created
by the gold discoveries in the distribution of purchasing
power in the world—that the movement of prices in
France in advance of incomes (so far as this is a fact)
is to be attributed, and not to any tendency in prices
during a depreciation of money to rise more rapidly
than the incomes by the expenditure of which alone
they can be raised.

And here we may remark, as bearing on the practical purpose which M. Chevalier had in view in this
discussion—the change of the monetary standard in
France from gold to silver—that the consideration
here urged goes directly to the root of his argument.
If the sufferings of the French workmen during the
period of transition be the result of a depreciation
of the standard, then of course the disaster may be
avoided by substituting for gold, as our author recom-
mends, a metal such as silver, of which the value is
steady ; but if, as we contend, the evil in question be
the result of the increased purchasing power of other
nations, it is plain that the proposed remedy must be
futile.   No change in the Mint regulations of France
will prevent the nations which are in possession of the
new gold from appropriating an increased proportion
of the aggregate wealth of the world.   To effect this,
it would be necessary not merely to deprive gold of
its character as a standard, but to annihilate its purchasing power altogether, to dethrone it from its
position as the universal equivalent of commerce.

As we have already intimated, we conceive that the
gold movement, whatever may be its effect in particular

cases, will, on the whole, operate favourably for the
industrial classes of society, by throwing into their
hands an increased share of the purchasing power of
the world. It is this which we regard as the great
redeeming incident of the gold discoveries. In almost
every other aspect in which we contemplate the occurrence, it is fraught with inconvenience, hardship, and
injustice, introducing uncertainty into mercantile dealings, disturbing contracts which were designed to be
fixed, stimulating the spirit of commercial speculation,
already too strong, and bringing unmerited loss upon
classes who have the strongest claims on our sympathy,
and whom upon social grounds it is most desirable to
sustain.

If we inquire who the people are who will suffer by
the impending monetary changes, the answer is, in the
first place and principally, those whose incomes consist
in fixed sums of money, or whose property depends
on fixed contracts expressed in the current gold coin of
the realm. Adopting the assumption of M. Chevalier
(which with him we make for the sake of distinctness,
and not as expressing a matured opinion), that the fall
in the value of gold will be 50 per cent., then the loss
to the holders of all such incomes will be to the extent
of one-half of their means. They will receive the
same nominal amount as at present, the same number
of bank-notes, which will be exchangeable for the
same number of sovereigns of the same weight and
fineness ; but these bank-notes or sovereigns will only
procure one-half as much of the necessaries, comforts,
and luxuries of life as they would do in the absence
of a depreciation of money. This is surely a serious

matter, and its gravity is not diminished when we
consider who the persons are that by the course of
events (always supposing the production of gold to
continue) will be placed in this position. They are,
in the first place, fundholders and mortgagees, a class
who, whatever may be the popular idea upon the
subject, really deserve as much consideration and
sympathy as any other in the community. For
of what is a large portion of funded property, and of
property lent on mortgage, composed ? To a very
large extent, as is well known, of trust money,
constituting as such, the provision made for widows
and orphans, for younger children and minors, and
others who from their age, sex, or circumstances are
incapacitated for taking part in the active pursuits of
life. The persons thus provided for are also very frequently persons whose social rank is rather in advance
of their pecuniary means of supporting it, with whom,
therefore, a reduction of income will frequently necessitate, not merely a curtailment of physical enjoyment,
but a descent in the social scale, a loss of caste and
position, with the many distressing mortifications which
such a loss involves. Again, trust money includes the
property of endowed bodies, of charitable and benevolent institutions, schools, hospitals, and churches, all
which, with the fall in the value of gold, will be
deprived of a corresponding proportion of their income,
and thus find abridged their means of public useful-
ness. Further, the depreciation of money will fall
heavily on those, not confined to any class, but in
general the most deserving of all classes, who seek
to provide against the precariousness of uncertain

incomes, by adopting the practice of life assurance. All contracts of this kind are purely monetary contracts, and as such based ultimately upon gold ; and with the fall in the value of gold, every person in whose favour a life is insured will be damnified to the full extent of the depreciation. He will receive indeed the same nominal sum for which he bargained; but this sum will be worth less to him for all the practical purposes of life. Instead of representing, as is commonly imagined, secure affluence, and pensioned idleness— interests which may well bear some additional pressure —the interests at stake in funded or mortgage property, as well as those at stake in life assurance, are among the most helpless as well as the most important which society comprises. It would be nearer the truth to say that they represent the classes on whom a pecuniary loss will inflict the maximum of harm.

But the loss from the depreciation of money will not be confined to the recipients of fixed money incomes. Those also will be sufferers by the change, though in a less degree and for a temporary period, whose remuneration is determined more by custom than by competition ; and this description includes a much larger number of persons than is commonly supposed. It includes, *e.g.*, two of the three learned professions, the medical and the legal, and a not unimportant portion of the third. It includes also the large number of officials, whether civil or military, whether in public or private employment, who are hired on yearly salaries. With respect to this large class, although their remuneration will probably in the end be brought into harmony with the altered state

of pecuniary affairs, yet during the period of transition
the adjustment will always be in arrear of events;
and those who are comprised in it will suffer accordingly.   The rise in prices will be very palpable before
a doctor's or barrister's fee will be increased, or salaries
in the Civil Service raised.

On the other hand, it must be remembered (and
although M. Chevalier has not overlooked this side of
the question, he has scarcely, we think, given it its
due weight) that for every loss of this kind there is,
from the nature of the case, a corresponding gain.   If
the national creditor be mulcted to the extent of one-
half of his property, the tax-payer pockets an equal
sum ; if the mortgagee loses, the mortgagor gains ;
if the professional classes are curtailed in their earnings, the public who employ them obtain their services
so much the more cheaply.   There is thus in all cases
a set-off; and this being so, it might seem as if, whatever were the case with individuals, with the community as a whole there would be neither loss nor
gain, neither benefit nor injury.   But we must not
lightly acquiesce in so indiscriminate a conclusion ; for,
putting aside entirely the substantial injustice involved
in the discharge of obligations in a sense different from
that in which they were incurred ; putting aside all
the dangers of a change affecting deeply an extensive
mass of interests, and opening to society an ordeal
which M. Chevalier thinks sufficiently formidable to
deserve the epithet 'revolutionary;' putting these
considerations aside, and considering solely the effect
of the pecuniary transfer, the question still remains,
whether the changes of condition thus produced are,

on the whole, salutary or the reverse ; whether they
conduce to the gain or loss—social and moral as well
as purely economical—of the nation in which they
occur.   We have already stated our opinion that the
effect of the gold discoveries will be to improve the
physical status of the great body of the people ; and
this we regard as a gain on the whole sufficient to outweigh all the concomitant evils.   Yet we are far from
thinking those evils either trifling or few.   It affords
slight matter for congratulation that a large number of
respectable people in narrow circumstances, many of
them old and helpless, should be deprived of one-half
of their livelihood in order that tax-payers may be
discharged from a portion of their fair liabilities ; or
that the recipients of charitable endowments, widows
and orphans, the sick and infirm, the needy in mind
and in body, should be stinted in their supplies for the
purpose of relieving landlords of their encumbrances :
and as little do we think it a matter for rejoicing that
the mercantile and manufacturing classes should be
aggrandized at the expense of physicians, barristers,
and members of the Civil Service.   It may be said,
indeed, that such a transfer of property tends to
strengthen the motives to enterprise and accumulation,
and thus to promote the growth of national wealth.
But, before conceding much weight to this argument,
we may ask if the strengthening of such motives be
at present such a social desideratum, either in Great
Britain or in the United States (the countries which
will reap the largest profit from the movement), as
to be worth procuring at such a cost.

It seems to us that the instincts of commercial

enterprise are already sufficiently strong in the Anglo-
Saxon race, and that it is not so much more wealth
that we want, as a higher sense of the responsibilities of wealth, and that more judicious expenditure of it which would accompany more just per-
ceptions. If this be so, we may well doubt if the
pecuniary disturbances with which we are threatened,
are likely to prove as purely beneficial as those whose
faith in progress is more robust than our own are
accustomed to describe them. The mode in which
wealth is distributed is always of more importance
than its aggregate amount; and a process which
increases the aggregate amount of wealth only by
operating on its distribution, is therefore, at best, a
questionable specific. We have seen what the nature
of the impending changes is. They will in many
instances increase, instead of mitigating, existing inequalities of condition. They will enrich the cosmopolitan merchant at the expense of the petty trader.
They will enrich the commercial classes, as a whole,
at the expense of possessors of fixed incomes, of the
professional classes, and of salaried *employés*. Landlords will probably, on the whole, be gainers; they
will lose temporarily where the outstanding leases
are long, but they will gain permanently through the
lightening of their fixed encumbrances; the balance
of gain being obtained by encroaching on the incomes
of their mortgagees. The tendency of the movement,
as amongst the middle and higher portions of society,
will thus be to aggrandize the wealthy at the expense
of the indigent; to tax the more liberal and enlightened for the benefit of the more narrow-minded and

selfish ; to enrich those whose command of wealth is
perhaps already somewhat in advance of their sense
of its responsibilities, from the means of classes at
once more necessitous and more cultivated. These
are the evils of the change, and against these we have
to set the benefit to the working classes, and the
ultimate gain to the world from the opening of new
and fertile regions to man's industry, and the extension
of his dominion over the earth.

That good will on the whole predominate, we
believe; but let us not, on this account, close our
eyes to the serious cost at which this preponderance
of good will be obtained. To a very great extent
the cost is inevitable and must be met, but something may be done towards lessening the evils of
the crisis by giving timely warning of its approach.
Means may be found in the framing of settlements
and leases, and in the selection of investments, to
mitigate its severity; the grand rule being, to avoid
as much as possible purely monetary securities, such
as the funds, mortgages, preference shares, and, in
general, investments the returns on which do not rise
with the advance in prices and salaries. The foresight of Lord Burleigh, warned by the changes which
he saw around him, effected in the sixteenth century
the partial substitution of corn for money rents, and
in this way the incomes of colleges and other institutions have been preserved, which but for this
precaution would have long since dwindled into
insignificance.* The plan adopted under the Tithe

* [The example of Lord Burleigh may be commended to the wise people
who are now, in the full flow of depreciation, recommending the compul-

Commutation Act, for regulating rent-charge by the price of agricultural produce, suggests another means by which the crisis may be moderated. A permissive law, facilitating arrangements of this kind, would be free from all objection on the score of justice, and might be attended with public advantage. But, after all is said, I fear it must be confessed that the great evils of the transition are not of a kind that can be largely alleviated. In the main they must be borne, and the sufferers must endeavour to console themselves with the reflection, that while "the individual withers," "the world is more and more."

POSTSCRIPT.

The reader will probably be interested to learn the course of the gold movement since the foregoing essays were written. To enable him to appreciate this in connection with what had gone before, it will be well to state here the leading facts of the production and distribution of the new gold from the outset down to the present time. These I am enabled to set forth in a form at once brief and authentic, thanks to a series of carefully prepared

---

sory sale of corporate property in land and the investment of the proceeds in the funds, and this *in the interest of the corporations !* Lord Burleigh was no political economist, but he was an extremely shrewd man, and knew what he was about. The supporters of the above proposal no doubt consider themselves strong in political economy, and would gladly make the science responsible for their projects. Whatever may be thought of their economic pretensions, one can at least have no difficulty in admitting that they too may know what they are about. Some very large fortunes have been made within the last few years ; and it would, no doubt, be extremely convenient for some people that land in large quantities should suddenly be thrown upon the market.

articles which have been recently published on this subject in the *Economist.*[*]

The first facts to be noted are (1) the total stock of gold in the world at the date of the Californian and Australian discoveries, and (2) the rate at which the production of gold was taking place in the period immediately preceding. These were as follows :—

The total (estimated) stock of gold in the world in 1848, was 560,000,000*l.*

As for the annual production, it had varied considerably since the beginning of the century. In 1800 it was, according to the best estimates, rather over 3,000,000*l.* But at a later period important discoveries of gold were made in Asiatic Russia, and for the five or six years ending 1848 the annual produce would seem to have varied from 5*l.* to about 8,000,000*l.*

Such was the state of things immediately preceding 1848. In that year the Californian discoveries took place, and these were followed by the discoveries in Australia in 1851. For these three years the annual average production is set down by the *Economist* at 9,000,000*l.*, but from this date the production suddenly rose to, for 1852, 27,000,000*l.*, and continued to rise till 1856, when it attained its maximum of 32,250,000*l.* At this stage a decline in the returns occurred, the lowest point reached being in 1860, when they fell to 18,683,000*l.*, but from this they rose again, and for the last ten years have maintained an average of about 20,500,000*l.* ; the returns for the year 1871 being 20,811,000*l.*

The total amount of gold added to the world's

---

[*] See the *Economist*, June 29th, August 3rd and 31st, 1872.

stock by this twenty years' production has been about 500,000,000*l.*, an amount nearly equal to that existing in the world at the date of the discoveries : in other words, the stock of gold in the world has been nearly doubled since that time.

As regards the distribution of this enormous sum, those who desire details will find them very fully and carefully tabulated in the articles of the *Economist* to which reference has just been made. For my present purpose it will suffice to indicate the main currents of the movement; and these can only be given for the period since 1858, that being the year when specie imports began to be regularly published by the Board of Trade. Since that year the production of gold has been about 300,000,000*l.*, and this has been distributed through three principal channels. The first and largest is that of which the tributaries, flowing from Australia and California, and in the latter case passing through the United States, converge on England, whence the body of the stream passes on to the Continent of Europe, and in large part finally to the East. About 190,000,000*l.*, out of the 300,000,000*l.* produced since 1858, have been thus disposed of. The stream of next importance is that which passes from the new gold countries direct to the East, and chiefly to India, by which way some 50,000,000*l.* have been carried off. This disposes of the whole of the Californian and Australian production, with the exception of 26,000,000*l.*, retained by Australia for her own purposes. Lastly, there is the Russian supply, which appears to have passed in large part to France, whence, in greater or less amount, it has been transferred to other Continental countries.

These have been the principal channels of distribution; but an important consideration remains—in what proportions have the various countries permanently absorbed the gold thus flowing through the channels of commerce? The following are the results arrived at by the *Economist*, still, the reader will recollect, for the period between 1858 and the present :—

Retained in England	£68,000,000	
„ in Continental Europe (chiefly in France)	105,000,000	
„ in Portugal and some other countries not included in the last entry . .	12,000,000	
„ in South America	8,000,000	
„ in India and the East	90,000,000	
„ in Australia	26,000,000	
* Total production since 1858	£309,000,000	

The only other point connected with the movement which it will be needful here to refer to is the net addition which, as the result of the whole, has accrued to our own currency. As has been seen, it follows from the figures given by the *Economist*, that of the whole amount of gold passing through England since 1858 (about 190,000,000*l.*) 68,000,000*l.* have been retained in the country. The question arises, how has this sum been disposed of? The *Economist* answers that 28,000,000*l.* have been absorbed by our currency;

* So the figures are set down by the *Economist;* yet no place is given in the table to the United States; which, including California, must surely (notwithstanding the existence of an inconvertible currency) have retained some portion of the supplies.

60,000,000*l.* having been coined from the new gold,
and 32,000,000*l.* of this having gone abroad. The
28,000,000*l.* thus added to our gold circulation would,
as the *Economist* remarks, of course be a maximum
sum. Taking it at 25,000,000*l.*, and accepting Mr.
Newmarch's estimate of the coin in circulation in
1857 as 75,000,000*l.*, this would bring our gold currency
at the present time up to 100,000,000*l.*—rather more
than double the amount estimated by Mr. Newmarch
as in circulation a few years previous to 1848. Assuming the facts to stand thus, our gold circulation
would have been about doubled since the gold discoveries. This, however, only accounts for, at most,
28,000,000*l.* out of the 68,000,000*l.* retained in one
form or another in the country since 1858 ; and here a
question arises as to what has become of the remaining
40,000,000*l.* retained at home, but not entering into
the circulation ? The answer given to this question
by the *Economist* appears to me, I confess, the least
satisfactory part of its statement. It in effect amounts
to this, that, allowing for 12,000,000*l.* as probably
existing in the form of foreign coin, partly in the
reserves of the Bank of England, and partly in the
hands of exchange dealers, the remainder—28,000,000*l.*
—has been used up for purposes of art and manufacture; in other words, that the United Kingdom
has, in this way, consumed about 2,000,000*l.* of gold
annually since 1858. As far as appears, there are no
grounds for supposing such a consumption except the
difficulty of otherwise accounting for the gold. For
my part, in presence of M. Chevalier's facts and arguments on this subject, I find it quite impossible to

accept this explanation, and should even prefer to believe, were there no other alternative, that a considerable portion of the missing sum had somehow escaped from the country without getting into the Government returns.

The foregoing statements give an outline of the movement during the period under review, so far as *gold* is concerned; but the real character of its effects on the monetary systems of the world cannot be understood without taking into account the simultaneous operations in silver. For example, one of the most important considerations connected with the subject is the proportions in which the additions made to the monetary stock have been absorbed by the different commercial countries. From the table given above it would seem as if the Continent of Europe was the largest absorbent—larger even than India and the East; but in point of fact the greater portion of the 105,000,000*l.* of new gold retained by Continental Europe has been employed in substitution for silver formerly existing in her currencies, the silver thus parted with having in the main been passed on to the East. The addition therefore made to the metallic currencies of the Continent, as the result of the gold movement, is greatly less than the mere gold statistics would indicate; while the addition made to Oriental currencies is very much greater. I have no data from which to estimate the precise amount thus transferred, nor is there any need here to go into details. A single fact will suffice to give an idea of the scale on which this silver movement has been proceeding. I find that the amount of silver which passed to the

East by way of Egypt alone during the last fifteen
years has amounted to no less than 95,000,000*l.* ; of
this the greater portion was taken from the currencies
of Europe, and principally from that of France, and
the whole has been added, over and above the
90,000,000*l.* of gold stated above, to the currencies of
India and the East. The largest absorbents, therefore, of the vast additions now being made to the
monetary stock of the world have not been the countries of Continental Europe, but Oriental countries,
mainly India and China. We thus find, in conformity
with the mode of distribution described in the third of
the foregoing essays, that, although England and the
United States receive the chief portion of the new
supplies in the first instance, yet of these only a small
part is retained permanently in their currencies. The
rest is passed on to the Continent of Europe and to
Asia ; while, again, of the portion sent to the Continent
probably the largest part finds its way ultimately to
the East, not indeed always in the form in which it
entered the Continent,—not, that is to say, as gold,—
but in that of silver, into which it has been transmuted
on the way.

V.

CO-OPERATION IN THE
SLATE QUARRIES OF NORTH WALES.*

The public must now be tolerably familiar with the
story of the Rochdale Equitable Pioneers, and of
the numerous societies, founded upon the same principles, which in various parts of the country have
already accomplished such great things for the working
people, and given earnest for the future of still
greater achievements in their behalf. It has heard
something also of other and more genuine examples
of "co-operation,"—where associates not only trade
but "work" together, where the labourers are also
the capitalists, and wages and profits return to the
same hands; experiments which, small as have been
the actual fruits they have hitherto yielded, form
yet, in the opinion of those who have most deeply
pondered the problem of industrial reform, the most
solid grounds of hope for the future permanent elevation of the labouring class.† But there is, besides

* *Macmillan's Magazine*, January 1865.

† See an article of great interest in the *Westminster Review* for April
1864, entitled "Strikes and Industrial Co-operation," in which the whole
subject is handled with remarkable ability and knowledge.

these, a third species of "co-operation," prevailing
throughout some large industries in Great Britain,
which has not, so far as I am aware, received any consideration in the numerous and instructive discussions
which have within the last few years taken place upon
this subject, but which is nevertheless well worthy
of attention. I refer to the method of employing
labour which prevails extensively in mining and other
analogous occupations, and is known as the " bargain "
or "contract" system. Having lately had an opportunity of witnessing this system in the slate quarries
of North Wales, I propose to describe briefly the
method and its results. It will, I think, be seen that
it is a genuine instance of "co-operation"—one, moreover, which exhibits the beneficial tendencies of that
plan in some respects in even a more striking light
than other and better known examples.

The mountains of North Wales, as is well known,
constitute the principal source of the wealth of that
region. They are extremely metalliferous, containing
lead and copper ore, besides sulphur ; but their most
important constituent is the slate formation. Veins
of this rock, varying in thickness from four and five
to four and five hundred yards, and traceable, in
some instances, for a length of many miles, traverse
the country, but more especially the mountain ranges
of Caernarvon and Merioneth. The importance of the
industry to which they give occasion may be judged
from the fact, that three slate quarries—those of Penrhyn, Llanberis, and Festinog—give employment to
not fewer than 7,000 men, representing a population
of perhaps 20,000 persons. These are, indeed, by

much the most extensive of the slate quarries in that region, but they form but a small fraction of the whole number. It is impossible to wander in any direction over the mountains of those two counties without finding abundant evidence how widely the popular enterprise is engaged in this branch of production. No mountain side is so inaccessible that the slate prospector has not reached it, and the most secluded glens and passes are heard to echo the thunder of the quarrier's blast.

The great majority of the slate quarries are worked by companies — either private co-partneries or joint stock companies; but a few, and notably the two largest—the quarries of Penrhyn and Llanberis—are in the hands of individuals, the proprietors of the mountains where the slate-formation occurs. In the former case the capitalist or capitalists working the quarry pay a royalty, which is generally one-twelfth of the produce. It must be observed that the slate does not, as is frequently supposed, and as might be inferred from a cursory glance at a slate quarry, constitute the mass of the mountain in which the quarry is cut. It runs in distinct veins which, on rising towards the surface, deteriorate,—a circumstance to which is due the risk which this mode of employing capital so largely involves; for it is always difficult to say from the appearance of the vein at the surface what may be its quality at a lower depth. Before this can be known, a mass of from two or three to sometimes twenty or even thirty yards in vertical depth must be removed—a tedious and costly operation, which must be completed before slate-quarrying, properly so called,

begins, and which is often performed to no purpose ;
the quality of the rock, when thus ascertained, not
proving such as to justify the further prosecution of
the work.   Cases have been mentioned to the writer
of quarries having been abandoned after 20,000*l.*, of
others having been given up after 80,000*l.*, had been
expended on preliminary operations.   This incident
of slate-quarrying serves to explain what will be presently referred to—the unwillingness of the working
quarriers to embark their savings in this kind of
speculation.

The business of making slates is an exceedingly
simple operation—one, however, which not the less
demands from the workman no small amount of intelligence, exactness, and dexterity, besides a good deal of
practical acquaintance with the nature of the materials
with which he has to deal.   It consists in detaching
the slate formation in blocks from the mountain side ;
in sawing the blocks when thus detached into suitable
sizes ; lastly, in splitting and dressing, so as to bring
them into proper shape—a process which is performed
sometimes by machinery, but more generally by hand
labour.   It is to the industrial arrangements by which
this operation is carried out that it is desired now to
invite the reader's attention.   They are as follows :—
The portion of the slate which it is proposed to work
is divided into sections carefully marked out, which
are let out as "bargains" to as many small co-partneries, consisting generally of three or four working men.
These co-partneries "contract" to produce slates—
each from the section of the rock assigned to it—
according to sizes and shapes at so much per thousand.

The men who take part directly in these contracts
form, perhaps, a third of the whole quarrying population ; they are, as might be expected, the older, more
experienced, and better-off portion ; the remainder
are employed by them as labourers at fixed wages
under the name of "germyns," apparently the Welsh
equivalent for " navvies." The capital employed in
the undertaking is furnished principally by the proprietors or lessees, as the case may be, of the quarry ;
but a portion is also provided by the "contractors."
Thus the former supply the larger and more expensive
machinery, such as the tramways, waggons, steam-
engine, if there be one, pumps, slate-saws and planes,
&c., while the latter furnish the smaller tools, as well
as the gunpowder used in blasting. The practice,
moreover, being to pay wages monthly, this supposes,
on the part of the workmen—unless so far as they
may have recourse to the pernicious aid of the tally-
shop—an amount of saving sufficient, at least, to
support them during this interval of delay. The
relations of the actual workers having been established
on this footing, and the contracts entered into, the
functions of the principal capitalist or capitalists are
thenceforward of an extremely limited kind ; they
consist chiefly in keeping the machinery in proper
order, and seeing to the number and quality of the
slates turned out. As for the rest—the plan of operations adopted, the distribution of the labour, its super-
intendence and reward—of all this the "contractors"
undertake the sole and entire charge. It should be
added that the " contracts " are supplemented by an
understanding, doubtless originating in the felt neces-

sity of mitigating for the working men the inevitable
risks of such undertakings, to the effect that, where
from the inferior quality of the rock, as ascertained on
trial, the returns fall below a certain standard, the
reduced earnings of the " contractors " shall be aided
by a " poundage," or additional allowance, varying
inversely with the amount of their gains.   This
poundage, so far as I could make out, though for the
most part regulated by custom, is also in some degree
discretionary on the part of the owner of the quarry,
and is not the same for all districts.   It applies, however, only to the less fortunate class of " bargains ; "
the better " bargains " are amply remunerated within
the terms of the contract.

Such, in brief, are the arrangements under which
industry in the Welsh slate quarries is carried on.   I
think it will be seen at once that this "contract
system" constitutes a true case of "co-operation."   It
is at least certain that it fulfils what I venture to think
are the most important conditions of that method of
industry : there is associated effort ; there is common
interest in the results of the work ; and these results
depend, subject to the natural conditions of the case,
and the customary qualification of the strict contract
just indicated, directly on the energy, skill, and mutual
good faith with which the workers perform their part.
It has also been said that the " contractors " advance a
portion of the capital ; but I should not be disposed to
attach much importance to this as a distinctive feature
of the "contract system ;" for, though as a matter of
fact the men who take part in contracts have generally
accumulated some little capital, and though this cir-

cumstance no doubt facilitates in some degree their
proceedings in carrying out the undertaking, still the
possession of capital does not by any means constitute
an indispensable condition to becoming a contractor,
it being always easy for a man of good character to
obtain the requisite tools and materials on credit from
small shopkeepers established in the quarrying districts, and established chiefly with a view to supplying
such needs.   The only item of capital which in practice the contractor is in the habit of advancing is the
money expended on his own support during the
monthly interval that elapses before the returns to his
industry come in ; and, so far as this is concerned, the
" germyn " whom he employs—a labourer at fixed
wages—has an equally valid title to take rank as a
capitalist ; the earnings of the " germyn " being also
postponed for the same period of time.   The value
of the experiment, therefore, and that which entitles it
to be regarded as an example of " co-operative "
industry, lies, in my opinion, in the other conditions to
which I have referred—in the fact that the system
enlists working men in a joint undertaking, of which
the results for them depend in large part on the skill,
energy, and conscientious zeal with which it is carried
through.

And now let us endeavour to appreciate the bearing
of these conditions on the well-being of the quarrying
community.   We shall consider in the first place the
position of the contractor, who, as I have already said,
represents about a third of the whole quarrying population.   He will not, of course, for a moment be confounded with the important and generally wealthy

personage by whom our railways and great public
works are carried on. The latter, a capitalist pure
and simple, has no other relations with the actual
workers than that of paymaster. But the contractor
of the slate quarries is himself a manual worker—
generally, indeed, a skilled worker, taking to himself
the more difficult processes of the undertaking, but
still in the strictest sense a working man—working in
the same place, and often at the same operation, as the
labourer whom he employs, and socially in no respect
his superior. But, though a manual labourer, our
contractor is also something very different from the
ordinary labourer for hire. His remuneration is no
fixed sum, but depends upon the success of his
exertions, which he has therefore the strongest interest
to increase to the utmost. Nor, again, is he to be
confounded with the labourer at task-work. In the
first place, the undertaking in which he embarks is of
an altogether more important character than any that
falls to the lot of the ordinary task-work labourer.
Before he commits himself to his engagements, a
calculation, not altogether free from complication—
requiring, besides an acquaintance with arithmetic,
and a tincture of mathematics, some practical knowledge of the different qualities of certain rocks—
must be performed. Then the undertaking itself comprises several distinct operations — quarrying, cleav-
ing, dressing—the carrying out of which, effectively
and economically, calls for deliberation, forethought,
and organizing skill. Again, the contractor, while a
labourer himself, is also a purchaser of the labours of
others, holding towards his "germyn" the position

of a capitalist proper, and is thus led to look at the
business of production in some degree from the point
of view of an employer,—a circumstance which may
go some way in accounting for the noteworthy fact,
that in the districts of the slate quarries strikes are
unknown.   Lastly, and to this I attach the greatest
importance of all, the contractor is a member of a
partnership, acquiring rights and incurring responsibilities in relation to his fellow-contractors, taking
part in their labours on equal terms, sharing their
anxieties, and interested in common with them in the
ultimate result of their common efforts.

But the influence of the arrangements I have
described is not limited to the class which comes
immediately under their operation.   A circumstance
which gives especial importance to the status of the
contractor in the slate quarry is that, placed as nearly
as possible midway between the position of the
ordinary labourer and that of the capitalist pure and
simple, it forms an easy stepping-stone for the elevation of the masses from the precarious position of
dependence upon the general labour-market, — a
position which, if there be value in experience, is
absolutely incompatible with any substantial and permanent improvement of their state.

The mode in which the ascent is made will be illustrated by a remark made to the writer by the lessee of
the Dolwydellan slate quarry—a gentleman to whose
kindness he is indebted for most of the information
contained in this paper.   In reply to a question with
reference to a difference in the rates of wages prevailing in different localities, he observed that the men

before us would be very slow to leave their present
occupation even for the prospect of a considerable
advance in their wages—"because," he explained,
pointing to a large quarry hole filled with water, "so
soon as this is pumped dry, there is not a man amongst
them who does not know that he will have a chance
of a share in the new contracts which will then
be opened." Thus the labourers who have not yet
attained to the rank of contractors are ever working in
full view of an early promotion to this position, their
attainment of which, however, depends entirely on their
success in recommending themselves to the favourable
consideration of the owner of the quarry, as well as to
that—an equally important condition—of their own
fellow-workmen, without whose approval and co-
operation they would hope in vain to take advantage
of the opportunities which are daily opening. Even
the less important class of workmen, who are employed
in clearing away refuse, also pass occasionally into the
ranks of the quarriers proper, and ultimately into those
of the contractors, and thus feel in some degree the
stimulus which such prospects supply. The whole
society is thus kept constantly under the incentive of
the public opinion of the *élite* among its own members
—a state of things which serves to diffuse throughout
the entire organization an influence of the healthiest
kind.

Nor has the beneficent tendency of these arrangements failed to become effectual in the actual condition
of the population of the slate quarries. Their ordinary
earnings, according to information supplied to me from
various sources, may be set down as follows :—

For carters of refuse, from 12s. to 17s. per week.
For "germyns" (quarriers at fixed wages, many of whom are
   mere boys), 12s. to 20s. per week.

In the case of the contractors the variations are
much more considerable; the results ranging from 3l.
to 8l., and occasionally to 10l. per month. In a small
quarry near Dolwydellan which I visited, three contractors had just concluded a "bargain," in which they
had netted for the month of July the sum of 9l. each.
On the whole, so far as I could make out, the
earnings of the contractors average something like
5l. monthly.

These rates are, I should suppose, about equal to
those prevailing in corresponding occupations—I mean
occupations in which the toil, risk, and skill are about
the same—in the most favoured industrial districts in
England; and such a result is surely very creditable
to the industrial system of Wales. For it must be remembered that capital is very far from increasing with
the same rapidity in Caernarvonshire and Merionethshire as in (say) Lancashire and Staffordshire; while,
on the other hand, owing to the general ignorance of
the English language which prevails in the former
counties,—a circumstance which cannot but operate
in some degree as an impediment to emigration,—
the relief afforded by this safety-valve to the labour
market there is likely to be considerably less than
in other portions of the United Kingdom. The external conditions affecting wages in the Welsh counties
are therefore decidedly less favourable than they are
in the more progressive districts of England; and yet
the labouring classes in the former localities are, it

seems, comparing analogous modes of labour, equally
well off. The explanation, as will be anticipated, is
to be found in the slower movements of population in
the Welsh districts. In Caernarvonshire population
advanced in the decade 1851 to 1861 at the rate of
9 per cent.; in Merionethshire at the rate of 3 per
cent.; in both counties at an average rate of 6 per
cent.; while over the whole of England and Wales
population during the same period went forward at
the average rate of 12 per cent., and in the more
prosperous parts of the country—for example in Lancashire and Staffordshire—at the rates respectively of
20 per cent. and 23 per cent.*

The comparatively slow growth of capital in those
counties of North Wales is thus, as regards its effect
on the condition of the people, neutralized by a growth
of population proportionately slow; and the practical
result is a rate of remuneration fully up to the English
level. The defect in respect to material conditions is
compensated by greater vigour in the moral. Now, I
think it is impossible not to connect this satisfactory

---

* I do not give these figures as accurate exponents of the relative
growth (by way of natural increase) of population in the several districts.
No doubt the results in all instances have been much modified both
by emigration and by migration within the limits of Great Britain. So
far as the former cause is concerned, the probability is, for the reason
stated, that, could its effect be ascertained (unfortunately the Emigration
Reports do not distinguish the natives of Wales), the result would considerably strengthen my case. And as regards the latter, though there
is no doubt a considerable Welsh movement towards the manufacturing
centres of England, this proceeds in the main from the agricultural districts; while, to be set against this, there is an Irish immigration into
Wales. On the whole, I think the figures I have given may be accepted
for the purpose for which they are adduced, as corroborative illustrations of tendencies which there are independent grounds for believing
to exist.

state of things with the *régime* of industry under
which it has come to pass. Indeed, to what else can
it be ascribed? Religious influences, no doubt, are
powerful in North Wales. Nothing apparently can
exceed the activity and zeal of the Dissenting bodies;
and the good effect on the morals and general de-
meanour of the people is very observable. But, however compatible a strong sense of religion may be
with worldly prudence in those matters on which the
growth of population depends, the mundane virtue
can yet scarcely be regarded as a specific religious
result : certainly it is not one which it is usual to hear
inculcated from the pulpit. Nor can the fact be attributed to education in the ordinary sense of the word ;
for, notwithstanding the strongly pronounced literary
instincts of the Welsh people, literary education in
North Wales seems to be in a decidedly backward
state. Improvements, it is said, of an important kind
have in recent years been effected in the primary
schools ; but this has occurred since the mass of the
present generation of Welshmen have entered upon
active life. It is rare, out of the principal towns, to
find working people over the age of thirty who can
exchange more than a few words of English: hundreds
of thousands cannot accomplish even this little : and
even in the towns it is not uncommon to meet substantial shopkeepers who are unable to sign their
names to their own bills. In one quarry I was told
that some considerable number of the workmen were
unable to read and write. It is therefore not to the
superiority of their school instruction that the industrial population of these Welsh counties are indebted

for the remarkable circumspection and self-control which they display in their most important social relations. I can only regard this phenomenon, therefore, as the fruit of that practical training in habits of thrift and wise foresight which is provided for them in the industrial system under which they live.

It thus appears that, in point of pecuniary returns, the position of the Welsh quarriers does not suffer by comparison with that of workmen in analogous occupations even in the most prosperous districts of England—districts far more favourably circumstanced, as regards the physical conditions affecting the remuneration of the labourer, than those of the slate quarries. But mere pecuniary return affords after all but an inadequate criterion of the labourer's condition. Fully as important as the amount which he earns is the mode in which his earnings are spent; and it is here that the peculiar strength of the co-operative principle comes into play. Those who have watched the working of "co-operative stores" have been struck with their effect in awakening and stimulating the saving spirit among the working classes—a result which has been attributed to the strong temptations to frugality presented by those establishments, in the opportunities they afford for investing small sums at a fair rate of profit. In the particular form of co-operation, however, to which I have in this paper called attention, this incident of the co-operative plan as it is conducted elsewhere—the provision, that is to say, for small investments—does not exist. As I have already intimated, to qualify a man for taking part in a "bargain," no capital is needed beyond the moral capital of a good character. Even should he be in a position to decline the credit which is readily extended to him, the amount required for the purchase of such implements and tools as it falls to his share of the bargain to provide would be exceedingly small. Nor does he find in the other branches of industry flourishing around him those special opportunities which are wanting in his own. Co-operative stores have indeed, as I have been informed, been established in one or two localities in North Wales, and with excellent results : but they do not yet exist on such a scale that they can be supposed to have sensibly affected the habits of the people. As regards the larger operations of slate quarrying, they are, as it happens, peculiarly ineligible as a field for small investments. This will at once be understood if regard be had to what has been already stated—that the amount of capital required to start a slate quarry is very large, while the risk of the speculation is very great. The former obstacle might indeed be overcome by recourse to the joint-stock expedient, were the joint-stock plan capable of being applied with advantage to this branch of production ; but this seems not to be the case ; at least, so think the working quarriers, and their opinion would seem to be borne out by facts.* In the case of

* Numerous joint-stock companies are at present (1864) working quarries in North Wales ; but, as a rule, I understand they are not flourishing concerns ; all the most prosperous undertakings being in the hands of individuals or private co-partneries. The reasons for the superiority of the latter are apparent enough. There is no need that the business organizations of such an undertaking should be other than extremely simple. In Penrhyn Quarry, for example, where the operations are on an immense scale, the entire business of keeping the accounts, &c. is performed by two clerks. This cannot but give a great advantage to

the population of the slate quarries, therefore, there
seems to be an entire absence of those special incen-
tives to frugality and providence which have been
incidents of the co-operative plan in its better-known
forms. Nevertheless frugality and providence are
found to characterize this population in a remarkable
degree. The mere fact that, according to the prevailing custom, wages are paid at so long an interval as
once a month, implies of itself a considerable fund of
accumulated savings existing among the body of the
people. But this would give but an inadequate idea
of their saving disposition. It is, I am assured, quite
common to find in the ranks of the contractors men
who have laid by from one to three and four hundred
pounds. In one quarry which I visited, a man was
pointed out to me—a manual labourer—who was
known to be in receipt of between 80*l.* and 100*l.* a
year, independently altogether of his current earnings
—the return on capital saved and invested. This, no
doubt, was an extraordinary case, but not, I was
assured, by any means without a parallel. Well,
where is the field for the investment of these considerable accumulations ? A portion goes into agricul-

individuals and small co-partneries over the necessarily more cumbrous
organization of a joint-stock company. Again, the special knowledge and
singleness of design which are so essential in this branch of industry are
much more likely to be realized by individuals, or associations consisting of
a few partners, than by a more numerous body. In addition to the reasons
mentioned in the text, it is probable that some distrust of the Saxon
enters into the Welsh workman's reluctance to commit his savings to
undertakings which are carried on largely by Saxon capital : this seems
to be expressed in his proverb : "Os byth y gweli sais ac engine yn
dyfod ir gwaith pacia dy bethan." [When you see an Englishman with
his engine coming to the work, pack and be off.]

ture ; prosperous quarrymen turning farmers in their
latter days, or sometimes combining with farming pursuits occasional adventures in their old line.   Retail
trade again absorbs some.   But probably the largest
part of the funds finds its way into the associations
known as " building societies."   These "building societies " might with more propriety be called loan
societies ; their functions consisting in advancing
money to be invested in building speculations, which,
though for the most part undertaken by the members,
are yet carried on on individual account, resembling in
this respect the " Vorschussvereine " described by Professor Huber in his interesting paper on " Co-operation." *   These societies are extremely popular with
the workmen ; and as to their range of operations, the
reader will be able to form some notion when I state
that several considerable towns in North Wales have
been almost entirely built by the capital supplied
through this agency.   Thus the pretty town of Bethesda, within five miles of Bangor, is almost entirely
the creation of the enterprise of working men deriving
their funds from this source.   Llandudno, Rhyll, and
Upper Bangor owe their existence in large part to the
same cause.   As to the substantial comfort in which
the people of the quarry districts live, no one who has
visited these districts will, I think, feel any doubt.
Nor is it comfort merely.   The style and finish of the
workmen's houses are very remarkable, more particularly in Bethesda and the neighbourhood of the Penrhyn quarries, where the elegant model furnished by
Colonel Pennant in his own village has been turned to

* Published in the " Social Science Transactions " for 1862.

excellent account. A feature in the architecture is
the variety of modes in which the staple material is
brought into requisition. Roofing is but a small part
of the purposes to which the slate is applied : there
are slate door-posts, slate window-settings ; the ground
story is generally flagged with slate, which makes its
appearance besides in many places where one would
little expect to find it. I know not whether the
extreme cleanliness of the Welsh is to be attributed in
any degree to the advantages of this material; but
they are certainly pre-eminent in this virtue. The
exquisite neatness of some of the cottages in Bethesda
and Trefriw is such as I imagine would not easily
be matched out of Holland. The kitchen-parlour is
quite a marvel of cleanliness, tidiness, and order—
with its slate floor swept till it shines, its " varnished
clock " clicking " behind the door," and its furniture,
though mostly made of common wood, polished to
such brightness that it does not pale even before the
constellations of brass knobs which glitter all around.
In the village where I was staying I have watched an
old woman who lived on the opposite side of the
street come out in showery weather to scrub her door-
slab clean as fast as it was soiled by the footsteps of
each careless passer-by : the apparition would follow on
the clearing away of a shower almost with the regu-
larity of the lady in the toy barometer. Nor should
we omit to say that some attempt at a library is rarely
absent from these quarriers' cottages. The selection
may not contain the newest publications, and is not
perhaps very choice ; but at least it shows literary
aspirations—a soul for something above the quarry.

The Bible, generally in Welsh, I observed, held a constant and honoured place in the literary store.

The simplicity of character and kindness of heart among the poorer classes of Welsh people are very striking and attractive. In illustration of these qualities I may mention an admirable trait, which may, I think, be fairly connected with their co-operative system.

The occupations of the slate quarry involve, as may readily be believed, no small amount of risk to the limbs and lives of those who engage in them ; the accidents from blasting, falling in of rocks, &c. being unfortunately very numerous, and frequently fatal ; and, as might be expected, there is no lack of provision against such disastrous contingencies. Besides the ordinary friendly societies which flourish in immense numbers all over the country, no quarry of any importance is without its sick club. Numerous associations exist framed with a special view to compensate for the losses incident to mutilation and death. But such machinery does not satisfy the cravings of the fraternal feeling that subsists among the workmen. The assistance from this source is almost invariably supplemented, where the accidents are of a serious nature involving calamitous consequences to the family of the injured man, by voluntary contributions raised among his fellow-workmen. " As a class," writes a correspondent, himself extensively engaged in this business, to whom I have already expressed my obligations,—" As a class, quarriers are very liberal. If by accident a father of a family is killed, the wife will go through the quarry and frequently gets (if

her husband has been a man of good character) from
10*l.* to 20*l.* At other times collections are made in
the chapels, and almost in every instance they show
great liberality." He adds that these occurrences are
unfortunately very frequent ; several such calls on the
workman's pocket having quite recently been made in
a single quarry in the short space of a few months.

Such, then, is the "contract system" of the slate
quarries, and such are its fruits. Divested as it is of
certain extraneous advantages which accompany other
forms of "co-operation," it sets, as it seems to me, in
all the stronger light the inherent virtue of the principle itself—the principle of combining the exertions of
labourers towards a common result in which they have
a joint interest—an interest varying with the success
of their common efforts. The results here obtained
are obtained not so much through the increased force
of the external inducements to prudent or righteous
conduct, as by strengthening the character of the
workman, calling into action qualities of mind which
in the ordinary condition of the labourer's life lie
dormant, enlarging his mental horizon, stimulating his
reflective powers, widening his sympathies—in a word,
developing those principles and habits which furnish
the only solid basis for any permanent improvement of
his state.

How far the particular arrangement which I have
described admits of being extended to other departments of production is what actual experiment can
alone determine. *Primâ facie*, it would seem that
one condition only was indispensable to its adoption—
the possibility of splitting up the work to be done into

a number of small and independent tasks. It is at all events certain that the success of the plan in the instances in which it has been tried has been remarkably great; and this, considered with reference to commercial, no less than to social results. As an expedient for the practical solution of the labour-problem, the weakness of the " contract system " seems to me to lie in the fact that under it the labourer and the capitalist are still distinct persons; the two capacities do not coalesce in the same man. The difficulty which, under the ordinary relations of labour and capital, occurs in settling the rate of wages might equally occur under the " contract system" in settling the terms of the contract. That it does not in practice arise is to be ascribed, I imagine, chiefly to the circumstance to which I have already adverted—the double capacity in which the contractor acts, as at once employer and employed; and, for the rest, to the general intelligence which the system engenders

POLITICAL ECONOMY AND LAND.*

VARIOUS as have been the schemes recently offered to public notice for the settlement of the Irish land question, one feature is noticeable as more or less prominently characterizing them all—a profound distrust of Political Economy. Just in proportion as a plan gives promise of being effective, does the author feel it necessary to assume an attitude, if not of hostility, then of apology, towards this science. It is either sneered at as unpractical and perverse, or its authority is respectfully put aside as of no account "in a country so exceptionally situated as Ireland." This state of opinion is perfectly intelligible. In its earlier applications to practical affairs Political Economy found itself inevitably in collision with numerous regulative codes, partly the remnants of feudalism, partly the products of the commercial doctrines of a later age, but all founded on the principle of substituting for individual discretion the control of those in power. It thus came naturally to be

* *Fortnightly Review*, January 1870.

identified with the opposite principle; and was known
to the general public mainly as a scientific development of the doctrine of *laissez-faire*. The Free-trade
controversy of course gave great prominence to this
side of the system, and of late the idea that all
Political Economy is summed up in *laissez-faire* has
been much fostered by the utterances of some public
men and writers, who have acquired a certain reputation as political economists, chiefly, it would seem,
through the pertinacity with which they have enforced
this formula, insisting on its sufficiency, not merely in
the domain of material interest, but over the whole
range of human life. If *laissez-faire* is to be taken
as the sum and substance of economic teaching, it
follows evidently enough that intervention by the
State to determine the relative status of those holding
interests in the soil involves an economic heresy of
the deepest dye; and it is not strange, therefore, that
those who accept or defer to this idea of the science
should, in attempting to deal with the Irish problem,
evince some susceptibility in reference to Political
Economy. In effect, it is very evident that two
courses only are open to economists of this hue.
Either they must hold by their maxims, and, doing
so, remit the solution of the Irish difficulty to civil
war and the arbitrament of armed force; or, accepting
the plea of Ireland's exceptional condition, they must
be content to put aside their science for the nonce,
and legislate as if it were not. The latter is the
course that fortunately has for the most part been
taken. Economic laws—so it seems now to be agreed
upon by thinkers of this school—do not act except

where circumstances are favourable, and have no business in a country so unfortunately situated as Ireland. This is one view of the relation of Political Economy to such questions as that presented by the present state of Ireland. In my opinion, it is a radically false, and practically a most mischievous view; one, therefore, against which, alike in the interest of the peace of Ireland and for the credit of economic science, I am anxious with all my energy to protest. I deny that economic doctrine is summed up in *laissez-faire;* I contend that it has positive resources, and is efficacious to build up as well as to pull down. Sustained by some of the greatest names—I will say by every name of the first rank in Political Economy, from Turgot and Adam Smith to Mill—I hold that the land of a country presents conditions which separate it economically from the great mass of the other objects of wealth,—conditions which, if they do not absolutely and under all circumstances impose upon the State the obligation of controlling private enterprise in dealing with land, at least explain why this control is in certain stages of social progress indispensable, and why in fact it has been constantly put in force, wherever public opinion or custom has not been strong enough to do without it. And not merely does economic science, as expounded by its ablest teachers, dispose of à *priori* objections to a policy of intervention with regard to land, it even furnishes principles fitted to inform and guide such a policy in a positive sense. Far from being the irreconcilable foe, it is the natural ally of those who engage in this course, at once justifying the principle

of their undertaking, and lending itself as a minister
to the elaboration of the constructive design.

As regards the main ground on which the distinction
between land and other forms of wealth depends,
little more needs be done than unfold the argument
contained in a few weighty sentences in which Mr.
Mill has summed up the case :—" Moveable property
can be produced in indefinite quantity, and he who
disposes as he likes of anything which, it can be fairly
argued, would not have existed but for him, does no
wrong to anyone. It is otherwise with regard to land,
a thing which no man made, which exists in limited
quantity, which was the original inheritance of all
mankind, and which whoever appropriates keeps others
out of its possession. Such appropriation, when there
is not enough left for all, is, at the first aspect, an
usurpation on the rights of other people." Where
wealth is provided by human industry, its having value
is the indispensable condition to its existence—to its
existence at least in greater quantity than suffices for
the producer's own requirements ; and the most obvious means of rendering this condition efficacious as a
stimulus to industry is to recognize in the producer a
right of property in the thing he has produced. This,
I take it, is, economically speaking, the foundation on
which private property rests, and is, if I mistake not,
the most solid and important of all the reasons for the
institution. It is one which applies to all the products
of human industry—a category comprising (with some
unimportant exceptions) moveable wealth in every form,
as well as some forms of immoveable wealth, but which
obviously can have no application to a commodity

which "no man has made."* It has been urged,
indeed, that this reasoning is not rigorous, and that
strict logic would require us to extend the description
given of land to every form of wealth, moveable as
well as immoveable, elaborated by the hand of industry
or still lying crude in the earth, since, in the last resort,
all is traceable alike to materials furnished by nature—
which "no man has made." But this is to fall into the
error of the Physiocrates, and to confound wealth with
matter. The street and palace, the corn and cotton,
the goods that fill our warehouses, whatever be the
form imparted to them by industry, all, no doubt,
derive their material existence in the last resort from
things which no man has made : no man has made the
matter of which they are composed ; but, as *wealth*,
as things possessing exchange value, they exist, not
through the liberality of nature, but through the
labour and enterprise of man. According to the
economic formula, their value (omitting the, in most

---

* [To guard against misapprehension, it may be as well to state that
I do not recognize in this argument any proof of a "natural right" to
property in anything, even in that which our hands have just made. If it
is right it should belong to us, it is not (if we go to the root of things)
because we have made it, but because it is expedient that property so
acquired should belong to him who so acquires it. The distinction is all-
important. If the product belonged to us in virtue of the fact of our
having produced it, that fact being past and unalterable, there could be
no limitation to our right in the absence of voluntary cession upon our
part, and we should in strict justice be entitled to prescribe its destination
to all future ages. On the other hand, belonging to us only in virtue of
considerations of expediency, our right to the product will be limited by
the expediency from which our right springs. The distinction, then,
between landed property and property in the products of industry is not
that in the latter case there is a "natural right" to property which does
not exist in the former, but that there are grounds of expediency for
recognizing the right in the one case which have no place in the other.]

instances, infinitesimal portion of it which covers rent)
corresponds to their cost of production.   It is not so
with land, which possesses value, and often high value,
even in its crudest form ; with respect to which, therefore, whatever other reasons may be urged in favour
of giving it up to private ownership, that reason cannot
be urged which applies to the mass of the other objects
of wealth—namely, that this mode of proceeding forms
the natural and most effective means of encouraging
industry useful to man.

It will be said, however, that the fact in question
is after all pertinent to the controversy only while land
remains in a state of nature, and that my argument
ceases to have practical force as soon as the soil of
a country has been brought under cultivation and is
improved by industry.   This exception, I admit, is
to a certain extent well founded—only let us carefully
note to what extent.   Of the labour employed on land,
all that is directed to the raising of the immediate
produce, and of which the results are realized in this
produce — that is to say, the great bulk of all the
labour applied to the land of a country—finds its
natural remuneration in these results, in this immediate
produce.   Such labour, recompensed as it is by the
immediate returns, and leaving the soil substantially as
it found it, cannot form a ground for rights of property
in the soil itself.   No more can labour employed, not
upon the cultivated soil at all, but in extrinsic operations—in making roads, bridges, harbours, in building
towns, and in general in doing things which, directly
or indirectly, facilitate the disposal of agricultural
produce.   It is very true indeed that labour thus

employed affects the value of land ; and there are writers who have relied upon this fact, as identifying in principle landed with other property, showing as it does a connection between the value of land and labour expended.* Unfortunately for the analogy they seek to establish, the labour that is expended is expended, not upon the land whose value it affects, but upon other things ; and the property which results accrues, not to those who exert or employ the labour, but to other persons. The fact, instead of making good the analogy, brings into sharp contrast the things compared. A bale of cloth, a machine, a house, owes its value to the labour expended upon it, and belongs to the person who expends or employs the labour : a piece of land owes its value, so far as its value is affected by the causes I am now considering, *not* to the labour expended upon it, but to that expended upon something else—to the labour expended in making a railroad, or building houses in an adjoining town; and the value thus added to the land belongs, not to the persons who have made the railway or built the houses, but to some one who may not even have been aware that these operations were being carried on—nay, who perhaps has exerted all his efforts to prevent their being carried on. How many landlords have had their rent-rolls doubled by railways made in their despite ?†
In considering the above exception, therefore, we must

* [In particular Mr Carey, the American economist, and M. Bastiat, who has borrowed his doctrine of rent from Mr. Carey. That doctrine owes such plausibility as it possesses entirely to overlooking the distinction here pointed out.]

† [" Pourrait-on sérieusement considérer cette rente, qui est exclusivement attribuée aux propriétaires, comme la rémunération d'avances et de travaux auxquels les propriétaires n'ont contribué que pour une part, et

put aside as irrelevant to the question all the industry
expended upon land of which the effects are limited to
the immediate crop, as well as all that employed in
the general material development of the country, apart
from the cultivation of the soil ; and we thus narrow
the argument to the effects of the labour directed to
the permanent improvement of the cultivated soil
itself—to rendering this a more efficient instrument
for productive purposes than nature gave it to us. So
far as this has been done—so far as the productive
qualities of the soil have been permanently improved
—so far, undoubtedly, the value added to the soil by
such operations, and property in this value, when it
vests in the producer, rests economically upon the
same foundation as property in corn, or wine, or
houses. The transformation of the Lincolnshire fens
and the lagoons of Holland into tracts of golden
wheat land has been referred to by Lord Dufferin :
the reclamation of bog and hill-side by Irish peasant
occupiers equally illustrates the principle ; and the
mention of this last instance will at once indicate what
a very short way the analogy in question will carry
those who have urged it towards the goal they seek.
On the assumption that property in land were measured by the value added to land by human labour—
to land as distinct from its products—and that this
property vested in the person who created the value,
landed property would, thus conditioned, be assimi-
lated in principle to property in other things. As

qui avait un but tout autre que celui d'accroître la valeur des propriétés
foncières."—*Précis de la Science Économique et de ses principales Applica-*
tions, par A. E. Cherbuliez : 1862. An admirable treatise, too little known
in this country.]

matters actually stand, I need scarcely say none of these conditions is fulfilled. Property in land is not measured by the value which industry has added to the land, but is co-extensive with the whole value of the commodity, from whatever causes arising; while the property in such results as human labour has fixed in the soil does not pass to him whose exertions have produced them, but to him who happens at the moment to be legal owner of the improved ground. The fact, in short, does not advance us a step towards the required assimilation : it merely shows us this, that there is a portion of landed property which man has made, which is strictly the product of human industry ; which, therefore, would rest on the same footing as property in other industrial products, were only the laws of landed property something wholly different from what they are.

It follows, then, that the distinction drawn between property in land and property in other things, founded on the fact that " no man made the land," by no means terminates (as might at first be supposed) with land in a state of nature : unless so far as the existing value of land is due altogether to the industry expended upon it—unless in such rare instances as the lagoons of Holland or the fens of Lincolnshire, or reclamations of waste land previously valueless—the distinction applies equally to all lands, cultivated or wild. Property in cultivated, no less than in wild land, consists largely in value which no human industry employed upon the land has created. The ordinary economic considerations, therefore, which apply to and justify property in other forms of wealth, do not apply here. There may be good reasons for the institution of property in land—on that I am not for the moment concerned to express an opinion—but they are not the reasons which support the institution in its other forms ; in particular, landed property is wanting in that foundation—in the judgment of most people, I apprehend, the strongest of all those on which property rests— the expediency of securing the labourer in the fruit of his toil.

The argument, as thus far conducted, carries me, I admit, no further than to this negative conclusion. It rebuts an *à priori* objection to legislative action in such cases as Ireland presents, founded upon an assumed analogy between land and other kinds of wealth. To exhibit the positive reasons which explain and vindicate a policy in the direction contemplated we must go a step further, and bring into view the causes which determine the existence and growth of agricultural rent, and, in relation to these causes, the position occupied by the owners of land on the one hand, and by the general community on the other.

The phenomenon of agricultural rent, let me briefly explain, is, economically considered, of this nature :— it consists of the existence in the returns to agricultural industry of a value over and above what is sufficient to replace the capital employed in agriculture with the profit customary in the country. This surplus value arises in this way. The qualities of different soils being different, and the capital applied even to an area of uniform fertility not being all equally productive— farms differing besides in respect of their situation, proximity to market, and other circumstances—it hap-

pens that agricultural produce is raised at varying
costs; but it is evident that when brought to common
markets it will, quality for quality, command the same
price. Hence arises, or rather hence would arise in
the absence of rent, a vast difference in the profits
upon agricultural industry. The produce raised on the
best soils, or under other circumstances of exceptional
advantage, will bear a much larger proportion to the
outlay than that raised under less favourable circumstances ; but as it is clear that, in a community where
people engage in agriculture with a view to profit, even
this latter portion would need to carry such a price as
would give the producer the same profits which he
might obtain in other occupations (for otherwise he
would not engage in its production), it follows that all
the produce except this, sold as it is, quality for quality,
at the same price, must yield a profit over and above
the customary profit of the country. This surplus
profit is known to political economists as "rent," and
we may henceforth conveniently distinguish it from
the rent actually paid by cultivators as "economic
rent." Arising in the manner described, "economic
rent" cannot properly be said to owe its existence to
either labourer, capitalist, or landlord. It is rather a
factitious value incident to the progress of society
under external physical conditions which necessitate
the raising of raw produce at different costs.* This
being its essential nature, it is plain that, so long as
the rent paid by the cultivator of a farm does not
exceed what the amount of "economic rent" would
be, so long those engaged in agricultural industry will

* See Note at the end of this Essay.

be on neither a better nor a worse footing than those engaged in other occupations. The labourer will have the ordinary wages, the capitalist the ordinary profit of the country.* On the other hand, it is evident that if the cultivator be required to pay more than this—if the rent exacted from him encroach upon the domain of wages and profits—he is so far placed at a disadvantage as compared with other producers, and is deprived of the ordinary inducements to industry. It thus becomes a question of capital importance, what provision exists in the conditions of an industrial community to prevent this result; what security we have that—the land of a country being once given up to private speculation—the limits set by "economic rent" shall, in the main, be observed in the actual rent which landlords obtain. Does the principle of *laissez-faire*—that play of interests developed by competition which in manufacturing and trading operations maintains the harmony of individual with general interests —does this suffice to secure, under ordinary circumstances, the same harmony in the transactions of which land is the subject? If it shall appear that it does not, then, I think, a case will have been made out for the interposition of some other agency—public opinion, custom, or, failing these, direct State action—to supply that which the principle of unrestricted competition has failed to supply—to secure an end which cannot but be regarded as among the legitimate ends of government—the coincidence in an important field of human activity of the individual with the general well-being.

* This position, to be accurate, needs a qualification which it will receive further on. As it stands it is correct for the purposes of the argument.

The influence which is ordinarily supposed to suffice for this purpose is the competition with agriculture of other modes of investing capital. The farmer, we are told, before taking a farm, will consider what rent he can pay consistently with obtaining the usual returns upon his industry ; if the landlord demands more than is consistent with this, he will decline the bargain, and embark his means in some other occupation. Rent, it is said, can thus never rise for any length of time, or, as a general rule, above the level prescribed by the economic conditions of the case. But, as has often been pointed out, and as is obvious at the first blush, this argument supposes a state of things which exists in but few countries in the world, if indeed it exists, or ever can exist, in any. It supposes all farmers to be capitalists—capitalists on a scale implying the possession of disposable wealth in substantial amount ; and it supposes a variety of occupations other than agriculture, soliciting investment, into any of which— a landlord proving unreasonable—farmers can turn their capital. The countries in which these conditions are realized in the highest degree—rather, I should say, in which the nearest approximation to their realization has been attained—are England and Scotland ; and yet it is very evident that in England and Scotland the uncontrolled play of the principle of competition in dealing with land is not found sufficient for keeping the relations of landlord and tenant in a satisfactory state. If it be, then what is the meaning of the current language upon this subject ? of "good" and "bad" applied to landlords in a sense in which the same epithets are never applied to traders in

other commodities than land; of such phrases as
"what a good landlord would do"—this being
assumed to be something quite different from what
his pecuniary interest would lead him to do; of the
constant appeal to the moralities of the landlord and
tenant relation ?* What is the meaning of landlords,
of English landlords, boasting that they do not let
their lands at a competition rent ? † What, again,
is the meaning of courts of law deferring to local
customs, and overriding and modifying the strict
terms of a contract ? The whole state of feeling
and all the current language in reference to this subject imply a deeply-felt conviction that the exigencies
of this relation are not, even in England and Scotland,
satisfactorily met by mere commercial motives, but
that public opinion and custom, custom in some instances enforced by law, are needed to supplement
and qualify the mere commercial rule.

In England and Scotland the interposition of these
agencies to qualify the action of competition in transactions of which land is the subject is more or less
masked; in almost all other fully-peopled countries
it is open and undisguised. In Asia the land has
never, as a general rule, been given up to private
speculation : it has remained in the hands of the

---

* It will be said, perhaps, that the phrase "good and bad employers"
is used with a similar connotation. In general, I think the words mean
no more than persons employing largely or scantily at the market rates.
If they mean more than this, it is when used by those who regard labour
as an exceptional commodity, the remuneration of which should not be
left to the play of competition. The exception thus proves the rule.

† ["Farms in England," says Lord Derby in a recent speech, "are
habitually let at a lower rent than they would fetch if competed for in
open market."]

State; and the condition of the agricultural population has accordingly varied with the greater or less
degree of enlightenment or of sound moral feeling
existing in the rulers. Over Europe, wherever the
land is not owned by the cultivators, custom or law
very generally regulates or largely modifies the relations of landlord and tenant. The position of the
cultivators is one not determined by contract, but, to
a large extent, resting on status. In fact it would be
intolerable were it otherwise; for nowhere in Europe,
England and Scotland excepted, has an approximation
ever been made towards a state of society in which
are fulfilled the conditions that alone render tolerable
the commercial treatment of land—in which the cultivators are capitalists, and a practical alternative to
rural occupation exists for large masses of the people.
The soil is over the greater portion of the inhabited
globe cultivated by very humble men, with very little
disposable wealth, and whose career is practically
marked out for them by irresistible circumstances as
tillers of the ground. In a contest between vast
bodies of people so circumstanced and the owners
of the soil—between the purchasers without reserve,
constantly increasing in numbers, of an indispensable
commodity, and the monopolist dealers in that commodity — the negotiation could have but one issue,
that of transferring to the owners of the soil the whole
produce, *minus* what was sufficient to maintain in the
lowest state of existence the race of cultivators. This
is what has happened wherever the owners of the soil,
discarding all considerations but those dictated by self-
interest, have really availed themselves of the full

strength of their position. It is what has happened under rapacious governments in Asia; it is what has happened under rapacious landlords in Ireland; it is what now happens under the bourgeois proprietors of Flanders;* it is, in short, the inevitable result which cannot but happen in the great majority of all societies now existing on earth where land is given up to be dealt with on commercial principles unqualified by public opinion, custom, or law.

It seems to me that I have made out my case, and shown that the incidents attaching to land not only separate it economically from wealth in other forms, not only therefore rebut *à priori* objections to special land legislation founded on assumed economic analogies, but—regard being had to the conditions of industrial society actually prevailing in the world—furnish positive reasons for this course,—for setting limits, where public opinion and custom are not efficacious for the purpose,—for setting limits by law to the free action of competition in dealing with this commodity. So far as to the general principle. I turn now to consider its application to Ireland.

The discussions on the Irish question, whatever differences of opinion they may have disclosed, have at least made one point clear : no settlement of Irish land can be effectual which still leaves with landlords the power of indefinitely raising rent. I think it may be said that amongst those who know the country, and have seriously grappled with the problem, there is a very general agreement upon this point. The end

---

* See M. Laveleye's Essay, " Cobden Club Essays," vol. i. pp. 255, 256.

may be approached by different paths and realized
in different forms. Compulsory leases, recognition
and extension of tenant-right, simple fixity of tenure,
are amongst the modes ; arbitration courts, the opinion
of official experts, the prices of produce, have been
suggested as the methods of procedure ; but in
whatever manner, through whatever machinery, the
plans that really promise to be effectual involve at
bottom the principle of depriving landlords of the
power of raising rent—the principle, therefore, of
imposing on the State the obligation of saying what
a "fair rent" is. It is very evident that this must
be so—that the landlord, with the power still left him
of raising his rent at will, could easily defeat the most
stringent provisions of the most apparently drastic
land code. Of what avail to the cultivator would be
a right of occupancy if the landlord can attach to that
right impossible conditions ? Of what advantage the
right of selling the good-will of his farm, if the rent
can be raised at the landlord's discretion against the
incoming tenant ? Where would be the gain from
leases if the limits of the rent are not known ? The
regulation of rent is thus of the very essence of the
case; it is felt to be so by all who have really grasped
the problem ; and yet it will be found that this topic
has in general been kept rather carefully in the back-
ground. The reason for this hesitancy it is not
difficult to guess. Few Englishmen can hear without
something of a cold tremor a proposal to fix rent by
law. And yet the consequences are perhaps unfor-
tunate. For all the reserve, it is felt that the efficacy
of the several competing schemes really depends

in the last resort upon this condition. *Omne ignotum pro mirifico.* Imagination magnifies the difficulty which is kept so carefully out of sight. Conscious that it lies behind, people hesitate to venture into what they expect will prove an economic *cul-de-sac;* or, if they must choose, the danger is they will choose the scheme, not which is most efficacious, nor even which is least revolutionary, but which best contrives to veil this terrible bugbear. Now, if the fixing of rent by State authority be really indispensable to an effective settlement of this question, it is surely well that the fact be frankly accepted. I have already shown that Political Economy furnishes no presumption against the propriety of this course. Let us now see if it cannot practically help the solution. *

According to some who pass for authorities, Political Economy has very little to say upon this subject. The worth of land is so much money as it will bring; and to seek a criterion for rent—nay, to attempt to conceive rent at all—otherwise than as it is determined by the market, is in the opinion of these wise persons a hopeless, if not an absurd undertaking. Had they reflected that what they pronounce to be an impossibility is, in point of fact, performed by not a few landlords in Ireland—by every landlord there who does not let his lands on the admittedly ruinous principle of competition—they might have seen reason to distrust

* [Throughout the discussions on the Irish Land Act the Government again and again denied their intention to interfere with the landlord's power of raising his rent ; but nothing is more certain than that the Act does interfere, though in a circuitous and indirect way, with this power ; and further, that it owes whatever success it has achieved to the knowledge shared alike by tenants and landlords that this power resides in the new law.]

the accuracy of scientific knowledge which led to
conclusions so flagrantly at variance with fact. Unless,
however, in what I have said above on the doctrine
of rent I have very grossly misrepresented economic
teaching, Political Economy is involved in no such
conflict with fact as the view in question would imply.
On the contrary, it recognizes in the returns from land
the existence of an element—that which I have designated "economic rent"—which is no other than the
"fair valuation rent" of good landlords.* It not only
recognizes this element, but can state the conditions
determining its amount and the laws of its growth.
The "fair valuation rent" of the popular platform
admits, in short, of being reduced to strictly scientific
expression. The only point really debatable is as to
the means of practically determining the entity in
question in given cases. But, as I have just said,
the thing is in fact done every day, with sufficient
accuracy for practical purposes, by those who manage
Irish estates; and that can scarcely be an insoluble
problem which scores of landlords and land-agents
solve every year.

In approaching the practical problem, there are two
parts that will need to be kept distinct—the first
starting of the new system, and the keeping it going
after it has been started. Over and above the determination of a fair rent, the former will involve the
much more serious practical difficulty of appraising
tenants' past improvements. Some able writers have

---

* The "fair valuation rent" *plus* the returns on permanent improvements of the soil, as will presently be more particularly explained *post*,
pp. 211, 212.

expressed themselves as if this latter difficulty might
be evaded by permitting to occupiers the sale of their
good-will. This would no doubt be so, were the
question of rent once settled; but with this still open,
the value of the occupation right would be uncertain,
while the settlement of the rent plainly cannot take
place till the abatement in consideration of tenants'
improvements is known. Thus the necessity of an
independent valuation of tenants' improvements, wherever landlord and tenant cannot themselves come to
an agreement, is inherent in the case. Questions of
this kind, involving, as they often will, disputes about
minute details, can obviously only be satisfactorily
dealt with by authorities adjudicating in the localities,
and taking evidence in disputed cases from competent
persons who have inspected the farms. Complicated
and delicate questions no doubt they will be, demand-
ing from those to whom the settlement is entrusted no
small amount of patience, sagacity, and firmness; but
questions not less complicated and delicate have already
been unravelled by Englishmen in India; and it is
hard to see why the same qualities of mind which have
threaded their way through the mazes of Hindu
customary law to results of order and substantial justice
should not be equal to dealing with the problem, analogous, but less complicated, and less remote from
English modes of thought, presented by Irish land.

These will be the initiatory difficulties; but these
once surmounted, past improvements once ascertained,
existing rents once adjusted to existing circumstances,
there is no reason that the future working of the status
principle should not be brought under general rules,

and reduced to a system. Confining our attention to
rent, with which alone I am at present concerned, the
problem, as I conceive it, will then lie in such an
adjustment of this element from time to time as shall
satisfy and reconcile the two following conditions :—
(1) to secure to the cultivators, so long as they fulfil the
conditions of their tenure, the due reward of their
industry ; and (2) to do substantial justice to the reasonable expectations of those who, on the faith of Acts of
Parliament and the past policy of the country, have
embarked their fortunes in Irish land.

And here we must endeavour to attain to some
definite conception of what constitutes the due reward
of the industry of the cultivator. I have already
stated what I conceive to be the economic basis of
property—the right of the producer to the thing he
has produced. Accepting this as our principle, the
point to be determined will be the amount of the
produce which is properly referable to the industry of
the cultivator. To bring the question to a clear issue,
I will take an extreme, but not absolutely impossible,
case : I will suppose a farm which owes nothing of
any kind to the landlord's outlay, on which the whole
capital, fixed and circulating, in buildings, fences,
manure, and wages, has been advanced by the cultivator ; and I will suppose, further, that the soil of
this farm is of the worst quality compatible with
profitable cultivation. These conditions being supposed, how much of the wealth produced from the
farm represents the due reward of the cultivator's
exertions ? I answer, the whole ; and for this reason,
that less than the whole would, according to the terms

of the hypothesis, leave the cultivator without that
ordinary remuneration which the conditions of industrial production in the country warrant — without,
therefore, such an adequate motive for his industry,
as cultivator of the soil, as in a healthy condition of
society would exist. In short, my imaginary farm
represents the possible case in which, in conformity
with Ricardo's theory, land under a *régime* of capitalist farmers would yield no rent. Passing from this
peculiar case, I will vary the hypothesis by supposing
the farm to be no longer entirely composed of the
worst cultivable land, but to be, we will say, of average
natural fertility, while the other conditions remain as
before ; the entire capital and labour being supplied
by the farmer. Under such circumstances,— and still
recognizing the principle that the producer is entitled
to what he produces,—how far will the tenants' claim
to the produce extend ? Many people would say, on
my principle, to the whole, and would regard the
result as a *reductio ad absurdum* of the principle. But
I hold this conclusion to be unwarrantable.

In a society constituted according to the principles
of modern industrial civilization, in which each member
enjoys the general advantages arising from separation
of employment and exchange, we are bound, I think,
in estimating the effect of a man's labour, to distinguish
the value from the commodity. In a state of patriarchal isolation the goods which the labour of a family
produces are wholly unaffected by anything which
other people do, and therefore rightly belong in absolute property to the family. But when the producer is
a member of an industrial society, the commodity he

makes may acquire a value—a power of commanding
the labour and goods of other people—not by reason of
what he has done, but through an importance given to
his industrial function by the circumstances of society.
Social circumstances may cause what he produces to
bear a higher value than his labour would naturally
give it, were others free to take advantage of the situation which society has permitted him to occupy. He
may, in short, be the monopolist of a favoured situation, in the advantages arising from which, as they
are no part of the fruit of his toil, he can, on the principle on which we proceed, have no right to property.
Such advantages, so far as they are peculiar to the
situation, are not properly the result of his labours, but
of the social circumstances which have made the situation specially advantageous, and, on the principle we
have recognized, would belong not to him, but to
society at large. Now the case I have put will be
found to fall within this reasoning. The corn and
roots and grass which constitute the agricultural
return, no doubt result, nature assisting, from the
labours of the cultivator; but the value of these
things—the power they confer of commanding the resources of society—is not measured by those labours,
but depends on causes extrinsic to the cultivator's
operations. The produce bears the price it does, not
in virtue of what the farmer has done, but because
society needs food—needs food in quantities which
can only be obtained by bringing lands under cultivation inferior to the best on his farm. That portion
of the value of his produce which is due to this
circumstance is, so far as he is concerned, an accident;

something to which he has no more right than anyone
else. As it does not result from his exertions, so it
offers no encouragement to his industry ; his claim to
it is therefore wanting in that basis which constitutes
the justification of property from the economic point
of view. My conclusion, then, is that the due reward
of the cultivator's industry, even where he supplies
the entire labour and capital employed in production,
is not necessarily co-extensive with the whole produce
of his farm. It is only so on the supposition that he
enjoys in raising it no exceptional advantages arising
out of his relations with other people. But where
he enjoys such exceptional advantages,—that is to
say, where he farms land better than the worst that
yields the current profit of the country,—the principle of property, economically considered, is satisfied
by his retaining so much of the produce as shall
give him the average remuneration, leaving to
society the remainder to be disposed of as it shall
think fit.

The other element of the problem is to do substantial justice to the reasonable expectations of the landlord. I say " reasonable " expectations, because if
the State is to be bound, not by what landlords might
reasonably expect when investing their money in land,
but by what they actually expected, or do now expect,
there is an end to the question ; nothing remains but
to recognize their right of property in its most absolute
sense, and lend the power of the empire to its maintenance. *Risu solvuntur tabulæ.* But if this extreme
ground is not to be maintained, then the claims of the
landlord and tenant are reconciled, become in fact the

correlatives of each other; for "reasonable" expectations must be bounded by the considerations set by
public policy; and public policy manifestly requires
that agriculture should enjoy the advantages common
to other industries in the country,—a result which is
only attained when the ordinary rewards of industry
are left with the cultivators of the soil. So much as
to the nature of the problem.

Let me here recall to the reader the nature of
"economic rent," and the causes to which it owes its
existence. It is that portion of the value of the
returns from land which remains after the outlay of
production has been replaced with customary profit;
and its existence results from a permanent discrepancy
between the price of agricultural produce and the cost
of production of a large portion, the price being
regulated by the highest standard of cost, and being
consequently more than sufficient to remunerate the
outlay on all produce raised at a cost less than this.
These being the causes which determine "economic
rent," the amount will evidently be measured by the
extent of the discrepancy; and consequently will vary,
the price of produce being given, with the productiveness of the soil, or, the productiveness of the soil
being given, with the price of produce. Now these
phenomena—the prices of agricultural produce and
the productiveness of the soil as indicated by its average yield—are already made the subject of record
in our official statistical returns. Here then we have
two available criteria which measure the growth of
"economic rent." Let us see how far they will help
us in the solution we are in search of.

The definition of "economic rent" as being so much of the value of the produce as exceeds the due remuneration of the cultivator's industry, might seem to identify this element with that which is properly, on the principle of distribution just laid down, the landlord's share; and the inference would be just, if we were to include in the cultivator's industry, not merely the capital and labour employed in raising the annual crops, but also that employed in adding to the productive qualities of the soil. But, as economists are aware, when the results of labour and capital are once made a part of the land itself, the returns upon them are governed, not by the laws of profit, but by those of rent, and become in practice inextricably blended with the rent due to natural fertility; while for the same reason they are distinguished from the returns which accrue on the ordinary annual outlay. In describing, therefore, "economic rent" as the value which remains in excess of what is needful for the due remuneration of the cultivator's industry, it must be understood that that industry only is spoken of which is employed in the direct production of the annual returns. Bearing this in mind, and having regard to what the tenant may do in the way of permanent improvement of the soil, it will be seen that the future growth of the landlord's share will not be commensurate with the future growth of "economic rent," and will not consequently follow the same indications. "Economic rent" gives us the maximum which the landlord's share can possibly attain; but in determining the amount which in the actual circumstances is properly his, we must discriminate the causes on which the productiveness of agriculture depends. What we want, in short, is some test which shall enable us to detach from the general value of the raw produce of the country that portion of. it which is the result of causes external to the cultivator's operations. It is this portion only which society, in sanctioning private property in land, has consented to give up to the landlord.

Of the two criteria just mentioned—prices of produce and the productiveness of the soil—the former, agricultural prices,* plainly cannot be affected (at least in a way to raise rent) by any conduct on the tenant's part. An advance of price of a durable kind can only arise from one or both of two conditions—either from a fall in the value of money, or from such an augmented demand for food as should necessitate for its satisfaction the bringing under cultivation, without contemporaneous improvement in the art of agriculture, less fertile soils than any now cultivated. The latter contingency is one exceedingly unlikely to occur; but the former is at the present moment in process of realization, and amongst the causes immediately affecting the pecuniary interests of landlords is perhaps the most important. Changes in the price of produce can thus only occur as the result of causes operating through society at large; it follows that all such changes would indicate grounds for a corresponding change in the pecuniary amount of the landlord's share. This

---

* [Which should of course include the price of all that is raised from the soil—butcher's meat for example. M. Laveleye mentions (Cobden Club Essays, p. 245) that in Belgium, where rents have doubled in thirty years, the price of corn has hardly increased. The advance is due to other products, and in a large degree to the advance in live stock.]

has been generally recognized by the advocates of
fixity of tenure in Ireland, and may be taken as a
settled point in the controversy. It remains to consider whether this criterion alone adequately satisfies
the justice of the case.

The only other cause which can affect economic
rent being the productiveness of the soil, it might
seem as if—unless where the landlord undertakes or
concurs with the tenant in undertaking improvements
of a permanent kind (cases which might easily be
provided for by special arrangements between the
parties)—I say it might seem, excluding such cases,
as if all future increase of productiveness in the soil
must necessarily be the result of the action of the
tenant, and that consequently all future augmentation
of economic rent, not referable to an advance in prices,
should properly be assigned to him. But plausible
as this inference is, I think it may be shown to be
unwarrantable.

Let us consider the following case. Suppose some
country village, at present of small account, to grow
into a town of some importance. It would naturally
soon be connected by railways with the chief industrial
centres of the country, and, as an inevitable consequence, agricultural rent in the neighbourhood would
greatly rise : it would rise for two reasons. First,
because the local demand would raise the local prices,
and, thus far, the criterion of prices would assign the
increase to the landlord ; but it would rise, secondly,
because the proximity of a town and the facilities
offered by railway communication would greatly
cheapen production. The farmer would now be able

to procure his ploughs and harrows, his threshing
and reaping machines, his artificial manures, his tiles
for draining, on greatly cheaper terms than before.
Farming at greater advantage, he would be able (and
that irrespective of any advance of price) to cultivate
soils which formerly it would not have paid to cultivate, and in general to employ with profit a larger
capital on his farm.* The soil, without supposing any
change in its physical properties, would now yield a
larger return, and in effect become more productive.
The larger capital employed upon it would yield a
larger return, while of this increase a portion would
be obtained at a lower cost than the current prices
(without supposing any advance beyond what had
previously prevailed) would suffice to remunerate.
These are conditions which imply an advance in
"economic rent"—an advance not due to prices, and
not indicated by prices ; and the question is, to what
cause is this result to be attributed—to the industry
of the tenant, or to the progress of society in the
locality ?   The tenant is very evidently a co-operator
in the result.   Without his capital and industry the
increased produce could not be obtained ; but that
capital and industry would find their due reward in
a corresponding augmentation of wages and profits ;
and the fact we have to deal with is the existence
of a new increment over and above this due remuneration.   It is with this part of the phenomenon only
that we are concerned ; and the point to be determined is its proper cause.   Now it seems to me, for

* I have to thank my friend Professor Waley for having called my
attention to the importance of this aspect of the case.

the same reasons which apply to the phenomenon of
rent in other cases, that it is properly referable, not
to the action of the cultivator, but to the progress
of society.

The principle involved in this illustration is of very
great importance, since it represents an influence that
is constantly operating in all progressive countries,
and which cannot but operate in Ireland if it is not to
remain for ever in the slough of despond. Every
fresh invention in the arts of productive industry
applicable to agriculture, every extension of railway
communication, every new development of internal
trade, of external commerce, would be attended with
consequences analogous in character to those which
happened in the rural environs of our imaginary town.
If Englishmen desire an illustration on a grand scale,
they have only to look around them. The immense
growth of rent in England and Scotland within a
century is wholly unexplained by any corresponding
rise in the price of produce, and is far from being
adequately explained by the improvements effected in
the permanent qualities of the soil, considerable as
these have been. The phenomenon only becomes
intelligible when we take account of the influence of
industrial and commercial progress generally in cheapening agricultural production. Here, then, we find a
source of growth for " economic rent," born of circumstances extrinsic to the tenant's sphere, and which
should, therefore, on the principle of discrimination we
have adopted, properly accrue to swell the landlord's
share. But augmentations of rent thus arising would
not be accompanied with any corresponding advance,

nor, necessarily, with any advance at all in agricultural prices.

I am, therefore, brought to the conclusion that the criterion of prices, taken simply, and without reference to other circumstances, would fail to furnish an adequate basis for the periodical adjustment of rent. Its adoption would, in effect, transfer to the tenant that for which the State has permitted and encouraged the landlord to pay. I own the considerations just adduced, not to mention others that might be urged in the same sense, go strongly—at least so it seems to me—to show the fundamental impolicy of giving up land to private speculation. But that is not the question here. Land in Ireland has been given up to be thus dealt with; and, this being the policy of the country, those who have embarked their fortunes in this venture are entitled to be protected in its legitimate fruits.

There is, therefore, need of some criterion to supplement that of prices, some criterion which shall mark the growth of rent proceeding from causes not embraced by price, nor yet identical with the operations of the tenant in improving the soil. In a word, we want a test which shall discriminate so much of the increased productiveness of the soil as arises from enhanced efficacy of the productive instrument itself, from that increased productiveness which is, so to speak, the agricultural expression of the progress of the age. After some consideration I am inclined to think that such a test may be found in the average yield per acre of the staple produce of the soil over the whole country—information supplied already by

Irish agricultural statistics. This average productiveness would not, I think, in the main, be very seriously affected by the permanent outlay of tenants, for it must be remembered that a large portion of their improvements are in the nature of reclamations of waste land; and such land will, from the nature of the case, be the least productive in the country. Thus the effect of tenants' improvements would largely be to bring down the average level of productiveness throughout Ireland. On the other hand, there would be improvements, such as thorough draining, effected in the better lands, which would tend to raise the level. As between the two modes of influence I strongly incline to think that the tendency to depress the level would prevail; though I do not believe the preponderance in this direction would be so great as seriously to affect the correctness of the test.* This, however, might be matter for investigation. But proceeding on the assumption that, so far as tenants' improvements are concerned, an equilibrium would result, any positive advance in the average yield per acre over the country could only be referred to causes of that general kind which

---

* Applied to *land under tillage* in Ireland since 1847—the period from which the present system of statistics dates—the criterion shows a very great decline in the productiveness of the soil ; but the explanation of this is to be found in the fact of its being partially applied. The newly-reclaimed land is always, at least in the first instance, brought under tillage ; and since 1847 a large portion of the soil of Ireland, as is well known, has been converted from tillage to pasture ; the portion so converted being, as a general rule, land of superior quality. Thus the test, confined to tillage land, would necessarily show a decline of productiveness. Were the returns from the grass lands, as measured by the increase of stock, taken into account, I have no doubt the balance would be more than redressed.

are incident to the progress of society.* I would, therefore, be disposed to combine this index with that of prices in seeking a rule for periodical readjustments of rent. Not that I would propose to fix those who might be charged with the duty of re-valuation absolutely to the results obtained from these data. It would obviously be necessary, particularly at first, to apply any general rule with discrimination and regard to local circumstances. But, I believe, the data in question constitute the main elements of a sound rule, the perfecting of which could only be the work of time and experience.

If these conclusions possess any value, they are applicable to all plans for the settlement of Ireland, which partially or generally, directly or indirectly, involve control by the State of the landlord's power over rent. But the plan which I have had mainly

---

* Those who have not firmly seized the doctrine of rent will probably see in the proposal to deprive the cultivator of any portion of the results accruing from the increased efficiency of his labours, a violation of equality as between him and those engaged in other industrial occupations. I will ask those who think so to consider what would be the effect of increased efficiency of industry, say in some manufacturing operation. Would it not be a proportional fall in the price of the commodity affected by the improvement? Now if a similar fall took place under similar circumstances in agriculture, the cultivator of the soil and the manufacturer would be on a footing of equality. But, in point of fact, this does not happen; and why? Simply because, owing to the limited extent of the better soils, competition cannot be brought to bear in the one case as in the other. Notwithstanding the immense progress made in the art of agriculture, assisted as this has been by the action of free trade, no serious impression has been made on agricultural prices, while the prices of manufactured articles steadily fall as new improvements come into operation. The deduction, therefore, made from the cultivator's profits of what is due to the exceptional position he occupies, so far from disturbing equality as between him and those engaged in other industries, is the necessary condition towards establishing equality.

in view in this speculation is that which has been propounded by Mr. George Campbell in his work on Irish land.* In this work Mr. Campbell has unfolded a scheme for the solution of the Irish problem incomparably (in the writer's judgment) the best deserving of attention of any that have solicited public notice—a scheme of which the characteristic and peculiar merits are that, at the cost of a minimum of disturbance to the actual machinery of Irish society, it would accomplish what would be a real and effective security of tenure for the Irish Tenant—would accomplish this in a manner suited to the ideas and habits of the country, while combining with this end the further considerable advantage of reserving for landlords under the new system a place and function in the national economy. Mr. Campbell's proposal proceeds upon the plan of distinguishing those parts of the country, or more properly those farms, where tenants now hold their land under definite contracts—where, in effect, the English system of managing property prevails—from those on which what may be called the Irish practice is followed : that of letting land from year to year, the task of providing for the permanent requirements of the farm being left to the occupier. With the state of things

* "The Irish Land," by George Campbell, Chief Commissioner of the Central Provinces of India. (Trübner & Co.) 1869. [I have allowed my remarks on Mr. Campbell's proposal to remain, partly because the principle of his scheme, though not its form or modes of procedure, has been embodied in the Irish Land Act, and therefore the comments which I have made on it are to a large extent applicable to that measure ; and partly also because the objections urged against Mr. Campbell's plan continue still to be urged against all legislation with similar aim, and their refutation consequently cannot yet be considered as out of date or superfluous.]

existing on farms in the former category Mr. Campbell
does not propose to interfere. But the tenants occupying under the latter conditions—a description which
it is scarcely necessary to say covers the mass of the
cultivators of Ireland—he would place upon a new
footing, constituting them tenants under status, in
contradistinction to those in the other category who
would be regarded as tenants under contract. Once
upon the footing of status, no tenant would be evicted
except for defined reasons, of which the non-payment
of rent, subdivision or sub-letting without the landlord's permission, are the chief; nor could his rent
be raised against him except with the sanction of an
authority representing the State. With a view to
the working of the system, Mr. Campbell proposes the
creation of a court or commission with large discretionary powers under an Act of Parliament prescribing
its duties and mode of procedure. It would be the
business of this court, in the first place, to settle
the present position of tenants under status, to consider their claims on the score of past outlay on their
farms, and, due allowance made for these, to settle
the rent; and it would fall to the same commission
to readjust the rent from time to time in conformity
with the changing circumstances of the country, either
at periodical re-valuations or on the requirement of
either landlord or tenant. By such provisions security
of tenure at fair rents would be realized for the cultivators of Ireland. But it is very far from Mr.
Campbell's aim that his plan should work as a cast-
iron system, stereotyping Irish society in its existing
form. He would permit, where circumstances rendered

this advisable, the re-appropriation by landlords of
land in possession of tenants, but only on the terms
of compensating the dispossessed tenant for his improvements, and indemnifying him for the inconvenience he sustained by dispossession ; while, subject
to the sanction of the landlord, the transference of
farms from tenant to tenant would take place with
perfect freedom.   In providing for transactions of this
kind, Mr. Campbell takes custom and Irish ideas
as his guide ; indeed, the recognition of custom as at
once the outcome of history and the surest starting-
point of reform may be said to be the *idée mère* of
his whole scheme.   He, therefore, naturally has recourse to the tenant-right of Ulster, in the legalization
and extension of which he finds the practical solution
of the thorny question of compensation for tenant's
improvements.   By a most ingenious argument Mr.
Campbell shows that, on any view of the case which
does not amount to practical confiscation of the tenant's
interests, this is what compensation in the case of small
farmers, as those under status would almost universally be, must come to.   In this opinion those who
look closely into the matter will be apt to agree with
Mr. Campbell.   When we have to deal with improvements on a substantial scale, carried on upon farms
of considerable extent, there would be little practical
difficulty in arriving at a tolerably correct estimate
of their value ; but when the problem is to ascertain
the worth of a thatched shed, or a gateway, or of a
rood of reclaimed bog in a farm of ten acres, there is
really no other criterion possible than this—how much
will another tenant give for them ?

I venture to offer two suggestions in the way of corollary to Mr. Campbell's plan. It would only be in keeping with the whole principle of his scheme, that, where the State has once charged itself with determining the tenants' rent, no higher rent than that named by the State should be recoverable in a court of law. A provision to this effect would effectually prevent sub-letting, at least in the usual form of that practice. The occupier, it is true, could sell his right of occupancy; and it will no doubt be urged against Mr. Campbell's plan that the sum paid for this by the incoming tenant would, in effect, amount to an increased rent—the objector will doubtless add, on the authority of Adam Smith and Lord Dufferin— of the worst kind. The value of this objection I shall presently consider ; but, before doing so, let me state my second suggestion, which is that the occupancy right should only be disposable to an incoming tenant. I believe that this restriction would be attended with very beneficial consequences. It would, in the first place, render impossible the mortgaging of the good-will ; and secondly, it would indirectly, but I believe very effectually, restrain competition for land within healthy limits. The intending purchaser of the occupancy of a farm might, of course, still raise the money for the purchase of the tenant-right on his personal credit. This is a use of his position and circumstances with which it would be neither possible nor proper to interfere ; but, in order to obtain the farm, one of two things he must have— either cash to pay for the good-will, or credit to induce some capitalist to lend him the money necessary for that purpose; either, that is to say, he must already be the master of realized property, or his character must be such as to make those who know him believe that he is likely to be a prosperous man. The restriction of competition for land to persons satisfying these conditions would render absolutely impossible, under the system of status-tenancy, anything at all resembling, or in any respect analogous to, the impossible rents promised by pauper peasants when the whole population enter the list of competition.

It appears then that, even conceding the argument that the purchase of the occupancy right would for the incoming tenant be equivalent to an increase of rent, still this increase—supposing the practice limited by the restriction I have indicated—would fall greatly short of what rents may attain under the present *régime*. But then we are told that the vice of the practice lies in the form, that the sale of the good-will is in effect a fine paid on entry, and that this has been condemned by Adam Smith. The use so constantly made of Adam Smith's authority in this connection, I must plainly say, does him flagrant injustice—injustice which it is difficult to conceive how· anyone should commit who had really studied his excellent remarks on the tenure of land. The ruling thought of all that he has said on this subject is the supreme importance of security of tenure for the tenant, as the essential foundation and mainspring of all agricultural progress. He eulogizes leases, and, failing leases, customs, or whatever conduces to realizing this indispensable condition. " It is those laws and customs," he tells us, " which have perhaps contributed more to

the present grandeur of England than all their boasted
regulations of commerce taken together." What he
says upon the subject of fines is wholly irrelevant to
the issue in the present case. He is comparing leases
at full rent with leases in which a portion of the rent
is fined down—that is to say, alternatives either of
which offers equal security to the tenant—and his
decision is in favour of that one in which no fine
is paid. What relevancy has a judgment on such
a point to the question involved in the tenant-right
controversy, where the alternative lies, not between
different modes of attaining equal security, but between
absolute security obtained through a fine accompanied
by a moderate rent, and no security accompanied by a
high rent without a fine ? Had the issue in the Irish
controversy really come under Adam Smith's review,
no one, who knows anything of the spirit pervading
the "Wealth of Nations," can doubt what his decision
would have been. At all events, his authority would
need to be greater even than it is to outweigh the
overwhelming force of the argument from Irish
experience. The universal testimony borne to the
prosperity of the tenant farmers in Ireland, wherever
the custom of Ulster prevails—a prosperity all the
more conspicuous from its contrast with the general
wretchedness of the same classes in other parts of
the country,—and the almost equally universal recognition of the connection between the system and
the results, are facts which no statesman can overlook.
Mr. Caird, with all his strong and undisguised prepossessions in favour of Scotch farming, was unable
to resist the evidence ; and the *Times* Commissioner,

in his singularly impartial descriptions written from direct observation, has recently confirmed the most favourable accounts of the system. In presence of such facts it is idle to talk of Adam Smith, or any other authority. All that has been said, or that can be said, against the practice of tenant-right really amounts to this—that the incoming tenant would be better off if he could get the farm with the advantages of the custom while keeping the money which is the price of those advantages. No doubt he would; and so, and in a still greater degree, would be the purchaser of a peasant property if he had not to pay the purchase-money; and yet peasant proprietors, working at this disadvantage, have contrived notwith-standing to cultivate their farms to some purpose. In neither case can a man spend his capital and have his capital; but he may in either case have that which is worth to him more than capital—the peace of mind that is born of security, the enterprise inspired by the prospect of reaping where he has sown.

[There is a mode of reasoning on this question which, if it is not positively fallacious, at least suggests a fallacy against which it may be well to insert a warning here. It is said * that a farmer at a full rent will, with a given capital, be able to work a larger farm than he would were he to employ a portion of his capital in purchasing his farm or in fining down the rent; and that, having regard to the existing price of land, he will, by adopting the former course, derive a larger income from his whole capital. The fact may

---

* See Judge Longfield's Essay on 'The Tenure of Land in Ireland,' "Cobden Club Essays," vol. i.

be so; but, inasmuch as there are farmers, nevertheless, who prefer a smaller farm which is their own property to a larger one at a full rent, this only shows that the position of proprietor is regarded by some as sufficiently advantageous to compensate for a certain loss on annual revenue. Of this, affecting as it does the person concerned only, farmers may be allowed to be themselves the best judges; and true policy will lie in removing all obstacles to their making the freest possible choice. But the line of reasoning to which I have referred implies that there is more than this in the matter; that, looking at the question from the point of view of public interest, an economic gain results from the farmer's remaining a tenant at a full rent, an economic loss from his becoming a proprietor. What is suggested is that the capital of the community available for agriculture is diminished by the adoption of the latter course, and here it is that the fallacy intrudes itself. The farmer who purchases his farm no doubt reduces thereby the amount of his own capital available for cultivation, but he does not curtail in any degree the capital of the community applicable for this purpose; for the purchase-money of his farm, in passing from his hands, at once becomes in the hands of the vendor a fund disposable for productive purposes. He will seek to derive an interest from it, and he can do this in no other way than by investing it. One, and not an improbable mode of investment, would be to lend it on mortgage, in which way, it is conceivable, the same capital might come back to the hands of the very farmer who had parted with it. It will perhaps be said that the farmer proprietor would be

thus brought under a rent in another form ; but there
would be this distinction between his position now and
formerly ; that, whereas he was formerly a tenant paying rent and subject to all the insecurity of that position, he is now an owner subject to a fixed rent-charge.
I have supposed the capital rendered disposable by
the farmer's purchase to be invested on mortgage ;
but it is of no consequence what supposition we make
with regard to the mode of investment. Suppose it
were invested in the Funds, it would still be disposable
in the hands of the vendor of stock, and, however it
might for a time pass from hand to hand, must ultimately, if it is to yield a revenue, find its way to the
sustenance of some branch of production—doubtless
to the sustenance of whatever branch had most need
of it. If agriculture were that branch, then, in the
absence of artificial obstacles, to the support of agriculture it would go. If it did not go back to agriculture this would only be because the interests of
the community were better served by a different disposition of the fund.]

Perhaps the greatest danger of the present moment
is that on which so much English legislation has made
shipwreck—the danger that our statesmen, meaning
well but embarrassed by their position, will be drawn
into the middle course of a weak compromise—a
compromise which will solve nothing, but embroil
everything. The plan recommended by Mr. Caird,
a high authority in practical agriculture, fulfils in a
remarkable manner the conditions of such a settlement. The inducements which he holds out to landlords to grant leases would be simply inappreciable,

when weighed against the reasons which would still
remain, from their point of view, for refusing them;
and what would be the value of leases without some
guarantee against an indefinite rise of rent? But
while his plan would wholly fail to give a sense of
security to the tenant, it would be very effectual in
hampering the action of the landlord. What landlord
would care to take an active part in working his estate
when he could only do so by passing his transactions
with his tenants through the ordeal of public advertise-
ment in leading newspapers, and waiting for the
expiration of a five years' notice to quit before getting
possession of his land? Of two things, one. The
material development of the country may, on plausible grounds, be entrusted to the initiative either of
landlord or of tenant. There is something to be
said for both plans. The landlord has naturally the
advantage of the tenant-farmer—at least of the Irish
tenant-farmer as he now exists—in enterprise and
command of capital. On the other hand, enterprise
and capital may, as others think, be developed in
a far higher degree by giving real security to the
tenant. But a system for which there is absolutely
nothing to be said is that which would fail to evoke
either of these motive powers; which would shackle
the landlord without freeing the tenant, and under a
net of inducements and counter-inducements, of checks
and counter-checks, would stifle all vigorous life.
Such, I venture to think, would be the effect of
the solution of the Irish problem recommended by
Mr. Caird. But such a result could scarcely prove
definitive. Things have gone too far for that. The

attempt to accomplish it would, however, immensely
aggravate all the dangerous elements of the situation,
and probably in the end involve us in extreme courses,
which might now be avoided.

NOTE TO P. 197.

[This is what Mr. Mill has since, in the programme of the Land Tenure
Reform Association, designated "the unearned increase" from land, all
future additions to which he proposes on certain conditions to appropriate
to the State.   The discussions which have arisen on this proposal of
Mr. Mill's have, by the flagrant weakness of the arguments employed
against it, brought into strong light the essential soundness of Mr. Mill's
position.   Thus, one of the principal of those arguments is derived
from a supposed analogy between Land and Stocks—*e.g.* the public funds.
It is urged that the public funds, like land, rise in value with the progress
of society ; that the advance in their price which has occurred since they
were first created has been "unearned" by the fundholder ; and that
therefore the same principle which applies to the "unearned increase"
from land would require us to mulct the fundholder of this portion of his
property.   The argument is founded upon a gross confusion, which
perhaps it may be well to clear up.   A rise in the price of stocks, where
it is due to the progress of society, represents a larger *capitalized* value
of *the same annual sum :* it merely indicates a change in the relation of
capital to interest.   But land rises in value, not merely from this cause,
but also because rent, the annual return, rises.   A rise in the price of
stocks, so far as it is due to the progress of society, would be shared by
all stocks in an equal degree.   The stockholder, consequently, unless so
far as the advance gives him greater confidence in the stability of his
property, derives no advantage from the change.   His income remains as
before.   He may indeed sell it for a higher price ; but, on reinvesting the
price, he would have to pay proportionally higher for whatever productive
fund he chose to buy.   To deprive stockholders of the increase in the
capitalized value of their stock would not be to keep their means of living
at the same point at which it stood before the advance in price took
place, but to reduce it below that point just in proportion to the amount
abstracted.   In other words, the recognition of their right to all increase
in the capitalized value of their income is the condition of leaving
that income unimpaired.   The case of land is totally different.   The
capitalized value of a given rent rises with the progress of society
precisely as the price of stocks rises.   So far the landlord stands on
the same footing with the fundholder.   *But then his rent rises also ;* and
this makes all the difference.   While the fundholder's income remains the
same as society progresses, the landlord's steadily rises : his means of

living steadily increase. The capitalized value of his estate consequently increases not simply *pari passu* with the increase in the price of stock, that is to say with the increase in the capitalized value of a given yearly sum, but in this proportion compounded with the increase in his annual rents. Now, it is to the increased value of land incident to the increase of annual rent, and to this alone, that Mr. Mill's proposal applies.

Another argument relied upon by Mr. Mill's opponents is the analogy to the case of land supposed to be furnished by the advance in the price of works of art and objects of *vertu* which also occurs with the progress of society. But surely the case must be felt to be desperate when such an argument is seriously put forward. Conceding the analogy to be perfect, is it not sufficient to reply *de minimis non curat lex?* Special legislation on such a subject as the land of a country may surely be permissible where it would not be worth the legislator's while to regulate by special enactment the irregular gains of a few picture-dealers. But in truth the cases are not analogous. In the first place picture collectors perform a useful social function by cultivating the public taste in the direction of art; the increase in the value of their property is therefore not altogether "unearned." And, secondly, pictures differ from land in this, that they do not *as a rule* rise in value with the progress of society. A few rise in value, and a great many more fall. The picture-dealer takes his chance : and it would be gross injustice, while compelling him to bear his losses, to compel him also to relinquish the occasional gains which form their natural compensation.]

POLITICAL ECONOMY AND LAISSEZ-FAIRE.*

GREAT BRITAIN, if not the birthplace of Political Economy, has at least been its early home, as well as the scene of the most signal triumphs of its manhood. Every great step in the progress of economic science (I do not think an important exception can be named) has been won by English thinkers; and while we have led the van in economic speculation, we have also been the first to apply with boldness our theories to practice. Our foreign trade, our colonial policy, our poor-laws, our fiscal system, each has in turn been reconstructed from the foundation upwards under the inspiration of economic ideas; and the population and the commerce of the country, responding to the impulse given by the new principles operating through those changes, have within a century multiplied themselves manifold. This London, in the midst of which we find ourselves, what is it but a mighty monument of economic achievement?—the greatest practical illus-

* An Introductory Lecture delivered in University College, November 1870.

tration which the world has seen of the potent influence of those principles which it is the business of the political economist to expound ? In view of such facts, one might expect that, if there was on the globe a spot where a keen interest would be felt in the study of Political Economy—where the science which unfolds the laws of industry and commerce would be held in honour—it would be London. Now I wish to call your attention to a singular fact, for singular it surely is. In this vast London, so energetic, so enterprising, so enlightened ; in this great centre of the world's commerce ; in this metropolis of the country which has produced Adam Smith, Ricardo, Malthus, Mill ; which has produced, again, Pitt and Huskisson, Peel, Cobden and Gladstone ; in this focus of economic activity and power ; the systematic study of economic science is almost without practical recognition. I wish to be accurate, and I therefore say "almost," and I use the qualification "practical" ; for in London there are, I believe, three chairs from which Political Economy, or matter connected with Political Economy, is taught—two in King's College and one here. But what is the number of students attracted from this great population to study Political Economy under those chairs ? I have no exact statistics upon the point, and the subject is perhaps of too delicate a nature to warrant me in going into details. But I am certainly not overstating the case when I say, that the aggregate number of students attending all the public economic schools in London falls very much short of a hundred individuals—one hundred individuals, that is to say, out of a population of three millions! I wish I could say that we in this college could claim one-half, or even a quarter, of this not very overwhelming grand total.

I do not know whether it is necessary to go into comparisons in order to point the significance of these figures; but I will venture to mention one other case, as it has come under my own personal observation. In the not very flourishing town of Galway, with which I have had till lately an official connection, there is a chair of Political Economy. The number of students who during my time attended the lectures from that chair varied ordinarily from six to ten persons. Now, if we compare the proportion which these numbers bear to the population from which they were drawn with the proportion which, let us say, the sixty or one hundred students attending London chairs bear to the population of this metropolis, and if we take this proportion as an indication of the interest felt in economic studies in the two places, we arrive at this rather surprising result—that in that remote, and I regret to say decaying, Irish town, the degree of interest taken in economic science is many times, perhaps five or six times, greater than here—greater, that is to say, in the "*ultima Thule*" of Connaught than in this metropolis of modern industrial civilization.

Now it seems to me that this is a very remarkable fact, and one that deserves the attention of those who, in this country, have charged themselves with this branch of speculation. I have called attention to it, partly in the hope that those who have better opportunities of acquainting themselves with the opinions

of the London public than I have may take it into
consideration, and partly with a view to bring under
your notice such a partial explanation of the phenomenon as occurs to myself. Let me say here, in
passing, that there is one explanation of the fact,
which to many people will seem the sufficient and
obvious one, which, nevertheless, I cannot allow to
be either a satisfactory or a complete account of the
matter. I shall possibly be told that the reason the
people of London are not attracted to the lectures
delivered from its economic chairs is simply that those
lectures are not attractive; that, in short, the fault
lies, not with the people of London, but with those
who fail to set Political Economy before them in an
interesting light. The facts may be as this explanation
suggests, at least I have no desire to deny them, so far
as my own particular share in the transaction is concerned : but I submit that the allegation fails to meet
the point. The professors of Political Economy in
London are not the creators, but the creatures, not the
cause, but the effect, of the requirements of the people
of London with respect to this subject. I do not deny
that there is a connection between the mode in which
a subject is taught and the interest taken in it, that the
public taste may be sensibly influenced by the quality
of those who occupy the seats of learning in a country.
But, conceding this, I still hold that the public cannot
escape from its responsibilities towards science and
learning by sheltering itself under an alleged incompe-
tency on the part of those to whom it has intrusted
their interests. If the teachers of Political Economy
in London are not up to the mark, why does not

London supply itself with better? Why is London
content to have Political Economy inadequately taught?
And thus I am brought back to the fact which I have
proposed for consideration : that, in this great centre
of English commercial and political life, Political
Economy, the one science which is pre-eminently an
English product, which has been built up by English
thinkers, and applied, with most striking effect, by
English statesmen, is, as a branch of liberal education,
all but practically ignored.

There are those who would probably explain this
singular state of things by reference to a supposed
distaste or inaptitude for abstract speculation characteristic of the average English mind. I will not undertake to say that there may not be some slender basis
of truth in this view. Englishmen are apt to value
themselves on being a practical people ; and, as every
excellence is said to have its compensating defect, it
is conceivable that this English virtue may have a tendency to run to excess, and that it may have issued
in a mental habit unfavourable to the cultivation of
economic science, which, it must be admitted, shares
the attributes common to all scientific knowledge.
Certainly, the very slender attention bestowed in
London on some other branches of philosophical speculation—I may instance mental philosophy and jurisprudence—affords some countenance to this view.
Still, I cannot admit this to be a complete account of
the matter. English distaste for abstract speculation,
assuming it to exist, is, at all events, not so strong
that it may not be overcome by the prospect of practical advantage. What do we see in the Universities ?

Branches of learning of the most abstract character, others, if not abstract, at all events as far removed as learning can conceivably be from utilitarian ends, but nevertheless pursued with extraordinary eagerness. And why? For no other reason, that I know of, than because certain large pecuniary prizes are attached to success in them. But this is perhaps a somewhat coarse illustration of the facility with which the practical English mind may be drawn contrary to its natural bent. More creditable evidence may be found in the large and increasing attention now given to the physical sciences; for physical science, though deriving its data from particular facts, nevertheless, as science, consists, not in statements regarding particular facts, but in abstract doctrines. What is a law of nature but a relation between phenomena considered apart from all particular exemplifications of the relation?—that is to say, an abstract doctrine. Yet this has not prevented the keenest possible pursuit of physical knowledge. In short, let it once be made clear that abstract speculation is not barren speculation, that scientific doctrines have a real bearing on the practical concerns of life—and by practical concerns of life I do not mean simply making money, but all that concerns human beings in shaping their conduct in the world—let this only be made clear, and I think we have no reason to suppose that a fair proportion of the community will not be drawn to their cultivation. And this brings me to what, it seems to me is the true explanation, or at least one principal cause, of that indifference towards economic studies of which the limited attention given to them in the seats of learning in London affords so remarkable an indication. I seem to observe in the literature and social discussions of the day signs of a belief that Political Economy has ceased to be a fruitful speculation. Nay, I fear I must go further, and admit that it is even regarded by some energetic minds in this country as even worse than unfruitful—as obstructive, a positive hindrance in the path of useful reform. I am anxious to state, as accurately as I can, what I understand to be the precise nature of those injurious prepossessions. Before attempting to prescribe remedies, it will be well to make a careful diagnosis of the disease.

Few persons of decent education will now deny that vast benefits have accrued to the world, and in an especial degree to this country, from the study of economic science. I have already referred to the great practical reforms that have been accomplished in obedience to its teaching in the principal departments of our public life. And over and above such tangible achievements, candid people will acknowledge that its influence has been felt throughout the whole range of our legislative and administrative systems, and with largely beneficial effect. We are all now very familiar with such commonplaces as that individuals are the best judges of their own interests; that monopolies should not be permitted in trade; that contracts should be free; that taxation should be equal, and should be directed to the maintenance of the revenue, not to the guidance of commerce; and the like. These seem now to be very trite maxims, but a century ago they were paradoxes; and, in truth, they represent nothing less than a revolution in the modes

of governing and administering the country, the result
of the new modes of thought introduced by economic
study. Well, the benefits conferred by economic
science being thus evident and palpable, it may seem
surprising that opinions such as I have just hinted at
should obtain, and obtain not merely amongst the
ignorant, but among well-informed and instructed
people. How are we to reconcile the recognition
which must be accorded to the past achievements of
this science with the beliefs in its present unfruitfulness,
still more with the opinion held by some of our more
advanced social thinkers, that it has become an obstacle
in the forward path of reform ?

I put the question thus broadly, because it is only
when these impressions are brought into juxtaposition
with the admitted facts of the case that the attitude
of a large portion of the educated classes towards this
study can be understood. It is too easily assumed by
economists that, the past services of their science once
established, its importance as a branch of modern
education must be forthwith acknowledged. But this
by no means follows. Not a few schemes of doctrine
may be named which have been useful in their time,
but which, having served their purpose, have ceased to
possess interest for those who desire to take part in
the working life of the world ; nay, the burthen of
which on the memory might even be felt by such as
an encumbrance and a drag. The rules of chivalry
once served a very useful purpose. The doctrines of
the scholastic logic for many centuries greatly aided
the progress of the speculative intellect. Numerous
systems of dogmatic theology, now extinct or becoming

so, have for a time served as scaffolding for moral ideas more or less valuable. The theory of the social contract, fanciful and barren as it may now seem to us, was potent among the active forces which produced the great intellectual ferment of the last century in France. Yet a knowledge of all or of any of these phases of thought would scarcely be considered as an indispensable part of the mental equipment of an educated man in the present day. Now this consideration may help us to understand the attitude taken towards Political Economy by a large number of instructed and active-minded people. It is not denied that the science has done some good; only it is thought that its task is pretty well fulfilled. The process of abolishing monopolies and removing impediments to industry is thought to have well-nigh reached its natural termination; or, if there is work to be done, then it is held to be work of a different order from most of that which has been hitherto accomplished—work, in the carrying out of which the maxims of economic science not only cannot help us, but may even prove an obstruction. These opinions, it is evident, must connect themselves with the idea entertained of economic science by those who hold them; and this brings me to what I regard as the root of the matter—the notion prevailing among the great majority of educated people respecting the nature and functions of Political Economy.

That notion, I imagine, takes somewhat this shape. Political Economy has of course to do with wealth; so far there is no question in dispute. But what is the problem concerning wealth which it undertakes to solve? I think the prevailing notion is that it undertakes to show that wealth may be most rapidly accumulated and most fairly distributed—that is to say, that human well-being may be most effectually promoted—by the simple process of leaving people to themselves; leaving individuals, that is to say, to follow the promptings of self-interest unrestrained either by the State or by public opinion, so long as they abstain from force and fraud. This is the doctrine commonly known as *laissez-faire;* and, accordingly, Political Economy is, I think, very generally regarded as a sort of scientific rendering of this maxim,—a vindication of freedom of industrial enterprise and of contract, as the one and sufficient solution of all industrial problems. Such, I apprehend, is the current notion; and it must be owned that it falls in very well with most of what is known respecting the practical applications of the science. How far this view is well founded I shall presently examine; but I wish first to show how it has produced that indifference towards the study amongst a large proportion of educated people, and that hostility on the part of a few, to which I have in the preceding remarks called your attention.

You will observe, then, that, taking the foregoing as a correct description of the scope and functions of economic science, its utility, with a view to the practical requirements of a country, will entirely depend upon what those requirements happen to be. If the industrial system of a country be of that character which was universal in Europe eighty or a hundred years ago, if trade and industry be hampered in all directions by artificial rules and restrictions, obviously there will be great scope for a scheme of doctrine embodying and expounding the principle of *laissez-faire*. But if this is not the case, if all, or nearly all, the reforms covered by this maxim have been already carried, then Political Economy, as its scientific expression, can, it is evident, have little relevancy to the practical work of the country. How, then, stands the case with regard to ourselves? Do we find State action here in the sphere of industry greatly overdone? Are the legal restraints on individual enterprise, still unremoved, of a serious kind? Is our trade still in shackles? Is our freedom of contract injuriously restricted? I think most candid people will acknowledge that, while something may still be needed in some or all of these directions, it is not of a very formidable character, and that this little may safely be trusted for its accomplishment to the impetus which still remains from the movement which carried the greater economic reforms. Looking around us on the social needs of the time, we are bound, I think, to confess that we do not find much work of a merely negative sort to do; and we must therefore acknowledge that, if Political Economy be merely what a widely prevalent opinion supposes it to be, if the sum and outcome of its teaching be *laissez-faire*, the field for its activity, in this country at least, must henceforth be a narrow one. Under these circumstances, it is not strange if the interest felt in the study is of a languid sort. Where the opinion prevails that *laissez-faire* marks the limit of industrial reform, that when we have set individual enterprise free we have done all that in such matters can be done,

Political Economy will naturally be regarded with a good-natured tolerance in consideration of its past services, combined with a profound indifference, based on the conviction that it has become in the course of events a practically obsolete scheme of thought. Such, it seems to me, is in point of fact the state of feeling on this subject amongst a large number of educated people in this country at the present time.

Amongst a large number, but not universally; for there are those whose faith in *laissez-faire* is not quite so absolute as that of the majority; who hold that there are ends to be compassed in social and industrial life which can only be reached through the action of society as an organized whole; and that, while the mere negative and destructive part of industrial reform has been well-nigh completed, a work of positive and reconstructive reform still lies before us. What will be the attitude of this section of thinkers towards a speculation putting itself forward as a scientific vindication of the principle of "letting things alone"? Inevitably one of hostility. When people think they see before them a field for useful action, in which good may be done by measures of a positive kind, they naturally feel impatient of a system propounding *laissez-faire* as the last word of human wisdom. Thus, if I have correctly seized the current impression respecting this branch of speculation, we have found at least a partial explanation of the phenomenon which I have proposed for consideration. People neglect Political Economy because they regard it as practically obsolete, as out of relation to the actual work of the time; or they oppose it because they

think it has begun to be obstructive; and the view
taken by depreciators and opponents is in each case
the natural result of the conception they have formed
of the study. And here it is that I join issue with
both classes. I altogether deny the correctness of
their view of the science; and, as the most effectual
means of exploding it, I shall now endeavour to show
that the maxim of *laissez-faire* has no scientific basis
whatever, but is at best a mere handy rule of practice,
useful, perhaps, as a reminder to statesmen on which
side the presumption lies in questions of industrial
legislation, but totally destitute of all scientific authority.

In proceeding to argue this point, I must ask you,
in the first place, to note what this doctrine of *laissez-
faire*, if it is to be taken as a scientific principle, really
means. The implied assertion, as I understand it,
is this : that, taking human beings as they are, in the
actual state of moral and intellectual development they
have reached ; taking account, further, of the physical
conditions with which they are surrounded in the
world; lastly, accepting the institution of private
property as understood and maintained in most
modern states,—the promptings of self-interest will
lead individuals, in all that range of their conduct
which has to do with their material well-being, spontaneously to follow that course which is most for
their own good and for the good of all. Such is
the assertion with which we have now to deal ; and
you will at once see that it involves the two following
assumptions : first, that the interests of human beings
are fundamentally the same—that what is most for

my interest is also most for the interest of other
people; and, secondly, that individuals know their
interests in the sense in which they are coincident
with the interests of others, and that, in the absence
of coercion, they will, in this sense, follow them.   If
these two propositions be made out, the policy of
laissez-faire—the policy, that is to say, of absolute
abstention on the part of the State in all that concerns
material well-being—follows with scientific rigour.
But can they be made out ?   For my part I am
disposed to accept the first one ; I am disposed to
believe that human interests, well understood, are
fundamentally at one : only let me in passing suggest
a caution.   Let us not confound the statement that
human interests are at one with the statement that
class interests are at one.   The latter I believe to
be as false as the former is true, and, moreover, to
be one of those plausible optimist falsities against
which it especially behoves us in the present day to
be on our guard.   But accepting the major premiss
of the syllogism, that the interests of human beings
are fundamentally the same, how as to the minor ?—
how as to the assumption that people know their
interests in the sense in which they are identical with
the interests of others, and that they spontaneously
follow them *in this sense?*   It is a remarkable thing
that Bastiat, the great apostle of *laissez-faire*, in the
work he has devoted to the glorification of this
principle, absolutely overlooks this indispensable step
of the argument—wholly fails to prove his minor
premiss.   He thus states the case :—" Human interests," he says, are either " naturally harmonious," or

"naturally antagonistic." *   If antagonistic, then the
solution of the social problem must lie in some form
of constraint. But if human interests be harmonious,
then, he argues, the solution must lie in leaving
people free to follow them—in the unqualified adoption, that is to say, of the principle of *laissez-faire*.
Now I beg you to mark the strange assumptions
that underlie this reasoning. Human interests are
naturally harmonious : *therefore* we have only to leave
people free, and social harmony must result ; as if it
were an obvious thing that people knew their interests in the sense in which they coincide with the
interests of others, and that, knowing them, they
must follow them ; as if there were no such things
in the world as passion, prejudice, custom, *esprit de
corps*, class interest, to draw people aside from the
pursuit of their interests in the largest and highest
sense !   Here is a fatal flaw on the very threshold of
Bastiat's argument ; and it is a flaw which no follower
of Bastiat has repaired—which, for my part, I believe
to be irreparable. Nothing is easier than to show
that people follow their interest, in the sense in
which they understand their interest. But between
this and following their interest in the sense in which
it is coincident with that of other people, a chasm
yawns. This chasm in the argument of the *laissez-
faire* school has never been bridged. The advocates
of the doctrine shut their eyes and leap over it.

For, to examine the question more nearly, and to
come at once to the important point—granting that

---

* As if even this were necessarily true ; as if it might not be that some
human interests were in harmony and some opposed.

people may, in a certain sense, be trusted to see most
clearly their own interest, and to pursue with avidity
what they so regard, what is it that people understand to be their interest? What did landlords, as
a class, understand to be their interest down to
1846, when they maintained the Corn Laws as indispensable to their rents, and the prop of their
political power? What do the same class now understand as their interest, when they avail themselves
of the power given them by the law to put their
estates in settlement, create life-interests, entails, col-
lateral charges, interposing endless artificial obstacles
between the land of the country and the living people
who inhabit it, to the practical exclusion from the
possession of land of the enormous majority of
Englishmen? What do Irish landlords understand
to be their interest when they are only withheld by
fear of assassination, or by law, from evicting their
tenants in order to consolidate their estates? What
did employers in former days understand to be their
interest when they enacted statutes of labourers?
or, in more recent times, when a ten hours' Act has
become necessary to protect women and children
against the consequences of an unscrupulous pursuit
of gain? What is the notion those farmers form of
their interest who employ the gang system as described in recent parliamentary reports? or, again,
those members of trades-unions, who pass rules against
task-work and in favour of uniform wages for the
skilful and the inept, the idle and the industrious,
rules against machinery and in favour of inefficient
methods of manual labour, rules against the admission

of their fellows to sharing with themselves the opportunities of a livelihood offered by the market, rules,
in a word, against the most efficacious use of man's
power over nature, and the fair distribution of the
proceeds of toil—what, in the idea of these trades-
unionists, is their interest? To give one instance
more, what was the notion of their interest entertained
by the slaveholding aristocracy in the Southern
States of the American Union, who, seeing with their
own eyes the exhausting and ruinous effects of the
system they upheld; seeing its influence in preventing the rise of a skilled industrial class, and
in thus almost wholly excluding manufacturing industry from the States where it prevailed; seeing its
effects in consigning to lawless barbarism more than
a half of the entire rural population,—nevertheless
rose in arms to maintain it, and not merely to
maintain, but to extend it far and wide over the
continent of America? Or, turning from particular
examples to broad results, can any one seriously
consider the present condition of the inhabitants of
these islands—these islands where industrial freedom
has for nearly half a century had greater scope than
in any previous age or in any other country, but
where also the extremes of wealth and poverty are
found in harsher contrast than they have been ever
found elsewhere; where one man consumes more
value in a single meal than goes to feed and clothe
the family of another for a month; where the entire
land of the country is owned by less than a hundred
thousand persons out of a population of thirty
millions; where one in every twenty persons is a

pauper; where the great bulk of the agricultural
population look forward with calm resignation to
spending their old age in a workhouse; while the
artisan population of the towns find themselves about
once in ten years in the midst of a frightful commercial catastrophe, which consigns hundreds of
thousands to ruin—I ask if any one can seriously
consider this state of things, and yet repose in
absolute satisfaction and confidence on his maxim of
laissez-faire? Nor is it merely the co-existence of
this state of things with an unparalleled freedom in
all directions of industrial and commercial enterprise
that we have to consider. The truly significant
circumstance is that the policy in question, the policy
expressed by *laissez-faire*, has been steadily progressive
for nearly half a century, and yet we have no sign
of mitigation in the harshest features of our social
state. I beg of you to consider the lesson taught
by the repeal of the Corn Laws. That was one of
the most important steps ever taken in carrying out
the policy of *laissez-faire*—as all economists believe
a thoroughly sound and wise step. Well, now,
observe what the repeal of the Corn Laws has done
for us, and also what it has not done for us. It has
given an immense impulse to our general trade; our
exports and imports have, since the passing of the
measure, enormously increased; our wealth and population have advanced with unexampled rapidity.
But the able men who led the agitation for the repeal
of the Corn Laws promised much more than this.
They told us that the Poor Laws were to follow the
Corn Laws; that pauperism would disappear with

the restrictions upon trade, and the workhouses ere
long become obsolete institutions. I fear this part
of the programme has scarcely been fulfilled. Those
ugly social features, those violent contrasts of poverty
and wealth, that strike so unpleasantly the eye of
every foreign observer in this country, are still pain-
fully prominent. The signs of the extinction of
pauperism are not yet very apparent. In a word,
"the grand final result" promised by Bastiat as the
double goal towards which *laissez-faire* conducts mankind—"the indefinite approximation of all classes
towards a level which is always rising; the equalization of individuals in the general amelioration"—
seems as yet, with all our freedom of trade, scarce
perceptibly nearer—nay, one might be tempted to
say, seems further off than ever. I say this is a
significant fact, and one fitted, it seems to me, to
abate our confidence in mere *laissez-faire* as the
panacea for industrial ills.

There is then no evidence, either in what we know
of the conduct of men in the present stage of their
development, or yet in the large experience we have
had of the working of *laissez-faire*, to warrant the
assumption that lies at the root of this doctrine.
Human beings know and follow their interests according to their lights and dispositions; but not necessarily,
nor in practice always, in that sense in which the
interest of the individual is coincident with that of
others and of the whole. It follows that there is no
security that the economic phenomena of society, as at
present constituted, will always arrange themselves
spontaneously in the way which is most for the

common good. In other words, *laissez-faire* falls to
the ground as a scientific doctrine. I say as a scientific
doctrine; for let us be careful not to overstep the
limits of our argument. It is one thing to repudiate
the scientific authority of *laissez-faire*, freedom of contract, and so forth; it is a totally different thing to set
up the opposite principle of State control, the doctrine
of paternal government. For my part I accept
neither one doctrine nor the other; and, as a practical
rule, I hold *laissez-faire* to be imcomparably the safer
guide. Only let us remember that it is a *practical
rule*, and not a doctrine of science; a rule in the
main sound, but like most other sound practical rules,
liable to numerous exceptions; above all, a rule which
must never for a moment be allowed to stand in
the way of the candid consideration of any promising
proposal of social or industrial reform. It is from
this point of view that the argument I have been
urging assumes a practical aspect. *Laissez-faire*,
freedom of contract, and phrases of like import, have
of late become somewhat of bugbears with a large
number of people. It is enough to mention them,
to discredit by anticipation the most useful practical
scheme. What did we hear during the discussions
on the Irish Land Bill? Political Economy again
and again appealed to as having pronounced against
that measure. Now, what did this mean? Simply
that the Bill interfered with freedom of contract,
violated the rule of *laissez-faire*—charges perfectly true,
and which would have been decisive against the
Bill had these phrases really possessed the scientific
authority which members of Parliament supposed

them to possess. Now, it is against this understanding
of the doctrine that my argument is directed. So
understood, I hold it to be a pretentious sophism, destitute of foundation in nature and fact, and rapidly becoming an obstruction and nuisance in public affairs.

Well, if Political Economy is something else than
the doctrine of *laissez-faire*, what is it? If it possesses capabilities in relation to positive and reconstructive, no less than in relation to negative and
destructive, reform, I may fairly be required to point
them out. And this is what, in the further remarks
I have now to offer you, I shall attempt to do. If
then I am asked what is Political Economy, I say
it is the Science of Wealth; and for those who clearly
apprehend what science, in the modern sense of the
term, means, this ought sufficiently to indicate at once
its province, and what it undertakes to do. Unfortunately, many who perfectly understand what science
means when the word is employed with reference to
physical nature, allow themselves to slide into a
totally different sense of it, or rather into acquiescence
in an absence of all distinct meaning in its use, when
they employ it with reference to social existence. In
the minds of a large number of people everything is
Social Science which proposes to deal with social
facts, either in the way of remedying a grievance,
or in promoting order and progress in society. Now
I am anxious here to insist upon this fundamental
point: whatever takes the form of a plan aiming at
definite practical ends—it may be a measure for
the diminution of pauperism, for the reform of land-
tenure, for the extension of co-operative industry, for

the improvement of the coinage ; or it may assume a
more ambitious shape, and aim at reorganising society
under spiritual and temporal powers, represented by a
high priest of humanity and three bankers—it matters
not what the proposal be, whether wide or narrow in
its scope, severely judicious or wildly imprudent—if
its object be to accomplish definite practical ends, then
I say it has none of the characteristics of a science,
and has no just claim to the name. Consider the
case of any recognized physical science—Astronomy,
Dynamics, Chemistry, Physiology—does any of these
aim at definite practical ends ? at modifying in a
definite manner, it matters not how, the arrangement
of things in the physical universe ? Clearly not. In
each case the object is, not to attain tangible results,
not to prove any definite thesis, not to advocate any
practical plan, but simply to give light, to reveal laws
of nature, to tell us what phenomena are found together, what effects follow from what causes. Does
it result from this that the physical sciences are without bearing on the practical concerns of mankind ? I
think I need not trouble myself to answer that
question. Well, then, Political Economy is a science
in the same sense in which Astronomy, Dynamics,
Chemistry, Physiology, are sciences. Its subject-matter
is different ; it deals with the phenomena of wealth,
while they deal with the phenomena of the physical
universe ; but its methods, its aims, the character of
its conclusions, are the same as theirs. What Astronomy does for the phenomena of the heavenly bodies ;
what Dynamics does for the phenomena of motion ;
what Chemistry does for the phenomena of chemical

combination ; what Physiology does for the phenomena of the functions of organic life ; that Political Economy does for the phenomena of wealth : it expounds the laws according to which those phenomena co-exist with or succeed each other; that is to say, it expounds the laws of the phenomena of wealth.

Let me here briefly explain what I mean by this expression. It is one in very frequent use ; but, like many other expressions in frequent use, it does not always perhaps carry to the mind of the hearer a very definite idea. Of course I do not mean by the laws of the phenomena of wealth, Acts of Parliament. I mean the *natural* laws of those phenomena. Now what are the phenomena of wealth ? Simply the facts of wealth ; such facts as production, exchange, price ; or again, the various forms which wealth assumes in the process of distribution, such as wages, profits, rent, interest, and so forth. These are the phenomena of wealth ; and the natural laws of these phenomena are certain constant relations in which they stand towards each other and towards their causes. For example, capital grows from year to year in this country at a certain rate of progress ; in the United States the rate is considerably more rapid ; in China considerably slower. Now these facts are not fortuitous, but the natural result of causes ; of such causes as the external physical circumstances of the countries in question, the intelligence and moral character of the people inhabiting them, and their political and social institutions ; and so long as the causes remain the same, the results will remain the same. Similarly, the prices of commodities, the rent of land, the rates of wages, profits, and interest, differ in different countries; but here again, not at random. The particular forms which these phenomena assume are no more matters of chance than the temperature or the mineral productions of the countries in which they occur are matters of chance ; or than the fauna and flora which flourish on the surface of those countries are matters of chance. Alike in the case of the physical and of the economic world, the facts we find existing are the results of causes, between which and them the connection is constant and invariable. It is, then, the constant relations exhibited in economic phenomena that we have in view, when we speak of the laws of the phenomena of wealth ; and in the exposition of these laws consists the science of Political Economy. If you ask me wherein lies the utility of such an exposition of economic laws, I answer, in precisely the same circumstance which constitutes the utility of all scientific knowledge. It teaches us the conditions of our power in relation to the facts of economic existence, the means by which, in the domain of material well-being, to attain our ends. It is by such knowledge that man becomes the minister and interpreter of Nature, and learns to control Nature by obeying her.

And now I beg you to observe what follows from this mode of conceiving our study. In the first place, then, you will remark that, as thus conceived, Political Economy stands apart from all particular systems of social or industrial existence. It has nothing to do with *laissez-faire* any more than with communism ; with freedom of contract any more than with paternal government, or with systems of *status.* It stands apart from all particular systems, and is moreover absolutely neutral as between all. Not, of course, that the knowledge which it gives may not be employed to recommend some and to discredit others. This is inevitable, and is only the proper and legitimate use of economic knowledge. But this notwithstanding, the science is neutral, as between social schemes, in this important sense. It pronounces no judgment on the worthiness or desirableness of the ends aimed at in such systems. It tells us what their effects will be as regards a specific class of facts, thus contributing data towards the formation of a sound opinion respecting them. But here its function ends. The data thus furnished may indeed go far to determine our judgment, but they do not necessarily, and should not in practice always, do so. For there are few practical problems which do not present other aspects than the purely economical—political, moral, educational, artistic aspects—and these may involve consequences so weighty as to turn the scale against purely economic solutions. On the relative importance of such conflicting considerations Political Economy offers no opinion, pronounces no judgment, thus, as I said, standing neutral between competing social schemes; neutral, as the science of Mechanics stands neutral between competing plans of railway construction, in which expense, for instance, as well as mechanical efficiency, is to be considered; neutral, as Chemistry stands neutral between competing plans of sanitary improvement; as Physiology stands neutral between opposing systems of medicine. It supplies the means, or, more correctly, a portion of the means, for estimating all ; it refuses to identify itself with any.

Now I desire to call particular attention to this characteristic of economic science, because I do not think it is at all generally appreciated, and because some serious and indeed lamentable consequences have arisen from overlooking it. For example, it is sometimes supposed that, because Political Economy comprises in its expositions theories of wages, profits, and rent, the science is *therefore* committed to the approval of our present mode of industrial life, under which three distinct classes, labourers, capitalists, and landlords, receive remuneration in those forms. Under this impression, some social reformers, whose ideal of industrial life involves a modification of our existing system, have thought themselves called upon to denounce and deride economic science, as forsooth seeking to stereotype the existing forms of industrial life, and of course therefore opposed to their views. But this is a complete mistake. Economic science has no more connection with our present industrial system than the science of mechanics has with our present system of railways. Our existing railway lines have been laid down according to the best extant mechanical knowledge ; but we do not think it necessary on this account, as a preliminary to improving our railways, to denounce mechanical science. If wages, profits, and rent find a place in economic theories, this is simply because these *are* the forms which the distribution of wealth assumes as society is now constituted. But it comes equally within the province of the economist to exhibit the working of any proposed modification of

this system, and to set forth the operation of the laws
of production and distribution under such new conditions. And, in connection with this point, I may
make this remark, that, so far from its being true that
economic science has done its work, and thus become
obsolete for practical purposes, an object of mere
historical curiosity, it belongs, on the contrary, to a
class of sciences whose work can never be completed,
never at least so long as human beings continue to
progress; for the most important portion of the data
from which it reasons is human character and human
institutions, and everything consequently which affects
that character or those institutions must create new
problems for economic science. Unlike the physicist,
who deals with phenomena incapable of development,
always essentially the same, the main facts of the
economist's study—man as an industrial being, man as
organized in society—are ever undergoing change.
The economic conditions of patriarchal life, of Greek
or Roman life, of feudal life, are not the economic
conditions of modern commercial life; and had Political
Economy been cultivated in those primitive, ancient, or
mediæval times, while it would doubtless have contained
some expositions which we do not now find in it, it must
also have wanted many which it now contains. One
has only to turn to the discussions on currency and
credit which have accompanied the great development
of our commerce during the last half-century, to see
how the changing needs of an advancing society evolve
new problems for the economist, and call forth new
growths of economic doctrine. At this moment one
may see that such an occasion is imminent. Since

the economic doctrines now holding their place in our
text-books were thought out, a new mode of industrial organization has established itself in this and
other countries. Co-operation is now a reality, and,
if the signs are not all deceptive, bids fair to trans-
form much of our industry. Now the characteristic
feature of co-operation, looked at from the economic
point of view, is, that it combines in the same person
the two capacities of labourer and capitalist; whereas
our present theories of industrial remuneration pre-
suppose a division of those capacities between distinct
persons. Obviously, our existing theories must fail
to elucidate a state of things different from that contemplated in their elaboration. We have thus need of
a new exposition of the law of industrial remuneration
—an exposition suited to a state of things in which
the gains of producers, instead of taking the form of
wages, profits, and rent, are realized in a single composite sum. I give this as an example of the new
developments of economic theory which the progress
of society will constantly call for. Of course it is an
open question whether this *is* the direction in which
industrial society is moving; and there are those,
I know, who hold that it is not towards co-operation,
but rather towards "captains of industry" and organization of workmen on the military plan, that the
current is setting. It may be so; and in this case the
economic problem of the future will not be that which
I have suggested above; nevertheless, *an* economic
problem there still will be. If society were organized to-morrow on the principles of M. Comte, so long
as physical and human nature remain what they are,

the phenomena of wealth would exhibit constant
relations, would still be governed by natural laws;
and those relations, those laws, it would still be important to know. The function of the economist would
be as needful as ever.

A far more serious consequence, however, of
ignoring the neutral attitude of this study in relation
to questions of practical reform is the effect it has had
in alienating from it the minds of the working classes.
Instead of appearing in the simple guise of an expositor of truths, the contributor of certain data towards the solution of social problems—data which of
themselves commit no man to any course, and of
which the practical cogency can only be determined
after all the other data implicated in the problem are
known—instead of presenting itself as Chemistry,
Physiology, mechanical science present themselves,
Political Economy too often makes its appearance,
especially in its approaches to the working classes, in
the guise of a dogmatic code of cut-and-dried rules, a
system promulgating decrees, " sanctioning " one social
arrangement, "condemning" another, requiring from
men, not consideration, but obedience. Now when
we take into account the sort of decrees which are
ordinarily given to the world in the name of Political
Economy—decrees which I think I may say in the
main amount to a handsome ratification of the existing
form of society as approximately perfect—I think we
shall be able to understand the repugnance, and even
violent opposition, manifested towards it by people who
have their own reasons for not cherishing that un-
bounded admiration for our present industrial arrange-

ments which is felt by some popular expounders of so-called economic laws. When a working man is told that Political Economy "condemns" strikes, hesitates about co-operation, looks askance at proposals for limiting the hours of labour, but "approves" the accumulation of capital, and "sanctions" the market rate of wages, it seems not an unnatural response that "since Political Economy is against the working man, it behoves the working man to be against Political Economy." It seems not unnatural that this new code should come to be regarded with suspicion, as a system possibly contrived in the interest of employers, which it is the workmen's wisdom simply to repudiate and disown. Economic science is thus placed in an essentially false position, and the section of the community, which is most vitally interested in taking to heart its truths, is effectually prevented from even giving them a hearing. I think it, therefore, a matter not merely of theoretic, but of the utmost practical importance, that the strictly scientific character of this study should be insisted on. It is only when so presented that its true position in relation to practical reforms, and its really benevolent bearing towards all sorts and conditions of men, will be understood, and that we can hope to overcome those deep-seated but perfectly natural prejudices with which the most numerous class in the community unfortunately regard it.

And now I trust I have made it clear that the branch of knowledge, with whose interests I am charged in this college, possesses other claims upon our attention than those which rest upon its past services; that it has a real and vital connection with

all existing problems which involve the material
interests of human beings, as well as a field for development in new directions, which can never fail so
long as society continues to progress. Above all, I
trust I have placed it beyond doubt that, rightly
conceived, economic science can never be an obstacle
to the fair consideration and discussion of any plan
of human improvement. Those schemes only need
fear Political Economy which are conceived in ignorance of human nature, or of the laws of the physical
universe. And surely it is a singular position which
those social reformers take up who deliberately slight
or neglect this study. They desire, they tell us, to
improve the condition of their fellow-creatures. They
have perhaps drawn up elaborate and highly complex
plans for achieving this end ; but they object to have
their proposals tested by scientific methods. Better
they think to take a leap in the dark, than to examine
beforehand by the lamp of science the ground to
which they invite us to commit ourselves. In a
striking passage of an admirable address, Professor
Huxley has pointed out how all true education, so far
as education is an art, is but a mode of acquiring
knowledge which Nature herself, where we omit this
means of acquiring it, is pretty sure to bring home
to us after her own rude fashion. The teaching of
Nature, says Professor Huxley—

"Is harsh and wasteful in its operation. Ignorance is
visited as sharply as wilful disobedience—incapacity meets
with the same punishment as crime. Nature's discipline
is not even a word and a blow, and the blow first ; but the
blow without the word. It is left to you to find out why
your ears are boxed.

"The object of what we commonly call education—that education in which man intervenes, and which I shall distinguish as artificial education—is to make good these defects in Nature's methods; to prepare the child to receive Nature's education, neither incapably, nor ignorantly, nor with wilful disobedience; and to understand the preliminary symptoms of her displeasure without waiting for the box on the ear. In short, all artificial education ought to be an anticipation of natural education. And a liberal education is an artificial education which has not only prepared a man to escape the great evils of disobedience to natural laws, but has trained him to appreciate and to seize upon the rewards, which Nature scatters with as free a hand as her penalties."

What is it then that those persons ask us to do who would dispense with the study of Political Economy? Simply to deprive ourselves of the aids of artificial education in the most complicated, most difficult, and most momentous concerns of life. Rather than take the trouble to understand "the preliminary symptoms of Nature's displeasure" in the government of her economic kingdom, they think it better we should rush into action and learn—by having our ears boxed. I do not know whether you will feel inclined to hearken to their advice. But I pray you to understand that the *soufflets* administered by Nature in punishment of economic ignorance are by no means trifling penalties. They are known by the names of bankruptcies, commercial crises, conflicts of capital and labour, Sheffield outrages, excess of population, pauperism, internal insurrections, international jealousies often issuing in foreign wars. This metropolis in its eastern quarter could just now supply some striking illustrations. Ireland, with its wretched peasantry, demoralized by centuries of industrial insecurity, could

furnish a few more. What is it that led France to
surrender her liberties into the hands of a saviour
of society? What but the spectre of socialism—
that rank growth of economic ignorance? Thus
economic ignorance, when it has conceived, brings
forth socialism, and socialism breeds despotism, and
despotism, when it is finished, issues in war, misery,
and ruin. Other causes, no doubt, have contributed
to the terrible catastrophe which we now witness
and deplore; but most assuredly economic ignorance
is deeply responsible in the matter. These horrors,
then, are some of the chastisements which Nature
administers to those who choose to remain in ignorance of the signs of her displeasure in economic
affairs. Would it not be as well to avoid them?
Nay, would it not be even worth while to seize on
some of the rewards which here, no less than in
her physical realm, Nature scatters with as free a
hand as her penalties?

M. COMTE AND POLITICAL ECONOMY.

Of the writers who during the last half century have contributed to place Social Philosophy on the footing which it now holds, none deserve more deference on questions of classification and method than Auguste Comte. Opinions will differ as to the value of his views on the regeneration and reorganization of society, but M. Comte has rendered services to the cause of social and historical speculation which are quite independent of the system of doctrines distinctively connected with his name. Even those who reject what are known as Positivist doctrines, and who feel themselves in imperfect sympathy with the spirit of Positivism, may gratefully acknowledge that social studies have taken a new place in the domain of speculative thought since M. Comte devoted to them his mind and life, and may recognize in his work an achievement not without analogy to that accomplished by Bacon in a different though neighbouring field. In neither case, they will probably

* *Fortnightly Review*, May 1870.

think, did the value of the performance consist in the positive contributions made to our knowledge, whether of physical nature by Bacon, or of the principles of social union by M. Comte,—though it will be allowed that our obligations to M. Comte on this score are vastly greater than any which can be credited to the author of the " Novum Organum,"— but in the distinctness and vividness of the conception which each alike had formed of the path of investigation to be followed in the pursuit of that knowledge which each had taken for his special goal, and in what was the consequence of this : the strength of conviction and the unfaltering faith with which each delivered his message.   Bacon's dreams of a New Atlantis to be reached by experiment and induction were not more in advance of the current speculation of his time than were the analogous dreams of M. Comte of a society regenerated by Positive Philosophy. While the poet was singing that—

"Through the ages one increasing purpose runs,"

the French philosopher believed that he had divined that purpose, and could lay bare its scope.   And he not only conceived the design, but, in the opinion of eminent judges, took important steps towards its realization.

The high authority, then, of M. Comte in the domain of Social Philosophy will scarcely be disputed—certainly will not be disputed by the present writer ; and it must therefore be allowed that the absolute proscription by him of a branch of social inquiry carries with it a certain presumption—some will think a weighty presumption—against the legiti-

macy of the speculation falling under this ban. Now
this presumption, whatever may be its weight, lies,
it must be frankly admitted, against the branch of
study which it is the purpose of the following pages
to promote.* It was M. Comte's opinion that Political
Economy, as cultivated by the school of Adam Smith's
successors in this country and in France, failed to
fulfil the conditions required of a sound theory by
Positive Philosophy, and was not properly a science.
He pronounces it to be defective in its conception,
"profoundly irrational" in its method, and "radically
sterile" as regards results.   Such an opinion, proceeding from a philosopher of M. Comte's eminence,
is a fact which ought not to be lightly passed by.
M. Comte, moreover, has supported this unfavourable
judgment by a train of elaborate argumentation; but,
so far as I know, his arguments have not yet been
seriously grappled with.   I am very sensible to what
an extant I shall leave myself open to the imputation
of presumption in venturing on a task which has been
avoided by so many incomparably better fitted than I
am for its effective discharge.   Nevertheless, the task
is one which I feel bound to undertake; for it seems
to me that I should be guilty of even greater presumption were I to enter upon an investigation such as I
propose to make the subject of the present volume,
without, at all events, attempting to do justice, so far
as my abilities permit, to M. Comte's views.   As a
preliminary step, therefore, to an examination of the

---

* [It should be stated that the present Essay was intended as the
preliminary chapter of a work on "The Logical Method of Political
Economy."]

character and method of Political Economy, I have
to ask the reader to follow me in an examination of
the grounds of M. Comte's judgment against the
scientific pretensions of this study.

And, in the first place, let me endeavour to state
the precise question on which M. Comte is at issue
with the student of economic science.   M. Comte
does not deny that the phenomena of wealth are
important elements in determining the condition and
progress of society; still less does he deny—on the
contrary, it is his emphatic assertion—that these
phenomena, like all others which in the aggregate
constitute the social state, are subject to invariable
law.   On the other hand, political economists—those
political economists, at least, whose views the present
writer shares—make no pretension to constitute Political Economy as the science of society.   It is fully
admitted that the subject-matter of their science is
but one among many elements which go to form the
aggregate social condition; and they are consequently
bound to acknowledge, as they do acknowledge, that
the most complete acquaintance with economic facts
and laws furnishes of itself no adequate basis for
general social speculation.   But agreeing thus far,
M. Comte and the political economists differ here :—
while admitting that economic phenomena are subject
to law, M. Comte denies that the law can be ascertained by study of the phenomena.   His position is,
that the facts of wealth are, in the form in which they
actually present themselves to our observation, so
inextricably interwoven with facts of a different order
—with facts, for example, of the intellectual, moral,

and political order—that the determination of the
laws which govern them is only possible when they
are considered in connection with such associated
facts; that consequently a science of Political Economy
is impossible ; just as for the same reason a science
of Psychology, or of Jurisprudence, or of any distinct
and separate order of social relations is impossible.
It was accordingly with him a fundamental canon of
philosophical method, that all investigations into the
structure and laws of society should proceed on the
principle of dealing with social facts, to use M. Comte's
language, in the *ensemble.* Society, he said, should be
contemplated in the totality of its elements ; and no
investigation should be undertaken into any portion
of those elements except in constant connection with
parallel investigations carried on contemporaneously
into all co-existing portions of the complex whole.
All isolated study of a single aspect of social life, of a
particular order of its relations apart from the rest, he
regarded as essentially vicious and doomed to failure
in advance.* Such a view is, of course, altogether
inconsistent with the existence of a science of wealth ;
and here, accordingly, the student of Political Economy
comes into collision with the teaching of M. Comte.
Instead of proceeding by the method of the *ensemble,*
and studying society in all its elements at once, the
political economist proceeds by an opposite rule : he
breaks up the aggregate social phenomenon into the
elementary groups of which it is composed, and, select-

---

* " Philosophie Positive," Leçons 47 and 48. See also the "Politique,"
vol. iii. p. 585 (1853), from which it will be seen that M. Comte's views on
this point underwent no change in his later years.

ing one of these, studies it apart from all the others. He does not indeed, as has been already intimated, confound the laws at which he thus arrives, the laws of this detached group, with the laws of society; but the laws of society itself, he holds, are only to be ascertained by working on the plan which he has adopted,— by making, that is to say, each distinct order of relations involved in the composite phenomenon of society the subject of a distinct and separate investigation, leaving it to the social philosopher properly so called—the speculator on society as a whole,—to combine the results of the labours of students of special branches in elucidation of the general problem.*

Such is the question at issue between the student of Political Economy and M. Comte. Now, adverting to the history of inductive research, it will at once be seen that the view taken by the political economist has this weighty presumption in its favour : it is in strict analogy with the course followed by all fruitful investigation from the dawn of scientific discovery to the present time.

* " Notwithstanding the universal *consensus* of the social phenomena, whereby nothing which takes place in any part of the operations of society is without its share of influence on every other part ; and notwithstanding the paramount ascendancy which the general state of civilization and social progress in any given society must hence exercise over all the partial and subordinate phenomena ; it is not the less true that different species of social facts are in the main dependent, immediately and in the first resort, on different kinds of causes ; and therefore not only may with advantage, but must, be studied apart : just as in the natural body we study separately the physiology and pathology of each of the principal organs and tissues, though every one is acted upon by the state of all the others ; and though the peculiar constitution and general state of health of the organism co-operates with, and often preponderates over, the local causes, in determining the state of any particular organ."—MILL'S *System of Logic*, vol. ii. p. 480.   3rd Ed.

When men first began to speculate on the facts of the universe, the line of investigation they fell into was precisely that which M. Comte holds to be the proper one in sociological inquiry. They contemplated nature in the *ensemble*, and propounded the question, What is the origin of all things? But so long as the problem remained in this form, nothing valuable issued from the efforts to solve it beyond the discipline afforded to the minds thus employed— nothing but a series of vague guesses more or less ingenious, yielding, it may be, some satisfaction to the speculative intellect, but incapable of throwing any light on the real relations of objective existence. In time, however, and by slow degrees, the spirit of the *ensemble* gave way to another spirit—that of specialization and detail. Influenced mainly by the practical necessities of life, in some degree also by the exceptional conspicuousness of certain phenomena, people turned from speculation on the universe as a whole to observation and reasoning upon certain limited orders of facts. Thus geometry arose out of the practical requirement of measuring the earth; and, beginning as an art, grew into a science, taking as its subject-matter the particular class of relations brought into view in that practical operation. The order followed in the genesis of the science of geometry is typical of the whole course of scientific development. In each case practical exigencies, or exceptional conspicuousness, have called attention to phenomena of a special kind—to the movements of the heavenly bodies, to the play of mechanical forces, to the composition of material substances, to the structure or functions of the human body—from the investigation of which have arisen the sciences of Astronomy, of Mechanics, of Chemistry, of Anatomy, of Physiology. Each science, called into existence by the anxiety to explain striking experiences, or to provide and justify practical expedients, has taken in charge some special and limited order of relations, has detached these from the mixed and heterogeneous body of physical phenomena, and has made them the subject of isolated and special study. The laws of the various orders of physical relations have thus been determined; and the rays of scientific light emanating from the separate investigations of perfectly independent workers have been made to converge in elucidation of the actual composite facts of the outer world.

This has been the course of development in physical science, the method by which the secrets of external nature have been unlocked. It has been a method, not of study in the *ensemble*, but of study through the elements—of analysis followed by synthesis. In perfect analogy with this mode of proceeding is the political economist's conception of the path of inquiry to be followed in dealing with the facts of social life. He proposes to break them up into their elementary groups, and he takes one of these groups— the phenomena of wealth—as the subject of his special investigation. It may be remarked, moreover, that, in selecting this particular group of phenomena, he has been influenced by considerations in all respects analogous to those which have determined the separate treatment of the various classes of physical phenomena. Political Economy, like Geometry, Astronomy, Mechanics, Chemistry, had its origin in practical exigencies, and made its *début* as an art. It aimed at the practical object of enriching particular nations by means of trade. For this purpose highly complicated machinery—encouragements for particular industries, prohibitions of others, bounties, drawbacks, in a word the whole body of commercial regulations known as the Colonial and Mercantile systems— was brought into play. These expedients, if they favoured some interests, damaged others : the conflict of interests brought on discussion ; and the argument rapidly passed from attack and defence of practical plans to examination of the natural laws governing the order of relations which it was the purpose of these plans to control. The limits of the debate were not at first, perhaps, very distinctly defined, but by degrees they grew clear. The facts of wealth became detached for the purposes of discussion from the other classes of facts with which in actual existence they were blended ; and Political Economy, as the science of those facts, emerged. As regards origin and mode of development, therefore, the parallel between Political Economy and the physical sciences is complete ; nor have I any reason to suppose that M. Comte would dispute the general correctness of the description I have given : indeed, he frankly admits that the precedents of physical science are against him.* What, then, is his line of argument ? It is this: he contends that the cases are not similar; that the problems presented, on the one hand by physical nature, on the

* " Philosophie Positive," vol. iv. pp. 353–54. Edit. 1839.

T

other by social life, are so radically discrepant that
the method applicable to the one must be, not only
modified, but reversed, in dealing with the other.
To follow in social inquiry the precedents of physical
research is, according to M. Comte, in oblivion of
essential distinctions, to practise a "blind imitation."
This is the position which we are now called upon to
consider.

Most people who take an interest in questions of
the kind we are now discussing are familiar with
M. Comte's classification of the sciences. As is known,
it proceeds upon the plan of arranging the various
branches of scientific knowledge in the order indicated
by the relative complexity of their subject-matter.
Thus it places first in the scale the sciences which deal
with the most simple order of relations—number and
extension. After these comes Mechanics, as involving
relations one degree more complex; next to Mechanics,
Astronomy, which is followed by Physics, and so on
through the whole circle of scientific knowledge;
each science, according to its place in the scale,
representing a degree of complexity greater than those
preceding and less than those following it. It results
from the principle of the arrangement that the organic
sciences, having for their subject-matter the complex
phenomena of the vegetable and animal world, should
occupy the later portion of the scale, and that Sociology, or the science of human society, as concerned
with the most complex of all phenomena, should conclude and crown the whole. As regards the merits
or demerits of this classification—a question on which
the highest authorities are not agreed—it would be

unbecoming in me to pretend to express an opinion.
I only refer to it in order to render M. Comte's argument against Political Economy intelligible. As has
been said, then, the sciences are arranged in the order
indicated by the degree of complexity in their subject-
matter ; those occupying the first or lower portion of
the scale embracing phenomena but little complex,
while the phenomena embraced by the sciences in the
later portion are complex in a high degree. It is on
this distinction that M. Comte grounds his argument
for disregarding in sociological speculation the precedents furnished by physical research. According to
him, the method of investigation that has been followed
in the study of physical nature—the method, that is to
say, which proceeds by breaking up composite phenomena into the elementary groups composing them,
studying apart the elementary groups, determining
their laws, and afterwards combining these laws in
explanation of the original aggregates,—this method,
according to M. Comte, owes its efficacy to the un-
complex character of the phenomena submitted to the
process. As phenomena become more complex, the
method, he contends, becomes less suitable, less efficacious, till at length a point is reached at which it fails
altogether, and it becomes necessary to adopt a contrary mode of procedure, the mode of procedure,
namely, which he describes as investigation through
the *ensemble*. This point in the scale of the sciences
coincides, he tells us, with that at which the transition
is made from inorganic to organic nature. The method
of investigation by disintegration and separate study
should thenceforth give way to that which proceeds by

treatment in the *ensemble*. Accordingly, he holds that
the organic sciences generally should be cultivated in
conformity with this principle; but in the study of
social phenomena, the most complex and intricate of
all, the rule becomes absolute and imperative.*

And here one is led to ask why the method of
specialization should lose its efficacy as problems become more complex? The very opposite is what one
would naturally expect. If a problem involving no
more than two or three distinct elements can only be
resolved by the process of analysis and separate consideration of the parts, the necessity for this would
seem to be still more urgent as the elements engaged
became more numerous. M. Comte's reason for
reversing this inference is very peculiar.† He says
that as phenomena become more complex, the elements
composing them become more *solidaires*. In the
physical universe, the complexity of the phenomena is
not great, and consequently their "solidarity" is but
"slightly pronounced:" "the elements are here better
known to us than the *ensemble*." But the reverse is
the case with the organic world, and more especially

* As to the nature of the complexity of social phenomena see Mill's
"Logic," vol. ii. p. 475 *et seq.* 3rd Edit.

† This argument has appeared to me so weak—indeed, M. Comte's
whole case against Political Economy is, as it seems to me, so weak—that
I have felt it difficult at times to repress the suspicion that his reasons
for rejecting it were not purely and simply of a philosophical kind.
"Il s'agit malheureusement," he says in one passage, "et sans que rien
puisse m'en dispenser, de tenter une création philosophique qui n'a
jamais été jusqu'ici ébauchée ni convenablement conçue par aucun de
mes prédécesseurs." "Sociology" could not be constructed in its entirety
by M. Comte if Political Economy were a legitimate speculation. But
M. Comte felt it to be his mission to construct Sociology in its entirety.
The conclusion seems evident.

with that portion of the organic world which constitutes the social organism. The phenomena are here
characterized by a very high degree of complexity, and
therefore, says M. Comte, by a very high degree of
solidarity : "the *ensemble* of the subject is better known
to us and more accessible than the parts." On the
fundamental principle, then, of inductive logic, which
requires us to proceed from the known to the unknown,
from the better to the less known, we are bound, in
dealing with the phenomena of organic nature, but more
especially with the phenomena of society, to begin our
investigations with the study of aggregates, and only
after we have determined *their* laws to address ourselves
to those of the less known elements. M. Comte admits
that this mode of proceeding must "gravely augment"
the fundamental difficulties already incident to the
extreme complication of the subject-matter; but this,
he conceives, is only a reason for reserving the study
of society for "the highest scientific intelligences."

In attempting to criticise this argument, it becomes
necessary to assign a distinct meaning to its several
propositions. We encounter, in the first place, the
expression, "the *ensemble* of society," and the statement that this is better known to us than the
"elements." In the most obvious meaning of the
word the statement is manifestly not true. By the
ensemble of society most people would, I think, understand the aggregate of the human beings composing
society—of those human beings considered in their
social relations ; and by the "elements," the individual
social men and women. In this sense I say it is
manifestly untrue that we know society better in its

ensemble than in its "elements,"—so manifestly so, that it cannot for a moment be supposed that this was M. Comte's meaning. When, for example, an Englishman travels in France, it is not with the *ensemble* of French society that he comes into contact, but with certain railway officials and hotel proprietors, exemplifying a very limited range of French social existence. As he prolongs his residence he may extend his knowledge; but the course which his acquisitions take will, I need scarcely say, be in the opposite direction to that which M. Comte's maxim affirms. Nor can a French philosopher attain a knowledge of French social existence by any different path; he, too, must proceed from individuals to classes, and from classes to the social whole. But there is another sense in which M. Comte's language may be understood. Social phenomena, like all other phenomena, meet us not simple, but composite. We do not encounter purely religious, or purely industrial, or purely political men and women. Social acts, social situations, can rarely be referred to any single influence. Human beings, as they exist, are not abstract, but historical, human beings, in a greater or less degree under the influence of all the causes that have been affecting the race from its origin down to the present time. Thus regarded, society, or more properly social phenomena, may be said to present themselves to us in the *ensemble;* and thus understood, the statement that we know society through its *ensemble*, not through its elements, is undoubtedly true. If this be M. Comte's meaning, the proposition cannot be disputed; but then it must be

remarked that the assertion is equally true as applied
to the phenomena of the physical universe. Physical
forces also act in constant conjunction. Unless we
effect the separation by artificial means we encounter
no purely chemical, or purely optical, or purely
mechanical phenomena, but phenomena in the production of which a variety, greater or less, of physical
forces concur—that is to say, we know physical nature
also through its *ensemble.* We are thus brought back
to the point from which we started : why are we
—the phenomena of social life and those of physical
nature being made known to us under similar conditions—to reverse in our study of society the method
of investigation which has been found efficacious in
dealing with the physical world ?

M. Comte's reply at this stage of the argument
resolves itself into the doctrine I have already stated,
that the solidarity of phenomena varies directly with
their complexity. It is true, he seems to admit, that
we know physical nature equally with social through its
ensemble ; but the *ensemble,* in the former case, is composed of fewer elements, and these, in proportion as
they are fewer, are less *solidaires*—are therefore more
easily broken up and submitted to separate examination. Hence arises an increased facility of applying
the method of disintegration and separate study in
their case. But, in the first place, this does not meet
the difficulty, since the answer admits that physical
nature *is* known to us through its *ensemble*—an admission which, on M. Comte's principles, seems to draw
with it the obligation of studying physical nature
through this, its most familiar manifestation. Waiving,

however, this point, I wish to examine M. Comte's position, which is really the root of his whole argument against Political Economy, that phenomena in proportion as they are more complex are more *solidaires*. If this assumption be not well founded, there is absolutely nothing for his reasoning to rest upon.

To test the doctrine, let us consider it in a concrete case. I take the instance of water, a composite physical phenomenon exemplifying a variety of physical laws. Considered chemically, its complexity is of the lowest degree, containing as it does but two elements, oxygen and hydrogen. According to M. Comte's doctrine, water, being chemically of the lowest degree of complexity, ought to exhibit, in the relation of its chemical elements, the lowest degree also of solidarity. The fact, I need scarcely say, is exactly the reverse. As everyone knows, the solidarity—by which I understand intimacy of relationship, closeness of interdependence—existing between the elements composing water is of an extremely intense kind, so much so that the analysis of water constituted an epoch in chemical history. On the other hand, if we take a phenomenon of greater complexity, say water in combination with lime, we find the solidarity diminish as the number of the elements is increased; the water or the lime being much more easily detached from the hydrate of lime than the elements composing the water, or than those composing the lime, are from each other. Nor is this a solitary example : rather it represents a rule holding extensively throughout chemical combination. In inorganic chemistry the salts are in general easily decomposed, while the less

complex elements composing them—the oxides of the
metals and the acids—are mostly of very difficult
analysis. And in organic compounds a similar rule
prevails. So far, therefore, the relation between complexity and solidarity appears to be the reverse of that
for which M. Comte contends. The case just considered illustrates the incidents of complexity within
the range of a single order of relations. How stands
the fact when the orders of relation exemplified in
the phenomena are different? For example, water
possesses—besides chemical—mechanical, optical, electrical, and other physical properties. Is it true that, as
between these several orders of physical phenomena,
the solidarity is, as M. Comte asserts, "little pronounced" — that the chemical, mechanical, optical,
and electrical attributes of water are but slightly interdependent — less interdependent than, for example,
physiological and moral qualities in a human being, or
political and industrial conditions in a body politic?
No one denies that here also there is solidarity; but
the question is, not as to the existence of solidarity, but
as to the degree. What M. Comte had to show was
that the solidarity of co-operating agencies was greater
in the case of the phenomena of society than in that of
the phenomena of the physical world— so much greater
as to necessitate in their case an inversion of the
method of investigation practised in the study of
physical nature; but to establish this he has not
advanced a particle of proof. For my part, I can
imagine no more eminent example of the solidarity
of forces than that presented by the most ordinary
phenomena of the physical world—the ebb and flow of

the tides, the succession of the seasons, the freezing
and thawing of water, a shower of rain, a drop of dew.
Yet this has been no bar in the study of these phenomena to the employment of methods which M. Comte
would nevertheless exclude from the domain of social
science on the ground that its phenomena are *solidaires.*

So much for the grounds of general philosophy on
which M. Comte relies in refusing to recognize Political Economy as a science; and he finds, as he
conceives, corroboration of the soundness of the view
he has taken in the history and actual condition of
economic speculation.   M. Comte opens his criticisms
on the history and existing state of Political Economy
with the remark, that its scientific pretensions could
not well have been otherwise than inane, considering
the sort of persons by whom it has been cultivated.
These have, he tells us, nearly all proceeded "from
the ranks of advocates and *littérateurs:*"*—"Strangers
by their education, even with regard to the least
important phenomena, to every idea of scientific observation, to every notion of natural law, to every sentiment of true demonstration, it was impossible for them,
whatever might have been the intrinsic force of their
intelligence, to apply duly to the complicated problems
of society a method of reasoning the simplest applications of which they were wholly ignorant of,—
destitute, as they were, of any other philosophical
preparation than certain vague and inadequate precepts
of general logic."   From this sweeping characterization
he excepts Adam Smith, and Adam Smith alone,

* " Philosophic Positive," vol. iv. p. 266.

whose judgment is commended in having avoided
the "vain pretension" of founding a special science,
and in confining the aim of his work to the elucidation
of some detached points of social philosophy. But
with the single exception of the "Wealth of Nations,"
the whole dogmatic portion of the pretended science
presents, according to M. Comte, the simple metaphysical character—a phrase which, as M. Comte's readers
are aware, supplies the strongest form of reprobation
known to the Comtian vocabulary. Of the truth of
this conclusion, if further evidence were needed, ample
is found in "the avowal, spontaneous and decisive, of
the respectable Tracy," implied "in the insertion of
his treatise on Political Economy between Logics and
Ethics, as a fourth part of his general treatise on
Ideology."

The impression which these comments will leave on
readers acquainted with the leading economical writers
of France and England, will scarcely, I should think,
be favourable to M. Comte's candour and sagacity.
It is, in fact, quite evident that M. Comte had no
effective knowledge of the branch of science which
he denounced ; and it is scarcely credible that he
could even have remembered, as he wrote the passage
from which I have made the above extracts, who its
cultivators had been ; for the list includes, to mention
no others, the names of Turgot, Hume, Bentham,
Ricardo, and the two Mills. There need be no hesitation in saying—and the remark implies no disrespect
to M. Comte—that any one of these writers had quite
as accurate a conception of what constitutes a law of
nature, and of the sort of proof by which a law of

nature is established, as M. Comte himself. It would
seem, indeed, as if M. Comte's mind lost its proper
balance and edge on coming into contact with Political
Economy. Not only does he forget what is due to the
able thinkers who preceded him, and who—could he
have believed it—were his fellow-labourers in building
up that science of society of which he wished to
constitute himself the sole and exclusive founder, but
his sense of logical cogency seems to fail him : I know
not how else to account for his reference to the collo-
cation of topics adopted by M. Destutt de Tracy in
his treatise on Ideology, as " decisive" evidence of
the unpositive character of Political Economy. What
M. Comte's reasons were for excepting Adam Smith
from the general condemnation passed upon the
cultivators of economic science, it is not easy to
surmise. One is almost tempted to believe that his
acquaintance with the eminent masters in the science
was confined to the author of the "Wealth of Nations."
Had he known, for example, and to mention no other
instances, Turgot's brief but pregnant " Essai sur la
Formation et la Distribution des Richesses"—a work
for which his biographer Condorcet, not unreasonably,
prefers the claim of being " the germ of the ' Wealth
of Nations'"—or Ricardo's " Principles of Political
Economy and Taxation," it is not easy to believe
that he could have committed himself to a distinction not less unjust than invidious. Two works more
thoroughly saturated with the severest spirit of the
Positive Philosophy would not easily be found in the
literature of scientific speculation.

But, passing from the personal question, M. Comte

proposes to try the Positive character of economical speculation by two tests, "continuity" and "fecundity." These qualities, he remarks, are the least equivocal symptoms of really scientific conceptions. "When the work of the present time, instead of presenting itself as the spontaneous sequel and gradual consummation of former work, takes, in the case of each new author, a character essentially personal, and the most fundamental notions are incessantly brought into question; when the dogmatic constitution of a science, far from engendering any sustained progress, results habitually in the sterile reproduction of illusory controversies, ever renewed, never advancing; when these indications are found, there we may be certain we have to do, not with positive science, but with theological or metaphysical dissertation. Now is not this the spectacle which Political Economy has presented for half a century? If our economists are in reality the scientific successors of Adam Smith, let them show us in what particulars they have effectively improved and completed the doctrine of that immortal master, what discoveries really new they have added to his original felicitous *aperçus?*"

The tests proposed are indubitably sound. The challenge is a fair one. If Political Economy cannot make good its pretensions by the criteria of continuity and fecundity, it deserves to be relegated to the limbo to which M. Comte consigns it.

But in proceeding to the ordeal it is necessary to distinguish. There would, it must at once be admitted, be no difficulty in showing that a great deal of writing on economical subjects, now no less than

when M. Comte published his criticisms, is of the
sort which he describes as "metaphysical,"—that is to
say, vague, "personal," full of "sterile and illusory
controversies;" it must further be acknowledged that
this style of writing prevails to a far larger extent in
the discussions of Political Economy than in those of
any physical science. The least reflection, however,
will show, what has often been pointed out, that this
incident of economic speculation is quite inevitable.
It results from two circumstances : first, the intimate
relation in which social questions, economic included,
stand to personal and class concerns, and through
them to general politics, and the keen interest consequently felt in such questions by the general public;
and, secondly, the absence of a technical nomenclature,
and the necessity which hence arises for employing
popular language in the exposition of the doctrines
of social and economic science. The inevitable consequence of this state of things has been to attract to
the discussion of such topics a crowd of unqualified
persons. The incident, however, is not peculiar to
Political Economy; and, if a science is to be made
responsible for all the unscientific and superficial argumentation to which it gives occasion, Sociology would
have quite as much, perhaps rather more, to answer
for than economic science. The question, therefore,
cannot be decided by extracts drawn at random from
the miscellaneous literature of economic discussion :
it is not by extracts from such sources, but by the
doctrines of the science as expounded in the works
of acknowledged masters, that the issue must be
determined. From the writings of M. Comte's *avocats*

and *littérateurs* I must appeal to those of Malthus, of Say, of Ricardo, of Tooke, of Senior, of Mill. These I take to be the veritable scientific successors of Adam Smith—after him and Turgot, the true founders and accredited expositors of economic doctrine. Limiting the controversy to this arena, I venture to assert that a more remarkable example of continuity of doctrine, of development of seminal ideas, of original *aperçus* extended, corrected, occasionally re-cast, of new discoveries supplementing, sometimes modifying, the old—in short, of all the indications of progressive science—will not easily be found even in the history of physical speculation.*

The portion of economic science which Adam Smith carried furthest, and in which he left least for his successors to correct or supplement, is probably the theory of production. With true instinct, he fixed on labour and land as the great original sources of wealth. Of these agencies, that furnished by nature being a constant force, he saw that the progress of wealth must depend on the progressive efficiency of that other which man contributed. The problem of production thus resolved itself into ascertaining the conditions determining the efficiency of human industry. These conditions he grouped under three leading categories—division of labour, machinery, and

---

* " L'économie politique," says M. Courcelle-Seneuil, " bien que jeune encore, présente une suite de travaux dont l'objet, le but et la méthode, sont les mêmes, qui forment un corps, établissent une tradition et des croyances communes, une science enfin dans laquelle les conceptions, même fautives et imparfaites, servent à élever des théories moins fautives et moins imparfaites ; dans laquelle chaque vérité découverte est recueillie et conservée et chaque erreur signalée comme un écueil à éviter."

the accumulation of capital. Such, stated in a few words, is the theory of production propounded in the " Wealth of Nations." It has been submitted by his successors to a searching criticism ; but it has emerged from the ordeal, in the main, unaffected as regards the essence of the doctrines, though more or less modified in detail. Land—though, without doing much violence to language, we may extend the term to cover all that the land contains, all the material objects, therefore, which form the subject-matter of wealth, and even those productive powers resident in the earth—can yet scarcely be understood as comprising the forces in general of physical nature. Adam Smith, at all events, did not so employ the term ; and, accordingly, his generalization of the sources of wealth into land and labour is defective in not paying sufficient regard to the part performed in production by these latter agencies. As he overlooked their co-operation, so he necessarily failed to perceive the conditions on which it was rendered, and the consequences involved in the varying efficacy of those conditions—an omission which has been supplied by his successors, with important consequences in the general theory of economic development. Again, his conception of capital has been carefully sifted by more than one later writer, and has been cleared in the process of discussion of some extraneous elements which obscured the true nature of the functions performed by that agent of production. Division of labour, again, which he regarded mainly in its more obvious applications, has been shown to be a particular case of a larger principle, co-operation, which embraces not merely the class of phenomena adverted to by Adam Smith, but the great transactions of international commerce, and industrial organization in its most extended sense. Subject to modifications of this minor kind, however, the doctrines of Adam Smith, in the theory of production, have been retained, and remain an integral portion of the existing body of economic science.

Passing to another field, and turning to his speculations on the phenomena of exchange value, one may with great truth apply to them what M. Say has said of his entire work : " The more we extend our knowledge of Political Economy, the more highly we shall appreciate both what he has done and what he has left for others to do." There are passages in the " Wealth of Nations " which touch the very core of the true theory of value. When, for example, he says : " The real price of everything, what everything really costs to the man who wants to acquire it, is the toil and trouble of acquiring it. What everything is really worth to the man who has acquired it, and who wants to dispose of it, is the toil and trouble which it can save to himself, and which it can impose upon other people : "—when, again, he says : " Labour was the first price—the original purchase-money that was paid for all things," * he expressed truths which had only need to be firmly grasped to unravel for him the complications of this

* Turgot also saw in industrial production the original act of exchange : " L'homme est encore seul ; la nature seule fournit à ses besoins, et déjà il fait avec elle un premier *commerce* où elle ne fournit rien qu'il ne paie par son travail, par l'emploi de ses facultés et de son temps."— *Valeurs et Monnaies*, quoted by M. Courcelle-Seneuil, vol. i. p. 304, note.

most intricate order of phenomena. But he has hardly laid hold on the clue when he lets it go, and proceeds to exclude from the operation of the principle he had enunciated all stages of social existence except the earliest—that "rude state of society which precedes the accumulation of stock and the appropriation of land." The doctrine of value, as he finally developed it, though vitiated by a defective analysis of the elements of cost, nevertheless had the great merit of connecting the phenomena with cost as its governing principle, and the further still higher merit—in which I think he was entirely original—of bringing into view the conception of "natural," as distinguished from "market" values—that "central price towards which the prices of all commodities are continually gravitating." These were considerable achievements, as those will acknowledge who are acquainted with the failure of even the most able of his predecessors to get beyond superficial generalizations—one might say the commonplaces of the subject—in this fundamental branch of Political Economy,* or who observe the futile efforts to excogi-

---

* Turgot's exposition of the doctrine of value (*Formation et Distribu-tion des Richesses*, §§ 33—35) does not go beyond proximate causes, namely, the reciprocal wants and means of buyers and sellers in a given market ; in modern phrase, demand and supply. But incidentally in another part of his work (§ 61), he falls into a groove of thought which all but leads him up to the principle of "natural price" and "cost of production." "C'est lui" [the capitalist], he writes, "qui attendra que la vente des cuirs lui rende, non seulement toutes ses avances, mais encore un profit suffisant pour le dédommager de ce que lui aurait valu son argent s'il l'avait em-ployé en acquisition de fonds ; et de plus du salaire dû à ses travaux, à ses soins, à ses risques, à son habileté même ; car sans doute, à profit égal, il aurait préféré vivre sans aucune peine d'un revenu d'une terre qu'il aurait pu acquérir avec le même capital." But having thus touched on the true solution, he afterwards (§ 67) recurs to his former position :

tate a theory of the numerous modern writers who rush into economic speculations with no better guidance than the light of nature. In this form the theory was accepted by Say * without substantial change, but in the hands of Ricardo it underwent important modifications, and in effect was recast. Starting from Adam Smith's conception of "natural price," and of cost as the regulator of this, he did much to elucidate the position by simply excluding from his exposition of the subject all that was inconsistent with these primary assumptions. But he did more than this. His clearer view of the nature of exchange value, and the firmer grasp he had attained of the bearing of that " first price," that " original purchase-money," on all the secondary results in the play of industrial exchange flowing from the necessity of its payment, enabled him to show that the same principle which governed exchanges in primitive societies, and which Adam Smith imagined was peculiar to such societies, obtained equally, though masked by the more complicated machinery of advanced civilization, in all stages of industrial development; and finally enabled him to bring within the scope of his general theory a class of phenomena of which the theory, as left by Adam

"Ce sont toujours les besoins et les facultés qui mettent le prix à la vente," &c.

* M. Say's doctrine of value—so far as a distinct doctrine can be elicited from his very contradictory statements—differed in some respects from Adam Smith's ; but Ricardo has shown (Works, p. 172) that where he differed, it was to go wrong. The essentials of Adam Smith's doctrine, that value was governed by cost of production, and that cost of production consisted of wages, profits, and rent, in such sense that a rise or fall of any of these elements necessitated a corresponding rise or fall of value—all this M. Say fully held.

Smith, failed to give any intelligible account—the phenomena of agricultural prices;—a generalization from which he was immediately led to his celebrated doctrine of rent. From the facts of value, as presented within the limits of a single industrial community, Ricardo advanced to the more complicated phenomena presented by international exchange; and here, again, with unfailing instinct, he laid his hand on the salient elements of the problem; though it was reserved for Mr. Mill, by his theory of the "equation of international exchange," first propounded in his "Essays on Unsettled Questions in Political Economy,"* to complete this portion of the docrine. In the more important and fundamental speculation, however, on the governing principle of "natural value" in domestic transactions, Ricardo left little for his successors to supply. Mr. Senior improved the exposition by giving a name—Abstinence—to an element of cost, not unrecognized by Ricardo, and implied in his exposition, but not brought into sufficient prominence by him; and Mr. Mill, in his chapter on the "ultimate elements of cost of production," has effected some modifications in detail, and given greater precision to some of the conceptions involved; but in essentials the doctrine remains as it came from the master's hand.

In the field of foreign trade, Adam Smith achieved important results, though mainly of a negative kind. His onslaught on the mercantile theory of wealth, and his advance from the destruction of that fetish to the

---

* "Un travail," says M. Cherbuliez of Geneva, "le plus important et le plus original dont la science économique se soit enrichie depuis une vingtaine d'années."

establishment of the doctrine of Free Trade, are among his best-known exploits. Yet it is nevertheless true that Adam Smith wholly failed to give a rational account of the principle which occasions and governs the interchange of commodities between nations, and by consequence to explain in what consists, or what measures, the gain of foreign trade. His language on this subject, in not a few passages, exhibits all the vacillation and contradiction of the mercantile school. While alive to the important and fundamental truth that "consumption is the sole end and purpose of production," and drawing the sound inference that "the interests of producers ought to be attended to only so far as they promote the interests of consumers," the main tenor of his exposition of the nature and effects of foreign trade is nevertheless conceived distinctly from the producer's stand-point. Foreign markets are regarded as beneficial, because affording a "vent for surplus productions," and the gain of commerce is supposed to lie mainly in its conducing to maintain a high range of mercantile profit. On the whole, it must be said, in spite of some admirable maxims and pregnant hints which occur throughout the discussion, that the theory of foreign trade, as developed in the "Wealth of Nations," constitutes a mass of confused thought and misapprehended fact. The whole of this portion of the science was still essentially chaotic, and, notwithstanding the partial elucidations effected by M. Say in his exposition of the doctrine that "products are the markets for products," remained in this condition until here again the genius of Ricardo, by a few masterly generalizations, introduced order and light into the jarring elements. One of these, known to economists as the doctrine of "comparative cost," set forth, for the first time, the fundamental conditions which determine the profitableness of international exchange. Adam Smith's negative conclusions were not only corroborated but supplied with a basis in the general theory of the subject, while the small element of truth contained in the doctrine of the Mercantile school was ascertained and discriminated. Phenomena, moreover, which Adam Smith had wholly overlooked, and which his doctrine would have been powerless to explain— for example, the continued importation of a commodity produced under less favourable conditions than those available for its production in the importing country— were brought into view, and shown to be the necessary consequences of the fundamental law which governed this province of exchange. The theory of foreign trade, thus for the first time placed upon a rational foundation, has since been taken up by Mr. Mill, at whose hands it has received important additions and modifications, but additions and modifications, as Mr. Mill himself is careful to point out, which are all in the nature of developments of the original doctrine—all, therefore, of that kind which are the natural incidents and best evidence of progressive science.

Let me briefly trace the history of one important economic doctrine more. The true nature and functions of money, as employed within the limits of a single country, were apprehended with great clearness by Adam Smith. When he distinguished the coin of a country—" the great wheel of circulation "—from the

goods which it circulates ; when he likened the use of
paper money to the substitution for this wheel of
another, less costly and more convenient; and, by a
still more apt image, to a road through the air which
should enable the people of the country to turn to the
purposes of cultivation the space previously occupied
by the ordinary highway; when, following out this
illustration, he showed how the conversion was effected
through the substitution, by means of interchange with
foreign countries, of productive capital for the barren
gold ; when he set the subject of a mixed currency in
this light,—he supplied or suggested principles adequate
to explain the most important phenomena of domestic
circulation.   These principles have all been accepted
by his successors, and are to be found in all good text-
books of Political Economy : some of their consequences, too, have been embodied in legislative
measures.   But the same weakness of his general doctrine on the side of international exchange which
excluded him from clear insight into the movements of
cosmopolitan commerce, disabled him also in his
attempt to deal with the phenomena of international
money.   On the causes regulating the distribution of
gold and silver throughout the world, and the relative
range of prices amongst commercial nations, Adam
Smith has thrown little or no light ; but, as the reader
will anticipate, his shortcomings were here again supplemented by the same able thinker who had solved
the general problem of international trade—a problem
of which the question of international money was but
a part.   In other directions, also, monetary doctrines
have progressed since the time of Adam Smith.   It

would be strange indeed were it otherwise. The disturbance of monetary relations caused by the great wars following on the French Revolution, the suspension of cash payments for twenty years by the Bank of England, the immense development of credit which has signalized the last half-century, have brought to light monetary phenomena of a range and complexity unknown in the earlier period. The investigations of the Bullion Committee of 1810, and the admirable labours of Mr. Tooke, preserved in his "History of Prices," have turned these opportunities to excellent account, and shed new light over the whole of this extended and intricate field ; which has been still further elucidated by the discussion arising out of the controverted question of the policy of the Bank Act of 1844.

Such, then, in four capital departments of Political Economy, has been the course of speculation since the publication of the "Wealth of Nations;"* and there would be no difficulty in extending the illustration to other doctrines of the science. But I think I may stop here, and ask if there is nothing in all this but "the reproduction of sterile controversies, ever renewed, never advancing?" Is this a spectacle of purely theological and metaphysical dissertation? Is it

---

* In the foregoing argument I have drawn my illustrations mainly from the works of English economists ; not that I have any wish to ignore what has been done by other schools, but because the capital discoveries in the science have, so far as I know, been made by Englishmen. This, I observe, is freely admitted by one of the most eminent of recent contributors to economic speculation on the Continent. M. Cherbuliez, of Geneva, writes :—"On peut considérer Adam Smith comme le fondateur d'une école, de cette école Anglaise, à laquelle la science est redevable de presque tous les théorèmes importants dont elle s'est enrichie depuis le commencement de ce siècle."—*Précis de la Science Économique,* vol. i. p. 30.

true that the successors of Adam Smith have nothing
to show of effective contribution to the doctrines of
their master, no really new discoveries to add to his
"felicitous *aperçus*"?   Are we not, on the contrary,
justified in affirming that Political Economy presents,
and that in a very eminent degree, one at least of
those symptoms which M. Comte has declared to be
among the least equivocal evidences of really scientific conceptions—continuity of doctrine?

The other criterion by which M. Comte proposes to
try Political Economy is fecundity, or the test of
fruit.   And here it is probable many people would
meet his challenge by adducing the general results
of modern industrial and commercial legislation—such
results, for example, as the extinction of trade corporations, the abolition of usury laws, the more or less
extensive adoption by the leading nations of Europe
of the principle of free trade, English colonial policy,
English financial, monetary, and poor-law reforms—
achievements which, it will scarcely be denied, may
be fairly credited to Political Economy.   They are
unquestionably in general conformity with its principles; and they were carried into effect by men more
or less under the influence of, some of them deeply
imbued with, the spirit of its teaching.   Nevertheless
I must demur to the test of fecundity as thus understood.   More than one even of the physical sciences
might find themselves in straits if required to make
good their pretensions by a criterion of this sort.
Geology is counted a science, yet amongst practical
miners, whether in Wales and Cornwall or in California
and Australia, empirical experience, coupled with

native sagacity, stands, if I have not been misin-
formed, for much more than the most profound geological knowledge. Zoology, Botany, perhaps also
Biology, if brought to the same test, might find themselves in similar difficulties; and I rather think Professor Max Müller would find it no easy matter to
establish the scientific character of those philological
studies of which he is the learned advocate, by the
criterion of fruit in this sense of the word. Are we
then to say that these several branches of scientific
knowledge have borne no fruit—that they have no
results to show in evidence of their scientific pretensions? Rather, I think, it behoves us to consider
whether such results as those of which examples have
been given above—applications, that is to say, of
scientific principles to the practical arts of life—
constitute the proper fruit of a science. It is in this
sense that M. Comte applies the test to Political
Economy, and even in this sense, as has been seen,
Political Economy emerges triumphant from the
ordeal; but the criterion, as thus understood, is vicious,
and ought not to be accepted. Practical applications
of scientific principles are, I submit, not the proper
fruit, but the accidental consequences of scientific
knowledge; or if fruit, then fruit of the kind typi-
fied by the apple of Atalanta, against the attractions of which Bacon warns the aspirant in the
scientific race as apt to draw him aside from the
nobler pursuit. It is not in such tangible results that
we shall find the genuine fruit of science; these may,
and in the end generally will, come in abundant supply,
but they are not of the essence of the plant; it is not

in these, but in that power which is the end and aim
of scientific knowledge—the power of interpreting
nature, of explaining phenomena. This is a test from
which no true science will shrink, and by the result
the scientific claims of Political Economy, as of all
other subjects of speculation, must stand or fall. Now
the question is, has Political Economy given evidence
of fecundity as thus understood ? Has it increased
our power of interpreting the facts of industrial and
commercial life ? To deny this would, it seems to me,
be as futile as to make a similar denial respecting any
of the physical sciences. M. Comte, indeed, does not
go this length. On the contrary, he admits, if not in
terms, at least by implication, that Political Economy
is equal to the interpretation of economic phenomena.
But his objection is, that it has not succeeded in preventing the injurious consequences which are incident
to some of the laws it expounds. To state, for
example, the effects of the extended use of machinery
in the production and distribution of wealth, if the
exposition be unaccompanied by the suggestion of
practical remedies for the industrial evils incident to
the process, is, according to M. Comte, a proceeding
" vraiment dérisoire," equivalent to proclaiming " the
proper social impotency " of economic science—a
complaint which, it seems to me, is about as philosophical as if we were to condemn the science of
electricity, because, in spite of lightning-conductors,
houses are sometimes struck by lightning, or to re-
proach mechanical science because railway-trains come
into collision, or to denounce astronomy because it is
powerless to prevent eclipses. Political Economy, it

must be owned, has no panacea to offer for the cure
of social evils, but it has that to offer which it is
in the nature of science to furnish—light as to the
causes on which those evils, so far as they proceed
from economic agencies, depend. It reveals the laws
according to which wealth is produced, accumulated,
and distributed ; according to which capital increases,
and profit declines, and rent grows, and wages, prices,
and interest fluctuate ; according to which, in a word,
economic phenomena are governed ; it thus extends
our power of interpreting nature, and, "by obeying,
of conquering her;" and, in doing so, it has given
evidence of fecundity in the only sense in which
fecundity can be properly required of a science.

A great deal has been made by M. Comte of the
divergence of view on fundamental points revealed by
the discussions of economic science. The fact, whether
to be regretted or not, cannot be denied ; but it may
be asked what there is in the controversies of
economists that has not been paralleled again and
again in the history of every physical science?
What, for example, has been the history of chemical
progress but a succession of controversies upon points
of the most fundamental character; controversies
which have not yet been closed? There is, indeed,
no little analogy between the course of Chemistry
in this respect and that of Political Economy. While
Adam Smith and the French Physiocrats were dis
cussing the fundamental problem as to the nature
and ultimate sources of wealth, a parallel controversy
was raging between the followers of Stahl in England,
and those of Lavoisier in France, on the most funda-

mental of chemical problems—the nature of combustion. Both controversies, after periods of about equal duration, were closed by the definitive triumph of English views in Political Economy, of French views in Chemistry; but closed only to be opened again on new,.but still fundamental issues. There are French economists who refuse to accept the doctrines of population and rent propounded by Malthus and Ricardo. And there are chemists, English and French, who, holding by the theory of Lavoisier as to the primary character of chemical combinations, reject the subtle speculations of a more modern school. At the present moment, as I learn from a recent article in the *Revue des deux Mondes,* there are no less than three distinct positions taken by chemists on the question of the molecular constitution of bodies :—

"Can it be said," asks the writer, "that the theory of atomicity reigns now without challenge in chemical science? No, we have not reached that point. There are still amongst *savans* of the highest authority some declared partisans of the theory of Lavoisier. There are chemists who, while abandoning the ancient doctrines, refuse to accept the new, and for the moment acknowledge no general idea of a kind to guide investigators. One may foresee, however, that the principle of atomicity will, at no distant day, rise superior to opposition and doubt." *

With such facts before us it will scarcely be maintained that divergence of view amongst the cultivators of a science on even fundamental points is inconsistent with its positive character; and we can, therefore,

* See an article in the *Revue des deux Mondes,* 15th July, 1869, by M. Edgar Savenez : 'L'Évolution des Doctrines chimiques depuis Lavoisier.'

afford to admit the existence of English and French
schools of Political Economy, without being forced to
take rank as outcasts from the Positive pale, among
metaphysical and theological dissertators. We may
even go further than this, and contemplate the possibility of economic generalizations which shall supersede
some now holding their place in our text-books.
Whatever may ultimately become of our existing
doctrines of value, of rent, of profits, of international
trade, they can scarcely meet a harder fate than befell
the phlogistic theory of combustion, or than seems
likely to befall the binary theory of chemical combination. Those doctrines, as they stand, do in fact explain
a vast number and variety of the phenomena of wealth
presented by modern industrial societies. This alone,
on Positive principles, constitutes a valid title, at all
events, to the claim of provisional acceptance. Subsequent examination will show whether they do not
also satisfy the second condition required for their
definite recognition as natural laws.

The above considerations will probably be deemed
a sufficient answer to M. Comte on the criterion of
fecundity as applied to Political Economy; but in connection with this topic, that philosopher has some
remarks on the subject of scientific prevision as practicable in the social sciences, the bearing of which on
Political Economy it may be well here briefly to
examine.

M. Comte has laid it down as the attribute of a
true social science, that it be able to establish a
" rational filiation in the succession of events, so as to
permit, as for every other order of phenomena, and

within the general limits imposed by a superior complication, a certain systematic prevision of their ulterior
succession." The point to which I wish to call attention is the extent to which Political Economy satisfies
the condition here required of a social science.

That in a certain sense " prevision " is attainable in
the phenomena treated by Political Economy will be
at once seen if we consider that its principles have
been frequently taken as a guide in practical legislation. It is true the rules by which a practical art is
conducted may be empirical ; but this character cannot
be attributed to the conclusions of Political Economy :
the common objections to it lie, indeed, all in the
opposite direction. It cannot be denied, for example,
that the doctrine of Free Trade is a product of
systematic reasoning : true or false, it is at least no
rule of thumb. We had no experience of Free Trade
when Adam Smith and Turgot preached it. The
announcement, then, that free trade would enrich a
country, like the announcement that water would
ascend in the exhausted tube of a pump, formed a
distinct prediction—a prediction that certain effects
would follow from certain causes ; and a prediction
which, wherever the experiment has been tried,* has
been verified by the event. It is clear, therefore, that
to this extent Political Economy lays claim, and not
without valid grounds, to the power of prediction.†

---

* Using the term ' experiment ' in the loose sense in which alone experiments in social science are possible. See Mill's " Logic," ii. p. 456, &c.

† " Elle peut prévoir les conséquences de tel ou tel acte, et c'est dans
cette faculté de prévoir les fruits à venir qu'elle trouve, comme la physique,
la contre-épreuve de la théorie, le signe de leur certitude."— *Traité
d'Économie Politique*, par J. G. Courcelle-Seneuil, vol. i. p. 10.

But the faculty contemplated by M. Comte, in the passage I have quoted, would seem to comprehend something more than this. It was to be a power of foreseeing, not merely a single consequence, however general and wide-reaching, but a train of consequences depending by " rational filiation " on an original cause. Can it be said that Political Economy satisfies this requirement ? Before answering this question, let us observe what the requirement involves.

We have seen that Political Economy has pre-dicted certain results as flowing from the policy of Free Trade; but it is not more certain that freedom of trade favours the best distribution of industrial forces, and thus conduces to the augmentation of wealth, than it is that an accelerated growth of capital promotes an accelerated increase of population ; while it is equally certain that, where other things are equal, density of population is attended with certain economic advantages—advantages which in their turn converge to the same result, intensifying the original impulse towards augmented wealth and population. Further it might be shown, remembering that the material well-being of a people depends in the last resort upon their habits as affecting their disposition and power to keep their numbers within the limits of the means of support ;—remembering again that the habits of a people are liable to be modified by changes in its condition if these be sufficiently long continued ; —I say it might be shown, having regard to these considerations, that a Free-trade policy would have a tendency, not merely to enrich a country and augment the number of its people, but also, through an action upon their habits, to raise permanently the standard of well-being among the population whose numbers it had contributed to increase. This, perhaps, will suffice for the purpose of illustration; but if the reader desires to see examples of this mode of reasoning on social affairs applied to actual questions of momentous interest, he has only to turn to Mr. Mill's celebrated chapters in the second volume of his "Political Economy" on the "Influence of the Progress of Society on Production and Distribution." In such instances, then, we find a "rational filiation" established in the succession of economic influences.

But does it amount to prevision of the actual order of economic events, and would it justify a distinct prediction of a remote economic result? At this point I think the answer must be in the negative; and for this reason : the realization of the results described is contingent in each case on the action of contemporaneous agencies influencing the course of events, but not included in the economic premisses. In short, the economic prevision is a prevision, not of events, but of tendencies—tendencies which would be liable, in a greater or less degree, or even completely, to be counteracted by others of which it takes no account.*

* "It is evident, in the first place, that Sociology, considered as a system of deductions *à priori*, cannot be a science of positive predictions, but only of tendencies. We may be able to conclude, from the laws of human nature applied to the circumstances of a given state of society, that a particular cause will operate in a certain manner unless counteracted ; but we can never be assured to what extent or amount it will so operate, or affirm with certainty that it will not be counteracted, because we can seldom know, even approximatively, all the agencies which may co-exist with it, and still less calculate the collective result of so many combined elements. The remark, however, must here be once more repeated, that

This incapacity, however, of forecasting events, let it be noted, argues no imperfection in economic science ; the imperfection is not here, but in those other cognate sciences to which belongs the determination of the non-economic agencies which are the unknown quantities in the problem. When these cognate social sciences shall have been brought up to the same stage of advancement which has been attained by Political Economy, something approaching to that systematic prevision of events contemplated by M. Comte will be possible. Meanwhile it is no slight gain, in speculating on the future of society, to have it in our power to determine the direction of an order of tendencies exercising so wide, constant, and potent an influence on the course of human development as the conditions of wealth. It is to hold in our hand one, and that not the weakest, of the threads of destiny.

So much for that highest form of scientific fruit— "forecast of the future." The principle, however, of establishing a filiation in events may take the more modest form of explaining the past ; and here, it seems to me, we have a field in which if abundant fruit has not been reaped, it is only because the ground

knowledge insufficient for prediction may be most valuable for guidance. It is not necessary for the wise conduct of the affairs of society, no more than of anyone's private concerns, that we should be able to foresee infallibly the results of what we do. We must seek our objects by means which may perhaps be defeated, and take precautions against dangers which possibly may never be realized. The aim of practical politics is to surround any given society with the greatest possible number of circumstances of which the tendencies are beneficial, and to remove or counteract, as far as practicable, those of which the tendencies are injurious. A knowledge of the tendencies only, though without the power of accurately predicting their conjunct result, gives us to a certain extent this power."—MILL'S *System of Logic*, vol. ii. p. 477. Third edition.

has not been adequately cultivated. That Political
Economy—assuming that it fulfils its limited purpose
of unfolding the natural laws of wealth—is capable
of throwing light on the evolutions of history, will
scarcely be denied, if only it be considered how large
a proportion of all human existence is absorbed in the
mere pursuit of physical well-being, how extensively
the material interests of men prevail in determining
their political opinions and conduct, and in how many
subtle ways worldly considerations gain an entrance
into the heart and conscience, and help to give the cue
to moral and religious ideas. It is scarcely possible, I
say, to reflect on this, and not perceive that to the right
interpretation and correct exposition of the conduct of
men in past times—that conduct which makes history
—a knowledge of the laws of wealth, a knowledge of
the direction in which, in a given epoch, material
interests draw the men who live in it, forms an indispensable qualification. Obvious, however, as this reflection is, the truth (except in a few eminent instances)
has been all but wholly ignored. Speaking generally,
it is not yet supposed—notwithstanding Mr. Buckle's
admirable efforts to raise the standard of requirement
on this point—that a knowledge of Political Economy
is any necessary part of the equipment of an historian.
It is impossible to doubt that the consequences of this
view of things to historic study have been very
serious ; that many precious indications, which to a
student furnished with the economic key would have
opened light through not a few of the dark but important crises of history, have been wholly lost to us—
thrown away upon investigators who, however rich in

erudition, perhaps embarrassed with their riches, were unprovided with this potent instrument. Our historians have but rarely been economists, and I fear it must be acknowledged that our economists have quite as rarely been profound students of history; and it has thus come to pass that this important field of economic research has as yet produced but scanty fruit.

NOTE ON AN ESSAY BY FREDERIC HARRISON, WRITTEN IN REPLY TO THE FOREGOING, WHICH APPEARED IN THE "FORTNIGHTLY REVIEW" FOR JULY 1870.

I quite agree with Mr. Harrison that the comparing of opinions by the disciples of two parallel schools of thought, " where there is mutual respect, no spirit of rivalry, and an active sense of a common purpose," may be as useful in eliciting truth, as controversy, in the theological sense of the term, is generally efficacious in hiding it ; and I trust I shall not be thought oblivious of this, or unappreciative of the gracious and highly flattering terms in which he has recognized my attempts to deal with a difficult problem, if I desire to append some observations in vindication of my own accuracy on some points on which he has impugned it. I am quite content that the arguments I have used in defence of the scientific pretensions of Political Economy against the attacks of Comte should be taken subject to whatever modification of their force or scope Mr. Harrison's strictures may be thought to have shown that they require ; but on one or two points his criticisms amount to a challenge of my accuracy in stating Comte's doctrine. On a question of this kind those only are qualified to judge who are students of Comte's writings, and even they may not find it convenient to verify at once the passages on which the issue turns. I am anxious, therefore, to lay before the readers of Mr. Harrison's Essay and mine the means of judging between us upon this part of the case.

At p. 40 Mr. Harrison corrects me in these terms :—

" Comte *does not* 'contend that the problems presented, on the one hand, by physical nature, and, on the other, by social life, are so radically discordant that the method applicable to the one must be, not only modified, but reversed, in dealing with the other.' He is speaking of the *inorganic*, not of the *physical* world. Comte insists that the organic phenomena of all sorts—zoological, physiological, moral, and social— cannot be pursued by a method which is very useful in the inorganic," &c. (The italics are Mr. Harrison's.)

It seems to me that most readers would by " physical," in the passage quoted from my Essay, understand " inorganic." Those sciences which deal with the physical phenomena of the organic world, as zoology, botany, &c., are, I think, more commonly called " natural sciences ; " the term " physical " being rather reserved for the sciences dealing with inorganic nature, such as astronomy, dynamics, chemistry, &c. But however this may be, it was, I submit, scarcely open to Mr. Harrison to fix upon this passage and proceed to comment upon it in language which implied that I was ignorant of the true character of Comte's distinction, when the page from which he quoted contained the following :—

" As has been said, then, the sciences are arranged in the order indicated by the degree of complexity in their subject-matter. . . . As phenomena become more complex, the method [of disintegration and separate study], he contends, becomes less suitable, less efficacious, till at length a point is reached at which it fails altogether, and it becomes necessary to adopt a contrary mode of procedure, the mode of procedure, namely, which he describes as investigation through the *ensemble*. *This point in the scale of the sciences coincides, he tells us, with that at which the transition is made from inorganic to organic nature.* The method of investigation by disintegration and separate study should thenceforth give way to that which proceeds by treatment in the *ensemble*. Accordingly he holds that the organic sciences generally should be cultivated in conformity with this principle."

Again, at p. 45, Mr. Harrison writes :—

" I turn to the reasoning of Professor Cairnes against what he says is M. Comte's position—' that phenomena, in proportion as they are more complex, are more *solidaires*.' For my own part, I cannot find in Comte any such doctrine, at least so stated."

Now I beg to call Mr. Harrison's attention to the following passage :*—

"Mais on doit, à ce sujet, reconnaître, en principe, que *le consensus devient toujours d'autant plus intime et plus prononcé qu'il s'applique à des phénomènes graduellement plus complexes* et moins généraux ; en sorte que, suivant ma hiérarchie scientifique élémentaire, l'étude des phénomènes chimiques forme, par sa nature, à ce titre, comme à tout autre, une sorte d'intermédiaire fondamental entre la philosophie inorganique et la philosophie organique, ainsi que chacun peut aisément s'en convaincre. D'après ce principe, il reste néanmoins incontestable que, conformément aux habitudes philosophiques prépondérantes, *c'est surtout aux systèmes organiques, en vertu de leur plus grande complication, que conviendra toujours essentiellement la notion scientifique de solidarité et de consensus*, malgré son universalité nécessaire."

If M. Comte does not here state that "phenomena, in proportion as they are more complex, are more *solidaires*," I must confess myself incompetent to interpret him. I may add that the same doctrine is implied (as I read his words) in the whole tenor of his exposition of sociological method.

The passage just quoted supplies an answer to another of Mr. Harrison's criticisms. At p. 41 he writes :—

"'But why,' says Professor Cairnes, 'the method of *ensemble* in studying the organic world?' Why? Because the organic world is an *ensemble*. Every organism is an *ensemble*. Every organic system and order is an *ensemble*. The organic means something which has a complex function over and above that of any of its elements. The study of the organic is simply the study of this complex function (*i.e.* of an *ensemble*)."

Now, whatever be the merit of this answer, what I am concerned here to show is that it is not Comte's : not only is it not Comte's answer, it is inconsistent with Comte's answer. Mr. Harrison says the organic world must be studied in the *ensemble*, "because it is an *ensemble*. Every organism is an *ensemble* ;" but according to M. Comte (as will be seen by reference to the passage just quoted), the reason for this is that the phenomena comprised in the organic world are "more complex," and, "in virtue of their greater complication," more "*solidaires*," than those of the inorganic world— a reason which, a little reflection will show, by no means runs

* " Philosophie Positive," vol. iv. p. 350. Edit. 1839.

on all fours with the former. For example, as M. Comte
states the case, one can see why the study of chemical phenomena should occupy an intermediate position between
organic and inorganic philosophy. It is intermediate, because
—the whole distinction turning on a question of degree—the
phenomena it deals with are more complex than other inorganic phenomena, less complex than organic. But how
does this accord with Mr. Harrison's rendering of the argument? Where is the room for a middle term between
organic and inorganic if the distinction turns upon the consideration of the presence or absence of organic character,
of "complex function"? Are chemical phenomena semi-
organic? Do they exhibit "complex function" in a rudimen-
tary form? If not, how is Mr. Harrison's statement of the
argument consistent with assigning chemical studies an
intermediate place?

Further, if the fact of "organic character," of "complex
function," be the ground of the distinction, the reasons for
the method of the *ensemble* will be strong or weak according
as the phenomena to be dealt with partake of this character,
manifest this "complex function." Now does Mr. Harrison
contend that a society is an organism in a stricter sense than
an individual man; that the adaptation of structure to function is *more* complete in the case of a nation than in that
of a human being? I hardly think he will say so; nay, I am
sure he will admit that the reverse is the fact; but, if so, his
reason for the method of the *ensemble* has less force in relation
to social investigations than in relation to the study of individual life—is less applicable to sociology than to biology—
a conclusion which exactly reverses one of Comte's most
frequently reiterated opinions. Comte held that the reasons
for studying social facts in the *ensemble* are incomparably
stronger than those which apply to biological investigations.
This is entirely in harmony with his doctrine as I have stated
it; social phenomena being "more complex" than biological;
but, as it seems to me, absolutely irreconcilable with Mr.
Harrison's exposition.

IX.

BASTIAT.*

Science belongs to no country; yet the method of
cultivating a science cannot but be affected by the
habits of philosophic thought which prevail among
its cultivators; and this influence will obviously be
stronger in proportion as the subject-matter of science
comes more directly into contact with human intelligence and will. I have lately pointed out in this
Review† that, even in a speculation so eminently
positive as Chemistry, there is room for difference
of opinion on problems of a fundamental kind, and
that in England and France opposing schools have
ranged themselves round conflicting theories from
the infancy of chemical science down to the present
hour. It is not, then, strange that similar phenomena
should manifest themselves in Political Economy, so
much more closely connected than Chemistry with
human conduct and pursuits; and we need not be
surprised if we find in France modes of thinking on
this subject more or less out of relation with those

* *Fortnightly Review*, October 1870.   † *Ante*, p. 301.

which prevail among ourselves. The fact unquestionably is so; but it is important that we should not overrate its extent or significance. Indeed, I think, it must be considered as no slight testimony to the influence of the scientific point of view in keeping speculation straight, that, in spite of the divergent tendencies of national philosophies, the most characteristic doctrines of the English school of Political Economy should have found some of their most powerful champions and most skilful expositors on the other side of the Channel; and that such men as Say, Duchâtel, Garnier, Courcelle-Seneuil, and Cherbuliez, while contributing not a few original and important developments to economic doctrine, should have been the interpreters to their countrymen of Adam Smith and Malthus, Ricardo and Mill. In effect, the main stream of economic thought has in both countries flowed in the same channels; while the idiosyncrasies of the national mind have, on each side, made themselves felt in producing certain eddies of speculation apart from the main current. No one can be at any loss in finding examples of aberrations due to this cause among ourselves. Among French political thinkers one of the most noteworthy is presented by the writings of Bastiat.

The name of Bastiat is, perhaps, the most familiar in this country of all French economists; a result to which several circumstances have contributed besides the merit of his writings. At a critical period of our reforming career he threw himself with extraordinary ardour into our contests, and lent effective assistance to the side that has triumphed. He is known on

more than one occasion to have made himself the
generous defender of English policy and character
against the unreasoning prejudices of his countrymen.
He was, moreover, the friend of Cobden—in itself, in
the judgment of most, a sufficient voucher for economic acquirement; and he has been fortunate enough
to find excellent translators for his principal works.
This last circumstance cannot, indeed, be fairly separated from the merits of the writings themselves; and
it must be owned that these were in some respects of
a high and rare order. As examples of dialectical
skill in reducing an opponent to absurdity, of simple
and felicitous illustration, of delicate and polished
raillery, attaining occasionally the pitch of a refined
irony, the "Sophismes Economiques" might almost
claim a place beside the "Provincial Letters." The
petition of the candle-makers and other manufac-
turers of light to the Legislative Body, praying the
exclusion by legislative enactment of the light of the
sun, is alone almost enough to make a reputation in
this line; and Swift himself has hardly shown greater
art in the logical conduct of an absurd proposition
than that with which the reader, in this modest proposal, is led, step by step, from the avowed
premisses of Protection, through a series of the most
natural and irrefragable deductions, straight to the
preposterous conclusion advocated by the petitioners.

"What we pray for is, that it may please you to pass a law
ordering the shutting up of all windows, skylights, dormer-
windows, outside and inside shutters, curtains, blinds, bull's-
eyes—in a word, of all openings, holes, chinks, clefts, and
fissures, by or through which the light of the sun has been

allowed to enter houses, to the prejudice of the meritorious manufactures with which we flatter ourselves we have accommodated our country—a country which, in gratitude, ought not to abandon us now to a strife so unequal. . . . . .

" And, first, if you shut up as much as possible all access to natural light, and create a demand for artificial light, which of our French manufactures will not be encouraged by it ?

" If more tallow is consumed, then there must be more oxen and sheep ; and, consequently, we shall behold the increase of artificial meadows, meat, wool, hides, and, above all, manure, which is the basis and foundation of all agricultural wealth.

"If more oil is consumed, then we shall have an extended cultivation of the poppy, of the olive, and of colewort. These rich and exhausting plants will come at the right time to enable us to avail ourselves of the increased fertility which the rearing of additional cattle will impart to our lands.

"Our heaths will be covered with resinous trees. Numerous swarms of bees will, on the mountains, gather perfumed treasures, now wasting their fragrance on the desert air, like the flowers from which they are derived. No branch of agriculture but will then exhibit a cheering development. . . . . .

" If you urge that the light of the sun is a gratuitous gift of nature, and that to reject such gifts is to reject wealth itself under pretence of encouraging the means of acquiring it, we would caution you against giving a death-blow to your own policy. Remember that hitherto you have always repelled foreign products, *because* they approximate more nearly than home products to the character of gratuitous gifts. To comply with the exactions of other monopolists, you have only *half a motive ;* and to repulse us simply because we stand on a stronger vantage-ground than others, would be to adopt the equation $+ \times + = -$; in other words, it would be to heap *absurdity* upon *absurdity.* . . . . .

  *   *   *   *   *   *

. . . . ." Make your choice, but be logical ; for as long as you exclude, as you do, coal, iron, corn, foreign fabrics, *in proportion* as their price approximates to *zero,* what inconsistency would it be to admit the light of the sun, the price of which is already at *zero* during the entire day !"

But it was not on the "Sophismes Économiques" that Bastiat would have been content to take the verdict of posterity as to his pretensions as an economist. Indeed, whatever might be the controversial and literary merits of these admirable tracts, they added nothing to already familiar economic truths. The theory of Free Trade had been fully thought out by a succession of able writers before Bastiat took it in hand, and all that he here could do was what, in fact, he did—furnish new and apt illustrations of a familiar doctrine, or, by well-selected instances, reduce opponents to glaring absurdity. But in 1848 the advent of the democratic republic brought other questions to the front, and stirred controversies more fitted to try the metal of a philosophic thinker. Socialism had raised its grim visage, and was propounding those solutions of the social problem, the mere recollection of which has since so often sufficed to frighten France from her propriety. Louis Blanc, Considérant, Leroux, Proudhon, were thundering against the existing industrial order ; and for those who cared to maintain that order the need of the hour was a philosophy adapted to the popular apprehension, which should be capable of furnishing a plausible reply to their attacks. At this time Bastiat was at the height of his reputation in Paris. He had frankly and sincerely accepted the Revolution, though sensible of the unpreparedness of the country for the new *régime*, and alive to the inevitable dangers incident to this state of things. His views, however, did not extend beyond

political changes, and while recognizing the generous
aims of the Socialists, he shrank with horror from their
subversive proposals. He accordingly came forward
eagerly to defend the menaced social structure. In a
series of clever brochures—" Propriété et la Loi,"
" Propriété et Spoliation," " Justice et Fraternité,"
"Capital et Rente," " Maudit Argent,"—he propounded
his reply to the "despotic organizers"—"ces pétrisseurs
de l'argile humaine." As he wrote, his ideas took
firmer hold of his mind, and gradually shaped themselves into a system. The needed philosophy was, he
thought, to be found in a recast of Political Economy,
and the " new exposition" he undertook to furnish in
his " Harmonies Économiques." Unfortunately, Bastiat
did not live to complete this work ; but enough was
accomplished to render perfectly clear the essential
character of the conception and the general scope of
his design. The English reader has now an opportunity of studying it in Mr. Stirling's excellent
Translation.

Political Economy, as treated by the predecessors
of Bastiat—by Adam Smith and his successors in this
country, by Say and his successors in France—aimed at
unfolding the natural principles—natural in the sense
of having their foundation in the nature of man and
of his environments—which govern the facts of material
well-being. Those economists did not, indeed, hold
themselves precluded from pointing out, when occasion
offered, the moral and social bearing of their doctrines ;
but, in general, they recognized the distinction between
such practical lessons as they believed deducible from
their expositions and the doctrines of the science

which they taught. In effect, Political Economy, in their hands, was a positive science, in the modern sense of that expression; its methods were combined induction and deduction; its conclusions embodied hypothetical truths of precisely the same character as those of any of the deductive physical sciences; and its purpose was to explain phenomena. As thus constituted, however, Political Economy did not meet the need which it was the object of Bastiat to satisfy. What he aimed at supplying was, not a positive science, not a body of doctrines which should simply *explain* the facts of wealth, but one which, while explaining, should also *justify* those facts,—should justify them, that is to say, as manifested in the results of those fundamental institutions of modern society, private property, freedom of industry, of contract, and of exchange. As his biographer, M. de Fontenay, puts it, his aim was—

"To combine together and fuse into one the two distinct aspects of Fact and of Right; to recur to the formula of the Physiocrats—'La science des faits au point de vue du droit naturel;' to prove that *that which is*, in its actual *ensemble*, and still more in its progressive tendency, is conformable to *that which ought to be*, according to the aspirations of the universal conscience."

In Bastiat's own words, he sought—

"To demonstrate the Harmony of those laws of Providence which govern human society," by showing "that all principles, all motives, all springs of action, all interests, co-operate towards a grand final result, ... the indefinite approximation of all classes towards a level which is always rising; in other words, the *equalization* of individuals in the general

amelioration." * "* The conclusion of the Economists," he says
in another place, "is for liberty. But, in order that this conclusion should take hold of men's minds and hearts, it must
be solidly based on this fundamental principle :—Interests,
left to themselves, tend to harmonious combinations, and to
the progressive preponderance of the general good."†

Such was the scheme of renovated economic
science propounded by Bastiat; and the question
which I desire here to consider is, how far this conception of the inquiry represents a legitimate philosophical speculation, and, more particularly, how far
the actual treatment of economic questions from this
point of view by Bastiat has resulted in what all will
allow to be among the primary and main ends of
economical investigation—the elucidation of the facts
of wealth.

And here the first remark that occurs is, that, as set
forth in the above extracts, the problem of Political
Economy is not properly the problem of a science at
all. Not only is it not *the* problem of a science, it is
not even a scientific problem ; for I apprehend it is of
the essence of all scientific investigation that the
conclusion be left free to shape itself according to
the results of the inquiry. Science has no foregone
conclusions ; but to prove a foregone conclusion is
the problem of Political Economy, as propounded by
Bastiat. What Bastiat proposes to do is, not to
ascertain what the consequences of a given set of
social arrangements are—that would have been a
scientific investigation—but *to prove that they are of a
certain kind;* to prove that "left to themselves, human

* Stirling's "Translation," p. 105.   † Ibid. p. 7.

interests are harmonious." By the very form in which he states his case, he constitutes himself the advocate of a system, instead of the expositor of a science.

But his conception of the problem involves a still graver error : as we have seen, it was of the essence of his scheme to "fuse together the two distinct aspects of Fact and Right." The "harmony" of human interests which he undertook to establish was not a mere coincidence of certain manifestations of material well-being with certain others, but extended to the moral consequences involved—an extension of view which, according to his biographer, constituted the great merit of his speculation. In effect, Bastiat, however widely separated from his opponents on the question of practical policy, was thoroughly at one with them on the most fundamental article of his philosophic creed : he and they alike accepted the doctrine of "natural rights." They differed, indeed, in their interpretation of the code of nature, but they were quite agreed as to its existence, and as to the obligation of bringing their doctrines to the test of its maxims. A new order of ideas thus found entrance among the premisses of economic science ; and the appeal, which had formerly been to facts,—to facts exclusively, mental or physical,—as the ground and evidence of doctrine, was henceforth extended to " rights," *" les plus simples éléments de la justice,"* *" bonne équité,"* and phrases of similar import.* It was

---

* His Essay on Free Trade opens with this announcement :—" Exchange is a natural right, like Property. Every citizen who has created or acquired a product, *ought* to have the option either of applying it immediately to his own use, or of ceding it to whosoever, on the surface of the globe, consents to give him in exchange the object of his desires.

thus that Fact and Right were fused. The principle
of value, as understood by Bastiat, was not simply
the law to which the facts of value conform, but such
a presentation of that law as should reconcile the
facts with what the expositor held to be the dictates
of natural justice. The problem involved in the
payment of interest on capital was not simply the
determination of the physical and mental conditions
which render possible the permanent payment of
interest, and which govern its amount and fluctuations,
but such a mode of presenting the practice as should
amount to its moral vindication,—to show that it is
"natural, just, legitimate, as useful to him who pays
as to him who receives it."* And so of the other
problems of the science. Political Economy, in short,
became in Bastiat's hands one more example of that
style of reasoning on political and social affairs which
flourished so luxuriantly in France during the latter
half of the last century, and is not yet quite extinct,
of which the "Social Contract" may be taken as the
type, and the "Declaration of the Rights of Man" as
the best known practical outcome—a species of hybrid
philosophy, consisting, to borrow the language of Mr.
Mill, "of attempts to treat an art like a science, and
to have a deductive art." "I speak," says Mr. Mill,
"of those who deduce political conclusions, not from
laws of nature, not from sequences of phenomena,
real or imaginary, but from unbending practical maxims.

To deprive him of this faculty, while he makes no use of it contrary to
public order or good morals, and solely to satisfy the convenience of
another citizen, is to legalize spoliation, is to do violence to the law of
justice."

* "Œuvres Complètes," vol. v. p. 26.

Such are all who found their theory of politics on what is called abstract right."*

Now is such a mode of speculation philosophically legitimate? It seems to me not, and for this reason —that, from the very form in which the problem is stated, the argument is involved from its outset in a *petitio principii.* The question, What is? and the question, What ought to be? are distinct questions. It may be that the answers to them coincide; that *that which is,* is also *that which ought to be;* but, then, this is a thing to be proved, not to be taken for granted; and it can only be proved by working out each problem independently of the other. Instead of this, Bastiat formally identifies them—"fuses" them into one. But fusion of the questions implies fusion of the answers;—that is to say, it is assumed that the same form of words which tells us what is, will tell us also what ought to be. Such a scheme of speculation, it is obvious, could only be worked out in one way—namely, through the instrumentality of terms capable of lending themselves at need to either point of view—capable either of simply expressing a matter of fact, or of connoting with the fact expressed a moral judgment. And such, in truth, is Bastiat's method of proceeding. Availing himself of the double meaning of such "passionate" terms as "principle," "value," "worth," "service," and the like, he has produced a theory which affects to cover both solutions—at once to explain and to justify the facts to which it applies. The economic vocabulary unfortunately lends itself only too readily to this sort of theorizing, and few

* " System of Logic," vol. ii. p. 466. Third ed.

writers have entirely escaped illusion from this cause. Bastiat's distinction is that he has contrived so to propound the problem of Political Economy that it can only be answered by an *équivoque.*

It may be added, that even though the questions of Fact and Right, of Science and Morality, were conceived and argued as distinct, there would still be strong, and, I venture to think, decisive reasons against combining them in the same scheme of speculation. To mention one reason only : such a mode of investigation would present the constant temptation to sacrifice one solution to the other, the scientific to the moral, or the moral to the scientific. The student would be constantly solicited to overlook or ignore, or, on the other hand, to strain or overrate, data, according asthey might seem to involve conclusions in one branch of the speculation in conflict with, or corroborative of, conclusions deemed to be of more importance in the other. Investigation, thus pursued, would no longer be disinterested ; science would lose its singleness of purpose. This objection would lie against the combined treatment of the two problems even if they were conceived and discussed as distinct. But the objection to Bastiat's method goes far deeper than this : that method not merely combines science and morality, it confounds them.

Passing from the question of the logical legitimacy of Bastiat's conception of Economic Science, let us consider now the results which have accrued from this mode of conceiving and dealing with the problems of wealth. What, in a word, have been the scientific fruits of Bastiat's method ? What new light have his speculations shed on the facts which form the subject-matter of his inquiry?

The doctrine on which Bastiat founded his pretensions as an original thinker in Political Economy was his Theory of Value. According to him this theory comprised potentially the whole of Economic Science; and, in point of fact, all that is peculiar to his views flows directly from this source: his conception of value is the *idée mère* of his entire scheme. It is, then, in this doctrine that we shall find the fairest evidence of his work as an economist, and I shall make no apology for examining it at some length.

The following passages from Mr. Stirling's Translation of the "Harmonies" set forth with sufficient fulness the salient features of the doctrine.

" Let us analyse the co-operation of nature of which I have spoken. Nature places two things at our disposal—*materials* and *forces*.

" Most of the material objects which contribute to the satisfaction of our wants and desires, are brought into the state of *utility* which renders them fit for our use only by the intervention of labour, by the application of the human faculties. But the elements, the atoms, if you will, of which these objects are composed, are the gifts—I will add, the *gratuitous* gifts—of nature. This observation is of the very highest importance, and will, I believe, throw a new light upon the theory of wealth.

    *   *   *   *   *   *

" It is very evident, that, if man in an isolated state must, so to speak, *purchase* the greater part of his satisfactions by an exertion, by an effort, it is rigorously exact to say that, prior to the intervention of any such exertion, any such effort, the materials which he finds at his disposal are the *gratuitous* gifts of nature. After the first effort on his part, however slight it may be, they cease to be *gratuitous;* and if the language of Political Economy had been always exact, it would have been

to material objects in this state, and before human labour had
been bestowed upon them, that the term *raw materials*
(*matières premières*) would have been exclusively applied.

" I repeat that this *gratuitous* quality of the gifts of nature,
anterior to the intervention of labour, is of the very highest
importance.   I said in my second chapter that Political
Economy was the *theory of value ;* I add now, and by anticipation, that things begin to possess *value* only when it is given
to them by labour.   I intend to demonstrate afterwards that
everything which is *gratuitous* for man in an isolated state is
gratuitous for man in his social condition, and that the gratuitous
gifts of nature, *whatever be their* UTILITY, have no value.   I say
that a man who receives a benefit from nature, directly and
without any effort on his part, cannot be considered as rendering himself an *onerous service*, and, consequently, that he
cannot render to another any service with reference to things
which are common to all.   Now, where there are no services
rendered and received, there is no *value*.

" All that I have said of *materials* is equally applicable to
the *forces* which Nature places at our disposal.   Gravitation,
the elasticity of the air, the power of the winds, the laws of
equilibrium, vegetable life, animal life, are so many forces
which we learn to turn to account.   The pains and intelligence
which we bestow in this way always admit of remuneration,
for we are not bound to devote our efforts to the advantage of
others gratuitously.   But these natural forces, in themselves,
and apart from all intellectual or bodily exertion, are *gratuitous*
gifts of Providence, and in this respect they remain destitute
of *value* through all the complications of human transactions.
This is the leading idea of the present work.

" This observation would be of little importance, I allow,
if the co-operation of Nature were constantly uniform ; if
each man, at all times, in all places, in all circumstances,
received from Nature equal and invariable assistance.   In
that case, science would be justified in not taking into account
an element which, remaining always and everywhere the
same, would affect the services exchanged in equal proportions on both sides.   As in geometry we eliminate portions of
lines common to two figures which we compare with each

other, we might neglect a co-operation which is invariably present, and content ourselves with saying, as we have done hitherto, ' There is such a thing as natural wealth ; Political Economy acknowledges it, and has no more concern with it.'

" But this is not the true state of the matter. The irresistible tendency of the human mind, stimulated by self-interest, and assisted by a series of discoveries, is to substitute natural and gratuitous co-operation for human and onerous concurrence ; so that a given utility, although remaining the same as far as the result and the satisfactions which it procures us are concerned, represents a smaller and smaller amount of labour. In fact, it is impossible not to perceive the immense influence of this marvellous phenomenon on our notion of value. For what is the result of it ? This, that in every product the *gratuitous* element tends to take the place of the *onerous ;* that *utility*, being the result of two *collaborations*, of which one is remunerated and the other is not, value, which has relation only to the first of these united forces, is diminished, and makes room for a *utility* which is identically the same, and this in proportion as we succeed in constraining nature to a more efficacious co-operation. So that we may say that mankind have as many more *satisfactions*, as much more *wealth*, as they have less *value*. Now the majority of authors having employed these three terms, *utility, wealth, value*, as synonyms, the result has been a theory which is not only not true, but the reverse of true. I believe sincerely that a more exact description of this combination of natural forces and human forces in the business of production—in other words, a juster definition of value—would put an end to inextricable theoretical confusion, and would reconcile schools which are now divergent."

      *   *   *   *   *   *

" Thus, the definition of the word value, in order to be exact, must have reference not only to human efforts, but likewise to those efforts which are exchanged or exchangeable. Exchange does more than exhibit and measure values—it gives them existence. I do not mean to say that it gives existence to the acts and the things which are exchanged, but it imparts to their existence the notion of *value*.

" Now, when two men transfer to each other their present efforts, or make over mutually the results of their anterior efforts, they *serve* each other ; they render each other reciprocal *service*.

" I say, then, VALUE IS THE RELATION OF TWO SERVICES EXCHANGED." * [The italics and capitals are the author's.]

To appreciate this, Bastiat's principal contribution to economic science, we must endeavour to separate in the above exposition the doctrines which he held in common with the most eminent economists who preceded him from the element or elements which he has himself added to the theory. It may be at once stated that in the main positions taken by Bastiat there is nothing at issue between him and the leading economists of England and France. He appears, indeed, not to have been of this opinion himself, and to have thought that, in asserting the "gratuitousness of the gifts of nature," he was announcing a truth which had hitherto escaped universal observation ; and, strange to say, this claim seems to be admitted by some who have commented on his works in this country. But it is certain that on this point he deceived himself. Adam Smith has indeed expressed himself in some passages as if it were in agriculture only that nature gave anything to man except on the terms of what Bastiat would call " onerous services"— an error which Smith shared with the Physiocrats ; but Ricardo has called particular attention to this erroneous limitation of an important principle, and

* Stirling's " Translation," pp. 61-63.

has shown that, so far from this being true, it is, on the contrary, in agriculture only, or at all events mainly, that nature in her co-operation with man has set any limit to her munificence.

"Does nature," Ricardo asks, "nothing for man in manufacture? Are the powers of wind and water, which move our machinery, and assist navigation, nothing? The pressure of the atmosphere and the elasticity of steam, which enable us to work the most stupendous engines—are they not the gifts of nature? To say nothing of the matter of heat in softening and melting metals, of the decomposition of the atmosphere in the process of dyeing and fermentation, there is not a manufacture which can be mentioned, in which nature does not give her assistance to man, *and give it, too, generously and gratuitously.*" *

Say, again, though differing from Ricardo in many points, is at one with him here. In language quite as emphatic as any that Bastiat has used, he insists on the point :—

"It is thus that nature is almost always in partnership of labour with man and his instruments; and in this partnership, we gain so much the more in proportion as we succeed in saving our labour and that of our capital, which is necessarily costly, and get performed, *through the gratuitous services of nature,* a larger portion of what is to be done." And again he observes, "Of those wants, some are satisfied by the use which we make of certain things with which *nature has furnished us gratuitously,* such as the air, water, the light of the sun. We may name these things *natural wealth,* since nature alone is at the cost of them. So far as she gives them indifferently to all, no one is obliged to obtain them at the cost of any sacrifice whatever. They have, therefore, no exchangeable value."†

---

* Works. p. 40, *note.*   † Traité d'Économie Politique, vol. i. p. 36.

It would be idle to multiply quotations from later writers, who have, so far as I know without an exception, followed on this point the teaching of Ricardo and Say. Nor can it be alleged that, while recognizing the fact, there was any failure to appreciate its due significance. So far from this, it has been taken as the basis of no less fundamental a doctrine than that of cost of production—a doctrine which merely asserts in other words that exchange-value in commodities, susceptible of indefinite production at a uniform cost, finds its determining principle in the efforts of man; the utility derived from nature going for nothing in the result.

It is not, therefore, in the recognition of the gratuitous character of nature's services in her co-operation with the industry of man, that what is peculiar to Bastiat's views on value is to be found. It is not in this, but in an assumption with which he accompanies his recognition of this circumstance. Ricardo, Say, and the great majority of succeeding economists have held that, however gratuitous may be the gifts of nature, such gifts are not necessarily on that account incapable of acquiring value. In order to this, they must be not only gratuitous, but also in such abundance, and so accessible to all, that none who desire them need be without them. Water, they would say, when not produced by artificial process, is a gratuitous gift of nature; but water—spring water for example—may or may not have value according to circumstances. If in sufficient abundance for the wants of a neighbourhood, and also accessible to all who live there, it can have no value—none at least beyond what would represent the labour employed in drawing it from the spring; but water in insufficient supply, though a gift of nature, may have value, and this value will have no necessary relation to the human exertion employed in obtaining it. And what is true of water is true, they would say, of all natural objects : in particular it is true of the natural productive forces residing in the materials of the earth. These, though to the persons who are at liberty to take advantage of them "gratuitous gifts of nature," yet not being bestowed on man in unlimited quantity, not being after the appropriation of the soil of a country accessible to all, may and do acquire value, and enter as elements into the causes which give value to land. Now it is this position which Bastiat denies ; and of which his denial, together with the consequences which he draws from it, forms the ground of his claim to having reconstituted economic science. According to him, a gift once obtained gratuitously from nature—a spring of water, a field of natural fertility, a pearl picked up on the sea-shore— can never afterwards acquire value except in virtue of human effort bestowed upon it. " The materials and forces given by God to man gratuitously at the beginning have continued gratuitous, and are and must continue to be so through all our transactions ; for* in the estimates and appreciations to which exchange gives rise, the *equivalents* are *human services*, and not the *gifts of God*." † This was the capital assumption of Bastiat's economic philosophy, that alone in which his theory of value differed from that generally

* The reader will note the begging of the question in this "for," &c.
† Stirling's " Translation," p. 221.

accepted. On it all that is peculiar to his scheme of speculation rests; and, this failing, the entire fabric inevitably collapses.*

Perhaps the most singular circumstance about the speculation is that Bastiat should have thought the principle just stated self-evident. He was wholly unable to conceive that a gift of nature should be at once "gratuitous" and not "common to all." A gratuitous gift limited in supply, and capable of acquiring value, was for him an impossible thought. Again and again throughout his writings he rings the changes on the grotesqueness of such a supposition. " Who," he asks, "can have the audacity to exact payment for this portion of *superhuman* value ? " " The purchaser of corn must pay for it, though it has cost nothing to anybody, not even labour ! Who then dares to come forward to demand this pretended *value?* " Accordingly, in speaking of gratuitous gifts of nature, Bastiat always assumes that such gifts are " common to all."

" It is that portion only of utility," he says, " which is due to human labour that becomes the object of exchange, and, by consequence, of remuneration. This latter varies doubtless much in proportion to the intensity of the labour, of its skill, promptitude, and suitability to the circumstances of the case (*son à-propos*), of the need which is felt for it, of the momentary absence of competition, &c. But it is not the less true that the concurrence of natural laws, *belonging to all*, enters for nothing into the price of the product." †

Where natural laws, or forces, or objects " belong to all," the conclusion is irrefragable. No one will pay

---

* It should be stated that Bastiat's originality in this, the capital element of his theory, has been challenged by Mr. Carey in his work on Social Philosophy—it seems to me on good grounds.

† " Œuvres Complètes." vol. iv. p. 41. The italics are mine.

for what he can get from nature without payment; but
the question is, do natural laws, forces, and objects *in
all cases* "belong to all"? Those natural laws and
forces of the soil in particular, which constitute its
fertility, are they incapable of appropriation by some
to the exclusion of others? Are they incapable, in
virtue of such appropriation, of acquiring value in
exchange? This is the gist of the whole argument;
and it is, I repeat, in assuming this point in the sense
I have described, that Bastiat's special contribution to
the economic theory of value consists.

Bastiat's doctrine, then—keeping in view the facts
which it expressed, the form apart—resolved itself
into the statement that exchange-value under all circumstances is due to human effort as its sole and
exclusive cause—to human effort as distinguished from
natural gift and endowment, material or mental. What
was given to man by nature was not only, he conceived, gratuitous in its origin, but must, in all cases,
and (so long as exchange is free) under all circumstances, be incapable of acquiring value. Stated thus
nakedly, however, the doctrine is not easily reconcilable with some very obvious facts. For example,
the value of a pearl picked up accidentally on the
sea-shore; the high remuneration obtained by persons
endowed with natural gifts of an exceptional kind—
painters, singers, and *artistes* generally; above all,
the value of land possessing natural fertility or
peculiar advantages of situation;—value in these and
other similar instances does not seem to lend itself
very easily to the doctrine that all value consists in
and represents human effort. To give the theory

plausibility, it needed to be clothed in other words.
A term, in short, was wanting, which, while designa-
ting "effort," should be capable also of suggesting
other considerations fitted to meet cases of the above
kind. More than this, it was necessary (bearing in
mind the moral side of the problem as conceived by
Bastiat) that the term, while satisfying the conditions
indicated, should also be capable of conveying a moral
judgment on the facts to which it was applicable.
Such a term Bastiat found in the word "service;" and
it is in the uses to which he turns this word—as at
once universal solvent of economic difficulties, and
what Bentham would call a "sacramental" term in the
warfare with Socialism—that the peculiar character of
his speculation reveals itself.

In propriety of speech the term "service" should,
I apprehend, be limited to personal exertions made in
another's behalf. It is in this sense that it is commonly
used in economic writings, and, so understood, it is
a convenient economic term. But it is obviously possible, without doing any great violence to language,
to give it a wider signification. Thus, for example, if
a friend were to warn me that I was about to drink
poison, he might be said to render me a service,
though the effort involved in the announcement would
be quite inappreciable. Similarly, a musician might
be said to render a service to an audience whom he
gratified by the performance of a piece of music,
however slight the effort incident to the performance
might happen to be. And so, again, might the owner
of an island just risen from the sea, on which no
human being had ever set foot, be said to render a

" service " to the person to whom he should consent to transfer his property so circumstanced. Service, in short, may be understood to mean, not exclusively personal effort in another's behalf, but any act whereby another is served, *i.e.* benefited, wholly irrespective of whether the act consist in onerous exertion, in the passive surrender of property to another's use, or in a mere utterance of words from which some useful or pleasant consequence may flow. "Service" thus fulfilled the first of the conditions required ; and it is accordingly substituted by Bastiat for " human effort " in the exposition of his theory. " Value " is said to depend upon " service," and to vary with the magnitude of the "service ; " and all exchange is described as an "exchange of services." In a word, what Bastiat did was this : having been at infinite pains to exclude gratuitous gifts of nature from the possible elements of value, and pointedly identified the phenomenon with " human effort " as its exclusive source, he designates human effort by the term " service," and then employs this term to admit as sources of value those very gratuitous natural gifts the exclusion of which in this capacity constituted the essence of his doctrine. I acknowledge it seems scarcely credible that a writer of Bastiat's distinguished reputation should put forward an elaborate speculation, purporting to be "a new exposition of economic science," in which principles established or accepted by a succession of eminent predecessors are challenged, and which should after all resolve itself into so gross a fallacy as this; but a few quotations will show whether I have overstated the case.

" To make an effort in order to satisfy another's want is to render him a service. If a service is stipulated in return, there is an exchange of services . . . . If the exchange is free, the two services exchanged are worth each other . . . . Less effort implies less service, and less service implies less value." *

So far he is propounding (doubtless in vague and somewhat equivocal terms, and without the due limitations) the doctrine of cost of production, and to this he for some time adheres; but, further on, we find this passage :—

" I take a walk along the sea-beach, and I find by chance a magnificent diamond. I am thus put in possession of a great value. Why? Am I about to confer a great benefit on the human race? Have I devoted myself to a long and laborious work? Neither the one nor the other. Why then does this diamond possess so much value? Undoubtedly because the person to whom I transfer it considers that I have rendered him a great *service*—all the greater that many rich people desire it, and that I alone can render it."

Here, it will be observed, he wholly abandons the idea of "effort" as the fundamental consideration. It is no longer "effort in satisfying another's want" that creates and measures the "service," but the capacity of the *natural object* in this respect in connection with the limitation set by *nature* to objects possessing this capacity. Further on, having to deal with the case of the high remuneration obtained by eminent *artistes*, he has these remarks :—

" Among the amusements which the people of Paris relish most is the pleasure of hearing the music of Rossini sung by Malibran or the admirable poetry of Racine interpreted by Rachel. There are in the world only two women who can

* Stirling's " Translation," pp. 44, 45.

furnish these noble and delicate kinds of entertainments, and unless we subject them to the torture, which would probably not succeed, we have no other way of procuring their services but by addressing ourselves to their good-will. Thus the services which we expect from Malibran and Rachel are possessed of great value." *

The reason assigned, it will be observed, being the same as in the case of the diamond—the power of satisfying a widely felt desire, coupled with the limitation of the number of persons possessing the natural endowments which give the power.

These, however, are rather " fancy" cases : the real hitch lies in the application of the theory to value in the case of land. I beg the reader's attention to Bastiat's mode of dealing with this point :—

" Land," he says, " has value, because it can no longer be acquired without giving in exchange the equivalent of this labour [the labour expended upon it]. But what I contend for is that this land, on which its natural productive powers had not originally conferred any value, has still no value in this respect. This natural power which was gratuitous then is gratuitous now, and will be always gratuitous. We may say that the land has *value,* but when we go to the root of the matter we find that what possesses value is the human labour which has improved the land, and the capital which has been expended on it." †

But then comes the question, which he puts into the mouth of an objector, how is this doctrine reconcilable with the fact of the value attaching to natural fertility?

" Everyone," says the objector, " who purchases a land estate examines its quality, and pays for it accordingly. If of two properties which lie alongside each other, the one consists

---

* Stirling's " Translation," p. 121. † Pp. 249, 250.

of rich alluvium, and the other of barren sand, the first is surely of more value than the second, although both may have absorbed the same capital, and, to say truth, the purchaser gives himself no trouble on that score." *

The objection is fairly stated ; and now mark the answer :—

"The answer to the objection now under consideration is to be found in the theory of value explained in the fifth chapter of this work. I there said that value does not essentially imply labour ; still less is it necessarily proportionate to labour. I have shown that the foundation of value is not so much the *pains taken* by the person who transfers it as the *pains saved* to the person who receives it ; and it is for that reason that I have made it to reside in something which embraces these two elements—in *service*. I have said that a person may render a great service with very little effort, or that with a great effort one may render a very trifling service. The sole result is that labour does not obtain necessarily a remuneration which is in proportion to its intensity, in the case either of man in an isolated condition, or of man in the social state."†

In other words, the difficulty is surmounted through the equivocal meaning of "service," which, with curious *naïveté*, we are informed in this passage was selected by the philosopher expressly because its meaning was equivocal.

Now what is the significance and what the worth of a theory, of which the efficacy, as a means of elucidating phenomena, lies entirely in the shifting uses of an ambiguous term? After the concessions made in these passages, it is evident that there is no longer any question of fact between Bastiat and the

* Stirling's "Translation," p. 255.   † P. 256.

economists whose views he controverts. In entire disregard of what he had contended for as a fundamental principle, he here admits that value depends upon other conditions than human effort—upon such condition as the degree of satisfaction which the valuable object or act is capable of conferring; upon such condition, again, as the degree of limitation set to the supply of natural objects or of acts depending upon natural endowment; lastly, upon such condition as the natural superiority of some agents furnished by nature over others—for this is what the explanation in the passage last quoted obviously comes to. After these concessions, I say, there is no longer between Bastiat and those whom he so vehemently controverts anything that can be called a question of fact; and yet the issue is very far from being verbal merely. The real difference is not as to the facts, nor yet as to the names by which the facts are to be called, but as to the method of dealing with them—a difference again which resolves itself into the different aims with which Bastiat and those whom he opposes have gone into the inquiry. Thus Ricardo, seeking to ascertain the laws to which exchange-value in its various manifestations conforms, analyses the various conditions under which the phenomenon is found to present itself, classifies them according to their essential distinctions, marking these distinctions by distinct names, and is thus enabled to show in what way and under what circumstances each class contributes to the ultimate result—the phenomenon of value. Bastiat, aiming, not at the interpretation of facts, but at the defence of a system, proceeds by a wholly different

course—repudiates analysis, classification, distinctive
nomenclature ; nay, avowedly selects as the central
term of his doctrine a word which designates combinations of facts of the most diverse character. The
difference of aim leads to difference of method, and
issues in a different result; for whereas Ricardo's
doctrine *does* succeed in explaining a vast variety of
the most important and most complicated facts of
exchange-value, Bastiat's, I have no hesitation in asserting, fails to solve even the simplest case. Let us
test it by an example :—I desire to know if the recent
gold discoveries will lower the value of gold. How
am I helped to this by being told that value represents
" service," and is in proportion to " service " ? " Service " may import half-a-dozen things—effort exerted,
effort saved, satisfaction conferred by the possession
of natural objects, limitation of supply, and various
combinations of these—and its import in the case
in hand I have no means of determining. Gold, it is
true, is now obtained by less " effort" than formerly.
With Ricardo's doctrine before me I know what
interpretation to place upon that circumstance.
Enlightened by Bastiat's, I am precluded from drawing any inference whatever; for though the effort
of production has been diminished, it may not be on
effort that " service " in this case depends : " On peut
rendre un grand service avec un très-leger effort,
comme avec un grand effort on peut ne rendre qu'un
très-médiocre service." Take a simpler case still. A
machine is invented which cheapens the production of
cloth :—will this lower the value of cloth ? It would
be quite consistent with Bastiat's theory that it should

not do so, because it would be open to him to say, as he does say in the case of the diamond and of Madame Malibran's singing, that though the effort of production was diminished, the satisfaction which the commodity was capable of conferring remained unaffected. To tell me then that value represents "service" and varies with "service" is to tell me nothing, unless I am told further the elements of "service" which are operative in the given case. This is what Ricardo's theory in effect does : this is what Bastiat's theory fails to do ; and in this difference lies the entire difference between the two doctrines. It is much as if a chemist were to propound as a solution of the problem of the composition of bodies, that matter is composed of elementary atoms, òmitting to classify the various forms of matter according to their elementary constitution, or to say in what proportion in each class the elements combine. Such a generalization is no generalization in the scientific sense of the term : it is a mere confounding of a crowd of unanalysed phenomena under an ambiguous word.

So utterly, so glaringly inadequate is Bastiat's Theory of Value as a means of explaining phenomena, that its enunciation by a reasoner of Bastiat's remarkable acuteness would be altogether inexplicable had economic explanation been his principal object. But this, as we have seen, if an object with Bastiat at all, was quite secondary in his scheme. His paramount aim was, in truth, not economic, but moral ; he sought, not simply to explain, but also, and mainly, to justify the social facts which he undertook to expound. And this brings me to the second and more important *rôle* played by the term "service" in his theory. For service not merely designates a fact, but connotes a moral judgment. No one will deny that a man's services are properly his own—that he has a right to be remunerated for his services by him who requires to have them rendered to him; if, therefore, property is resolvable into the right to certain values, and values in all cases represent, and vary with, services, we have the moral sentiment at once enlisted in the support of property. To maintain property—property, let us say, in the ground-rent of houses in the centre of London—is to maintain the right of a man to the product of "services"—of "services" rendered to society by himself or by those from whom he has derived. To maintain freedom of contract is to maintain the right of one who has rendered "services" to exchange those "services" on such terms as he pleases against the "services" of others who are equally free. Thus all industrial and commercial operations under a *régime* of freedom were resolved by Bastiat into instances of the reciprocity of services—"*services pour services;*" than which, he asks, what can be more just? "*Services pour services*"—the phrase has the unmistakeable ring of an axiom of "natural justice." Like the "droit du travail," "a fair day's wages for a fair day's work," and other kindred expressions, it, so to speak, sounds in equity. Whatever can be brought under the formula of "*services pour services*" has already received its moral ratification. We see, then, what Bastiat really accomplished. By dint of such explanations as I have given examples of, he succeeded in bringing the principal phenomena of value within the comprehension of a single term; this term being one which, from its etymological associations, connoted a moral judgment on the facts to which it was applied. Armed with the shibboleth of *services pour services*, Bastiat felt himself strong to encounter Communists on their own ground, and was able to return in kind the bolts launched at him from the arsenal of the Rights of Man.

So much for the "new exposition of Political Economy," by which Bastiat proposed to defend social order menaced by socialistic attacks. The degree of faith which he placed in his specific is certainly surprising; for, however he may have failed to convince others, it is beyond question that he succeeded in fully convincing himself. He entirely believed that the Theory of Value set forth above contained the key to the social problem—furnished the sufficient foundation for a policy of the most rigid *laissez-faire*. Considered with reference to the practical purpose for which it was designed—as a corrective to the intoxicating appeals of socialistic writers—the antidote must, I think, be pronounced to be extraordinarily weak, a veritable pill to cure an earthquake. Nor would it seem that Bastiat's writings have produced any sensible impression upon the general course of economic thought in France. He has left no school, and even those who yield a general assent to his system for the most part qualify their adhesion by reservations on essential points. The most important of recent French treatises on Political Economy— those, *e.g.*, of M. Cherbuliez and of M. Courcelle-Seneuil—scarcely refer to him, and, when they do, it is for the purpose of refutation. It will, perhaps, occur to the reader that there was little need, under these circumstances, for the somewhat elaborate examination of his system of economic philosophy attempted in the foregoing pages. It may be said of Bastiat, however, as of some other eminent French thinkers, that Englishmen seem disposed to attach greater weight to his authority than it finds amongst his own countrymen; and it happens that his capital doctrine is in immediate contact with one of the most urgent of our own social questions—that of land-tenure reform. Since the free-trade controversy was settled, no question has come up for political discussion on which economic theory has a more direct and decisive bearing than on this. It is evident that the nature and extent of the prospective reform will mainly be determined by the economic standpoint from which the question is regarded—according, that is to say, as it is regarded from the standpoint of absolute property and commercial contract, or from that which recognizes a fundamental distinction between land and the ordinary products of industry. The latter view flows as an immediate corollary from the theory of rent propounded by Ricardo—one of those "pretty problems," by the way, which some eminent authorities would rank, as regards its social importance, with "the resolution of double stars," and "theories of irregular verbs." The former—the absolute property and commercial contract view of the case—can, on the other hand, only find its justification in some theory tantamount to Bastiat's, of which the capital feature is the identification of value, and, therefore, of property, in all its forms, as a phenomenon depending on the same causes, a product of the same essential conditions. Accept Bastiat's theory of value, and for any reform in land beyond the assimilation of real and personal property (for thus far it does carry us) we are without scientific warrant. The principle which governs contracts in the case of moveable wealth must be allowed to govern them in the case of land. The Irish Land Act, and all legislation in the same direction, are, of course, in this view, an injustice and a blunder. Such is one of the practical bearings of Bastiat's doctrine; and Bastiat's reputation in this country being what it is, it has seemed to me not out of place—more especially in the presence of fresh translations of his principal work—to attempt some estimate of the scientific value of his speculation.

APPENDICES.

A.

PRODUCTS OF VICTORIA—*Prices in Melbourne.**

	Sheep, wethers, each.	Cows and Heifers, each.	Bullocks, working, per pair.	Hay, per ton.	Bread, retail, per 4 lb. loaf.	Beef, retail, per lb.	Mutton, retail, per lb.	Butter, fresh, per lb.	Eggs, per dozen.	Turkeys, each.	Ducks, per couple.	Fowl, per couple.	Potatoes, wholesale, per cwt.	Potatoes, retail, per lb.	Carrots, per bunch.	Turnips, per bunch.	Cabbages, each.
	s. *s.*	£ £	£ £	£ £	*d.* *d.*	*d.* *d.*	*d.* *d.*	*d.* *d.*	*s.* *d.*	*s.* *s.*	*s.* *s.*	*s.* *s.*	*s.* *d.* *s.* *d.*	*d.*	*d.*	*d.*	*d.*
Pre-gold period	4 to 5	2 to 3	8 to 14	2 to 5	5 to 8	1 to 2	1 to 2	12 to 18	0 9	7 to 9	2 to 5	2 to 4	6 6 to 8 0	1	2	2	2
Single Average	4*s.* 6*d.*	£2 10*s.*	£11 0*s.*	£3 10*s.*	6½	1½	1½	15	0 9	8*s.* 0*d.*	3*s.* 6*d.*	3*s.* 0*d.*	7*s.* 3*d.*	1	2	2	2
1851	...	...	...	8 10	12	...	...	...	1 5	6 9	5 0	4 0	8 0	2½	1	1¾	4¼
1852	5 6	5 10	19 0	12 0	16	4	3¾	24	2 0	8 3	10 0	9 0	13 0	10	3¾	3½	8
1853	14 3	12 10	31 0	29 0	21	6½	6¼	43½	5 0	17 0	14 0	14 6	23 6	15	6¼	6	19
1854	25 3	8 15	30 0	33 0	19¾	8	8	49½	8 6	33 4	22 8	16 0	23 4	5⅓	9⅓	7¼	34
1855	16 8	8 7	...	15 0	20¼	6	5½	44	3 0	17 6	18 0	12 6	17 4	4	6	3¼	6
1856	18 4	7 0	29 5	8 0	17	5	5	39	4 11	17 6	16 6	12 0	10 0	3⅛	3⅜	2¼	4
August, 1858	25 0	7 5	22 10	7 10	...	6¼	5½	39	4 0	22 6	9 0	9 0	13 6	...	3	6	17
October, 1858	23 0	6 0	18 0	6 0	10½	9½	7	33	2 0	20 0	11 0	9 0	...	6	3¼	2½	10
	s. *d.*	£ *s.* *d.*	£ *s.*	£ *s.*	*d.*	*d.*	*d.*	*d.*	*s.* *d.*	*s.* *d.*	*s.* *d.*	*d.*	*s.* *d.*	*d.*	*d.*	*d.*	*d.*
Average of 1858	24 0	6 12 6	20 5	6 15	10½	8	6¼	36	3 0	21 3	10 0	9	13 6	6	3⅛	4¼	13½

The first line, showing prices in the pre-gold period, is taken from the tables in the "History of Prices," vol. vi. pp. 830-41, slightly altered in some instances in conformity with returns given by Mr. Westgarth. The remaining figures to 1856 are averages taken from the same tables. The two last quotations are taken from the local papers.

* Wool and Tallow have been omitted from this table by an oversight; but it may be stated that their prices have not differed very materially from those of home wool and tallow; the explanation of which is, that these articles are merely parts of a larger production, namely cattle, which, it will be seen, have advanced in a threefold proportion; the rise in beef and mutton compensating the comparatively stationary condition of the other elements of the products.

	PROVISIONS.			Butcher's Meat at Leadenhall and Newgate Markets, by the carcase.		RAW MATERIALS.			P.	METALS			
	Butter, Waterford, per cwt.	Bacon, Waterford, per cwt.	Pork, small, by the carcase, per 8 lbs.	Beef, per lb.	Mutton, per lb.	Leather, English Butts, 16.24, per lb.	Tallow, Home, per cwt.	Wool, Fleeces, South Down, per pack of 240 lbs.	Soda Ash, per cwt.	Copper, Toughcake, per ton.	Iron, British Bars, per ton.	Lead, English Pig, per ton.	Tin, English Bars, per ton.
	s. s.	s. s.	s. d.	d.	d.	s. d. s. d.	s. d.	£ s. £ s.	s. d.	s. d.	£ s. £ s.	£ s.	£
1849—January	70 to 78	54 to 57	4 5	4¾	5¾	0 9 to 1 4	44 0	10 0 to 11 0	9 11	79 10	6 0	15 15	80
" April	56 " 60	56 " 59	3 9	4⅜	5½	0 9 " 1 4	...	11 10 " 12 10	...	88 10	6 15 to 6 17	15 17	90
" June	68 " 70	60 " 64	3 10	4	5	0 9 " 1 4	40 6	11 12	9 9	79 10	5 10 " 6 10	15 8	74
" October	66 " 70	48 " 56	4 1	4⅝	5	0 9 " 1 4	39 8	11 12	9 11	84 0	6 0	15 17	74
1850—January	66 " 70	42 " 47	3 9	4¼	4⅞	0 9 " 1 4	38 1	12 10 to 13 10	10 3	84 0	6 0	15 17	81
" April	66 " 70	44 " 48	3 9	3⅞	4¾	0 9 " 1 4	...	12 10 " 13 10	...	88 10	5 17 " 5 18	18 10	81
" July	64 " 66	40 " 60	3 9	4⅛	4⅝	0 9 " 1 4	38 4	12 10 " 13 10	10 3	84 0	5 17 " 5 18	18 10	75
" October	72 " 76	46 " 52	4 1	4	4⅝	0 9 " 1 4	39 6	13 10 " 14 10	9 9	79 10	5 7 " 5 10	17 1	81
1851—January	78 " 80	43 " 45	3 10	4	4⅜	0 10½ " 1 4	39 7	13 10 " 14 10	9 7	84 0	5 15 " 5 16	17 10	84
" April	76 " 78	46 " 54	3 9	4	4⅜	0 11 " 1 4	...	14 0 " 14 10	...	84 0	5 15 " 5 16	17 12	85
" July	72 " 74	52 " 56	3 7	4	4⅜	0 10½ " 1 4½	40 3	14 0 " 14 10	9 4	84 0	5 7	17 0	85
" October	74 " 76	50 " 53	3 8	4	4¼	0 10½ " 1 4½	39 0	13 0 " 13 10	9 6	84 0	5 7	17 2	85
	s. d.	s. d.	s. d.	d.	d.	s. d.	s. d.	£ s. d.	s. d.	£ s. d.	£ s.	£ s. d.	£ s.
Average of three years, 1849, '50, '51	70 8	54 3	3 10	4⅛	4¾	1 0¾	39 10	12 17 5	9 10	83 12 6	5 17	16 16 7	81 5
1852—January	72 to 76	41 to 45	3 9	4⅜	4¾	0 10 to 1 4	38 3	13 0 to 14 10	8 6	88 10	5 2	16 17	90
" July	64 " 68	56 " 58	3 6	4⅝	5	0 10½ " 1 4½	41 4	14 10 " 15 10	8 5	102 10	5 10	17 10	88
1853—January	80 " 86	51 " 52	3 7	4⅞	5¾	0 10½ " 1 4	47 6	17 10 " 18 10	8 8	107 10	10 0	24 0	103
" July	84	64	5 0	5⅜	6	1 3 " 1 7	57 8	17 0 " 18 0	9 3	107 10	9 0	23 0	108
1854—January	104	60 to 63	4 8	5⅜	5¾	1 3 " 1 6	64 6	15 10 " 16 0	9 6	126 0	9 5 to 9 10	23 10	131
" July	100 to 104	58 " 61	4 8	5⅜	6⅜	1 3 " 1 6	65 0	12 0 " 12 10	8 6	126 0	10 10	24 15	120
1855—January	104	...	...	5⅝	5⅝	... ...	58 0	12 10 " 13 10	8 6	126 0	8 10	23 0	117
" July	100	...	...	5⅝	6	... ...	66 6	14 0 " 15 0	8 11	126 0	8 15	22 10	111
1856—January	104 to 108	...	...	5⅜	5⅝	... ...	54 9	14 10 " 15 0	9 3	126 0	8 17 to 9 2	25 15	130
" July	104	...	...	5⅜	6	... ...	57 6	17 10 " 18 0	9 5	107 10	8 15 " 9 0	25 15	130
1857—January	110 to 112	64 to 67	4 11	5⅜	6¼	2 0 to 2 7	58 6	21 0 " 22 0	9 6	135 0	8 17 " 9 2	23 2	147
" April	106	73 " 74	4 10	5⅛	5⅞	2 0 " 2 7	...	21 10 " 22 0	...	135 0	8 10 " 8 15	24 15	147
" July	98 to 102	74 " 78	4 5	5⅝	5⅞	1 11 " 2 6	60 6	19 10	10 6	117 0	8 5	25 5	131
" October	106 " 120	78 " 80	4 11	5⅝	5⅞	1 10 " 2 3	59 0	20 10 " 21 0	11 6	121 10	8 5 to 8 10	24 7	141
1858—January	106 " 112	54 " 58	4 7	5¼	5⅞	1 6 " 2 2	56 0	13 0	9 6	107 0	7 0 " 7 10	23 0	109
" April	112 " 114	56 " 60	3 8	4⅞	5⅜	1 2 " 1 10	...	13 0 to 14 0	...	107 0	7 0 " 7 10	22 10	113
" July	108 " 112	68 " 70	3 6	5⅝	5¼	1 2 " 1 10	52 0	14 10 " 15 0	10 3	107 10	7 0 " 7 5	21 15	119
" September	104 " 106	62 " 64	3 10	5⅝	5⅝	1 2 " 1 9	52 0	15 0 " 16 0	10 3	102 10	7 0 " 8 0	21 10	119
	s. d.	s. d.	s. d.	d.	d.	s. d.	s. d.	£ s. d.	s.	£ s.	£ s. d.	£ s. d.	£
Average price, 1858	109 3	61 6	3 10¾	5¼	5¾	1 6⅞	53 4	14 3 9	10	108 10	7 5 7¾	22 3 9	115

	No. 40 Mule Yarn, fair 2nd quality, per lb.	No. 30, Water Twist, fair 2nd quality, per lb.	7/8 Printer's 66 reed. 29 yards.	9/8 Shirting, 66 reed. 37½ yards.	30 m T cloths. 24 yards	29/30 Domestics. 60 yards.	Good Seconds, Water Twist. 20 yards.	Good Seconds, Mule Twist. 40 yards.	Frockings. (per yard)	Hucks. (per yard)	Drills. (per yard)	7/8 Linens. (per yard)	Sheeting. (per yard)	Bed Ticks. (per yard)
	d.	d.	s. d. s. d.	s. d. s. d.	s. d. s. d.	d. d.	d. d.	d. d.	d.	d.	d.	d.	s. d.	d.
1849—January	7¼	7¼	.. ..	.. ..	.. ..	..	..	..	4½	5½	5½	5½	2 2	9½
,, April	8¼	7¼	.. ..	.. ..	.. ..	..	..	..	4	5	5⅝	4¾	2 1	9¼
,, July	8½	7¼	.. ..	.. ..	.. ..	..	..	..	3¾	4¾	5	4¾	2 0	9
,, October	9	8¼	.. ..	.. ..	.. ..	..	..	..	3½	4¾	5	4¾	2 0	8¾
1850—January	10	9¼	.. ..	.. ..	.. ..	..	..	..	3⅝	4⅞	5⅛	5	2 1	9
,, April	10⅜	9½	4 9 to 5 3	8 0 to 8 9	3 9 to 4 0	1⅞ to 3¼	8⅛ to 8⅝	10⅛ to 10⅝	3¾	4⅞	5	5¼	2 1	9
,, July	11⅜	1[illegible]	.. ..	.. ..	.. ..	..	..	..	..	..	..	..	..	..
,, October	11¼	11¼	.. ..	.. ..	.. ..	..	..	..	..	5⅛	5¼	5¼	2 1½	9½
1851—January	12¼	11¼	.. ..	.. ..	.. ..	..	..	..	3¾	5¼	5½	5½	2 2	9½
,, April	11¼	10¼	4 6 ,, 5 0	8 3 ,, 9 0	4 1½ ,, 4 4½	2 ,, 4	9½ ,, 10	11¼ ,, 11½	..	..	..	..	..	..
,, July	9⅝	9¼	.. ..	.. ..	.. ..	..	..	..	3½	5	5¼	5¼	2 1	9
,, October	9	9½	.. ..	.. ..	.. ..	..	..	..	3¼	5¼	5½	5½	2 2½	9¼
Average price of three years, 1849, '50, 51	d. 10	d. 9½	s. d. 4 10½	s. d. 9 0	s. d. 4 0¾	d. 2½	d. 9	d. 10⅝	d. 3¾	d. 5	d. 5¼	d. 5⅛	s. d. 2 1⅛	d. 9⅛
1852—January	9	9½	4 4½ to 5 0	7 3 to 8 6	3 4 to 3 9	1⅞ to 4	7¾ to 8	8¼ to 8½	3⅝	5⅜	5¼	5¼	2 2	9
,, July	9¾	9¾	.. ..	.. ..	.. ..	..	..	..	3⅝	4⅝	4⅝	5	2 0	8¾
1853—January	9⅝	9¾	4 10½ ,, 5 3	7 6 ,, 8 9	3 4½ ,, 3 10½	1⅞ ,, 3	8⅛ ,, 8¾	9⅜ ,, 9¾	..	..	..	..	..	..
,, July	10¼	9½	.. ..	.. ..	.. ..	..	..	..	..	..	..	..	..	..
1854—January	9½	9¾	4 3 ,, 5 0	7 3 ,, 8 6	3 6 ,, 3 10½	1⅞ ,, 3	7¾ ,, 8⅛	9 ,, 9¼	3½	..	5¼	5¼	2 1	9
,, July	9¾	9½	.. ..	.. ..	.. ..	..	..	..	4	5½	5½	5¾	2 3	9½
1855—January	8¾	..	3 9 ,, 4 6	7 0 ,, 8 0	2 11 ,, 3 5	1¾ ,, 2⅞	7⅛ ,, 7⅞	8½ ,, 9	..	..	..	..	..	..
,, July	9¾	..	.. ..	.. ..	.. ..	..	..	..	..	..	..	..	..	..
1856—January	9¼	..	4 3 ,, 5 0	7 0 ,, 8 4½	3 1½ ,, 3 9	1⅞ ,, 2⅞	8¼ ,, 8½	9¼ ,, 9¾	3⅞	5¼	5¼	5½	2 2	9¼
,, July	10	..	.. ..	.. ..	.. ..	..	..	..	4⅛	..	5¼	5⅝	2 2	9¼
1857—January	11⅝	10¾	.. ..	.. ..	.. ..	..	..	..	..	..	..	..	2 3	..
,, April	12	11¾	4 7½ ,, 5 7½	8 6 ,, 9 9	3 9 ,, 4 3	2 ,, 3¼	2¼ ,, 9¾	11 ,, 11¾	..	..	..	6½	..	..
,, July	12½	11¾	.. ..	.. ..	.. ..	..	..	..	4⅜	5¾	5¾	6¼	2 4	9½
,, October	13⅜	13	.. ..	.. ..	.. ..	..	..	..	4⅛	5½	5½	6	2 3	9
1858—January	10¼	9¾	.. ..	.. ..	.. ..	..	..	..	..	..	..	..	..	..
,, April	11¼	10¼	4 4½ ,, 5 3	8 3 ,, 9 4½	3 9 ,, 4 7½	2⅛ ,, 3¼	8⅞ ,, 9⅛	10¾ ,, 11¼	3⅞	5¼	5⅛	5½	2 2	8¾
,, July	11⅝	11	.. ..	.. ..	.. ..	..	..	..	3⅝	..	..	..	..	..
,, September	11¼	11½	.. ..	.. ..	.. ..	..	..	..	4¼	5⅝	5¾	6¼	2 4	9½
Average price of 1858	d. 11⅓	d. 10¼	s. d. 4 9¾	s. d. 8 9¾	s. d. 4 2¼	d. 2⅝	d. 9	d. 11	d. 4	d. 5⅓	d. 5⅜	d. 5⅞	s. d. 2 2⅞	d. 8⅞

* Average prices during the early months of each year.

WEST INDIES.

	Sugar, B.P. good and fine, per cwt. (bond). s. d.	Sugar, B.P. Brown, per cwt. (bond). s. d.	Logwood (Jamaica), per ton. £ s. d.	Rum (Jamaica) 10 to 20, O.P. per gallon (bond). s. d.	Coffee, Jamaica, fine ord. to middling, per cwt. (in bond). s. d.	Turpentine, English Spirits, without casks. s. d.	Whiskey, Patent Still, per proof gallon (bond). † s. d.	Peas, per imperial quarter. s. d.	Beans, per imperial quarter. s. d.	Rye, per imperial quarter. s. d.	Oats, per imperial quarter. s. d.	Barley, per imperial quarter. s. d.	Wheat, per imperial quarter. s. d.
1849—January	22 26	20 22	5 15 3	2 10	35 0	30 3	1 5½	35 9 6	33 11	28 6	17 6	27 9	50 10
„ April	25 27	23 25	4 17 3	2 10	35 0	33 3	1 4½	29 10	32 1	26 5	...	...	45 1
„ July	25 29	23 24	4 15 4	2 8	36 0	31 9	1 4	33 8	29 1	28 2	16 5	23 5	43 3
„ October	24 27	23 24	4 15 4	2 8	50 0	30 9	1 4	31 11	26 1	25 4	...	...	38 11
1850—January	24 27	22 23	4 15 4	2 8	50 6	31 9	1 4	28 5	26 8	21 1	18 7	24 9	41 5
„ April	24 27	22 24	4 17 4	2 8	40 6	29 9	1 4	24 4	29 6	23 4	...	...	...
„ July	27 28	24 26	4 17 3	2 8	50 6	32 9	1 4	28 0	27 5	26 2	...	...	38 6
„ October	29 30	26 28	3 15 3	3 3	53 6	29 9	1 4	28 0	27 0	22 8	...	...	...
1851—January	26 33	28 27	3 15 3	3 3	42 6	33 9	1 4½	24 0	32 2	28 1	...	...	...
„ April	26 32	27 24	3 15 3	3 6	43 6	33 9	1 4½	20 0	31 1	28 1	...	...	...
„ July	25 28	24 23	3 15 3	3 6	42 6	33 9	1 4	24 2	27 8	25 0	...	...	...
„ October	25 29	20 20	3 15 3	3 4	40 6	34 3	1 4½	24 0	27 0	...	...	...	...
Average price of three years, 1849, 50, 51	27 0	23 10	4 1 10	2 6½	45 6	31 0	1 5½	29 0	28 7	25 9	17 6	25 3½	43 0
1852—January	22 26	18 0	3 11 7	2 6½	44 0	33 0	1 0	29 2	29 2	28 8	19 1	28 6	38 7
„ July	25 26	17 21	3 11 2	2 2	43 6	30 9	1 0	31 11	39 11	31 11	21 0	33 2	40 10
1853—January	23 29	21 25	4 11 7	4 0	50 0	43 3	2 1	32 2	45 6	29 1	21 11	36 0	45 0
„ July	25 28	23 25	5 11 6	3 3	53 0	60 0	2 5	41 2	45 1	36 10	27 5	34 9	60 11
1854—January	24 29	25 23	6 11 10	3 3	49 0	57 4	2 8	50 3	43 0	47 1	25 2	41 1	70 8
„ July	22 20	22 22	6 11 10	3 3	53 0	54 4	2 8	48 0	45 9	40 0	25 2	42 1	65 7
1855—January	...	...	...	...	...	...	...	...	...	...	...	...	71 8
„ July	...	...	...	...	...	...	...	...	...	...	...	...	77 8
1856—January	...	...	...	...	...	...	...	...	...	...	...	...	67 9
„ July	...	...	...	...	...	...	...	...	...	...	...	...	...
1857—January	37 41	37 34	5 15 7	4 9	44 6	43 9	2 1	40 9	39 10	39 0	23 3	35 10	56 9
„ April	37 42	37 37	5 15 6	4 8	43 6	39 9	2 2	39 9	45 6	37 7	25 10	36 10	47 7
„ July	43 47	43 39	5 15 5	4 8	50 8	43 9	2 2	43 9	45 10	41 0	25 3	31 0	44 3
„ October	34 42	30 34	5 15 5	4 6	58 6	39 1	2 2	39 9	39 8	35 4	27 0	34 0	43 0
1858—January	27 35	23 29	5 15 5	4 8	68 6	31 0	2 2	45 0	38 4	31 3	25 5	...	45 3
„ April	29 30	19 17	5 15 5	4 8	66 0	40 9	2 2	40 1	42 7	33 6	25 0	...	...
„ July	24 30	24 19	5 15 5	4 6	56 0	45 9	2 1	43 0	46 3	34 0	27 0	...	...
„ September	26 32	22 22	5 15 5	4 2	55 0	36 0	1 1	45 0	46 7	...	...	...	...
Average price of 1858	30	23 6	£5 5s.	3 7½	60 9	38 2¼	1 9¾	41 10¼	41 7¾	32 11	24 11½	34 5½	45 0½

* The figures in these columns represent averages. † The dates for Whiskey are January, March, October, and December for each year. ‡ After January 1856, twopence added to compensate change in law. § 15 to 25, O.P.

	Cotton Wool		Ashes, First Sort Pearl, U.S. per cwt.	Duty 1s. per load — Timber, Canadian pine, per load.	Resin, American, per cwt. P.	Tobacco, Maryland, per lb. bond.	Tobacco, Virginia, per lb. bond.	Beef, American and Canadian, per tierce.	Pork, American and Canadian, per barrel.	Indian Corn, Yellow American, per quarter.	Rice, Carolina (American dressed), per cwt.
	Middling Orleans, per lb.	Fair Orleans, per lb.									
1849—January											
,, April											
,, July											
,, October											
1850—January											
,, April											
,, July											
,, October											
1851—January											
,, April											
,, July											
,, October											
Average price of three years, 1849, '50, '51											
1852—January											
,, July											
1853—January											
,, July											
1854—January											
,, July											
1855—January											
,, July											
1856—January											
,, July											
1857—January											
,, April											
,, July											
,, October											
1858—January											
,, April											
,, July											
,, September											
Average price of 1858											

	Flax, Riga, P.T.R., per ton.	Hemp, St. Petersburg, clean, per ton.	Hides, Kips, Russia, dry, per lb.	Leather, 16.25, Foreign Butts, per lb.	Oils, Gallipoli, per 252 gallons.	Oil, Seal pale, per 252 gallons.	Oil, Palm, per 252 gallons.	Tallow, Russian, per cwt.
1849—January	34 to 40	30 to 30	0 9	0 1 2	42 10	26 12	30 10	44 0
,, April	34 ,, 40	28 ,, 28	0 8	0 1 2	42 5	31 5	34 10	39 6
,, July	34 ,, 40	30 ,, 30	0 9	0 1 1	41 5	32 15	39 10	38 6
,, October	34 ,, 38	30 10 31	0 9	0 1 1	44 5	39 5	32 15	
1850—January	34 ,, 42	31 10 28	0 9	0 1 1	47 5	37 5	31 17	38 8
,, April	38 ,, 46	30 ,, 30	0 9	0 1 1	41 5	38 2	30 5	39 0
,, July	38 ,, 46	30 ,, 30	0 9	0 1 1	43 15	37 5	30 5	40 0
,, October	38 ,, 46	31 ,, 31	0 9	0 1 10	43 5	32 17	28 5	
1851—January	39 ,, 48	,, 30	0 8	0 1 10	41 15	31 5	28 5	39 5
,, April	42 ,, 43	30 ,, 30	0 8	0 1 10	38 0	32 12	27 5	39 4
,, July	42 ,, 42	31 0 30	0 0	0 1 10	40 0	32		
,, October								
Average price three years, '50, '51	40 to	30 1 3	0 9 1	1 1 2	42 18 9	33 4 5	30 6 7	39 1
1852—January	42 to	31 10	8 8 0	0 1 1	44 0	32 5	26 17	37 5
,, July	42 ,,	30 15	8 8 0	0 1 1	46 17	35 15	28 12	44 4
1853—January	42 ,,	39	8 10 0	1 1 1	59 0	35 17	34 5	47 7
,, July		36 15	10 10 10	1 1 1	67 10	32 2	40 5	56 6
1854—January	35 ,,	42 12	0 1 0		63 5	43 5	42 5	64 5
,, July	35 ,,	62 12	0 1 0		52 15	40 0	46 5	65 0
1855—January	57 ,,	55 0			57 5	47 5	48 0	57 5
,, July	53 ,,	46 0	4 4 0	2 2 2	56 5	53 15	41 0	64 7
1856—January	53 ,,	43 0	2 2 0	2 2 2	53 0	56 5	43 5	54 4
,, July	52 ,,	33 0	2 2 0	2 2 2	49 5	48 2	73 10	56 5
1857—January	52 ,,	37 0	1 1 0	1 2 1	61 5	43 15	47 5	63 5
,, April	52 ,,	36 0	0 0 0	1 1 1	58 10	43 2	46 5	
,, July	55 ,,	34 0	0 0 0	0 1 1	57 0	45 0	40 0	62 5
,, October	56 ,,	32 0	0 0 0	3 3 0	62 10	35 5	39 15	58 8
1858—January	53 53	29 10 0	8 8 0	0 0 9	51 10	39 0	33 15	56 5
,, April	53	30 0 0	8 8 0	0 0 9	47 0	37 10	33 15	
,, July	58 50	29 0 0	8 8 0	2 2 9	45 5	38 2	39 15	53 5
,, September	50 0	70 0 0	0 0 0	2 2 0	45 5		39 15	51 1
Average price of 1858	55	29 12 6	9 1	1 6 1	47 6 1	38 10	39 6 3	53 9

WOOL.

	Steel, Swedish, in Kegs, per ton.	Iron, Swedish, per ton.	Tar, Stockholm, per barrel.	(Sheep's) Northern Germany Secunda, per lb.	German, 1st and elect. per lb.	Timber, Dantzic and Memel fir, per load (bond).	Tallow, St. Petersburg, New Y.C. per cwt.
	£ s. d.	£ s. d.	s. d.	d.	d.	s. d.	s. d.
1849—January	15 0 0	10 5 0 to 11 10 0	17 0 to 17 0	9 to 1	3 to 4 3	70 0 to 80 0	41 0 to 49 0
,, April	14 0 0	11 0 to 10 15	18 0 to 17 0	7½ to 1	4 to 4 10	75 0 to 60 0	38 3 to 33 0
,, July	14 0 0	12 0 to 0 12 0	17 0 to 16 0	7¾ to 1	6 to 3 0	75 0 to 60 0	38 0 to 38 0
,, October	14 5 0	12 10	16 0 to 16 0	5 to 2	6 to 4 10	70 0 to 60 0	39 0 to 37 0
1850—January	14 2 0	0 12 0	17 0 to 16 0	2 to 2	6 to 4 0	70 0 to 55 0	39 0 to 38 0
,, April	14 0 0	12 5 to 12 0	17 0 to 16 0	2 to 2	3 to 4 0	65 0 to 55 0	37 0 to 36 0
,, July	14 12 0	11 15 to 11 0	19 0 to 17 0	2 to 2	3 to 4 0	70 0 to 60 0	37 6 to 38 0
,, October	14 17 0	11 15 to 11 0	21 0 to 19 0	2 to 2	3 to 4 0	65 0 to 60 0	38 6 to 37 0
1851—January	14 17 0	11 15 to 11 0	19 0 to 20 0	2 to 2	3 to 4 0	75 0 to 50 0	37 0 to 40 0
,, April	14 17 0	11 15 to 11 0	18 0 to 17 0	2 to 2	3 to 4 0	65 0 to 50 0	37 3 to 37 0
,, July	14 17 0	11 15 to 11 0	17 0 to 16 0	2 to 2	3 to 4 0	65 0 to 50 0	37 0 to 37 0
Average price of three years 1849, '50, '51	14 9 9	11 18 11	17 9	1¾	8¼ 3	63 4	38 8
1852—January	14 0	11 15 5	16 10 to 16 0	2 to 2	4 to 3 0	60 0 to 45 0	36 6
,, July	15 0	11 0	14 6 to 14 0	2 to 2	4 to 3 0	65 0 to 52 0	46 0
1853—January	20 9	12 0	16 0 to 15 0	2 to 2	6 to 4 0	77 0 to 67 0	38 0 to 38 0
,, July	16 6	14 18 to 14 10	17 9 to 16 0	0 to 0	6 to 4 1	80 0 to 70 0	46 0 to 53 6
1854—January	16 6	18 to 17 10	24 0	0 to 0	4 to 4 0	95 0 to 65 0	62 0 to 62 0
,, July	17 6	17 10 to 17 10	31 0 to 28 0	0 to 0	4 to 4 0	90 0 to 80 0	65 0 to 65 0
1855—January	20 10	17 0 to 17 10	28 0 to 27 0	0 to 0	4 to 4 0	95 0 to 65 0	53 0 to 59 0
,, July	20 10	16 0 to 16 10	25 16 to 25 0	0 to 0	4 to 4 0	93 0 to 60 0	68 0 to 68 0
1856—January	21 0	15 0 to 14 0	16 0 to 15 0	2 to 2	6 to 4 0	80 0 to 57 0	50 0 to 55 0
,, July	21 5	14 0 to 14 0	18 16 to 15 0	2 to 2	6 to 4 0	77 0 to 57 0	54 6 to 59 0
,, January	22 0	14 0 to 14 0	17 15 to 13 0	2 to 2	4 to 4 0	72 0 to 49 0	57 0 to 57 0
1857—January	22 5	14 0 to 14 0	0 16 to 14 0	2 to 2	4 to 4 0	77 0 to 52 0	51 9 to 51 0
,, July	21 0	15 0 to 14 0	15 0 to 16 0	2 to 2	4 to 4 0	77 0 to 50 0	56 0 to 55 0
,, April	19 0	14 0 to 13 0	15 0 to 14 0	2 to 2	4 to 3 0	67 0 to 47 0	50 6 to 50 0
1858—September	20 13 9	14 2 6	14 9½	2	3	58 1¼	52 3
Average price of 1858							

A A

E.

PRODUCTS OF ASIA.—*Seventeen Commodities.*

	Cotton, Bengal, Madras, and Surat, per lb.	Hemp, Jute, per ton.	Silk (raw) China Tsatlee, per lb.	Rape, per last of 10 qrs.	Coffee, Native, Ceylon ordinary to good, per cwt. (bond).	Tea, Congou, per lb. (bond).	Tea, Hyson, per lb. (bond).	SUGAR, BENGAL. Brown, per cwt. (bond).	SUGAR, BENGAL. Yellow and White, per cwt. (bond).
	d. d.	£ s. £ s.	s. d. s. d.	£ £	s. d. s. d.	s. d. s. d.	s. d. s. d.	s. d. s. d.	s. d. s. d.
1849—January	2¾ to 3⅞	13 0 to 18 0	12 6 to 17 6	24 to 27	31 6 to 32 6	0 8 to 1 9	1 0 to 3 7	14 0 to 19 0	17 0 to 30 0
,, April	3 ,, 4⅛	13 0 ,, 18 0	12 0 ,, 17 0	28 ,, 30	32 6 ,, 34 0	0 8 ,, 1 9	1 0 ,, 3 7	16 0 ,, 22 0	20 6 ,, 28 0
,, July	3⅜ ,, 4⅛	13 0 ,, 17 0	12 0 ,, 17 6	32 ,, 34	30 6 ,, 33 0	0 8 ,, 1 9	1 0 ,, 3 7	18 0 ,, 26 6	22 0 ,, 35 0
,, October	3¾ ,, 4⅜	13 0 ,, 17 0	13 6 ,, 20 0	28 ,, 30	38 6 ,, 40 0	0 8¾ ,, 1 9	1 0 ,, 3 7	18 0 ,, 26 6	21 0 ,, 34 0
1850—January	3⅞ ,, 5	13 0 ,, 17 0	14 6 ,, 19 6	30 ,, 35	55 6 ,, 57 0	0 10½ ,, 1 9	1 3 ,, 3 7	17 0 ,, 27 0	21 6 ,, 34 0
,, April	4 ,, 5	13 0 ,, 17 0	16 0 ,, 20 0	32 ,, 36	52 0 ,, 52 6	0 9 ,, 1 9	1 4 ,, 3 7	21 6 ,, 29 6	25 0 ,, 33 0
,, July	4⅛ ,, 6⅛	13 0 ,, 19 0	15 0 ,, 21 0	32 ,, 37	43 0 ,, 43 6	0 10¼ ,, 1 7	1 2 ,, 3 6	16 0 ,, 18 0	23 0 ,, 33 0
,, October	4⅝ ,, 7	13 0 ,, 19 0	17 6 ,, 22 0	24 ,, 26	53 0 ,, 55 0	1 0 ,, 1 7	1 3 ,, 3 6	17 6 ,, 19 6	25 6 ,, 34 6
1851—January	4⅜ ,, 7	13 0 ,, 19 0	18 6 ,, 22 0	24 ,, 26	55 0 ,, 56 6	1 0 ,, 1 10	1 3 ,, 3 6	19 0 ,, 22 0	27 0 ,, 37 0
,, April	4¼ ,, 5⅞	10 0 ,, 16 0	18 6 ,, 22 0	26 ,, 30	42 0 ,, 43 0	1 0¼ ,, 1 10	1 3 ,, 3 6	18 0 ,, 21 0	25 0 ,, 35 0
,, July	2⅛ ,, 4⅜	10 0 ,, 16 0	18 6 ,, 22 0	26 ,, 31	37 0 ,, 38 0	0 10¼ ,, 1 8	1 2 ,, 3 6	16 0 ,, 19 0	24 6 ,, 34 0
,, October	2⅝ ,, 4	10 0 ,, 16 0	14 6 ,, 20 0	19 ,, 22	40 6 ,, 42 0	0 8¼ ,, 1 6	1 2 ,, 3 6	13 0 ,, 17 0	22 0 ,, 25 0
Average price of three years, 1849, '50, '51	d. 4⅜	£ s. d. 14 16 8	s. d. 17 7½	£ s. d. 28 14 2	s. d. 43 3	s. d. 1 3½	s. d. 2 4¼	s. d. 19 7	s. d. 27 9
1852—January	2⅝ to 4	10 0 to 16 0	14 6 to 19 6	19 ,, 22	38 6 to 40 0	0 7½ ,, 1 6	1 1 ,, 3 6	13 0 ,, 15 6	20 0 ,, 33 6
,, July	3½ ,, 4⅝	10 0 ,, 16 0	16 6 ,, 20 6	20 ,, 25	44 0 ,, 44 6	0 6½ ,, 1 6	1 1 ,, 3 6	12 0 ,, 15 0	21 0 ,, 34 0
1853—January	3 ,, 4⅛	13 0 ,, 15 17	16 6 ,, 20 6	20 ,, 25	46 0 ,, 47 0	0 10 ,, 2 0	1 0 ,, 3 0	16 0 ,, 19 0	25 6 ,, 30 0
,, July	3 ,, 4⅛	20 0 ,, 24 0	16 0 ,, 19 0	26 ,, 28	45 0 ,, 46 6	0 11½ ,, 2 0	1 4 ,, 3 0	17 0 ,, 21 0	25 0 ,, 31 0
1854—January	2¼ ,, 4⅛	20 0 ,, 24 0	10 6 ,, 20 0	30 ,, 36	49 6 ,, 50 0	1 2 ,, 1 10	1 4 ,, 3 0	18 0 ,, 21 0	25 6 ,, 30 6
,, July	2⅛ ,, 4⅛	20 0 ,, 25 0	7 0 ,, 18 0	30 ,, 36	.. ..	0 11 ,, 1 10	1 4 ,, 3 0	17 0 ,, 22 0	26 6 ,, 30 6
1855—January	2⅛ ,, 4⅛	.. ..	8 0 ,, 18 6	..	.. ..	0 9½ ,, 1 10	1 4 ,, 3 0	.. ..	.. ..
,, July	3⅛ ,, 4⅛	.. ..	8 0 ,, 18 6	..	.. ..	0 8½ ,, 2 4	1 5 ,, 3 6	.. ..	.. ..
1856—January	3¼ ,, 4⅛	.. ..	9 0 ,, 19 6	..	.. ..	0 9 ,, 2 4	1 6 ,, 3 6	.. ..	.. ..
,, July	4 ,, 5⅛	.. ..	9 6 ,, 25 6	..	.. ..	0 8½ ,, 2 4	1 6 ,, 4 0	.. ..	.. ..
1857—January	4⅝ ,, 5⅜	14 0 ,, 33 0	22 6 ,, 27 6	42 ,, 44	56 0 ,, 57 0	1 1 ,, 1 5	1 6 ,, 4 0	26 0 ,, 33 0	36 0 ,, 40 0
,, April	4¾ ,, 6	17 0 ,, 26 10	22 6 ,, 28 6	42 ,, 44	61 0 ,, 61 6	1 0½ ,, 1 5	1 6 ,, 4 0	26 0 ,, 34 0	37 0 ,, 41 0
,, July	4¾ ,, 6	18 0 ,, 26 0	24 0 ,, 29 0	42 ,, 44	64 0 ,, 65 0	1 1 ,, 1 5	1 6 ,, 4 0	31 6 ,, 38 0	44 0 ,, 49 0
,, October	5 ,, 7½	20 0 ,, 27 0	23 6 ,, 28 0	37 ,, 39	61 6 ,, 62 0	1 2 ,, 1 6	1 6 ,, 4 0	24 0 ,, 30 0	38 0 ,, 45 6
1858—January	3⅝ ,, 5¼	14 0 ,, 21 0	15 0 ,, 20 0	37 ,, 39	51 0 ,, 52 6	0 11 ,, 1 4	1 4 ,, 3 6	16 0 ,, 22 6	30 0 ,, 37 6
,, April	4 ,, 5⅜	13 10 ,, 19 0	17 6 ,, 19 6	37 ,, 39	50 0 ,, 54 0	0 9 ,, 1 6	1 2 ,, 3 6	15 0 ,, 21 0	29 0 ,, 35 0
,, July	4⅜ ,, 6	13 10 ,, 19 0	15 0 ,, 20 0	34 ,, 35	45 6 ,, 47 6	0 9½ ,, 1 5	1 4 ,, 3 0	12 6 ,, 20 6	29 0 ,, 34 0
,, September	4¼ ,, 6	13 10 ,, 19 0	15 0 ,, 20 0	34 ,, 35	48 0 ,, 50 0	0 9 ,, 1 4	1 3 ,, 3 0	16 0 ,, 22 6	31 0 ,, 35 0
Average price of 1858	d. 5	£ s. d. 16 12 3	s. d. 17 9	£ s. d. 35 13 4	s. d. 49 9	s. d. 1 1¼	s. d. 2 3⅛	s. d. 18 3	s. d. 32 6

	SUGAR, MAURITIUS.			SPICES.				
	Brown, per cwt. (bond).	Good and Fine Yellow, per cwt. (bond).	Rice, Bengal Yellow, and White, per cwt.	Black Pepper, (heavy and light), per lb. (bond).	Cinnamon, 1st, 2nd, and 3rd qualities, per lb. (bond).	Cloves, Amboyna and Bencoolen, per lb. (bond).	Cassia Lignea, ordinary to good, per cwt. (bond).	Sago, Pearl, per cwt.
	s. d. s. d.	s. d. s. d	s. d. s. d.	d. d.	s. d. s. d.	s. d. s. d.	s. s.	s. d. s. d.
1849—January	15 0 to 21 0	22 0 to 25 0	*9 6 to 13 0	2¾ to 3¼	1 6 to 4 0	1 2 to 2 0	.. ..	*17 0 to 25 0
,, April	15 6 ,, 24 0	25 0 ,, 28 0	*9 0 ,, 12 6	2⅝ ,, 3⅜	1 6 ,, 4 0	1 2 ,, 2 0	84 to 90	*17 0 ,, 25 0
,, July	19 0 ,, 25 0	25 0 ,, 28 0	*8 6 ,, 12 0	2⅝ ,, 3¼	1 6 ,, 4 0	1 2 ,, 2 0	86 ,, 93	*17 0 ,, 23 0
,, October	18 0 ,, 23 6	25 0 ,, 28 0	*8 0 ,, 11 0	2⅞ ,, 3⅜	0 9 ,, 4 3	1 2 ,, 2 0	95 ,, 99	*17 0 ,, 23 0
1850—January	18 0 ,, 24 6	25 6 ,, 28 0	*8 9 ,, 11 6	3⅛ ,, 3⅝	0 9 ,, 4 3	1 2 ,, 2 1	90 ,, 101	*19 0 ,, 25 0
,, April	17 0 ,, 22 6	24 0 ,, 26 0	*8 6 ,, 11 6	3⅛ ,, 4⅛	0 9 ,, 4 6	1 2 ,, 2 1	104 ,, 107	*19 0 ,, 26 0
,, July	17 0 ,, 22 0	24 0 ,, 26 0	*9 0 ,, 12 0	3⅜ ,, 3⅞	0 9 ,, 4 6	1 0 ,, 1 8	80 ,, 87	*19 0 ,, 26 0
,, October	19 6 ,, 24 6	25 6 ,, 28 6	*10 0 ,, 12 6	3⅜ ,, 3¾	0 9 ,, 4 6	1 0 ,, 1 8	98 ,, 103	*19 0 ,, 26 0
1851—January	21 6 ,, 27 0	29 0 ,, 31 0	*9 6 ,, 12 0	3¼ ,, 3⅞	0 9 ,, 4 0	0 10 ,, 1 6	102 ,, 106	*19 0 ,, 24 0
,, April	21 0 ,, 26 6	28 0 ,, 30 0	*8 0 ,, 11 0	3⅛ ,, 3⅜	0 9 ,, 3 6	0 10 ,, 1 6	92 ,, 96	*18 0 ,, 23 0
,, July	19 0 ,, 24 6	26 0 ,, 29 0	*8 3 ,, 10 6	3 ,, 3¼	0 10 ,, 3 6	0 10 ,, 1 6	94 ,, 96	*16 0 ,, 24 0
,, October	16 0 ,, 22 0	23 6 ,, 27 0	*8 3 ,, 10 6	3⅛ ,, 3¼	0 9 ,, 3 6	0 7 ,, 1 6	100 ,, 104	*15 0 ,, 24 6
Average of three years, 1849, '50, '51	s. 21	s. d. 26 6	s. d. 9 8½	d. 3¼	s. d. 2 6	s. d. 1 4½	s. d. 95 9	s. d. 21 1
1852—January	14 0 to 19 0	22 0 to 26 0	*8 6 to 10 6	3⅛ to 3½	0 10 to 3 3	0 6½ to 1 2	110 to 116	15 0 to 24 6
,, July	19 0 ,, 22 6	23 0 ,, 24 6	*8 6 ,, 10 6	3¼ ,, 4⅜	0 11 ,, 2 9	0 6½ ,, 1 2	94 ,, 95	15 0 ,, 24 0
1853—January	16 6 ,, 23 6	23 6 ,, 28 0	9 0 ,, 12 0	3¼ ,, 4⅛	1 4 ,, 2 10	0 7½ ,, 1 0½	108 ,, 117	16 0 ,, 24 0
,, July	17 0 ,, 23 0	23 0 ,, 27 6	11 6 ,, 15 0	4¼ ,, 5	1 4 ,, 2 8	0 8 ,, 1 2	130 ,, 140	18 0 ,, 23 0
1854—January	18 0 ,, 23 0	22 6 ,, 27 6	13 0 ,, 16 6	4¼ ,, 5	1 1 ,, 2 4	0 8 ,, 1 1	130 ,, 140	17 6 ,, 24 0
,, July	17 6 ,, 23 6	24 0 ,, 29 0	13 0 ,, 16 0	5⅜ ,, 6	0 11 ,, 2 1	0 8 ,, 1 1	130 ,, 137	17 6 ,, 24 0
1855—January	.. ..	.. ..	.. ..	..	.. ..	.. ..	.. ..	.. ..
,, July	.. ..	.. ..	.. ..	..	.. ..	.. ..	.. ..	.. ..
1856 January	.. ..	.. ..	.. ..	..	.. ..	.. ..	.. ..	.. ..
,, July	.. ..	.. ..	.. ..	..	.. ..	.. ..	.. ..	.. ..
1857—January	26 0 ,, 37 0	37 0 ,, 40 0	†9 6 ,, 13 0	4⅜ ,, 5	0 11 ,, 2 1	0 8 ,, 1 0½	100 ,, 115	†23 6 ,, 27 0
,, April	26 6 ,, 36 6	37 0 ,, 42 0	†10 3 ,, 13 6	4¼ ,, 5	0 11 ,, 2 1	0 8 ,, 1 4	115 ,, 125	†23 6 ,, 28 0
,, July	31 6 ,, 42 6	42 6 ,, 46 6	†11 6 ,, 14 6	5¼ ,, 5⅜	1 1 ,, 1 11	0 7¾ ,, 1 1	134 ,, 142	†22 0 ,, 24 0
,, October	25 6 ,, 33 0	33 0 ,, 42 0	†10 0 ,, 15 0	5¼ ,, 5⅝	1 1 ,, 1 11	0 7¾ ,, 1 1	142 ,, 155	†22 0 ,, 27 6
1858—January	17 0 ,, 25 0	25 6 ,, 33 0	†7 0 ,, 11 0	4¾ ,, 5¼	1 0 ,, 1 11	0 7¾ ,, 1 0½	100 ,, 110	†18 0 ,, 24 0
,, April	16 0 ,, 25 6	25 6 ,, 31 0	†6 6 ,, 10 6	5 ,, 6	1 0 ,, 1 11	0 7½ ,, 1 1¼	120 ,, 130	†18 0 ,, 23 0
,, July	15 0 ,, 24 0	24 0 ,, 36 0	†6 6 ,, 12 0	4½ ,, 5½	0 11 ,, 1 8	0 7 ,, 1 1¼	110 ,, 120	†17 0 ,, 21 0
,, September	18 0 ,, 26 0	26 0 ,, 32 0	†6 0 ,, 12 0	4½ ,, 5½	0 9 ,, 1 8	0 7 ,, 1 2½	90 ,, 105	†16 6 ,, 21 0
Average price, 1858	s. d. 20 9	s. d. 29 1	s. d. 8 6¾	d. 5⅛	s. d. 1 4	d. 10½	s. d. 110 6	s. d. 19 9¾

* Duty, 6*d*. per cwt. † Duty, 4½*d*. per cwt.

Date	Potatoes (York Regents) at Waterside Market, Southwark, per ton (s. d.)		Saltpetre, Bengal, per cwt. (s. d.)		Silk, Italian (Raw), all descriptions, per lb. (s. d.)		Indigo, Bengal, Oude and Madras, per lb. (s. d.)		Port (duty 5s. 6d. per gallon) per pipe (£ s. d.)		Sherry, duty 5s. 6d. per gallon) per butt (£ s. d.)	
	from	to	from	to	from	to	from	to	from	to	from	to
1849—January	155 0		25 6	27 6	13 0	21 0	1 11	3 0	17 0	52 0	12 0	76 0
,, April	140 0		25 6	28 0	12 6	23 0	1 11	5 0	17 0	52 0	12 0	76 0
,, July	190 0		26 6	28 0	12 0	23 0	1 11	6 0	17 0	52 0	12 0	76 0
,, October	75 0		26 0	28 0	15 0	26 0	1 11	6 0	17 0	52 0	12 0	76 0
1850—January	95 0		25 0	28 0	16 0	28 0	1 11	9 0	17 0	52 0	12 0	76 0
,, April	85 0		25 6	27 0	16 6	28 0	1 11	10 0	19 0	52 0	12 0	76 0
,, July	75 0		26 0	28 0	19 0	28 0	1 11	8 0	24 0	52 0	12 0	76 0
,, October	80 6		27 0	28 0	19 0	28 0	3 11	0 0	24 0	52 0	12 0	76 0
1851—January	97 0		26 0	29 0	19 0	28 0	3 11	6 0	24 0	52 0	12 0	76 0
,, April	80 0		25 0	29 0	19 0	28 0	2 11	8 0	24 0	52 0	12 0	76 0
,, July	100 0		25 6	29 6	19 0	25 0	1 11	9 0	24 0	52 0	12 0	76 0
,, October	70 0		25 0	29 0	18 0	25 0	1 11	9 0	24 0	52 0	12 0	76 0
Average price of three years, 1849, '50, '51 ..	103 6		27 2		21 4½		3 11		36 0 10		44 4	
1852—January	70 0		24 0	28 6	17 0	25 0	1 9	9 0	24 0	52 0	12 0	76 0
1853—July	97 6		25 0	29 0	19 0	27 0	1 9	9 0	24 0	52 0	12 0	76 0
1853—January	127 6		24 0	30 0	19 0	30 0	2 9	4 0	24 0	52 0	12 0	70 0
,, July	117 0		25 0	31 0	18 0	25 0	1 9	6 0	24 0	50 0	10 0	70 0
1854—January	140 0		27 6	36 0	20 0	30 0	1 9	6 0	26 0	50 0	18 0	80 0
,, July	80 0		21 0	28 0	19 0	24 0	2 9	3 0				
1855—January	112 6		21 0	32 0	18 0	27 0	1 9	0 0				
,, July	74 0		22 0	32 0	18 0	38 0	1 9	0 0				
1856—January	86 6		29 0	37 0	22 0	43 0	2 9	3 0	35 0	60 0	28 0	80 0
,, July	78 0		30 0	34 0	28 0	45 0	2 9	0 0	58 0	65 0	28 0	80 0
1857—January	110 6		39 0	45 0	32 0	45 0	1 9	0 0	42 0	75 0	30 0	85 0
,, April	127 0		38 0	41 0	32 0	50 0	1 9	3 0	42 0	75 0	30 0	85 0
,, July	105 0		36 0	65 0	32 0	37 0	2 9	6 0	42 0	75 0	27 0	85 0
,, October	140 0		55 0	42 0	38 0	36 0	2 9	0 0	42 0	65 0	28 0	80 0
1858—January	152 6		31 0	47 0	24 0	37 0	0 11	0 0	30 0		25 0	85 0
,, April	165 0		28 0	37 0	23 0	36 0	0 11	0 0				
,, July	150 0		34 0	48 0	24 0	37 0	0 11	0 0				
,, September	65 0		36 0	48 0	23 0	35 0	0 11	0 0				
Average price of 1858	133 1		36 9		29 10½		5 1½		54 10		55 0	

G.

RATIO OF PRESENT PRICES TO THE AVERAGE PRICES OF 1849, 1850, AND 1851.

(The latter being taken as 100*) deduced from the foregoing Tables.*

PRODUCTS OF VICTORIA.	1849, '50, and '51.	1858.
Cattle—Sheep, Cows, Bullocks	100	327·1
Hay	100	192·8
Bread	100	161·5
Butcher's Meat—Beef, Mutton	100	474·9
Butter	100	240·0
Farm-yard Produce—Eggs, Turkeys, Ducks, Fowl	100	312·8
Potatoes	100	186·3
Potatoes, retail	100	600·0
Garden Vegetables—Carrots, Turnips, Cabbages	100	349·1
PRODUCTS OF THE UNITED KINGDOM.		
Provisions—Butter, Bacon, Pork	100	123·1
Butcher's Meat—Beef, Mutton	100	122·2
Leather	100	148·0
Tallow	100	133·6
Wool	100	110·2
Soda Ash	100	102·0
Copper	100	129·1
Iron	100	124·4
Lead	100	131·8
Tin	100	141·5
Wheat	100	104·7
Barley	100	135·1
Oats	100	141·5
Rye	100	127·8
Beans	100	145·4
Peas	100	143·4
Cotton Manufactures (8 articles)	100	103·3
Linen Manufactures (6 articles)	100	105·8
Whiskey	100	123·3
Turpentine	100	120·5
Coffee	100	133·5
Rum	100	142·0
Logwood	100	128·3
Sugar (2 qualities)	100	104·7

PRODUCTS OF NORTH AMERICA.	1849, '50, and '51.	1858.
Cotton Wool—Middling Orleans, Fair Orleans ...	100	115·5
Ashes	100	114·8
Timber	100	120·1
Resin	100	152·6
Tobacco—Maryland, Virginian	100	127·8
Provisions—Beef, Pork	100	130·0
Indian Corn	100	118·0
Rice	100	108·9

PRODUCTS OF CONTINENTAL EUROPE.

Flax	100	135·6
Hemp	100	101·5
Hides	100	100·6
Leather	100	159·7
Tallow (2 qualities)	100	136·4
Timber	100	92·8
Wool (2 qualities)	100	103·8
Tar	100	83·2
Oils—Gallipoli, Palm, Seal	100	117·8
Iron	100	118·2
Steel	100	144·5
Wheat	100	104·7
Barley	100	135·1
Oats	100	141·5
Rape	100	124·2

PRODUCTS OF ASIA.

Cotton	100	114·1
Hemp	100	88·0
Silk	100	100·1
Rape	100	124·2
Coffee	100	115·0
Tea—Congou, Hyson	100	106·4
Sugar—Bengal (2 qualities), Mauritius (2 qualities)	100	104·8
Rice	100	88·6
Spices—Black Pepper, Cinnamon, Cloves, Cassia Lignea	100	97·2
Sago	100	94·7

COMMODITIES SUBJECT TO EXCEPTIONAL INFLUENCES.

Potatoes	100	122·2
Saltpetre	100	135·1
Silk	100	136·6
Indigo	100	130·0
Wine—Port, Sherry	100	138·1

ABSTRACT OF DR. SOETBEER'S TABLES.

Given in his Contributions to the Statistics of Prices in Hamburg.

1831—40	Percentage rates compared with the average of the years 1831—40.								
	18³¹⁄₄₀	18⁴¹⁄₅₀	1851	1852	1853	1854	1855	1856	1857
Coffee	100.0	68.5	75.6	74.4	83.8	88.5	82.7	86.2	95.4
,, Domingo	100.0	71.3	77.3	72.7	83.1	78.4	86.5	95.5	105.8
,, Java	..	..	..	..	..	..	..	..	..
Cocoa	..	100.0	88.4	105.0	105.0	98.3	125.1	149.9	265.0
Tea	100.0	110.7	86.5	79.8	85.8	89.7	84.8	83.4	94.0
Unrefined Sugar	100.0	83.3	75.8	71.4	82.3	85.5	96.8	122.6	127.8
Refined do.	100.0	82.4	74.7	72.2	77.2	79.7	82.2	112.6	116.5
Tobacco	100.0	99.0	112.0	94.4	85.7	84.6	84.6	98.7	120.7
Rice	100.0	85.5	65.1	70.9	77.9	93.0	103.5	86.0	76.7
Pepper	100.0	82.3	84.8	87.6	98.6	109.5	109.5	120.4	112.2
Almonds	100.0	95.0	99.1	89.2	94.1	99.7	110.1	111.6	120.8
Raisins	100.0	99.5	89.7	84.7	137.9	163.5	127.6	183.3	254.7
Currants	100.0	72.9	59.7	67.1	164.5	173.5	184.2	200.3	135.0
Wine	100.0	77.5	98.4	101.6	120.5	148.1	173.0	189.7	197.8
Rum	100.0	80.0	56.8	57.5	78.8	94.2	106.2	100.0	107.2
Geneva	100.0	90.2	134.0	137.5	147.0	170.0	189.0	166.5	161.0
Wheat	100.0	120.0	108.3	116.7	150.0	193.1	215.3	206.9	144.4
Rye	100.0	112.9	118.2	140.0	161.8	196.4	209.1	203.6	140.0
Barley	100.0	113.1	112.8	134.0	157.4	178.7	200.0	212.8	180.9
Oats	100.0	111.7	117.4	110.9	143.5	167.4	187.0	191.3	169.6
Wheatmeal	..	100.0	90.0	92.9	120.7	154.3	165.7	160.7	129.3
Herrings	100.0	79.8	67.5	107.9	113.5	98.4	104.8	118.3	132.5
Ham	100.0	106.0	93.7	127.3	141.0	147.6	160.0	156.5	159.4
Beef	100.0	110.5	113.4	124.7	142.9	149.8	174.5	172.9	175.3
Butter	100.0	108.4	105.0	105.8	131.4	140.4	146.3	154.0	155.5
Cheese	100.0	101.1	103.6	103.6	113.2	127.0	144.0	152.7	..
Indigo	100.0	83.9	91.5	89.0	91.5	86.6	87.8	97.6	103.7
Logwood	100.0	85.2	68.8	66.7	89.2	97.8	93.5	100.0	95.7
Saltpetre	100.0	97.9	89.1	89.4	91.3	140.8	152.3	164.2	145.8
Soda	..	..	..	..	..	..	..	..	..
Clover Seed	100.0	95.1	106.7	123.4	118.1	139.0	148.2	176.6	159.3
Rapeseed	100.0	..	..	..	..	..	..	..	..
Rapeseed Oil	100.0	101.0	98.9	94.3	103.1	124.1	159.2	148.7	142.8
Tar	100.0	106.2	112.5	103.1	100.0	164.1	171.9	118.7	104.7
Tallow	100.0	96.8	84.6	84.9	113.8	134.3	129.0	118.9	130.0
Wool	100.0	87.8	85.6	90.9	99.2	91.7	99.7	102.9	109.9
Cotton	100.0	70.6	83.3	73.1	81.8	77.8	77.0	84.1	105.6
Hemp	..	100.0	88.2	96.7	105.6	138.9	115.6	98.7	99.7
Linen	100.0	65.4	70.4	65.5	61.6	60.0	59.3	56.1	64.9
Rags	100.0	125.0	175.9	193.1	175.9	172.4	158.6	148.3	137.9
Skins	100.0	76.3	79.2	80.0	96.0	112.0	118.4	143.3	185.7
Calf Skin	100.0	98.0	83.8	78.4	87.6	95.2	102.1	109.2	135.1
Iron	100.0	91.2	72.0	74.2	109.7	122.6	110.8	114.0	112.9
Zinc	100.0	139.4	95.3	104.7	140.7	148.7	151.3	163.3	191.3
Lead	100.0	107.7	98.3	96.0	129.5	137.0	152.0	137.6	138.2
Copper	100.0	96.2	94.3	108.6	121.9	123.6	128.9	126.0	135.6
Tin	100.0	101.3	103.0	112.7	152.2	155.1	151.4	171.5	166.4
Pit Coal	100.0	100.0	85.7	85.7	114.3	128.6	128.6	128.6	100.0

The above table is framed on a basis of the average prices of 1831-40. This is represented by 100 in the first column ; the second column represents the average of prices with reference to this basis, during 1841-50, and the remaining columns the averages, with reference to the same basis, of each year from 1851 to 1857, inclusive. By comparing the first and second columns it will be seen that, on the whole, the prices of 1841-50 had fallen as compared with those of 1831-40, while by carrying the eye forward, the reader will find that after 1850 there is in the great majority of cases a rise, which in 1857 reaches a very high point, not only in relation to 1841-50, but in relation to 1831-40. The rise in prices thus shown is very much greater than that indicated by my tables, which is accounted for by the circumstance, that mine have been carried on to 1858, when the full effect of the reaction from the crisis of 1857 had been felt.

I.

STATEMENT OF THE CONCLUSIONS ARRIVED AT BY M. LAVASSEUR.

("JOURNAL DES ÉCONOMISTES," MARCH 1858.)

[*From the official statistics of French Prices, including all commodities produced or consumed in France from 1847 to 1856, inclusive.*]

NATURAL PRODUCTS.

	Per cent.	Per cent.
Actual increase in prices during the above period . . .		67·19
Proportion of increase due to war and scarcity	20	
Ditto to speculation	5	25·00
Increase in price of natural products		42·19

MANUFACTURED PRODUCTS.

	Per cent.	Per cent.
Actual increase in prices during the above period . . .		14·94
Proportion of increase due to war and scarcity	2	
Ditto due to speculation	5	7·00
Increase in price of manufactured products		7·94

By adding these results together and dividing by two, the average increase in price of all commodities is made out to be 25 per cent., from which 5 per cent. is deducted as an allowance "for the development of industry and the increase of consumers," thus bringing the advance in price, due to the depreciation of gold, to 20 per cent.

Exception might, I think, be taken to some of the principles by which M. Lavasseur arrives at this result ; *e.g.* the plan of averages is very apt to be deceptive, unless the commodities from which the averages are taken, are of equal or nearly equal importance ; and the principle of the last deduction of 5 per cent. as an allowance for "the development of industry and the increase of consumers," appears to me to be fallacious ; the development of industry and the increase of consumers having, except in the case of agricultural produce, a tendency to lower, instead of raising, price. But, passing by these considerations, the important fact remains, that French prices, comprehending those of all articles produced or consumed in France, have, after making liberal allowance for the effects of war, scarcity, and undue speculation, undergone since 1847 a marked rise, and that this rise has taken place (so far as the classification has been carried) in the manner according to which, supposing it to have proceeded from an increase of money, it might be expected to take place ; a fact which, I submit, affords a strong corroboration of the general truth of the views which I have advanced.

K.

EXTRACTS FROM DR. STRANG'S PAPER ON WAGES IN GLASGOW AND THE WEST OF SCOTLAND.

[*Read at the Meeting of the British Association in* 1858.]

AVERAGE RATE OF WAGES OF WORKERS IN FACTORIES (numbers not less than 30,000 in 1851, 1856, and 1858).

	1851.		1856.		1858.	
	s.	*d.*	*s.*	*d.*	*s.*	*d.*
Power-loom Weavers	8	9	10	9	9	9
Spinners	25	0	30	0	27	0
Winders	8	0	9	0	9	0
Warpers	12	0	17	0	16	6
Dressers	32	0	40	0	35	0
Tenters	30	0	40	0	38	0
Twisters	9	0	12	0	12	0
Mechanics	24	0	27	0	26	0
Labourers	12	0	17	0	15	0

WORKMEN IN MINES AND IRON WORKS (in number 31,900, total wages paid in 1854-5 1,976,000*l.*, ten hours a day).

	1852.		1854.		1856.		1858.	
	s.	*d.*	*s.*	*d.*	*s.*	*d.*	*s.*	*d.*
Miners	2	6	5	0	5	0	3	0
Blast furnace keepers ...	5	0	6	8	7	9	5	0
Do. assistants...	3	2	4	2	4	2	3	3
Do. fillers ...	2	8	3	10	4	2	3	9
Puddlers, including under hands	7	6	10	6	10	0	9	0
Rollers (chief rollers) ...	10	0	14	6	13	6	12	0
Labourers	1	6	2	1	2	0	2	0

ENGINEERS AND MECHANICS (per day).

Year.	Shillings.	Year.	Shillings.
1851	3'43	1855	3'99
1852	3'52	1856	4'00
1853	3'82	1857	3'97
1854	3'97	1858	3'92

WORKMEN ENGAGED IN THE BUILDING TRADE (ten hours a day).

QUARRIERS.		QUARRIERS.	
Year.	Shillings.	Year.	Shillings.
1851	16 per week.	1855	20 per week.
1852	16 „	1856	22 „
1853	17 „	1857	22 „
1854	19 „	1858	19–20 „

MASONS.

	s.	d.	
Summer of 1850 and '51	21	0	per week of 60 hours.
Winter do. do.	18	0	ditto.
Summer of 1852	21	0 & 18s.	ditto.
Do. 1853	23	9	ditto.
Do. 1854	25	0	ditto.
Do. 1855	25	0	ditto.
Do. 1856	25	0	ditto.

In September 1856, a change was made, and the rate fixed per hour, as follows :—

	d.		s.	d.	
September 19th, 1856 ...	5½	per hour or	26	11½	per week of 57 hours.
December 12th, „	5¼	„	24	11	ditto.
May 15th, 1857	5	„	23	9	ditto.
July 24th, „	5¼	„	24	11	ditto.
Aug. 7th, „	5½	„	26	1½	ditto.
Nov. 6th „	5	„	23	9	ditto.
March 1st, 1858	4¾	„	22	6¼	ditto.
August 1st, „	4¼	„	*22	6½	ditto.

CARPENTERS AND JOINERS.

s.		s.	
1851 ...... 21 per week of 60 hours.		1855.......... 24 per week of 57 hours.	
1852 ...... 24 ditto.		1856......... 24 ditto.	
1853 ...... 23 ditto.		1857 to Nov. 26 ditto.	
1854 ...... 24 ditto of 57 hours.		1858.........†24 ditto.	

COMMON LABOURERS (connected with all matters of house construction).

	s.	d.	
1850, '51, and '52	12	0	per week of 57 hours.
1853	14	0	ditto.
1854-5-6	17	0	ditto.
1857	16	0	ditto.
1858	15	9	ditto.

* Equal to 23s. 8¼d. per week of 60 hours.   † Equal to 25s. 3d. per week of 60 hours.

HAND-LOOM WEAVERS (per week, for men, boys, and girls).

	s.	d.		s.	d.
1851	5	8	1856	7	1
1852	6	9	1857	6	4
1853	7	0	1858	5	9

HAND-LOOM WEAVERS (fancy work).

		s.	d.	s.	d.	
1856	... ...	9	3	to 14	0	per week.
1858	... ...	7	0	to 5	9	„

Dr. Strang remarks that there has been a gradual diminution of hand-loom weavers during the last few years.

It will be desirable to add a few words in the way of explanation and comment on the tables now presented. And first, as to the standard of comparison which has been adopted. It appeared to me that, in selecting this, three leading considerations should be kept in view : first, that it should be taken from a period sufficiently long to allow, by the use of averages, of the elimination, as far as possible, of what is casual and exceptional ; secondly, that this period should exclude occasions of violent commercial agitation ; thirdly, that it should be continued to a point of time coinciding as nearly as possible with that at which the action of the new supplies of gold began to be felt. The period extending over 1849, 1850, and 1851, though not free from objection, appears to me, on the whole, to fulfil these conditions with tolerable fairness. It is in respect to the first that it principally errs, but the necessity of complying with the second and third (which I thought the more important conditions) left me no choice on this point ; for, had I extended the period from which the average is taken further back than 1849, it would have been brought under the influence of the powerfully disturbing occurrences of the years 1845, 1846, and 1847, including the Railway speculation of 1845 and 1846, the Irish famine of 1846 and 1847, and the commercial crisis of the last year ; while, on the other hand, to have carried it to a date later than 1851 would have been to bring it under the influence of the gold discoveries—that is to say, subjected that which was to be our standard of comparison to the action of the agency, the character of which it was our object to investigate. Indeed, with a view to American prices, the year 1851 is too late ; the demand springing up in California consequent on the gold discoveries, having previous to the close of that year produced a very decided effect on the American markets ; a circumstance which prevents the rise in American prices, as shown in the tables, from being as marked as it otherwise would be. If it be said that these objections might be obviated by taking a *longer* period *anterior* to 1845, this is true ; but, by doing so, we should have incurred others of a more serious kind. In the first place, there was to this course the practical objection arising from the difficulty of obtaining extensive returns of prices from so distant a period—a difficulty of which no one who has attempted to construct a table of prices on a large scale will think lightly; while it would have been further objectionable as not fulfilling the third of the three conditions which I have stated above—that of taking the standard of comparison from a period as close as possible to the epoch of the gold discoveries. To disregard this condition would be in no small degree to conceal the operation of the agency in question; there being a constant tendency in the progress of the mechanical arts and applied sciences to cheapen production, and thus, when any considerable period of time is allowed to elapse, to neutralize the effect of any cause, which, like the new gold, tends to raise prices. But, though not free from objection, I conceive the years 1849, 1850, and 1851 to form on the whole a fair basis of comparison; and this I think will appear from the following extracts from the Trade Reports of that time, which have been taken partly from the *Economist,* and partly from the 5th volume of the "History of Prices."

During the whole of 1848 the country was suffering from the depression consequent upon the reaction from the crisis of 1847, but by the close of that year and the opening of 1849 its prospects became more cheering. This is shown by the following extracts from the *Economist,* January 6th, 1849. *Lime Street, London.*—"At the close of this year, which has been so sadly eminent for dulness in the produce market, I have the pleasure to announce a decided improvement, which is more important for being so very unusual just at this period. The reports from our manufacturing districts are more favourable." *Manchester.*— "We have the satisfaction, at the termination of another remarkable and eventful year, of communicating to you the continuance of a decided improvement in the trade of this district." *Liverpool.*—"The wool-market continued in a state of great depression till the end of October. . . . During the past two months, however, we are glad to notice a considerable change for the better; a large business has been done both for the home trade and for export, and prices both of foreign and domestic wools have an upward tendency." On the other hand, the corn market is reported as at this time in a very depressed condition, "all classes holding back for the period of free trade becoming a great act; anticipating a still further reduction in value under its dreaded influence;" as were also the markets for colonial produce.

The anticipations, however, expressed in the passages I have extracted, of a general revival of commercial activity, were not realized during the first half of 1849, which must be regarded as a time of more than ordinary depression. About the middle of 1849, however, a decided improvement took place, as appears from the following report, dated October 31st, 1849:—"With the single exception of some branches of the cotton trade, I have the satisfaction of reporting a continued improvement up to a late period, and with every appearance of continued activity, at least for some months to come, to the extent to which it has now reached. The worsted stuff trade has been the one most active; this trade has never before reached anything like the extent to which it has now attained. Plain and fancy woollens have varied, ... but on the whole they have been very satisfactory. The silk trade has been brisk and prosperous." At the close of October (1849), the historian of prices informs us ("History of Prices," vol. v. p. 244)—that "there sprung up in the colonial markets a marked disposition to a speculative rise of prices. The tendency first manifested itself in coffee. . . . . From coffee the speculation gradually spread to several other articles." This buoyant state of the market, it appears, continued till the end of January 1850, at which time the reports announce that "the speculations in colonial produce appear to have in some measure subsided." The commercial character of 1849 appears thus to have been one of depression during the first half of the year, followed by a general revival of trade in the latter half, accompanied by a speculative rise of prices of certain markets : on the whole, we may consider the range of prices during this year as somewhat under the normal level.

At the opening of 1850 we are told, "the trade of the country was moderately active" ("History of Prices," vol. vi. p. 249) : and this representation is fully supported by quotations from the Trade Reports. Thus from Yorkshire the accounts say :—"I continue to receive very satisfactory reports as to the state of trade in all branches of manufactures throughout my district, except that portion engaged in spinning low numbers of cotton yarns, or manufacturing heavy cotton goods. The general condition of the factory workers, as regards employment and their ability, by good wages and low prices, to obtain food and clothing, is also satisfactory." (Ibid. p. 250.) The principal complaints at this time appear to have been in the cotton trade respecting the high price of raw cotton, which we are told "were general throughout 1850." In April 1850, the account from Lancashire was as follows :—"All the accounts I receive represent the woollen, worsted, flax, and silk mills to be in an active and prosperous state, and I have received similar good accounts of the larger portion of the different branches of trade in print works." (Ibid. pp. 250-1.) On July 6, 1850, the following reports appear in the *Economist:*—"Nothing has occurred during the past month to disturb the even and satisfactory course in which the commerce of the country appears to be now steadily proceeding. . . . The low prices of many foreign articles might have been expected to offer a sufficient inducement to speculative investment ; but such has not been the case, business having been in most instances restricted to the supply of the actual consumptive and export demand ; so great, however, is this demand at present for many of our silk, cotton, and woollen fabrics, that higher rates are obtainable than have been current for some years past ; and so far from the stocks of manufactured goods increasing, there is difficulty in getting orders executed except for forward delivery. From Liverpool the account at the same time was as follows :— "Throughout the manufacturing districts there is full employment, and trade is in the highest degree flourishing. At this season of the year

there is generally a large business doing in domestic wools, but the transactions have been to a greater extent than usual." From Manchester,
owing to the cause already adverted to, the scarcity and dearness of raw
cotton which continued throughout this year, the accounts were less favourable. In the review of this year's cotton trade (December 1850) given in
the " History of Prices," vol. v. pp. 255, 256, the following statements
appear :—" On the 1st of January, 1850, this quality (Middling Orleans)
was worth 6¼d. per pound, being 50 per cent. *higher* than at the commencement of 1849, and also of 1848. Speculators came freely into the market
early in 1850, basing their operations on the promising appearance of
trade in the manufacturing districts, and the unfavourable prospects of
the crop of American cotton. . . . . There was a trifling reaction in
August ; in September and October a recovery ; but in November a considerable fall, arising in apprehension of a war on the Continent. In
December, more activity ; and the year 1850 closed with a price of 7¼d.
per pound, or nearly 20 per cent. higher than at the opening." " In coffee,"
we are told, " there were considerable fluctuations during the year ;
the price in January 1850 having risen very considerably, under the
influence of bad crops from Brazil, and speculative purchases," falling in
June and rising again in September, from which time it rose steadily till
the end of the year. " In indigo and silk there were also some fluctuations arising out of reports of deficient crops." " In the sugar market the
year 1850 has been marked, on the whole, by a very steady maintenance of
prices." Of the ship-building trade we are told that " new British ships
have fully maintained our last quotations ; indeed, we have felt the want of
a larger supply of good vessels, which would have met with a ready sale
at fair prices if at hand." The review of this year is thus summed up :—
" As a general rule there was a disposition in the latter half of 1850, in all
the great markets of produce, to look forward to considerably higher
prices, on the twofold ground of increasing consumption, and of the
probable failure of the usual supplies." (Ibid. p. 258.)

The opening of the year 1851 is thus chronicled :—"The year 1851
opened with fair prospects. . . . . Prices of colonial produce were firm
and rising ; and already the export trade to the United States began to
exhibit the influence of the large consumption in California." (Ibid.
p. 258.) A reaction, however, from this favourable condition of things
occurred in the spring, and on April 3, 1851, there was the following
report from Yorkshire :—" In various branches there has been a considerable quantity of machinery either unemployed or working for a shorter
period than for many previous months. This has not been extended to
all branches of trade at the same time or in the same degree. . . . . In
the neighbourhood of Huddersfield nearly all branches of the woollen
trade are represented to be at this moment very flat and depressed."
(Ibid.) At Liverpool the price of cotton had fallen at the end of May to
a point as much as 60 or 70 per cent. below the prices current in the
previous January. " Throughout July, August, and September there was

great depression in the produce markets of London and Liverpool. Prices had failed to correspond with expectations formed, and had fallen considerably instead of having risen. . . . About the end of September, however, the markets began to revive. The reports from Manchester represent the home trade as decidedly better." (Ibid. p. 261.) "When the period arrived for taking a review of the twelve months, the retrospect was of a mixed character. . . . But, as a general rule, the close of 1851 was distinguished by a range of prices in almost every branch of trade and manufacture *lower* than had prevailed for a very long period."

On a survey of the three years we may say that they embraced a period of chequered character, not free from commercial vicissitudes, but undisturbed by commercial convulsion. The range of prices in 1849 was perhaps rather under the usual level, but on the other hand "in 1850 prices had in most cases risen considerably above their ordinary level." ("Hist. of Prices," vol. v. p. 265.) This high range of prices appears to have culminated in January 1851, from which point there was a decline, which appears to have touched its lowest range about August of this year, after which a revival set in ; prices, however, at the end of the year remaining still greatly depressed when compared with the high level they had attained at its opening. There is one important class of articles, indeed, which throughout the whole of this period continued at a low range, namely agricultural produce : this was owing principally to two causes, viz. favourable seasons and free trade which had at this time just come into force : but, on the other hand, there were others scarcely less important, which ruled throughout at prices much above what had been their usual level for many years previously, *e.g.* raw cotton and wool ; the former of these articles being maintained throughout the greater portion of the whole period at from 50 to 80 per cent. above what had for many years been the prevailing price ; and the latter also at what were considered very high rates.

Such being the grounds on which the years 1849, 1850, and 1851 have been taken as a standard of comparison, it remains that I should explain the principles on which the tables have been constructed, and the significance of the results which they embody.

And first as to the sources from which the foregoing returns have been taken : these are as follows, viz.—for agricultural produce, the Gazette returns, as given either in the Statistical Abstract published by Government, or in the *Economist;* for butcher's meat and potatoes, the Registrar-General's quarterly returns ; for cotton (American), a series of tables published lately by Mr. Spence of Manchester, entitled, "The Course of Corn, Cotton, and Money ;" the figures in the columns marked P in the tables have been furnished to me by private merchants extensively engaged in transactions with the articles to which they relate ; a few columns have been taken from the tables in the sixth volume of the "History of Prices," and the remainder from the Prices Current published weekly in the *Economist.* The prices are, as a general rule, the prices of the London markets, though in some instances they refer to others, but the locality of the market is evidently unimportant, provided the quotations for any given article refer throughout the whole period to the *same* market, and this rule has been always observed. The same principle obviously applies to foreign as well as to home commodities. The prices, *e.g.* of cotton wool, of tobacco, of tea, or of sugar, will always be higher (I speak of bond prices) in London than in the countries of their production, by the cost of transmission *plus* the profit on the capital invested in the trade, and these elements, it is true, will vary for short intervals, but taken over long periods they will on an average be the same. The variations of prices therefore in the London markets will on an average show the variations of prices in the markets of the producing countries.

Of articles subject to import duties, the prices quoted are, with one or two unimportant exceptions which are duly notified in a footnote, the *bond* prices.

From the commodities comprised in the tables silver has been designedly excluded, because, contrary to what is sometimes supposed, silver, of all articles, forms the most fallacious criterion of changes in the value of gold, owing to the circumstance that silver and gold, wherever a double standard of value exists, and to some extent even where it does not, are made to perform the same functions, and can be reciprocally substituted one for the other ; the effect of which is that a fall in the value of gold is always attended with a fall in the value of silver, though not necessarily to the same extent.

The tables have been constructed with a view to exhibit the operation of the principles which in the preceding paper I have endeavoured to establish ; the classification being made according to the countries in which the commodities are produced, and the mode of their production. To the complete carrying out of this principle several practical difficulties occur. Thus there is an important group of commodities which are not produced in any of the leading commercial countries of the world, and which do not therefore properly fall under any of the above heads— West Indian commodities. These are obviously too important to be omitted from any table purporting to represent the progress of prices, but, on the other hand, they do not conveniently fit into any of the departments laid down. As on the whole the least objectionable plan, I have added them as a distinct group to the productions of the United Kingdom ; for, although tropical commodities, they are the produce for the most part of British capital, and are more under the influence of our monetary system than that of any other country. Again, it will be found that there are many commodities which are common to several classes. Of these grain is by far the most important ; the others being cotton, rice, tallow, oils, rape, and a few more. It is, as I have pointed out (*ante*, pp. 70, 71), through the medium of such commodities that the most powerful corrective is supplied to that local divergence of prices which it is the object of these tables to illustrate. In proportion therefore as such commodities are found in the several tables, will the operation of the principles to which I call attention be neutralized, and the phenomenon in question be less striking.

The tables, though containing altogether about one hundred commodities, I must admit to be in a very incomplete state. It will be remembered, however, that *I do not base any theory upon them.* The theory which I have advanced stands on entirely independent grounds, namely, the conditions of production affecting different classes of commodities, the peculiar character of the monetary systems existing in different countries, the commercial channels by which the new gold is diffused, and lastly the principles of monetary science. In their present form I cannot even claim for these tables a verification of that theory : all that I assume for them is that they afford so extensive an illustration of the principles which I have advanced as to warrant me in feeling considerable confidence in their general soundness. Thus, if the reader will glance over Table G, which shows at one view the result of the comparison instituted in the previous returns, he will find that out of the whole number of commodities included in it, which amounts to nearly one hundred, only six have fallen since the epoch of 1849-51 : the remainder have all risen, and the greater number in a very marked manner ; and he will find further, that in this progress of prices the advance has on the whole taken place in the order in which, as I have endeavoured to show, prices may be expected to advance under an increase of the precious metals. Thus he will find Victorian prices to have advanced in the proportion of about 200 per cent., or rather more. He will find the movement in English and American prices on the whole greater than in the prices of Continental Europe, while these latter show a greater advance than prices in Asia. This local divergence of prices will be very remarkable if we take some leading commodities of British and American produce, and contrast them with some of the leading products of Asia. Thus, if we take provisions and butcher's meat, the metals, agricultural produce, raw cotton, and tobacco, and compare these with some principal Asiatic products, as cotton, silk, coffee, tea, sugar, rice, and spices, we shall find that while the prices of the former articles have risen from 15 to 45 per cent. as compared with their prices in 1849-51, the prices of the latter have in no case risen more than 15 per cent., and have in several cases positively fallen—in one important article, rice, by so much as 11 per cent. The only important Asiatic products in which a marked rise in price has taken place are saltpetre and indigo, and in both these cases the rise is owing to causes of an exceptional nature—in saltpetre to a greatly increased consumption during the last four years, consequent upon causes too numerous here to mention, combined with the obstacles presented to a rapid extension of the supply by the scarcity of the peculiar clays from which this article is principally obtained ; and in indigo owing to the interruption given to the operations of the indigo planters by the Mutiny, and to the speculative transactions to which this event gave occasion. It will be seen, too, that, on the whole, the other doctrines of the paper are pretty well borne out. Thus the advance in raw materials is much greater than in manufactured articles, while amongst raw materials the advance is more marked in animal than in vegetable products ; such articles, e.g., as leather, tallow, provisions, and butcher's meat showing a very remarkable rise.

I have appended to my own tables an abstract of the results arrived at by Dr. Soetbeer of Hamburg, in his " Beiträge zur Statistik der Preise," for which I am indebted to the kindness of the Archbishop of Dublin, as well as a statement of M. Levasseur's conclusions as to the progress of prices in France during the period of 1847 to 1856. It will be seen that the conclusions of both these writers, derived from independent data, and reached by modes of investigation entirely different from mine, concur in supporting not only the general position of a rise in prices, but also, *so far as they go*, the particular doctrines which I have ventured to advance respecting the mode in which this rise must take place. On the other hand Mr. Newmarch (the author, in conjunction with the late Mr. Tooke, of the fifth and sixth volumes of the " History of Prices "), in a communication made to the British Association at its meeting in Leeds in *September*, 1858, maintained that prices were then *rather lower than previous to the gold discoveries*, and that no depreciation in the value of money had up to that time taken place ; resting his conclusions on certain tables which he then produced. To account, however, for the discordance of Mr. Newmarch's conclusions as well with mine as with those of others who have investigated the same problem, it is only necessary to state, first, that the tables on which he based his conclusions contained *not more than twenty commodities*, and excluded almost all those in which the advance has been most marked ; and secondly, that the standard of comparison which he adopted was *a single quotation in January*, 1851 ; that being, as I have shown above, as well from Mr. Newmarch's own writings as from other authorities, *the culminating point of an ascending movement* in prices which had commenced in the beginning of the preceding year. Under these circumstances, the standard of comparison being exceptionally high, the object of comparison—that is to say, the prices in *September*, 1858—being (owing to the reaction consequent on the commercial crisis of the previous autumn) exceptionally low, and the comparison being limited to a select number of commodities, it is not strange that the conclusion should have been different from that of other writers who proceeded upon different principles.

For the returns of wages in Glasgow and the West of Scotland, given in Table K, I am indebted to Dr. Strang, who kindly allowed me to copy them from the valuable paper on that subject which he read before the British Association in September last. I had hoped to have extended this portion of the subject by adding to these some returns of wages in Ireland, but the materials which I have yet obtained for this purpose are not sufficiently extensive to be worth publication. It will be seen, however, that Dr. Strang's tables, so far as they go, fully support the general views advanced.

I cannot conclude without gratefully acknowledging the assistance I have received, while compiling these tables, from several gentlemen, both in this country (Ireland) and in England, to whom I have had occasion to apply for information, and who, as well by procuring me returns as by the observations with which in some instances they have accompanied them, have afforded me very material aid. I shall only further add that, as I cannot but fear that many inaccuracies may have found their way into the foregoing tables notwithstanding my anxiety to avoid them, I shall feel obliged to anyone who will do me the favour of pointing out any error he may detect, whether in the way of omission or of commission, and still more so if he will afford me the means of correcting it. Such criticism will be the more acceptable, as I purpose carrying on these tables with a view to exhibit the future progress of depreciation, and hope on some future occasion to be able to publish them in a form less incomplete and fragmentary than that in which, owing to unavoidable circumstances, they at present appear. [This intention the writer has been prevented from carrying into effect.]

THE END.

ONDON :

R. CLAY, SONS, AND TAYLOR, PRINTERS.

BREAD STREET HILL.

*MACMILLAN & CO.'S CATALOGUE of Works in
BELLES LETTRES, including Poetry,
Fiction, Works on Art, Critical and
Literary Essays, etc.*

Allingham.—LAURENCE BLOOMFIELD IN IRELAND ;
or, the New Landlord. By WILLIAM ALLINGHAM. New and
Cheaper Issue, with a Preface. Fcap. 8vo. cloth. 4*s*. 6*d*.

*The aim of this little book is to do something, however small, towards
making Ireland, yet so little known to the general British public,
better understood. Several of the most important problems of life,
Irish life and human life, are dealt with in their principles,
according to the author's best lights. In the new Preface, the
state of Ireland, with special reference to the Church measure, is
discussed. " It is vital with the national character. . . . . It has
something of Pope's point and Goldsmith's simplicity, touched to a
more modern issue."*—ATHENÆUM.

Arnold.—Works by MATTHEW ARNOLD :—

THE COMPLETE POETICAL WORKS. Vol. I. NARRATIVE
AND ELEGIAC POEMS. Vol. II. DRAMATIC AND LYRIC POEMS.
Extra fcap. 8vo. Price 6*s*. each.

*The two volumes comprehend the First and Second Series of the
Poems, and the New Poems. "Thyrsis is a poem of perfect
delight, exquisite in grave tenderness of reminiscence, rich in breadth
of western light, breathing full the spirit of gray and ancient Oxford."*—SATURDAY REVIEW. *"The noblest in it is clothed in
clearest words. There is no obscurity, no useless ornament: everything is simple, finished, and perfect."*—SCOTSMAN.

A

Arnold—*continued.*

ESSAYS IN CRITICISM.   New Edition, with Additions.   Extra fcap. 8vo. 6s.

> *The Essays in this Volume are—"The Function of Criticism at the Present Time;" "The Literary Influence of Academies;" "Maurice de Guerin;" "Eugenie de Guerin;" "Heinrich Heine;" "Pagan and Mediæval;" "Religious Sentiment;" "Joubert;" "Spinoza and the Bible;" "Marcus Aurelius." Both from the subjects dealt with and mode of treatment, few books are more calculated to delight, inform, and stimulate than these charming Essays.*

Bacon's Essays.—See GOLDEN TREASURY SERIES.

Baker.—(For other Works by the same Author, see CATALOGUE OF TRAVELS.)

CAST UP BY THE SEA ; OR, THE ADVENTURES OF NED GREY. By SIR SAMUEL BAKER, M.A., F.R.G.S., With Illustrations by HUARD. Fourth Edition. Crown 8vo. cloth gilt. 7s. 6d.

> *" An admirable tale of adventure, of marvellous incidents, wild exploits, and terrible dénoûments."—*DAILY NEWS. *"A story of adventure by sea and land in the good old style."—*PALL MALL GAZETTE.

Ballad Book.—See GOLDEN TREASURY SERIES.

Baring-Gould.—Works by S. BARING-GOULD. M.A. :—

IN EXITU ISRAEL. An Historical Novel. Two Vols. 8vo. 21s.

> *" Some of its most powerful passages — and fre. ously powerful they are—are descriptions of familiar c.... in the earlier days of the Revolution."—*LITERARY CHURCHMAN. *" Full of the in st exciting incidents and ably portrayed characters, abounding in beautifully attractive legends, and relieved by descriptions fresh, vivid, and truth-like."—*WESTMINSTER REVIEW

Baring-Gould—*continued.*

LEGENDS OF OLD TESTAMENT CHARACTERS, from the Talmud and other sources. Two vols. Crown 8vo. 16*s.* Vol. I. Adam to Abraham. Vol. II. Melchizedek to Zachariah.

Mr. Baring-Gould has here collected from the Talmud and other sources, Jewish and Mohammedan, a large number of curious and interesting legends concerning the principal characters of the Old Testament, comparing these frequently with similar legends current among many of the nations, savage and civilized, all over the world. " These volumes contain much that is very strange, and, to the ordinary English reader, very novel."—DAILY NEWS.

Barker.—Works by LADY BARKER :—

"Lady Barker is an unrivalled story-teller."—GUARDIAN.

STATION LIFE IN NEW ZEALAND. New and Cheaper Edition. Crown 8vo. 3*s.* 6*d.*

These letters are the exact account of a lady's experience of the brighter and less practical side of colonization. They record the expeditions, adventures, and emergencies diversifying the daily life of the wife of a New Zealand sheep-farmer; and, as each was written while the novelty and excitement of the scenes it describes were fresh upon her, they may succeed in giving here in England an adequate impression of the delight and freedom of an existence so far removed from our own highly-wrought civilization. " We have never read a more truthful or a pleasanter little book."—ATHENÆUM.

SPRING COMEDIES. STORIES.

CONTENTS :—A Wedding Story—A Stupid Story—A Scotch Story —A Man's Story. Crown 8vo. 7*s.* 6*d.*

"Lady Barker is endowed with a rare and delicate gift for narrating stories,—she has the faculty of throwing even into her printed narrative a soft and pleasant tone, which goes far to make the reader think the subject or the matter immaterial, so long as the author will go on telling stories for his benefit."—ATHENÆUM.

STORIES ABOUT :—With Six Illustrations. Second 'Edition. Extra fcap. 8vo. 4*s.* 6*d.*

Barker—*continued.*

This volume contains several entertaining stories about Monkeys, Jamaica, Camp Life, Dogs, Boys, &c. "There is not a tale in the book which can fail to please children as well as their elders." —PALL MALL GAZETTE.

A CHRISTMAS CAKE IN FOUR QUARTERS. With Illustrations by JELLICOE. Second Edition. Extra feap. 8vo. cloth gilt. 4s. 6d.

In this little volume, Lady Barker, whose reputation as a delightful story-teller is established, narrates four pleasant stories showing how the "Great Birth-day" is kept in the "Four Quarters" of the globe,—in England, Jamaica, India, and New Zealand. The volume is illustrated by a number of well-executed cuts. "Contains just the stories that children should be told. 'Christmas Cake' is a delightful Christmas book."—GLOBE.

Bell.—ROMANCES AND MINOR POEMS. By HENRY GLASSFORD BELL. Fcap. 8vo. 6s.

"Full of life and genius."—COURT CIRCULAR.

Besant.—STUDIES IN EARLY FRENCH POETRY. By WALTER BESANT, M.A. Crown. 8vo. 8s. 6d.

A sort of impression rests on most minds that French literature begins with the "siècle de Louis Quatorze;" any previous literature being for the most part unknown or ignored. Few know anything of the enormous literary activity that began in the thirteenth century, was carried on by Rulebeuf, Marie de France, Gaston de Foix, Thibault de Champagne, and Lorris; was fostered by Charles of Orleans, by Margaret of Valois, by Francis the First; that gave a crowd of versifiers to France, enriched, strengthened, developed, and fixed the French language, and prepared the way for Corneille and for Racine. The present work aims to afford information and direction touching the early efforts of France in poetical literature. "In one moderately sized volume he has contrived to introduce us to the very best, if not to all of the early French poets."—ATHENÆUM.

Book of Golden Deeds.—See GOLDEN TREASURY SERIES.

Book of Golden Thoughts.—See GOLDEN TREASURY SERIES.

Book of Praise.—See GOLDEN TREASURY SERIES.

Brimley.—ESSAYS BY THE LATE GEORGE BRIMLEY, M.A. Edited by the Rev. W. G. CLARK, M.A. With Portrait. Cheaper Edition. Fcap. 8vo. 2s. 6d.

George Brimley was regarded by those who knew him as "one of the finest critics of the day." The Essays contained in this volume are all more or less critical, and were contributed by the author to some of the leading periodicals of the day. The subjects are, " Tennyson's Poems," " Wordsworth's Poems," "Poetry and Criticism," " The Angel in the House," Carlyle's "Life of Sterling," "Esmond," "My Novel," "Bleak House," " Westward Ho!" Wilson's "Noctes Ambrosianæ," Comte's "Positive Philosophy." " It will," JOHN BULL says, "be a satisfaction to the admirers of sound criticism and unassuming common sense to find that the Essays of the late George Brimley have reappeared in a new and popular form. They will give a healthy stimulus to that spirit of inquiry into the real value of our literary men whose names we too often revere without sufficient investigation."

Broome.—THE STRANGER OF SERIPHOS. A Dramatic Poem. By FREDERICK NAPIER BROOME. Fcap. 8vo. 5s.

Founded on the Greek legend of Danaë and Perseus. "Grace and beauty of expression are Mr. Broome's characteristics ; and these qualities are displayed in many passages."—ATHENÆUM. " The story is rendered with consummate beauty."—LITERARY CHURCHMAN.

Bunyan's Pilgrim's Progress.—See GOLDEN TREASURY SERIES.

Burke.—EDMUND BURKE, a Historical Study. By JOHN MORLEY, B.A., Oxon. Crown 8vo. 7s. 6d.

" The style is terse and incisive, and brilliant with epigram and point. Its sustained power of reasoning, its wide sweep of observation and reflection, its elevated ethical and social tone, stamp it as

a work of high excellence."—SATURDAY REVIEW. *"A model of compact condensation. We have seldom met with a book in which so much matter was compressed into so limited a space."*—PALL MALL GAZETTE. *"An essay of unusual effort."*—WESTMINSTER REVIEW.

Burns' Works.—See GOLDEN TREASURY SERIES and GLOBE LIBRARY.

Carroll.—Works by "LEWIS CARROLL:"—

ALICE'S ADVENTURES IN WONDERLAND. With Forty-two Illustrations by TENNIEL. 33rd Thousand. Crown 8vo. cloth. 6s.

A GERMAN TRANSLATION OF THE SAME. With TEN-NIEL'S Illustrations. Crown 8vo. gilt. 6s.

A FRENCH TRANSLATION OF THE SAME. With TEN-NIEL'S Illustrations. Crown 8vo. gilt. 6s.

AN ITALIAN TRANSLATION OF THE SAME. By T. P. ROSSETTE. With TENNIEL'S Illustrations. Crown 8vo. 6s.

"Beyond question supreme among modern books for children."—SPECTATOR. *" One of the choicest and most charming books ever composed for a child's reading."*—PALL MALL GAZETTE. *" A very pretty and highly original book, sure to delight the little world of wondering minds, and which may well please those who have unfortunately passed the years of wondering."*—TIMES.

THROUGH THE LOOKING-GLASS, AND WHAT ALICE FOUND THERE. With Fifty Illustrations by TENNIEL. Crown 8vo. 6s. 23rd Thousand.

In the present volume is described, with inimitably clever and laughter-moving nonsense, the further Adventures of the fairy-favoured Alice, in the grotesque world which she found to exist on the other side of her mother's drawing-room looking-glass, through which she managed to make her way. The work is profusely embellished with illustrations by Tenniel, exhibiting as great an amount of humour as those to which "Alice's Adventures in Wonderland" owed so much of its popularity.

Carroll—*continued.*

PHANTASMAGORIA, AND OTHER POEMS. Fcap. 8vo. gilt edges. 6*s.*

"*Those who have not made acquaintance with these poems already have a pleasure to come. The comical is so comical, and the grave so really beautiful.*"—LITERARY CHURCHMAN.

Chatterton : A BIOGRAPHICAL STUDY. By DANIEL WILSON, LL.D., Professor of History and English Literature in University College, Toronto. Crown 8vo. 6*s.* 6*d.*

The author here regards Chatterton as a Poet, not as a "mere resetter and defacer of stolen literary treasures." Reviewed in this light, he has found much in the old materials capable of being turned to new account : and to these materials research in various directions has enabled him to make some additions. He believes that the boy-poet has been misjudged, and that the biographies hitherto written of him are not only imperfect but untrue. While dealing tenderly, the author has sought to deal truthfully with the failings as well as the virtues of the boy : bearing always in remembrance, what has been too frequently lost sight of, that he was but a boy;—a boy, and yet a poet of rare power. The EXAMINER *thinks this "the most complete and the purest biography of the poet which has yet appeared.*"

Children's Garland from the Best Poets.—See GOLDEN TREASURY SERIES.

Church (A. J.)—HORÆ TENNYSONIANÆ, Sive Eclogæ e Tennysono Latine redditæ. Cura A. J. CHURCH, A.M. Extra fcap. 8vo. 6*s.*

Latin versions of Selections from Tennyson. Among the authors are the Editor, the late Professor Conington, Professor Seeley, Dr. Hessey, Mr. Kebbel, and other gentlemen. "Of Mr. Church's ode we may speak in almost unqualified praise, and the same may be said of the contributions generally."—PALL MALL GAZETTE.

Clough (Arthur Hugh).—THE POEMS AND PROSE REMAINS OF ARTHUR HUGH CLOUGH. With a

Clough (Arthur Hugh)—*continued.*

Selection from his Letters and a Memoir. Edited by his Wife. With Portrait. Two Vols. Crown 8vo. 21*s.* Or Poems separately, as below.

The late Professor Clough is well known as a graceful, tender poet, and as the scholarly translator of Plutarch. The letters possess high interest, not biographical only, but literary—discussing, as they do, the most important questions of the time, always in a genial spirit. The "Remains" include papers on "Retrenchment at Oxford;" on Professor F. W. Newman's book, "The Soul;" on Wordsworth; on the Formation of Classical English; on some Modern Poems (Matthew Arnold and the late Alexander Smith), &c. &c. "Taken as a whole," the SPECTATOR *says, "these volumes cannot fail to be a lasting monument of one of the most original men of our age." "Full of charming letters from Rome," says the* MORNING STAR, *"from Greece, from America, from Oxford, and from Rugby."*

THE POEMS OF ARTHUR HUGH CLOUGH, sometime Fellow of Oriel College, Oxford. Third Edition. Fcap. 8vo. 6*s.*

"From the higher mind of cultivated, all-questioning, but still conservative England, in this our puzzled generation, we do not know of any utterance in literature so characteristic as the poems of Arthur Hugh Clough."—FRASER'S MAGAZINE.

Clunes.—THE STORY OF PAULINE: an Autobiography. By G. C. CLUNES. Crown 8vo. 6*s.*

"Both for vivid delineation of character and fluent lucidity of style, 'The Story of Pauline' is in the first rank of modern fiction."— GLOBE. *"Told with delightful vivacity, thorough appreciation of life, and a complete knowledge of character."*—MANCHESTER EXAMINER.

Collects of the Church of England. With a beautifully Coloured Floral Design to each Collect, and Illuminated Cover. Crown 8vo. 12*s.* Also kept in various styles of morocco.

In this richly embellished edition of the Church Collects, the paper is thick and handsome and the type large and beautiful, each Collect, with a few exceptions, being printed on a separate page. The dis-

*tinctive characteristic of this edition is the floral design which ac-
companies each Collect, and which is generally emblematical of the
character of the day or saint to which it is assigned; the flowers
which have been selected are such as are likely to be in bloom on the
day to which the Collect belongs. Each flower is richly but tastefully and naturally printed in colours, and from the variety of
plants selected and the faithfulness of the illustrations to nature,
the volume should form an instructive and interesting companion
to all devout Christians, who are likely to find their devotions assisted
and guided by having thus brought before them the flowers in their
seasons, God's beautiful and never-failing gifts to men. The Preface explains the allusion in the case of all those illustrations which
are intended to be emblematical of the days to which they belong, and
the Table of Contents forms a complete botanical index, giving both
the popular and scientific name of each plant. There are at least
one hundred separate plants figured. " This is beyond question,"
the ART JOURNAL says, " the most beautiful book of the season."
" Carefully, indeed livingly drawn and daintily coloured," says the
PALL MALL GAZETTE. The GUARDIAN thinks it " a successful
attempt to associate in a natural and unforced manner the flowers
of our fields and gardens with the course of the Christian year."*

Cowper's Poetical Works.—See GLOBE LIBRARY.

Cox.—RECOLLECTIONS OF OXFORD. By G. V. COX, M.A.,
late Esquire Bedel and Coroner in the University of Oxford.
Second and cheaper Edition. Crown 8vo. 6s.

*Mr. Cox's Recollections date from the end of last century to quite
recent times. They are full of old stories and traditions, epigrams
and personal traits of the distinguished men who have been at
Oxford during that period. The TIMES says that it "will
pleasantly recall in many a country parsonage the memory of
youthful days."*

Dante.—DANTE'S COMEDY, THE HELL. Translated by
W. M. ROSSETTI. Fcap. 8vo. cloth. 5s.

*" The aim of this translation of Dante may be summed up in one
word—Literality. To follow Dante sentence for sentence, line
for line, word for word—neither more nor less, has been my
strenuous endeavour."—AUTHOR'S PREFACE.*

Days of Old ; STORIES FROM OLD ENGLISH HISTORY.

By the Author of "Ruth and her Friends." New Edition.
18mo. cloth, gilt leaves. 3s. 6d.

*The Contents of this interesting and instructive volume are, " Cara-
doc and Dwa," a story of British life in the first century;
" Wolfgan and the Earl; or, Power," a story of Saxon England : and " Roland," a story of the Crusaders. " Full of truthful and charming historic pictures, is everywhere vital with moral
and religious principles, and is written with a brightness of description, and with a dramatic force in the representation of
character, that have made, and will always make, it one of the
greatest favourites with reading boys."—*NONCONFORMIST.

De Vere.—THE INFANT BRIDAL, and other Poems. By
AUDREY DE VERE. Fcap. 8vo. 7s. 6d.

*" Mr. De Vere has taken his place among the poets of the day.
Pure and tender feeling, and that polished restraint of style which
is called classical, are the charms of the volume."*—SPECTATOR.

Doyle (Sir F. H.)—Works by Sir FRANCIS HASTINGS DOYLE,
Professor of Poetry in the University of Oxford :—

THE RETURN OF THE GUARDS, AND OTHER POEMS.
Fcap. 8vo. 7s.

*" Good wine needs no bush, nor good verse a preface; and Sir Francis
Doyle's verses run bright and clear, and smack of a classic vintage.
. . . His chief characteristic, as it is his greatest charm, is the
simple manliness which gives force to all he writes. It is a characteristic in these days rare enough."*—EXAMINER.

LECTURES ON POETRY, delivered before the University of
Oxford in 1868. Crown 8vo. 3s. 6d.

*THREE LECTURES :—(1) Inaugural, in which the nature of Poetry
is discussed; (2) Provincial Poetry; (3) Dr. Newman's " Dream
of Gerontius." " Full of thoughtful discrimination and fine insight: the lecture on ' Provincial Poetry' seems to us singularly
true, eloquent, and instructive."*—SPECTATOR. *" All these dis-
sertations are marked by a scholarly spirit, delicate taste, and the
discriminating powers of a trained judgment."*—DAILY NEWS.

Dryden's Poetical Works.—See GLOBE LIBRARY.

Dürer, Albrecht.—HISTORY OF THE LIFE OF AL-
BRECHT DÜRER, of Nürnberg. With a Translation of his
Letters and Journal, and some account of his Works. By Mrs.
CHARLES HEATON. Royal 8vo. bevelled boards, extra gilt. 31s. 6d.

*This work contains about Thirty Illustrations, ten of which are pro-
ductions by the autotype (carbon) process, and are printed in permanent tints by Messrs. Cundall and Fleming, under licence from
the Autotype Company, Limited ; the rest are Photographs and
Woodcuts.*

Estelle Russell.—By the Author of "The Private Life of
Galileo." Crown 8vo. 6s.

*Full of bright pictures of French life. The English family, whose
fortunes form the main drift of the story, reside mostly in France, but
there are also many English characters and scenes of great interest.
It is certainly the work of a fresh, vigorous, and most interesting
writer, with a dash of sarcastic humour which is refreshing and
not too bitter. " We can send our readers to it with confidence."*
—SPECTATOR.

Evans.—BROTHER FABIAN'S MANUSCRIPT, AND
OTHER POEMS. By SEBASTIAN EVANS. Fcap. 8vo. cloth. 6s.

*" In this volume we have full assurance that he has ' the vision and
the faculty divine.' . . . Clever and full of kindly humour."*—
GLOBE.

Fairy Book.—The Best Popular Fairy Stories. Selected and
Rendered anew by the Author of "John Halifax, Gentleman."
With Coloured Illustrations and Ornamental Borders by J. E.
ROGERS, Author of " Ridicula Rediviva." Crown 8vo. cloth,
extra gilt. 6s. (Golden Treasury Edition. 18mo. 4s. 6d.)

" A delightful selection, in a delightful external form."—SPECTATOR.
*Here are reproduced in a new and charming dress many old
favourites, as " Hop-o'-my-Thumb," " Cinderella," " Beauty and
the Beast," " Jack the Giant-killer," " Tom Thumb," " Rumpel-
stilzchen," " Jack and the Bean-stalk," " Red Riding-Hood,"
" The Six Swans," and a great many others. " A book which
will prove delightful to children all the year round."*—PALL MALL
GAZETTE.

Fletcher.—THOUGHTS FROM A GIRL'S LIFE. By LUCY FLETCHER. Second Edition. Fcap. 8vo. 4*s.* 6*d.*

"*Sweet and earnest verses, especially addressed to girls, by one who can sympathise with them, and who has endeavoured to give articulate utterance to the vague aspirations after a better life of pious endeavour, which accompany the unfolding consciousness of the inner life in girlhood. The poems are all graceful; they are marked throughout by an accent of reality; the thoughts and emotions are genuine.*"— ATHENÆUM.

Freeman (E. A., Hon. D.C.L.) — HISTORICAL ESSAYS. By EDWARD FREEMAN, M.A., Hon. D.C.L., late Fellow of Trinity College, Oxford. Second Edition. 8vo. 10*s.* 6*d.*

This volume contains twelve Essays selected from the author's contributions to various Reviews. The principle on which they were chosen was that of selecting papers which referred to comparatively modern times, or, at least, to the existing states and nations of Europe. By a sort of accident a number of the pieces chosen have thrown themselves into something like a continuous series bearing on the historical causes of the great events of 1870—71. *Notes have been added whenever they seemed to be called for; and whenever he could gain in accuracy of statement or in force or clearness of expression, the author has freely changed, added to, or left out, what he originally wrote. To many of the Essays has been added a short note of the circumstances under which they were written. It is needless to say that any product of Mr. Freeman's pen is worthy of attentive perusal: and it is believed that the contents of this volume will throw light on several subjects of great historical importance and the widest interest. The following is a list of the subjects :—I. "The Mythical and Romantic Elements in Early English History;" II. "The Continuity of English History;" III. "The Relations between the Crowns of England and Scotland;" IV. "St. Thomas of Canterbury and his Biographers;" V. "The Reign of Edward the Third;" VI. "The Holy Roman Empire;" VII. "The Franks and the Gauls;" VIII. "The Early Sieges of Paris;" IX. "Frederick the First, King of Italy;" X. "The Emperor Frederick the Second;" XI. "Charles the Bold;" XII. "Presidential Government."— "All of them are well worth reading, and very agreeable to read. He never touches a*

*question without adding to our comprehension of it, without leaving
the impression of an ample knowledge, a righteous purpose, a clear
and powerful understanding."*—SATURDAY REVIEW.

Garnett.—IDYLLS AND EPIGRAMS. Chiefly from the Greek
Anthology. By RICHARD GARNETT. Fcap. 8vo. 2s. 6d.

*"A charming little book. For English readers, Mr. Garnett's
translations will open a new world of thought."*—WESTMINSTER
REVIEW.

Geikie.—SCENERY OF SCOTLAND, viewed in Connexion
with its Physical Geology. By ARCHIBALD GEIKIE, F.R.S.,
Director of the Geological Survey of Scotland. With Illustrations
and a New Geological Map. Crown 8vo. 10s. 6d.

*"Before long, we doubt not, it will be one of the travelling companions
of every cultivated tourist in Scotland."*—EDINBURGH COURANT.
"Amusing, picturesque, and instructive."—TIMES. *"There is
probably no one who has so thoroughly mastered the geology of
Scotland as Mr. Geikie."*—PALL MALL GAZETTE.

Gladstone.—JUVENTUS MUNDI. The Gods and Men of the
Heroic Age. By the Right Hon. W. E. GLADSTONE, M.P.
Crown 8vo. cloth extra. With Map. 10s. 6d. Second Edition.

*"This new work of Mr. Gladstone deals especially with the historic
element in Homer, expounding that element and furnishing by its
aid a full account of the Homeric men and the Homeric religion.
It starts, after the introductory chapter, with a discussion of the
several races then existing in Hellas, including the influence of the
Phœnicians and Egyptians. It contains chapters "On the Olympian
System, with its several Deities;" "On the Ethics and the Polity of
the Heroic Age;" "On the Geography of Homer;" "On the Characters of the Poems;" presenting, in fine, a view of primitive life and
primitive society as found in the poems of Homer. To this New
Edition various additions have been made. "To read these brilliant
details," says the* ATHENÆUM, *"is like standing on the Olympian
threshold and gazing at the ineffable brightness within." According
to the* WESTMINSTER REVIEW, *"it would be difficult to point out
a book that contains so much fulness of knowledge along with so
much freshness of perception and clearness of presentation."*

Globe Library.—See end of this CATALOGUE.

Golden Treasury of the best Songs and Lyrical
POEMS IN THE ENGLISH LANGUAGE.—See GOLDEN
TREASURY SERIES.

Golden Treasury Series.—See end of this CATALOGUE.

Goldsmith's Works.—See GLOBE LIBRARY.

Guesses at Truth.—By !TWO BROTHERS. With Vignette
Title, and Frontispiece. New Edition, with Memoir. Fcap. 8vo. 6s.
Also see Golden Treasury Series.

*These " Guesses at Truth " are not intended to tell the reader what
to think. They are rather meant to serve the purpose of a quarry
in which, if one is building up his opinions for himself, and only
wants to be provided with materials, he may meet with many
things to suit him. To very many, since its publication, has this
work proved a stimulus to earnest thought and noble action ; and
thus, to no small extent, it is believed, has it influenced the general
current of thinking during the last forty years. It is now no
secret that the authors were AUGUSTUS and JULIUS CHARLES
HARE. " They—living as they did in constant and free interchange •
of thought on questions of philosophy and literature and art ;
delighting, each of them, in the epigrammatic terseness which is the
charm of the 'Pensées' of Pascal, and the 'Caractères' of La
Bruyère—agreed to utter themselves in this form, and the book
appeared, anonymously, in two volumes, in 1827."*

Hamerton.—Works by PHILIP GILBERT HAMERTON :—

A PAINTER'S CAMP. Second Edition, revised. Extra fcap.
8vo. 6s.

BOOK I. *In England :* BOOK II. *In Scotland ;* BOOK III. *In France.*

*This is the story of an Artist's encampments and adventures. The
headings of a few chapters may serve to convey a notion of the
character of the book: A Walk on the Lancashire Moors ; the
Author his own Housekeeper and Cook ; Tents and Boats for the*

Hamerton—*continued.*

Highlands; The Author encamps on an uninhabited Island; A Lake Voyage; A Gipsy Journey to Glencoe; Concerning Moonlight and Old Castles; A little French City; A Farm in the Autunois, &c. &c. " *These pages, written with infinite spirit and humour, bring into close rooms, back upon tired heads, the breezy airs of Lancashire moors and Highland lochs, with a freshness which no recent novelist has succeeded in preserving.*"—NONCONFORMIST. " *His pages sparkle with many turns of expression, not a few well-told anecdotes, and many observations which are the fruit of attentive study and wise reflection on the complicated phenomena of human life, as well as of unconscious nature.*"—WESTMINSTER REVIEW.

ETCHING AND ETCHERS. A Treatise Critical and Practical. With Original Plates by REMBRANDT, CALLOT, DUJARDIN, PAUL POTTER, &c. Royal 8vo. Half morocco. 31*s.* 6*d.*

" *The work is one which deserves to be consulted by every intelligent admirer of the fine arts, whether he is an etcher or not.*"—GUARDIAN.

" *It is not often we get anything like the combined intellectual and æsthetic treat which is supplied us by Mr. Hamerton's ably written and handsome volume. It is a work of which author, printer, and publisher may alike feel proud. It is a work, too, of which none but a genuine artist could by possibility have been the author.*"—SATURDAY REVIEW.

Hervey.—Works by ROSAMOND HERVEY :—

THE AARBERGS. Two vols. Crown 8vo. cloth. 21*s.*

" *All who can relish the more delicate flavour of thoughtfulness and sentiment enriching the quiet tone of common life will accept with gratitude a story so refined and wholesome.*"—GUARDIAN. "*A singularly pleasant book.*"—DAILY NEWS.

DUKE ERNEST, a Tragedy; and other Poems. Fcap. 8vo. 6*s.*

" *Conceived in pure taste and true historic feeling, and executed with much dramatic force. . . . . Thoroughly original.*"—BRITISH QUARTERLY.

Higginson.—MALBONE: An Oldport Romance. By T. W. HIGGINSON. Fcap. 8vo. 2s. 6d.

This is a story of American life, so told as to be interesting and instructive to all English readers. The DAILY NEWS *says: " Who likes a quiet story, full of mature thought, of clear humorous surprises, of artistic studious design ? ' Malbone' is a rare work, possessing these characteristics, and replete, too, with honest literary effort."*

Home.—BLANCHE LISLE, and other Poems. By CECIL HOME. Fcap. 8vo. 4s. 6d.

Hood (Tom).—THE PLEASANT TALE OF PUSS AND ROBIN AND THEIR FRIENDS, KITTY AND BOB. Told in Pictures by L. FRÖLICH, and in Rhymes by TOM HOOD. Crown 8vo. gilt. 3s. 6d.

This is a pleasant little tale of wee Bob and his Sister, and their attempts to rescue poor Robin from the cruel claws of Pussy. It will be intelligible and interesting to the meanest capacity, and is illustrated by thirteen graphic cuts drawn by Frölich. " The volume is prettily got up, and is sure to be a favourite in the nursery." —SCOTSMAN. *" Herr Frölich has outdone himself in his pictures of this dramatic chase."*—MORNING POST.

Jebb.—THE CHARACTERS OF THEOPHRASTUS. An English Translation from a Revised Text. With Introduction and Notes. By R. C. JEBB, M.A., Fellow and Assistant Tutor of Trinity College, Cambridge, and Public Orator of the University. Extra fcap. 8vo. 6s. 6d.

The first object of this book is to make these lively pictures of old Greek manners better known to English readers. But as the Editor and Translator has been at considerable pains to procure a reliable text, and has recorded the results of his critical labours in a lengthy Introduction, in Notes and Appendices, it is hoped that the work will prove of value even to the scholar. " We must not omit to give due honour to Mr. Jebb's translation, which is as good as translation can be. . . . Not less commendable are the execution of the Notes and the critical handling of the text."—SPECTATOR. *" Mr. Jebb's little volume is more easily taken up than laid down."*— GUARDIAN.

Jest Book.—By MARK LEMON.—See GOLDEN TREASURY
SERIES.

Keary (A.)—Works by Miss A. KEARY:—

JANET'S HOME. Cheap Edition. Globe 8vo. 2*s.* 6*d.*

"*Never did a more charming family appear upon the canvas; and
most skilfully and felicitously have their characters been portrayed.
Each individual of the fireside is a finished portrait, distinct and
lifelike. . . . The future before her as a novelist is that of becoming
the Miss Austin of her generation.*"—SUN.

CLEMENCY FRANKLYN. Globe 8vo. 2*s.* 6*d.*

"*Full of wisdom and goodness, simple, truthful, and artistic. . . It
is capital as a story; better still in its pure tone and wholesome
influence.*"—GLOBE.

OLDBURY. Three vols. Crown 8vo. 31*s.* 6*d.*

"*This is a very powerfully written story.*"—GLOBE. "*This is a
really excellent novel.*"—ILLUSTRATED LONDON NEWS. "*The
sketches of society in Oldbury are excellent. The pictures of child
life are full of truth.*"—WESTMINSTER REVIEW.

Keary (A. and E.)—Works by A. and E. KEARY:—

THE LITTLE WANDERLIN, and other Fairy Tales. 18mo.
3*s.* 6*d.*

"*The tales are fanciful and well written, and they are sure to win
favour amongst little readers.*"—ATHENÆUM.

THE HEROES OF ASGARD. Tales from Scandinavian My-
thology. New and Revised Edition,illustrated by HUARD. Extra
fcap. 8vo. 4*s.* 6*d.*

"*Told in a light and amusing style, which, in its drollery and
quaintness, reminds us of our old favourite Grimm.*"—TIMES.

Kingsley.—Works by the Rev. CHARLES KINGSLEY, M.A..
Rector of Eversley, and Canon of Chester :—

*Mr. Canon Kingsley's novels, most will admit, have not only com-
manded for themselves a foremost place in literature, as artistic*

B

Kingsley (C.)—*continued.*

productions of a high class, but have exercised u₁ on the age an incalculable influence in the direction of the highest Christian manliness. Mr. Kingsley has done more perhaps than almost any other writer of fiction to fashion the generation into whose hands the destinies of the world are now being committed. His works will therefore be read by all who wish to have their hearts cheered and their souls stirred to noble endeavour ; they must be read by all who wish to know the influences which moulded the men of this century.

"WESTWARD HO !", or, The Voyages and Adventures of Sir Amyas Leigh. Sixth Edition. Crown 8vo. 6s.

No other work conveys a more vivid idea of the surging, adventurous, nobly inquisitive spirit of the generations which immediately followed the Reformation in England. The daring deeds of the Elizabethan heroes are told with a freshness, an enthusiasm, and a truthfulness that can belong only to one who wishes he had been their leader. His descriptions of the luxuriant scenery of the then new-found Western land are acknowledged to be unmatched. FRASER'S MAGAZINE *calls it "almost the best historical novel of the day."*

TWO YEARS AGO. Fourth Edition. Crown 8vo. 6s.

"*Mr. Kingsley has provided us all along with such pleasant diversions —such rich and brightly tinted glimpses of natural history, such suggestive remarks on mankind, society, and all sorts of topics, that amidst the pleasure of the way, the circuit to be made will be by most forgotten.*"—GUARDIAN.

HYPATIA ; or, New Foes with an Old Face. Fifth Edition. Crown 8vo. 6s.

The work is from beginning to end a series of fascinating pictures of strange phases of that strange primitive society : and no finer portrait has yet been given of the noble-minded lady who was faithful to martyrdom in her attachment to the classical creeds. No work affords a clearer notion of the many interesting problems which agitated the minds of men in those days, and which, in various phases, are again coming up for discussion at the present time.

Kingsley (C.)—*continued.*

HEREWARD THE WAKE—LAST OF THE ENGLISH. Crown 8vo. 6s.

Mr. Kingsley here tells the story of the final conflict of the two races, Saxons and Normans, as if he himself had borne a part in it. While as a work of fiction "Hereward" cannot fail to delight all readers, no better supplement to the dry history of the time could be put into the hands of the young, containing as it does so vivid a picture of the social and political life of the period.

YEAST : A Problem. Fifth Edition. Crown 8vo. 5s.

In this production the author shows, in an interesting dramatic form, the state of fermentation in which the minds of many earnest men are with regard to some of the most important religious and social problems of the day.

ALTON LOCKE. New Edition. With a New Preface. Crown 8vo. 4s. 6d.

This novel, which shows forth the evils arising from modern "caste," has done much to remove the unnatural barriers which existed between the various classes of society, and to establish a sympathy to some extent between the higher and lower grades of the social scale. Though written with a purpose, it is full of character and interest; the author shows, to quote the SPECTATOR, *"what it is that constitutes the true Christian, God-fearing, man-living gentleman."*

AT LAST : A CHRISTMAS IN THE WEST INDIES. With numerous Illustrations. Second and Cheaper Edition. Crown 8vo. 10s. 6d.

Mr. Kingsley's dream of forty years was at last fulfilled, when he started on a Christmas expedition to the West Indies, for the purpose of becoming personally acquainted with the scenes which he has so vividly described in " Westward ho !" "In this book Mr. Kingsley revels in the gorgeous wealth of West Indian vegetation, bringing before us one marvel after another, alternately sating and piquing our curiosity. Whether we climb the cliffs with him, or peer over into narrow bays which are being hollowed out by the trade-surf, or wander through impenetrable forests, where the tops of the trees form a green cloud overhead, or gaze down glens which

B 2

Kingsley (C.)—*continued.*

are watered by the clearest brooks, running through masses of palm and banana and all the rich variety of foliage, we are equally delighted and amazed."—ATHENÆUM.

THE WATER BABIES. A Fairy Tale for a Land Baby. New Edition, with additional Illustrations by Sir NOEL PATON, R.S.A., and P. SKELTON. Crown 8vo. cloth extra gilt. 5*s.*

"In fun, in humour, and in innocent imagination, as a child's book we do not know its equal." —LONDON REVIEW. *"Mr. Kingsley must have the credit of revealing to us a new order of life. . . . There is in the 'Water Babies' an abundance of wit, fun, good humour, geniality,* élan, *go."*—TIMES.

THE HEROES ; or, Greek Fairy Tales for my Children. With Coloured Illustrations. New Edition. 18mo. 4*s.* 6*d.*

"We do not think these heroic stories have ever been more attractively told. . . . There is a deep under-current of religious feeling traceable throughout its pages which is sure to influence young readers powerfully."—LONDON REVIEW. *"One of the children's books that will surely become a classic."* —NONCONFORMIST.

PHAETHON ; or, Loose Thoughts for Loose Thinkers. Third Edition. Crown 8vo. 2*s.*

"The dialogue of 'Phaethon' has striking beauties, and its suggestions may meet half-way many a latent doubt, and, like a light breeze, lift from the soul clouds that are gathering heavily, and threatening to settle down in misty gloom on the summer of many a fair and promising young life."—SPECTATOR.

POEMS ; including The Saint's Tragedy, Andromeda, Songs, Ballads, etc. Complete Collected Edition. Extra fcap. 8vo. 6*s.*

Canon Kingsley's poetical works have gained for their author, independently of his other works, a high and enduring place in literature, and are much sought after. The publishers have here collected the whole of them in a moderately-priced and handy volume. The SPECTATOR *calls "Andromeda" "the finest piece of English hexameter verse that has ever been written. It is a volume which many readers will be glad to possess."*

Kingsley (H.)—Works by HENRY KINGSLEY :—

TALES OF OLD TRAVEL. Re-narrated. With Eight full-page Illustrations by HUARD. Fourth Edition. Crown 8vo. cloth, extra gilt. 5s.

In this volume Mr. Henry Kingsley re-narrates, at the same time preserving much of the quaintness of the original, some of the most fascinating tales of travel contained in the collections of Hakluyt and others. The CONTENTS *are:—Marco Polo ; The Shipwreck of Pelsart ; The Wonderful Adventures of Andrew Battel ; The Wanderings of a Capuchin ; Peter Carder ; The Preservation of the " Terra Nova ;" Spitzbergen ; D'Ermenonville's Acclimatization Adventure ; The Old Slave Trade ; Miles Philips : The Sufferings of Robert Everard ; John Fox ; Alvaro Nunez ; The Foundation of an Empire. "We know no better book for those who want knowledge or seek to refresh it. As for the 'sensational,' most novels are tame compared with these narratives."—*ATHE-NÆUM. *" Exactly the book to interest and to do good to intelligent and high-spirited boys."—*LITERARY CHURCHMAN.

THE LOST CHILD. With Eight Illustrations by FRÖLICH. Crown 4to. cloth gilt. 3s. 6d.

This is an interesting story of a little boy, the son of an Australian shepherd and his wife, who lost himself in the bush, and who was, after much searching, found dead far up a mountain-side. It contains many illustrations from the well-known pencil of Frölich. "A pathetic story, and told so as to give children an interest in Australian ways and scenery."— GLOBE. *"Very charmingly and very touchingly told."—*SATURDAY REVIEW.

Knatchbull-Hugessen.—Works by E. H. KNATCHBULL-HUGESSEN, M.P. :—

Mr. Knatchbull-Hugessen has won for himself a reputation as an inimitable teller of fairy-tales. " His powers," says the TIMES, *"are of a very high order ; light and brilliant narrative flows from his pen, and is fed by an invention as graceful as it is inexhaustible." " Children reading his stories," the* SCOTSMAN *says, " or hearing them read, will have their minds refreshed and invigorated as much as their bodies would be by abundance of fresh air and exercise."*

Knatchbull-Hugessen—*continued.*

STORIES FOR MY CHILDREN. With Illustrations. Third Edition. Extra fcap. 8vo. 5*s.*

" *The stories are charming, and full of life and fun.*"—STANDARD. " *The author has an imagination as fanciful as Grimm himself, while some of his stories are superior to anything that Hans Christian Andersen has written.*"—NONCONFORMIST.

CRACKERS FOR CHRISTMAS. More Stories. With Illustrations by JELLICOE and ELWES. Fourth Edition. Crown 8vo. 5*s.* "*A fascinating little volume, which will make him friends in every household in which there are children.*"—DAILY NEWS.

MOONSHINE : Fairy Tales. With Illustrations by W. BRUNTON. Fourth Edition. Crown 8vo. cloth gilt. 5*s.*

Here will be found " *an Ogre, a Dwarf, a Wizard, quantities of Elves and Fairies, and several animals who speak like mortal men and women.*" *There are twelve stories and nine irresistible illustrations.* " *A volume of fairy tales, written not only for ungrown children, but for bigger, and if you are nearly worn out, or sick, or sorry, you will find it good reading.*"—GRAPHIC. "*The most charming volume of fairy tales which we have ever read. . . . We cannot quit this very pleasant book without a word of praise to its illustrator. Mr. Brunton from first to last has done admirably.*"— TIMES.

La Lyre Française.—See GOLDEN TREASURY SERIES.

Latham.—SERTUM SHAKSPERIANUM, Subnexis aliquot aliunde excerptis floribus. Latine reddidit Rev. H. LATHAM, M.A. Extra fcap. 8vo. 5*s.*

Besides versions of Shakespeare, this volume contains, among other pieces, Gray's " Elegy," Campbell's " Hohenlinden," Wolfe's " Burial of Sir John Moore," and selections from Cowper and George Herbert.

Lemon.—THE LEGENDS OF NUMBER NIP. By MARK LEMON. With Illustrations by C. KEENE. New Edition. Extra fcap. 8vo. 2*s.* 6*d.*

Life and Times of Conrad the Squirrel. A Story
for Children. By the Author of "Wandering Willie," "Effie's
Friends," &c. With a Frontispiece by R. FARREN. Crown 8vo.
3s. 6d.

*It is sufficient to commend this story of a Squirrel to the attention of
readers, that it is by the author of the beautiful stories of "Wandering Willie" and "Effie's Friends." It is well calculated to
make children take an intelligent and tender interest in the lower
animals.*

Little Estella, and other Fairy Tales for the Young. Royal
16mo. 3s. 6d.

" *This is a fine story, and we thank heaven for not being too wise to
enjoy it.*"—DAILY NEWS.

Little Lucy's Wonderful Globe.—See YONGE, C. M.

Lowell.—AMONG MY BOOKS. Six Essays. Dryden—Witch-
craft—Shakespeare once More—New England Two Centuries Ago
—Lessing—Rousseau and the Sentimentalists. Crown 8vo. 7s. 6d.

"*We may safely say the volume is one of which our chief complaint
must be that there is not more of it. There are good sense and lively
feeling forcibly and tersely expressed in every page of his writing.*"
—PALL MALL GAZETTE.

Lyttelton.—Works by LORD LYTTELTON :—

THE "COMUS" OF MILTON, rendered into Greek Verse.
Extra fcap. 8vo. 5s.

THE "SAMSON AGONISTES" OF MILTON, rendered into
Verse. Extra fcap. 8vo. 6s. 6d.

" *Classical in spirit, full of force, and true to the original.*"
—GUARDIAN.

Macmillan's Magazine.—Published Monthly. Price 1s.
Volumes I. to XXV. are now ready. 7s. 6d. each.

Macquoid.—PATTY. By KATHERINE S. MACQUOID. Two
vols. Crown 8vo. 21s.,

The ATHENÆUM *"congratulates Mrs. Macquoid on having made a great step since the publication of her last novel," and says this " is a graceful and eminently readable story."* *The* GLOBE *considers it " well-written, amusing, and interesting, and has the merit of being out of the ordinary run of novels."*

Malbone.—See HIGGINSON.

Marlitt (E.)—THE COUNTESS GISELA. Translated from the German of E. MARLITT. Crown 8vo. 7s. 6d.

" *A very beautiful story of German country life."*—LITERARY CHURCHMAN.

Masson (Professor).—Works by DAVID MASSON, M.A., Professor of Rhetoric and English Literature in the University of Edinburgh. (See also BIOGRAPHICAL and PHILOSOPHICAL CATALOGUES.)

ESSAYS, BIOGRAPHICAL AND CRITICAL. Chiefly on the British Poets. 8vo. 12s. 6d.

" *Distinguished by a remarkable power of analysis, a clear statement of the actual facts on which speculation is based, and an appropriate beauty of language. These Essays should be popular with serious men."*·—ATHENÆUM.

BRITISH NOVELISTS AND THEIR STYLES. Being a Critical Sketch of the History of British Prose Fiction. Crown 8vo. 7s. 6d.

"*Valuable for its lucid analysis of fundamental principles, its breadth of view, and sustained animation of style."*—SPECTATOR. " *Mr. Masson sets before us with a bewitching ease and clearness which nothing but a perfect mastery of his subject could have rendered possible, a large body of both deep and sound discriminative criticism on all the most memorable of our British novelists. . . . . His brilliant and instructive book."*—JOHN BULL.

Merivale.—KEATS' HYPERION, rendered into Latin Verse. By C. MERIVALE, B.D. Second Edition. Extra fcap. 8vo. 3s. 6d.

Milner.—THE LILY OF LUMLEY. By EDITH MILNER. Crown 8vo. 7s. 6d.

"*The novel is a good one and decidedly worth the reading.*"—
EXAMINER. "*A pretty, brightly-written story.*" — LITERARY
CHURCHMAN. "*A tale possessing the deepest interest.*"—COURT
JOURNAL.

Mistral (F.)—MIRELLE, a Pastoral Epic of Provence. Translated by H. CRICHTON. Extra fcap. 8vo. 6*s.*

"*It would be hard to overpraise the sweetness and pleasing freshness
of this charming epic.*"—ATHENÆUM. "*A good translation of
a poem that deserves to be known by all students of literature and
friends of old-world simplicity in story-telling.*" — NONCON-
FORMIST.

Brown, M.P.—MR. PISISTRATUS BROWN, M.P., IN
THE HIGHLANDS. Reprinted from the *Daily News*, with
Additions. Crown 8vo. 5*s.*

These papers appeared at intervals in the DAILY NEWS *during
the summer of* 1871. *They narrate in light and jocular style
the adventures "by flood and field" of Mr. Brown, M.P. and
his friend in their tour through the West Highlands, and will be
found well adapted to while away a pleasant hour either by the
winter fireside or during a summer holiday.*

Mrs. Jerningham's Journal. A Poem purporting to be the
Journal of a newly-married Lady. Second Edition. Fcap. 8vo.
3*s.* 6*d.*

"*It is nearly a perfect gem. We have had nothing so good for a
long time, and those who neglect to read it are neglecting one of
the jewels of contemporary history.*"—EDINBURGH DAILY RE-
VIEW. · "*One quality in the piece, sufficient of itself to claim a
moment's attention, is that it is unique—original, indeed, is not too
strong a word—in the manner of its conception and execution.*"
—PALL MALL GAZETTE.

Mitford (A. B.)—TALES OF OLD JAPAN. By A. B.
MITFORD, Second Secretary to the British Legation in Japan.
With Illustrations drawn and cut on Wood by Japanese Artists.
Two Vols. Crown 8vo. 21*s.*

*The old Japanese civilization is fast disappearing, and will, in a
few years, be completely extinct. It was important, therefore, to*

preserve as far as possible trustworthy records of a state of society which, although venerable from its antiquity, has for Europeans the charm of novelty ; hence the series of narratives and legends translated by Mr. Mitford, and in which the Japanese are very judiciously left to tell their own tale. The two volumes comprise not only stories and episodes illustrative of Asiatic superstitions, but also three sermons. The Preface, Appendices, and Notes explain a number of local peculiarities ; the thirty-one woodcuts are the genuine work of a native artist, who, unconsciously of course, has adopted the process first introduced by the early German masters. "They will always be interesting as memorials of a most exceptional society ; while, regarded simply as tales, they are sparkling, sensational, and dramatic, and the originality of their ideas and the quaintness of their language give them a most captivating piquancy. The illustrations are extremely interesting, and for the curious in such matters have a special and particular value."—PALL MALL GAZETTE.

Morte d'Arthur.—See GLOBE LIBRARY.

Myers (Ernest).—THE PURITANS. By ERNEST MYERS. Extra fcap. 8vo. cloth. 2s. 6d.

"*It is not too much to call it a really grand poem, stately and dignified, and showing not only a high poetic mind, but also great power over poetic expression.*"—LITERARY CHURCHMAN.

Myers (F. W. H.)—POEMS. By F. W. H. MYERS. Containing "St. Paul," "St. John," and others. Extra fcap. 8vo. 4s. 6d.

"*It is rare to find a writer who combines to such an extent the faculty of communicating feelings with the faculty of euphonious expression.*"—SPECTATOR. "'*St. Paul' stands without a rival as the noblest religious poem which has been written in an age which beyond any other has been prolific in this class of poetry. The sublimest conceptions are expressed in language which, for richness, taste, and purity, we have never seen excelled.*"—JOHN BULL.

Nine Years Old.—By the Author of "St. Olave's," "When I was a Little Girl," &c. Illustrated by FRÖLICH. Second Edition. Extra fcap. 8vo. cloth gilt. 4s. 6d.

It is believed that this story, by the favourably known author of " St. Olave's," will be found both highly interesting and instructive to the young. The volume contains eight graphic illustrations by Mr. L. Frölich. The EXAMINER *says : " Whether the readers are nine years old, or twice, or seven times as old, they must enjoy this pretty volume."*

Noel.—BEATRICE, AND OTHER POEMS. By the Hon. RODEN NOEL. Fcap. 8vo. 6s.

"It is impossible to read the poem through without being powerfully moved. There are passages in it which for intensity and tenderness, clear and vivid vision, spontaneous and delicate sympathy, may be compared with the best efforts of our best living writers." —SPECTATOR. *" It is long since we have seen a volume of poems which has seemed to us so full of the real stuff of which we are made, and uttering so freely the deepest wants of this complicated age."*—BRITISH QUARTERLY.

Norton.—Works by the Hon. Mrs. NORTON :—

THE LADY OF LA GARAYE. With Vignette and Frontispiece. New Edition. Fcap. 8vo. 4s. 6d.

"A poem entirely unaffected, perfectly original, so true and yet so fanciful, so strong and yet so womanly, with painting so exquisite, a pure portraiture of the highest affections and the deepest sorrows, and instilling a lesson true, simple, and sublime." — DUBLIN UNIVERSITY MAGAZINE. *" Full of thought well expressed, and may be classed among her best efforts."*—TIMES.

OLD SIR DOUGLAS. Cheap Edition. Globe 8vo. 2s. 6d.

" This varied and lively novel—this clever novel so full of character, and of fine incidental remark." — SCOTSMAN. *" One of the pleasantest and healthiest stories of modern fiction."*—GLOBE.

Oliphant.—Works by Mrs. OLIPHANT :—

AGNES HOPETOUN'S SCHOOLS AND HOLIDAYS. New Edition with Illustrations. Royal 16mo. gilt leaves. 4s. 6d.

" There are few books of late years more fitted to touch the heart, purify the feeling, and quicken and sustain right principles."— NONCONFORMIST. *" A more gracefully written story it is impossible to desire."*—DAILY NEWS.

Oliphant—*continued.*

A SON OF THE SOIL. New Edition. Globe 8vo. 2*s.* 6*d.*

"*It is a very different work from the ordinary run of novels. The whole life of a man is portrayed in it, worked out with subtlety and insight.*"—ATHENÆUM. "*With entire freedom from any sensational plot, there is enough of incident to give keen interest to the narrative, and make us feel as we read it that we have been spending a few hours with friends who will make our own lives better by their own noble purposes and holy living.*"—BRITISH QUARTERLY REVIEW.

Our Year. A Child's Book, in Prose and Verse. By the Author of "John Halifax, Gentleman." Illustrated by CLARENCE DOBELL. Royal 16mo. 3*s.* 6*d.*

"*It is just the book we could wish to see in the hands of every child.*" —ENGLISH CHURCHMAN.

Olrig Grange. Edited by HERMANN KUNST, Philol. Professor. Extra fcap. 8vo. 6*s.* 6*d.*

This is a poem in six parts, each the utterance of a distinct person. It is the story of a young Scotchman of noble aims designed for the ministry, but who "rent the Creed trying to fit it on," who goes to London to seek fame and fortune in literature, and who returns defeated to his old home in the north to die. The NORTH BRITISH DAILY MAIL, *in reviewing the work, speaks of it as affording "abounding evidence of genial and generative faculty working in self-decreed modes. A masterly and original power of impression, pouring itself forth in clear, sweet, strong rhythm. . . . Easy to cull, remarkable instances of thrilling fervour, of glowing delicacy, of scathing and trenchant scorn, to point out the fine and firm discrimination of character which prevails throughout, to dwell upon the ethical power and psychological truth which are exhibited, to note the skill with which the diverse parts of the poem are set in organic relation. . . . It is a fine poem, full of life, of music, and of clear vision.*"

Oxford Spectator, the.—Reprinted. Extra fcap. 8vo. 3*s.* 6*d.*

These papers, after the manner of Addison's "Spectator," appeared in Oxford from November 1867 *to December* 1868, *at intervals varying from two days to a week. They attempt to sketch several features of Oxford life from an undergraduate's point of view, and to give modern readings of books which undergraduates study. "There is," the* SATURDAY REVIEW *says, "all the old fun, the old sense of social ease and brightness and freedom, the old medley of work and indolence, of jest and earnest, that made Oxford life so picturesque."*

Palgrave.—Works by FRANCIS TURNER PALGRAVE, M.A., late Fellow of Exeter College, Oxford :—

ESSAYS ON ART. Extra fcap. 8vo. 6s.

Mulready—Dyce—Holman Hunt—Herbert—Poetry, Prose, and Sensationalism in Art—Sculpture in England—The Albert Cross, &c. Most of these Essays have appeared in the SATURDAY REVIEW *and elsewhere : but they have been minutely revised, and in some cases almost re-written, with the aim mainly of excluding matters of temporary interest, and softening down all asperities of censure. The main object of the book is, by examples taken chiefly from the works of contemporaries, to illustrate the truths, that art has fixed principles, of which any one may attain the knowledge who is not wanting in natural taste. Art, like poetry, is addressed to the world at large, not to a special jury of professional masters. "In many respects the truest critic we have."*—LITERARY CHURCHMAN.

THE FIVE DAYS' ENTERTAINMENTS AT WENTWORTH GRANGE. A Book for Children. With Illustrations by ARTHUR HUGHES and Engraved Title-page by JEENS. Small 4to. cloth extra. 6s.

"If you want a really good book for both sexes and all ages, buy this, as handsome a volume of tales as you'll find in all the market."—ATHENÆUM. *"Exquisite both in form and substance."* —GUARDIAN.

LYRICAL POEMS. Extra fcap. 8vo. 6s.

"A volume of pure quiet verse, sparkling with tender melodies, and alive with thoughts of genuine poetry. . . . Turn where we will throughout the volume, we find traces of beauty, tenderness, and truth ; true poet's work, touched and refined by the master-hand of a real artist, who shows his genius even in trifles."—STANDARD.

Palgrave—*continued.*

ORIGINAL HYMNS. Third Edition, enlarged, 18mo. 1s. 6d.

"*So choice, so perfect, and so refined, so tender in feeling, and so scholarly in expression, that we look with special interest to everything that he gives us.*"—LITERARY CHURCHMAN.

GOLDEN TREASURY OF THE BEST SONGS AND LYRICS. Edited by F. T. PALGRAVE. See GOLDEN TREASURY SERIES.

SHAKESPEARE'S SONNETS AND SONGS. Edited by F. T. PALGRAVE. Gem Edition. With Vignette Title by JEENS. 3s. 6d.

"*For minute elegance no volume could possibly excel the 'Gem Edition.'*"—SCOTSMAN.

Palmer's Book of Praise.—See GOLDEN TREASURY SERIES.

Parables.—TWELVE PARABLES OF OUR LORD. Illustrated in Colours from Sketches taken in the East by McENIRY, with Frontispiece from a Picture by JOHN JELLICOE, and Illuminated Texts and Borders. Royal 4to. in Ornamental Binding. 16s.

The SCOTSMAN *calls this "one of the most superb books of the season." The richly and tastefully illuminated borders are from the* Brevario Grimani, *in St. Mark's Library, Venice. The* TIMES *calls it "one of the most beautiful of modern pictorial works;" while the* GRAPHIC *says "nothing in this style, so good, has ever before been published."*

Patmore.—THE ANGEL IN THE HOUSE. By COVENTRY PATMORE.

BOOK I. *The Betrothal;* BOOK II. *The Espousals;* BOOK III. *Faithful for Ever. The Victories of Love. Tamerton Church Tower.* Two Vols. Fcap. 8vo. 12s.

"*A style combining much of the homeliness of Crabbe, with sweeter music and a far higher range of thought.*"—TIMES. "*Its merit is more than sufficient to account for its success. . . . In its manly and healthy cheer, the 'Angel in the House' is an effectual protest against the morbid poetry of the age.*"—EDINBURGH REVIEW.

" *We think his 'Angel in the House' would be a good wedding-gift to a bridegroom from his friends; though, whenever it is read with a right view of its aim, we believe it will be found itself, more or less, of an angel in the house.*"—FRASER'S MAGAZINE.

*** *A New and Cheap Edition in One Vol.* 18mo., *beautifully printed on toned paper, price* 2s. 6d.

Pember.—THE TRAGEDY OF LESBOS. A Dramatic Poem. By E. H PEMBER. Fcap. 8vo. 4s. 6d.

Founded upon the story of Sappho. "*He tells his story with dramatic force, and in language that often rises almost to grandeur.*"— ATHENÆUM.

Poole.—PICTURES OF COTTAGE LIFE IN THE WEST OF ENGLAND. By MARGARET E. POOLE. New and Cheaper Edition. With Frontispiece by R. Farren. Crown 8vo. 3s. 6d.

" *Charming stories of peasant life, written in something of George Eliot's style. . . . Her stories could not be other than they are, as literal as truth, as romantic as fiction, full of pathetic touches and strokes of genuine humour. . . . All the stories are studies of actual life, executed with no mean art.*"—TIMES.

Pope's Poetical Works.—See GLOBE LIBRARY.

Population of an Old Pear Tree. From the French of E. VAN BRUYSSEL. Edited by the Author of "The Heir of Redclyffe." With Illustrations by BECKER. Second Edition. Crown 8vo. gilt edges. 6s.

" *This is not a regular book of natural history, but a description of all the living creatures that came and went in a summer's day beneath an old pear tree, observed by eyes that had for the nonce become microscopic, recorded by a pen that finds dramas in everything, and illustrated by a dainty pencil. . . . We can hardly fancy anyone with a moderate turn for the curiosities of insect life, or for delicate French esprit, not being taken by these clever sketches.*"—GUARDIAN. "*A whimsical and charming little book.*" —ATHENÆUM.

Portfolio of Cabinet Pictures.—Oblong folio, price 42*s.*

This is a handsome portfolio containing faithfully executed and beautifully coloured reproductions of five well-known pictures :— " Childe Harold's Pilgrimage" and " The Fighting Téméraire," by J. M. W. Turner ; " Crossing the Bridge," by Sir W. A. Callcott ; " The Cornfield," by John Constable ; and " A Landscape," by Birket Foster. The DAILY NEWS *says of them, " They are very beautifully executed, and might be framed and hung up on the wall, as creditable substitutes for the originals."*

Raphael of Urbino and his Father Giovanni

SANTI.—By J. D. PASSAVANT, formerly Director of the Museum at Frankfort. Illustrated. Royal 8vo. cloth gilt, gilt edges. 31*s.* 6*d.*

To the enlarged French edition of Herr Passavant's Life of Raphael, that painter's admirers have turned whenever they have sought for information ; and it will doubtless remain for many years the best book of reference on all questions pertaining to the great painter. The present work consists of a translation of those parts of Passavant's volumes which are most likely to interest the general reader. Besides a complete life of Raphael it contains the valuable descriptions of all his known paintings, and the Chronological Index, which is of so much service to amateurs who wish to study the progressive character of his works. The illustrations, twenty in number, by Woodbury's new permanent process of photography, are from the finest engravings that could be procured, and have been chosen with the intention of giving examples of Raphael's various styles of painting. " There will be found in the volume almost all that the ordinary student or critic would require to learn."—ART JOURNAL. *" It is most beautifully and profusely illustrated."*—SATURDAY REVIEW.

Realmah.—By the Author of "Friends in Council." Crown 8vo. 6*s.*

Rhoades.—POEMS. By JAMES RHOADES. Fcap. 8vo. 4*s.* 6*d.*

CONTENTS :—*Ode to Harmony ; To the Spirit of Unrest ; Ode to Winter ; The Tunnel ; To the Spirit of Beauty ; Song of a Leaf;*

By the Rother; An Old Orchard; Love and Rest; The Flowers Surprised; On the Death of Artemus Ward; The Two Paths; The Ballad of Little Maisie; Sonnets.

Richardson.—THE ILIAD OF THE EAST. A Selection of Legends drawn from Valmiki's Sanskrit Poem, "The Ramayana." By FREDERIKA RICHARDSON. Crown 8vo. 7s. 6d.

"*It is impossible to read it without recognizing the value and interest of the Eastern epic. It is as fascinating as a fairy tale, this romantic poem of India.*"—GLOBE. "*A charming volume which at once enmeshes the reader in its snares.*"—ATHEN.EUM.

Robinson Crusoe.—See GLOBE LIBRARY and GOLDEN TREASURY SERIES.

Roby.—STORY OF A HOUSEHOLD, AND OTHER POEMS. By MARY K. ROBY. Fcap. 8vo. 5s.

Rogers.—Works by J. E. ROGERS :—

RIDICULA REDIVIVA. Old Nursery Rhymes. Illustrated in Colours, with Ornamental Cover. Crown 4to. 6s.

"*The most splendid, and at the same time the most really meritorious of the books specially intended for children, that we have seen.*"—SPECTATOR. "*These large bright pictures will attract children to really good and honest artistic work, and that ought not to be an indifferent consideration with parents who propose to educate their children.*"—PALL MALL GAZETTE.

MORES RIDICULI. Old Nursery Rhymes. Illustrated in Colours, with Ornamental Cover. Crown 4to. 6s.

"*These world-old rhymes have never had and need never wish for a better pictorial setting than Mr. Rogers has given them.*"—TIMES. "*Nothing could be quainter or more absurdly comical than most of the pictures, which are all carefully executed and beautifully coloured.*"—GLOBE.

Rossetti.—Works by CHRISTINA ROSSETTI :—

GOBLIN MARKET, AND OTHER POEMS. With two Designs by D. G. ROSSETTI. Second Edition. Fcap. 8vo. 5s.

C

Rossetti—*continued.*

> "*She handles her little marvel with that rare poetic discrimination which neither exhausts it of its simple wonders by pushing symbolism too far, nor keeps those wonders in the merely fabulous and capricious stage. In fact, she has produced a true children's poem, which is far more delightful to the mature than to children, though it would be delightful to all.*"—SPECTATOR.

THE PRINCE'S PROGRESS, AND OTHER POEMS. With two Designs by D. G. ROSSETTI. Fcap. 8vo. 6s.

> "*Miss Rossetti's poems are of the kind which recalls Shelley's definition of Poetry as the record of the best and happiest moments of the best and happiest minds. . . . They are like the piping of a bird on the spray in the sunshine, or the quaint singing with which a child amuses itself when it forgets that anybody is listening.*"—SATURDAY REVIEW.

Rossetti (W. M.)—DANTE'S HELL. See "DANTE."

Ruth and her Friends. A Story for Girls. With a Frontispiece. Fourth Edition. Royal 16mo. 3s. 6d.

> "*We wish all the school girls and home-taught girls in the land had the opportunity of reading it.*"—NONCONFORMIST.

Scott's Poetical Works.—See GLOBE LIBRARY.

Scouring of the White Horse; or, the Long VACATION RAMBLE OF A LONDON CLERK. Illustrated by DOYLE. Imp. 16mo. Cheaper Issue. 3s. 6d.

> "*A glorious tale of summer joy.*"—FREEMAN.   "*There is a genial hearty life about the book.*"—JOHN BULL.   "*The execution is excellent. . . . Like 'Tom Brown's School Days,' the 'White Horse' gives the reader a feeling of gratitude and personal esteem towards the author.*"—SATURDAY REVIEW.

Seeley (Professor). — LECTURES AND ESSAYS. By J. R. SEELEY, M.A. Professor of Modern History in the University of Cambridge. 8vo. 10s. 6d.

CONTENTS :—*Roman Imperialism:* 1. *The Great Roman Revolution;* 2. *The Proximate Cause of the Fall of the Roman Empire;* 3. *The Later Empire.*—*Milton's Political Opinions* — *Milton's Poetry*—*Elementary Principles in Art*—*Liberal Education in Universities*—*English in Schools*—*The Church as a Teacher of Morality*—*The Teaching of Politics: an Inaugural Lecture delivered at Cambridge.* " *He is the master of a clear and pleasant style, great facility of expression, and a considerable range of illustration. . . . The criticism is always acute, the description always graphic and continuous, and the matter of each essay is carefully arranged with a view to unity of effect.*"—SPECTATOR. " *His book will be full of interest to all thoughtful readers.*"—PALL MALL GAZETTE.

Shairp (Principal).—KILMAHOE, a Highland Pastoral, with other Poems. By JOHN CAMPBELL SHAIRP, Principal of the United College, St. Andrews. Fcap. 8vo. 5s.

" *Kilmahoe is a Highland Pastoral, redolent of the warm soft air of the western lochs and moors, sketched out with remarkable grace and picturesqueness.*"—SATURDAY REVIEW.

Shakespeare.—The Works of WILLIAM SHAKESPEARE. Cambridge Edition. Edited by W. GEORGE CLARK, M.A. and W. ALDIS WRIGHT, M.A. Nine vols. 8vo. Cloth. 4*l.* 14*s.* 6*d.*

*This, now acknowledged to be the standard edition of Shakespeare, is the result of many years' study and research on the part of the accomplished Editors, assisted by the suggestions and contributions of Shakespearian students in all parts of the country. The following are the distinctive characteristics of this edition :—*1. *The text is based on a thorough collation of the four Folios, and of all the Quarto editions of the separate plays, and of subsequent editions and commentaries.* 2. *All the results of this collation are given in notes at the foot of the page, together with the conjectural emendations collected and suggested by the Editors, or furnished by their correspondents, so as to give the reader a complete view of the existing materials out of which the text has been constructed, or may be amended.* 3. *Where a quarto edition differs materially from the received text, the text of the quarto is printed* literatim *in a smaller type after the received text.* 4. *The lines in each scene are numbered separately, so as to facilitate reference.* 5. *At the end of each*

C 2

*play a few notes, critical, explanatory, and illustrative, are added.
6. The Poems, edited on a similar plan, are printed at the end
of the Dramatic Works. The Preface contains some notes on
Shakespearian Grammar, Spelling, Metre, and Punctuation, and
a history of all the chief editions from the Poet's time to the present.
The* GUARDIAN *calls it an "excellent, and, to the student, almost
indispensable edition;" and the* EXAMINER *calls it "an unrivalled
edition."*

Shakespeare, Globe.—See GLOBE LIBRARY.

Shakespeare's Tempest. Edited with Glossarial and Explanatory Notes, by the Rev. J. M. JEPHSON. Second Edition.
18mo. 1s.

*This is an edition for use in schools. The introduction treats briefly
of the value of language, the fable of the play and other points.
The notes are intended to teach the student to analyse every obscure
sentence and trace out the logical sequence of the poet's thoughts;
to point out the rules of Shakespeare's versification; to explain
obsolete words and meanings; and to guide the student's taste by
directing his attention to such passages as seem especially worthy
of note for their poetical beauty or truth to nature. The text is in
the main founded upon that of the first collected edition of Shakespeare's plays.*

Smith.—POEMS. By CATHERINE BARNARD SMITH. Fcap.
8vo. 5s.

*"Wealthy in feeling, meaning, finish, and grace; not without passion,
which is suppressed, but the keener for that."*—ATHENÆUM.

Smith (Rev. Walter).—HYMNS OF CHRIST AND THE
CHRISTIAN LIFE. By the Rev. WALTER C. SMITH, M.A.
Fcap. 8vo. 6s.

*"These are among the sweetest sacred poems we have read for a long
time. With no profuse imagery, expressing a range of feeling
and expression by no means uncommon, they are true and elevated,
and their pathos is profound and simple."*—NONCONFORMIST.

Song Book, the.—See GOLDEN TREASURY SERIES.

Spenser's Works.—See GLOBE LIBRARY.

Spring Songs. By a WEST HIGHLANDER. With a Vignette
Illustration by GOURLAY STEELE. Fcap. 8vo. 1s. 6d.

"*Without a trace of affectation or sentimentalism, these utterances are perfectly simple and natural, profoundly human and profoundly true.*"—DAILY NEWS.

Stephen (C. E.)—THE SERVICE OF THE POOR; being
an Inquiry into the Reasons for and against the Establishment of Religious Sisterhoods for Charitable Purposes. By CAROLINE EMILIA STEPHEN. Crown 8vo. 6s. 6d.

Miss Stephen defines religious Sisterhoods as "associations, the organization of which is based upon the assumption that works of charity are either acts of worship in themselves, or means to an end, that end being the spiritual welfare of the objects or the performers of those works." Arguing from that point of view, she devotes the first part of her volume to a brief history of religious associations, taking as specimens—I. The Deaconesses of the Primitive Church; II. the Béguines; III. the Third Order of S. Francis; IV. the Sisters of Charity of S. Vincent de Paul; V. the Deaconesses of Modern Germany. In the second part, Miss Stephen attempts to show what are the real wants met by Sisterhoods, to what extent the same wants may be effectually met by the organization of corresponding institutions on a secular basis, and what are the reasons for endeavouring to do so. "It touches incidentally and with much wisdom and tenderness on so many of the relations of women, particularly of single women, with society, that it may be read with advantage by many who have never thought of entering a Sisterhood."— SPECTATOR.

Stephens (J. B.)—CONVICT ONCE. A Poem. By J. BRUNTON STEPHENS. Extra fcap. 8vo. 3s. 6d.

A tale of sin and sorrow, purporting to be the confession of Magdalen Power, a convict first, and then a teacher in one of the Australian Settlements; the narrative is supposed to be written by Hyacinth, a pupil of Magdalen Power, and the victim of her jealousy. The metre of the poem is the same as that of Longfellow's "Evangeline." "It is as far more interesting than ninety-nine novels out of a hundred, as it is superior to them in power, worth, and beauty. We should most strongly advise everybody to read ' Convict Once.' "—WESTMINSTER REVIEW.

Storehouse of Stories.—See YONGE, C. M.

Streets and Lanes of a City : Being the Reminiscences
of AMY DUTTON. With a Preface by the BISHOP OF SALIS-
BURY. Second and Cheaper Edition. Globe 8vo. 2s. 6d.

> *This little volume records, to use the words of the Bishop of Salisbury, "a portion of the experience, selected out of overflowing materials, of two ladies, during several years of devoted work as district parochial visitors in a large population in the north of England." Every incident narrated is absolutely true, and only the names of the persons introduced have been (necessarily) changed. The "Reminiscences of Amy Dutton" serve to illustrate the line of argument adopted by Miss Stephen in her work on "the Service of the Poor," because they show that as in one aspect the lady visitor may be said to be a link between rich and poor, in another she helps to blend the "religious" life with the "secular," and in both does service of extreme value to the Church and Nation. "One of the most really striking books that has ever come before us."*—LITERARY CHURCHMAN.

Sunday Book of Poetry.—See GOLDEN TREASURY SERIES.

Symonds (J. A., M.D.)—MISCELLANIES. By JOHN
ADDINGTON SYMONDS, M.D. Selected and Edited, with an
Introductory Memoir, by his Son. 8vo. 7s. 6d.

> *The late Dr. Symonds, of Bristol, was a man of singularly versatile and elegant as well as powerful and scientific intellect. In order to make this selection from his many works generally interesting, the editor has confined himself to works of pure literature, and to such scientific studies as had a general philosophical or social interest. Among the general subjects are articles on the Principles of Beauty, on Knowledge, and a Life of Dr. Pritchard ; among the Scientific Studies are papers on Sleep and Dreams, Apparitions, the Relations between Mind and Muscle, Habit, etc. ; there are several papers on*

the Social and Political Aspects of Medicine; and a few Poems and Translations, selected from a great number of equal merit, have been inserted at the end, as specimens of the lighter literary recreations which occupied the intervals of leisure in a long and laborious life. " Mr. Symonds has certainly done right in gathering together what his father left behind him."—SATURDAY REVIEW.

Theophrastus, Characters of.—See JEBB.

Thring.—SCHOOL SONGS. A Collection of Songs for Schools.

With the Music arranged for four Voices. Edited by the Rev. E. THRING and H. RICCIUS. Folio. 7*s*. 6*d*.

There is a tendency in schools to stereotype the forms of life. Any genial solvent is valuable. Games do much ; but games do not penetrate to domestic life, and are much limited by age. Music supplies the want. The collection includes the "Agnus Dei," Tennyson's "Light Brigade," Macaulay's "Ivry," etc. among other pieces.

Tom Brown's School Days.—By AN OLD BOY.

Golden Treasury Edition, 4*s*. 6*d*. People's Edition, 2*s*.

With Sixty Illustrations, by A. HUGHES and SYDNEY HALL, Square, cloth extra, gilt edges. 10*s*. 6*d*.

With Seven Illustrations by the same Artists, Crown Svo. 6*s*.

" We have read and re-read this book with unmingled pleasure. . . . We have carefully guarded ourselves against any tampering with our critical sagacity, and yet have been compelled again and again to exclaim, Bene! Optime!"—LONDON QUARTERLY REVIEW.
" An exact picture of the bright side of a Rugby boy's experience, told with a life, a spirit, and a fond minuteness of detail and recollection which is infinitely honourable to the author."—EDINBURGH REVIEW. *" The most famous boy's book in the language."*—DAILY NEWS.

Tom Brown at Oxford.—New Edition. With Illustrations.

Crown Svo. 6*s*.

" In no other work that we can call to mind are the finer qualities of the English gentleman more happily portrayed."—DAILY NEWS.
" A book of great power and truth."—NATIONAL REVIEW.

Trench.—Works by R. CHENEVIX TRENCH, D.D., Archbishop of Dublin. (For other Works by this Author, see THEOLOGICAL, HISTORICAL, and PHILOSOPHICAL CATALOGUES.)

POEMS. Collected and arranged anew. Fcap. 8vo. 7*s.* 6*d.*

ELEGIAC POEMS. Third Edition. Fcap. 8vo. 2*s.* 6*d.*

CALDERON'S LIFE'S A DREAM: The Great Theatre of the World. With an Essay on his Life and Genius. Fcap. 8vo. 4*s.* 6*d.*

HOUSEHOLD BOOK OF ENGLISH POETRY. Selected and arranged, with Notes, by Archbishop TRENCH. Second Edition. Extra fcap. 8vo. 5*s.* 6*d.*

*This volume is called a "Household Book," by this name implying that it is a book for all—that there is nothing in it to prevent it from being confidently placed in the hands of every member of the household. Specimens of all classes of poetry are given, including selections from living authors. The editor has aimed to produce a book "which the emigrant, finding room for little not absolutely necessary, might yet find room for in his trunk, and the traveller in his knapsack, and that on some narrow shelves where there are few books this might be one." "The Archbishop has conferred in this delightful volume an important gift on the whole English-speaking population of the world."—*PALL MALL GAZETTE.

SACRED LATIN POETRY, Chiefly Lyrical. Selected and arranged for Use. By Archbishop TRENCH. Second Edition, Corrected and improved. Fcap. 8vo. 7*s.*

" The aim of the present volume is to offer to members of our English Church a collection of the best sacred Latin poetry, such as they shall be able entirely and heartily to accept and approve—a collection, that is, in which they shall not be evermore liable to be offended, and to have the current of their sympathies checked, by coming upon that which, however beautiful as poetry, out of higher respects they must reject and condemn—in which, too, they shall not fear that snares are being laid for them, to entangle them unawares in admiration for aught which is inconsistent with their faith and fealty to their own spiritual mother."—PREFACE.

JUSTIN MARTYR, AND OTHER POEMS. Fifth Edition. Fcap. 8vo. 6*s.*

Trollope (Anthony). — SIR HARRY HOTSPUR OF HUMBLETHWAITE. By ANTHONY TROLLOPE, Author of "Framley Parsonage," etc. Cheap Edition. Globe 8vo. 2s. 6d.

The TIMES *says: " In this novel we are glad to recognize a return to what we must call Mr. Trollope's old form. The characters are drawn with vigour and boldness, and the book may do good to many readers of both sexes." The* ATHENÆUM *remarks: " No reader who begins to read this book is likely to lay it down until the last page is turned. This brilliant novel appears to us decidedly more successful than any other of Mr. Trollope's shorter stories."*

Turner. — Works by the Rev. CHARLES TENNYSON TURNER :—

SONNETS. Dedicated to his Brother, the Poet Laureate. Fcap. 8vo. 4s. 6d.

*" The Sonnets are dedicated to Mr. Tennyson by his brother, and have, independently of their merits, an interest of association. They both love to write in simple expressive Saxon; both love to touch their imagery in epithets rather than in formal similes; both have a delicate perception of rhythmical movement, and thus Mr. Turner has occasional lines which, for phrase and music, might be ascribed to his brother. . . He knows the haunts of the wild rose, the shady nooks where light quivers through the leaves, the ruralities, in short, of the land of imagination."—*ATHENÆUM.

SMALL TABLEAUX. Fcap. 8vo. 4s. 6d.

*" These brief poems have not only a peculiar kind of interest for the student of English poetry, but are intrinsically delightful, and will reward a careful and frequent perusal. Full of naïveté, piety, love, and knowledge of natural objects, and each expressing a single and generally a simple subject by means of minute and original pictorial touches, these Sonnets have a place of their own."—*PALL MALL GAZETTE.

Virgil's Works. — See GLOBE LIBRARY.

Vittoria Colonna. — LIFE AND POEMS. By MRS. HENRY ROSCOE. Crown 8vo. 9s.

The life of Vittoria Colonna, the celebrated Marchesa di Pescara, has received but cursory notice from any English writer, though in every history of Italy her name is mentioned with great honour among the poets of the sixteenth century. "In three hundred and fifty years," says her biographer, Visconti, "there has been no other Italian lady who can be compared to her." "It is written with good taste, with quick and intelligent sympathy, occasionally with a real freshness and charm of style."—PALL MALL GAZETTE.

Volunteer's Scrap Book. By the Author of "The Cambridge Scrap Book." Crown 4to. 7s. 6d.

"A genial and clever caricaturist in whom we may often perceive through small details that he has as proper a sense of the graceful as of the ludicrous. The author might be and probably is a Volunteer himself, so kindly is the mirth he makes of all the incidents and phrases of the drill-ground."—EXAMINER.

Wandering Willie. By the Author of "Effie's Friends," and "John Hatherton." Third Edition. Crown 8vo. 6s.

" This is an idyll of rare truth and beauty. . . . The story is simple and touching, the style of extraordinary delicacy, precision, and picturesqueness. . . . A charming gift-book for young ladies not yet promoted to novels, and will amply repay those of their elders who may give an hour to its perusal."—DAILY NEWS.

Webster.—Works by AUGUSTA WEBSTER :—

" If Mrs. Webster only remains true to herself, she will assuredly take a higher rank as a poet than any woman has yet done."—WESTMINSTER REVIEW.

DRAMATIC STUDIES. Extra fcap. 8vo. 5s.
"A volume as strongly marked by perfect taste as by poetic power."—NONCONFORMIST.

A WOMAN SOLD, AND OTHER POEMS. Crown 8vo. 7s. 6d.
" Mrs. Webster has shown us that she is able to draw admirably from the life ; that she can observe with subtlety, and render her observations with delicacy ; that she can impersonate complex conceptions and venture into which few living writers can follow her."—GUARDIAN.

Webster—*continued.*

PORTRAITS. Second Edition. Extra fcap. 8vo. 3*s.* 6*d.*

"*Mrs. Webster's poems exhibit simplicity and tenderness . . . her taste is perfect . . . This simplicity is combined with a subtlety of thought, feeling, and observation which demand that attention which only real lovers of poetry are apt to bestow.*"—WESTMINSTER REVIEW.

PROMETHEUS BOUND OF ÆSCHYLUS. Literally translated into English Verse. Extra fcap. 8vo. 3*s.* 6*d.*

"*Closeness and simplicity combined with literary skill.*" — ATHENÆUM. "*Mrs. Webster's 'Dramatic Studies' and 'Translation of Prometheus' have won for her an honourable place among our female poets. She writes with remarkable vigour and dramatic realization, and bids fair to be the most successful claimant of Mrs. Browning's mantle.*"—BRITISH QUARTERLY REVIEW.

MEDEA OF EURIPIDES. Literally translated into English Verse. Extra fcap. 8vo. 3*s.* 6*d.*

"*Mrs. Webster's translation surpasses our utmost expectations. It is a photograph of the original without any of that harshness which so often accompanies a photograph.*"—WESTMINSTER REVIEW.

THE AUSPICIOUS DAY. A Dramatic Poem. Extra fcap. 8vo. 5*s.*

Westminster Plays. Lusus Alteri Westmonasterienses, Sive Prologi et Epilogi ad Fabulas in S^u Petri Collegio : actas qui Exstabant collecti et justa quoad licuit annorum serie ordinati, quibus accedit Declamationum quæ vocantur et Epigrammatum Delectus. Curantibus J. MURE, A.M., H. BULL, A.M., C. B. SCOTT, B.D. 8vo. 12*s.* 6*d.*

IDEM.—Pars Secunda, 1820—1864. Quibus accedit Epigrammatum Delectus. 8vo. 15*s.*

When I was a Little Girl. STORIES FOR CHILDREN.

By the Author of "St. Olave's." Third Edition. Extra fcap. 8vo. 4*s.* 6*d.* With Eight Illustrations by L. FRÖLICH.

"*At the head, and a long way ahead, of all books for girls, we* place ' *When I was a Little Girl.*' "—Times. " *It is one of the choicest morsels of child-biography which we have met with.*"— Nonconformist.

Wollaston.—LYRA DEVONIENSIS. By T. V. Wollaston, M.A. Fcap. 8vo. 3s. 6d.

" *It is the work of a man of refined taste, of deep religious sentiment, a true artist, and a good Christian.*"—Church Times.

Woolner.—MY BEAUTIFUL LADY. By Thomas Woolner. With a Vignette by Arthur Hughes. Third Edition. Fcap. 8vo. 5s.

" *It is clearly the product of no idle hour, but a highly-conceived and faithfully-executed task, self-imposed, and prompted by that inward yearning to utter great thoughts, and a wealth of passionate feeling, which is poetic genius. No man can read this poem without being struck by the fitness and finish of the workmanship, so to speak, as well as by the chastened and unpretending loftiness of thought which pervades the whole.*"— Globe.

Words from the Poets. Selected by the Editor of " Rays of Sunlight." With a Vignette and Frontispiece. 18mo. limp., 1s.

" *The selection aims at popularity, and deserves it.*"—Guardian.

Wyatt (Sir M. Digby).—FINE ART. a Sketch of its History, Theory, Practice, and application to Industry. A Course of Lectures delivered before the University of Cambridge. By Sir M. Digby Wyatt, M.A. Slade Professor of Fine Art. 8vo. 10s. 6d.

" *An excellent handbook for the student of art.*"—Graphic. " *The book abounds in valuable matter, and will therefore be read with pleasure and profit by lovers of art.*"—Daily News.

Yonge (C. M.)—Works by Charlotte M. Yonge. (See also Catalogue of Works in History, and Educational Catalogue.)

THE HEIR OF REDCLYFFE. Eighteenth Edition. With Illustrations. Crown 8vo. 6s.

Yonge (C. M.)—*continued.*

HEARTSEASE. Eleventh Edition. With Illustrations. Crown 8vo. 6*s.*

THE DAISY CHAIN. Tenth Edition. With Illustrations. Crown 8vo. 6*s.*

THE TRIAL: MORE LINKS OF THE DAISY CHAIN. Fifth Edition. With Illustrations. Crown 8vo. 6*s.*

DYNEVOR TERRACE. Fourth Edition. Crown 8vo. 6*s.*

HOPES AND FEARS. Third Edition. Crown 8vo. 6*s.*

THE YOUNG STEPMOTHER. Third Edition. Crown 8vo. 6*s.*

CLEVER WOMAN OF THE FAMILY. Second Edition. Crown 8vo. 6*s.*

THE DOVE IN THE EAGLE'S NEST. Second Edition. Crown 8vo. 6*s.*

"*We think the authoress of ' The Heir of Redclyffe' has surpassed her previous efforts in this illuminated chronicle of the olden time.*"—BRITISH QUARTERLY.

THE CAGED LION. Illustrated. Crown 8vo. 6*s.*

"*Prettily and tenderly written, and will with young people especially be a great favourite.*"—DAILY NEWS. "*Everybody should read this.*"—LITERARY CHURCHMAN.

THE CHAPLET OF PEARLS; OR, THE WHITE AND BLACK RIBAUMONT. Crown 8vo. 6*s.*

"*Miss Yonge has brought a lofty aim as well as high art to the construction of a story which may claim a place among the best efforts in historical romance.*"—MORNING POST. "*The plot, in truth, is of the very first order of merit.*"—SPECTATOR. "*We have seldom read a more charming story.*"—GUARDIAN.

THE PRINCE AND THE PAGE. A Tale of the Last Crusade. Illustrated. 18mo. 3*s.* 6*d.*

Yonge (C. M.)—*continued.*

" *A tale which, we are sure, will give pleasure to many others besides the young people for whom it is specially intended.* . . . *This extremely prettily-told story does not require the guarantee afforded by the name of the author of ' The Heir of Redclyffe' on the title-page to ensure its becoming a universal favourite.*"—DUBLIN EVENING MAIL.

THE LANCES OF LYNWOOD. New Edition, with Coloured Illustrations. 18mo. 4*s.* 6*d.*

" *The illustrations are very spirited and rich in colour, and the story can hardly fail to charm the youthful reader*"—MANCHESTER EXAMINER.

THE LITTLE DUKE: RICHARD THE FEARLESS. New Edition. Illustrated. 18mo. 3*s.* 6*d.*

A STOREHOUSE OF STORIES. First and Second Series. Globe 8vo. 3*s.* 6*d.* each.

CONTENTS OF FIRST SERIES:—History of Philip Quarll— Goody Twoshoes—The Governess—Jemima Placid—The Perambulations of a Mouse—The Village School—The Little Queen— History of Little Jack.

" *Miss Yonge has done great service to the infantry of this generation by putting these eleven stories of sage simplicity within their reach.*" —BRITISH QUARTERLY REVIEW.

CONTENTS OF SECOND SERIES:—Family Stories—Elements of Morality—A Puzzle for a Curious Girl—Blossoms of Morality.

A BOOK OF GOLDEN DEEDS OF ALL TIMES AND ALL COUNTRIES. Gathered and Narrated Anew. New Edition, with Twenty Illustrations by FRÖLICH. Crown 8vo. cloth gilt. 6*s.* (See also GOLDEN TREASURY SERIES). Cheap Edition. 1*s.*

" *We have seen no prettier gift-book for a long time, and none which, both for its cheapness and the spirit in which it has been compiled, is more deserving of praise.*"—ATHENÆUM.

A BOOK OF WORTHIES.—See GOLDEN TREASURY SERIES.

Yonge (C.M.)—*continued.*

LITTLE LUCY'S WONDERFUL GLOBE. Pictured by FRÖLICH, and narrated by CHARLOTTE M. YONGE. Second Edition. Crown 4to. cloth gilt. 6s.

Miss Yonge's wonderful "knack" of instructive story-telling to children is well known. In this volume, in a manner which cannot but prove interesting to all boys and girls, she manages to convey a wonderful amount of information concerning most of the countries of the world ; in this she is considerably aided by the twenty-four telling pictures of Mr. Frölich. "'Lucy's Wonderful Globe' is capital, and will give its youthful readers more idea of foreign countries and customs than any number of books of geography or travel."—GRAPHIC.

CAMEOS FROM ENGLISH HISTORY. From ROLLO to EDWARD II. Extra fcap. 8vo. 5s. Second Edition, enlarged. 5s.

A SECOND SERIES. THE WARS IN FRANCE. Extra fcap. 8vo. 5s.

The endeavour has not been to chronicle facts, but to put together a series of pictures of persons and events, so as to arrest the attention, and give some individuality and distinctness to the recollection, by gathering together details at the most memorable moments. The "Cameos" are intended as a book for young people just beyond the elementary histories of England, and able to enter in some degree into the real spirit of events, and to be struck with characters and scenes presented in some relief. "Instead of dry details," says the NONCONFORMIST, *"we have living pictures, faithful, vivid, and striking."*

Young.—MEMOIR OF CHARLES MAYNE YOUNG, Tragedian. With Extracts from his Son's Journal. By JULIAN CHARLES YOUNG, M.A., Rector of Ilmington. New and Cheaper Edition. Crown 8vo. 7s. 6d. With Portraits and Sketches.

" There is hardly a page of it which was not worth printing. There is hardly a line which has not some kind of interest attaching

to it."—GUARDIAN. "*In this budget of anecdotes, fables, and gossip, old and new, relative to Scott, Moore, Chalmers, Coleridge, Wordsworth, Croker, Mathews, the Third and Fourth Georges, Bowles, Beckford, Lockhart, Wellington, Peel, Louis Napoleon, D'Orsay, Dickens, Thackeray, Louis Blanc, Gibson, Constable, and Stanfield (the list might be much extended), the reader must be hard indeed to please who cannot find entertainment.*"—PALL MALL GAZETTE.

MACMILLAN'S

GOLDEN TREASURY SERIES.

UNIFORMLY printed in 18mo., with Vignette Titles by Sir NOEL PATON, T. WOOLNER, W. HOLMAN HUNT, J. E. MILLAIS, ARTHUR HUGHES, &c. Engraved on Steel by JEENS. Bound in extra cloth, 4s. 6d. each volume. Also kept in morocco and calf bindings.

> "*Messrs. Macmillan have, in their Golden Treasury Series, especially provided editions of standard works, volumes of selected poetry, and original compositions, which entitle this series to be called classical. Nothing can be better than the literary execution, nothing more elegant than the material workmanship.*"—BRITISH QUARTERLY REVIEW.

The Golden Treasury of the Best Songs and
LYRICAL POEMS IN THE ENGLISH LANGUAGE. Selected and arranged, with Notes, by FRANCIS TURNER PALGRAVE.

> "*This delightful little volume, the Golden Treasury, which contains many of the best original lyrical pieces and songs in our language, grouped with care and skill, so as to illustrate each other like the pictures in a well-arranged gallery.*"—QUARTERLY REVIEW.

The Children's Garland from the best Poets.
Selected and arranged by COVENTRY PATMORE.

> "*It includes specimens of all the great masters in the art of poetry, selected with the matured judgment of a man concentrated on obtaining insight into the feelings and tastes of childhood, and*

D

*desirous to awaken its finest impulses, to cultivate its keenest sensi-
bilities."*—MORNING POST.

The Book of Praise. From the Best English Hymn Writers. Selected and arranged by Sir ROUNDELL PALMER. *A New and Enlarged Edition.*

" *All previous compilations of this kind must undeniably for the
present give place to the Book of Praise. . . . The selection has
been made throughout with sound judgment and critical taste. The
pains involved in this compilation must have been immense, embracing, as it does, every writer of note in this special province of
English literature, and ranging over the most widely divergent
tracks of religious thought."*—SATURDAY REVIEW.

The Fairy Book ; the Best Popular Fairy Stories. Selected and rendered anew by the Author of "JOHN HALIFAX, GENTLEMAN."

" *A delightful selection, in a delightful external form ; full of the
physical splendour and vast opulence of proper fairy tales."*—
SPECTATOR.

The Ballad Book. A Selection of the Choicest British Ballads. Edited by WILLIAM ALLINGHAM

" *His taste as a judge of old poetry will be found, by all acquainted with
the various readings of old English ballads, true enough to justify
his undertaking so critical a task."*—SATURDAY REVIEW.

The Jest Book. The Choicest Anecdotes and Sayings. Selected and arranged by MARK LEMON.

" *The fullest and best jest book that has yet appeared."*—SATURDAY
REVIEW.

Bacon's Essays and Colours of Good and Evil. With Notes and Glossarial Index. By W. ALDIS WRIGHT, M.A.

" *The beautiful little edition of Bacon's Essays, now before us, does
credit to the taste and scholarship of Mr. Aldis Wright. . . . It
puts the reader in possession of all the essential literary facts and
chronology necessary for reading the Essays in connection with
Bacon's life and times."*—SPECTATOR. " *By far the most complete
as well as the most elegant edition we possess."*—WESTMINSTER
REVIEW.

The **Pilgrim's Progress** from this World to that which is to come. By JOHN BUNYAN.

"*A beautiful and scholarly reprint.*"—SPECTATOR.

The **Sunday Book of Poetry for the Young.** Selected and arranged by C. F. ALEXANDER.

"*A well-selected volume of Sacred Poetry.*"—SPECTATOR.

A **Book of Golden Deeds** of All Times and All Countries. Gathered and narrated anew. By the Author of "THE HEIR OF REDCLYFFE."

"*. . . To the young, for whom it is especially intended, as a most interesting collection of thrilling tales well told; and to their elders, as a useful handbook of reference, and a pleasant one to take up when their wish is to while away a weary half-hour. We have seen no prettier gift-book for a long time.*"—ATHENÆUM.

The **Poetical Works of Robert Burns.** Edited, with Biographical Memoir, Notes, and Glossary, by ALEXANDER SMITH. Two Vols.

"*Beyond all question this is the most beautiful edition of Burns yet out.*"—EDINBURGH DAILY REVIEW.

The **Adventures of Robinson Crusoe.** Edited from the Original Edition by J. W. CLARK, M.A., Fellow of Trinity College, Cambridge.

"*Mutilated and modified editions of this English classic are so much the rule, that a cheap and pretty copy of it, rigidly exact to the original, will be a prize to many book-buyers.*"—EXAMINER.

The **Republic of Plato.** TRANSLATED into ENGLISH, with Notes by J. Ll. DAVIES, M.A. and D. J. VAUGHAN, M.A.

"*A dainty and cheap little edition.*"—EXAMINER.

The **Song Book.** Words and Tunes from the best Poets and Musicians. Selected and arranged by JOHN HULLAH, Professor of Vocal Music in King's College, London.

D 2

" A choice collection of the sterling songs of England, Scotland, and Ireland, with the music of each prefixed to the words. How much true wholesome pleasure such a book can diffuse, and will diffuse, we trust, through many thousand families."—EXAMINER.

La Lyre Française. Selected and arranged, with Notes, by GUSTAVE MASSON, French Master in Harrow School.

A selection of the best French songs and lyrical pieces.

Tom Brown's School Days. By AN OLD BOY.

" A perfect gem of a book. The best and most healthy book about boys for boys that ever was written."—ILLUSTRATED TIMES.

A Book of Worthies. Gathered from the Old Histories and written anew by the Author of "THE HEIR OF REDCLYFFE." With Vignette.

" An admirable addition to an admirable series."—WESTMINSTER REVIEW.

A Book of Golden Thoughts. By HENRY ATTWELL, Knight of the Order of the Oak Crown.

" Mr. Attwell has produced a book of rare value . . . . Happily it is small enough to be carried about in the pocket, and of such a companion it would be difficult to weary."—PALL MALL GAZETTE.

Guesses at Truth. By TWO BROTHERS. New Edition.

MACMILLAN'S

GLOBE LIBRARY.

Beautifully printed on toned paper and bound in cloth extra, gilt edges, price 4s. 6d. *each ; in cloth plain,* 3s. 6d. *Also kept in a variety of calf and morocco bindings at moderate prices.*

Books, Wordsworth says, are

> "the spirit breathed
> By dead men to their kind ; "

and the aim of the publishers of the Globe Library has been to make it possible for the universal kin of English-speaking men to hold communion with the loftiest "spirits of the mighty dead ; " to put within the reach of all classes *complete* and *accurate* editions, carefully and clearly printed upon the best paper, in a convenient form, at a moderate price, of the works of the MASTER-MINDS OF ENGLISH LITERATURE, and occasionally of foreign literature in an attractive English dress.

The Editors, by their scholarship and special study of their authors, are competent to afford every assistance to readers of all kinds : this assistance is rendered by original biographies, glossaries of unusual or obsolete words, and critical and explanatory notes.

The publishers hope, therefore, that these Globe Editions
may prove worthy of acceptance by all classes wherever the
English Language is spoken, and by their universal circulation justify their distinctive epithet; while at the same time
they spread and nourish a common sympathy with nature's
most "finely touched" spirits, and thus help a little to
"make the whole world kin."

The SATURDAY REVIEW *says: " The Globe Editions are admirable
for their scholarly editing, their typographical excellence, their com-
pendious form, and their cheapness." The* BRITISH QUARTERLY
REVIEW *says: "In compendiousness, elegance, and scholarliness,
the Globe Editions of Messrs. Macmillan surpass any popular series
of our classics hitherto given to the public. As near an approach
to miniature perfection as has ever been made."*

Shakespeare's Complete Works. Edited by W. G.
CLARK, M.A., and W. ALDIS WRIGHT, M.A., of Trinity College,
Cambridge, Editors of the "Cambridge Shakespeare." With
Glossary. pp. 1,075. Price 3s. 6d.

*This edition aims at presenting a perfectly reliable text of the complete
works of " the foremost man in all literature." The text is essentially the same as that of the "Cambridge Shakespeare." Appended
is a Glossary containing the meaning of every word in the text which
is either obsolete or is used in an antiquated or unusual sense.
This, combined with the method used to indicate corrupted readings,
serves to a great extent the purpose of notes. The* ATHENÆUM *says
this edition is "a marvel of beauty, cheapness, and compactness.
. . . For the busy man, above all for the working student, this is
the best of all existing Shakespeares." And the* PALL MALL
GAZETTE *observes: "To have produced the complete works of
the world's greatest poet in such a form, and at a price within the
reach of every one, is of itself almost sufficient to give the publishers
a claim to be considered public benefactors."*

Spenser's Complete Works. Edited from the Original
Editions and Manuscripts, by R. MORRIS, with a Memoir by J.
W. HALES, M.A. With Glossary. pp. lv., 736. Price 3s. 6d.

The text of the poems has been reprinted from the earliest known editions, carefully collated with subsequent ones, most of which were published in the poet's lifetime. Spenser's only prose work, his sagacious and interesting " View of the State of Ireland," has been re-edited from three manuscripts belonging to the British Museum. A complete Glossary and a list of all the most important various readings serve to a large extent the purpose of notes explanatory and critical. An exhaustive general Index and a useful " Index of first lines" precede the poems ; and in an Appendix are given Spenser's Letters to Gabriel Harvey. "Worthy—and higher praise it needs not—of the beautiful ' Globe Series.' The work is edited with all the care so noble a poet deserves."—DAILY NEWS.

Sir Walter Scott's Poetical Works. Edited with a

Biographical and Critical Memoir by FRANCIS TURNER PALGRAVE, and copious Notes. pp. xliii., 559. Price 3s. 6d.

" Scott," says Heine, " in his every book, gladdens, tranquillizes, and strengthens my heart." This edition contains the whole of Scott's poetical works, with the exception of one or two short poems. While most of Scott's own notes have been retained, others have been added explaining many historical and topographical allusions ; and original introductions from the pen of a gentleman familiar with Scotch literature and scenery, containing much interesting information, antiquarian, historical, and biographical, are prefixed to the principal poems. " We can almost sympathise with a middle-aged grumbler, who, after reading Mr. Palgrave's memoir and introduction, should exclaim—' Why was there not such an edition of Scott when I was a schoolboy ?' "—GUARDIAN.

Complete Works of Robert Burns.—THE POEMS,

SONGS, AND LETTERS, edited from the best Printed and Manuscript Authorities, with Glossarial Index, Notes, and a Biographical Memoir by ALEXANDER SMITH. pp. lxii., 636. Price 3s. 6d.

Burns's poems and songs need not circulate exclusively among Scotchmen, but should be read by all who wish to know the multitudinous capabilities of the Scotch language, and who have the capacity of appreciating the exquisite expression of all kinds of human feeling—rich pawky humour, keen wit, withering satire, genuine pathos, pure passionate love. The exhaustive glossarial index and the copious notes will make all the purely Scotch poems intelligible even to an Englishman. Burns's letters must be read by all who desire fully to appreciate the poet's character, to see it on all its many sides. Explanatory notes are prefixed to most of these letters, and Burns's Journals kept during his Border and Highland Tours, are appended. Following the prefixed biography by the editor, is a Chronological Table of Burns's Life and Works. "Admirable in all respects."—SPECTATOR. *"The cheapest, the most perfect, and the most interesting edition which has ever been published."*—BELL'S MESSENGER.

Robinson Crusoe. Edited after the Original Editions, with a Biographical Introduction by HENRY KINGSLEY. pp. xxxi., 607. Price 3s. 6d.

Of this matchless truth-like story, it is scarcely possible to find an unabridged edition. This edition may be relied upon as containing the whole of "Robinson Crusoe" as it came from the pen of its author, without mutilation, and with all peculiarities religiously preserved. These points, combined with its handsome paper, large clear type, and moderate price, ought to render this par excellence *the "Globe," the Universal edition of Defoe's fascinating narrative. "A most excellent and in every way desirable edition."*—COURT CIRCULAR. *"Macmillan's ' Globe' Robinson Crusoe is a book to have and to keep."*—MORNING STAR.

Goldsmith's Miscellaneous Works. Edited, with Biographical Introduction, by Professor MASSON. pp. lx., 695. Globe 8vo. 3s. 6d.

This volume comprehends the whole of the prose and poetical works of this most genial of English authors, those only being excluded which are mere compilations. They are all accurately reprinted from the most reliable editions. The faithfulness, fulness, and literary merit of the biography are sufficiently attested by the name of its author, Professor Masson. It contains many interesting anecdotes which will give the reader an insight into Goldsmith's character, and many graphic pictures of the literary life of London during the middle of last century. "Such an admirable compendium of the facts of Goldsmith's life, and so careful and minute a delineation of the mixed traits of his peculiar character as to be a very model of a literary biography in little."—SCOTSMAN.

Pope's Poetical Works. Edited, with Notes and Introductory Memoir, by ADOLPHUS WILLIAM WARD, M.A., Fellow of St. Peter's College, Cambridge, and Professor of History in Owens College, Manchester. pp. lii., 508. Globe 8vo. 3s. 6d.

This edition contains all Pope's poems, translations, and adaptations, —his now superseded Homeric translations alone being omitted. The text, carefully revised, is taken from the best editions; Pope's own use of capital letters and apostrophised syllables, frequently necessary to an understanding of his meaning, has been preserved; while his uncertain spelling and his frequently perplexing interpunctuation have been judiciously amended. Abundant notes are added, including Pope's own, the best of those of previous editors, and many which are the result of the study and research of the present editor. The introductory Memoir will be found to shed considerable light on the political, social, and literary life of the period in which Pope filled so large a space. The LITERARY CHURCHMAN *remarks: "The editor's own notes and introductory memoir are excellent, the memoir alone would be cheap and well worth buying at the price of the whole volume."*

Dryden's Poetical Works. Edited, with a Memoir, Revised Text, and Notes, by W. D. CHRISTIE, M.A., of Trinity College, Cambridge. pp. lxxxvii., 662. Globe 8vo. 3s. 6d.

*A study of Dryden's works is absolutely necessary to anyone who wishes to understand thoroughly, not only the literature, but also the political and religious history of the eventful period when he lived and reigned as literary dictator. In this edition of his works, which comprises several specimens of his vigorous prose, the text has been thoroughly corrected and purified from many misprints and small changes often materially affecting the sense, which had been allowed to slip in by previous editors. The old spelling has been retained where it is not altogether strange or repulsive. Besides an exhaustive Glossary, there are copious Notes, critical, historical, biographical, and explanatory; and the biography contains the results of considerable original research, which has served to shed light on several hitherto obscure circumstances connected with the life and parentage of the poet. "An admirable edition, the result of great research and of a careful revision of the text. The memoir prefixed contains, within less than ninety pages, as much sound criticism and as comprehensive a biography as the student of Dryden need desire."—*PALL MALL GAZETTE.

Cowper's Poetical Works. Edited, with Notes and Biographical Introduction, by WILLIAM BENHAM, Vicar of Addington and Professor of Modern History in Queen's College, London. pp. lxxiii., 536. Globe 8vo. 3*s.* 6*d.*

This volume contains, arranged under seven heads, the whole of Cowper's own poems, including several never before published, and all his translations except that of Homer's "Iliad." The text is taken from the original editions, and Cowper's own notes are given at the foot of the page, while many explanatory notes by the editor himself are appended to the volume. In the very full Memoir it will be found that much new light has been thrown on some of the most difficult passages of Cowper's spiritually chequered life. "Mr. Benham's edition of Cowper is one of permanent value. The biographical introduction is excellent, full of information, singularly neat and readable and modest—indeed too modest in its comments. The notes are concise and accurate, and the editor has been able to discover and introduce some hitherto unprinted matter. Altogether the book is a very excellent one."—SATURDAY REVIEW.

Morte d'Arthur.—SIR THOMAS MALORY'S BOOK OF KING ARTHUR AND OF HIS NOBLE KNIGHTS OF THE ROUND TABLE. The original Edition of CAXTON, revised for Modern Use. With an Introduction by Sir EDWARD STRACHEY, Bart. pp. xxxvii., 509. Globe 8vo. 3*s.* 6*d.*

This volume contains the cream of the legends of chivalry which have gathered round the shadowy King Arthur and his Knights of the Round Table. Tennyson has drawn largely on them in his cycle of Arthurian Idylls. The language is simple and quaint as that of the Bible, and the many stories of knightly adventure of which the book is made up, are fascinating as those of the "Arabian Nights." The great moral of the book is to "do after the good, and leave the evil." There was a want of an edition of the work at a moderate price, suitable for ordinary readers, and especially for boys: such an edition the present professes to be. The Introduction contains an account of the Origin and Matter of the book, the Text and its several Editions, and an Essay on Chivalry, tracing its history from its origin to its decay. Notes are appended, and a

Glossary of such words as require explanation. "It is with perfect confidence that we recommend this edition of the old romance to every class of readers."—PALL MALL GAZETTE.

The Works of Virgil. Rendered into English Prose, with Introductions, Notes, Running Analysis, and an Index. By JAMES LONSDALE, M.A., late Fellow and Tutor of Balliol College, Oxford, and Classical Professor in King's College, London ; and SAMUEL LEE, M.A., Latin Lecturer at University College, London. pp. 288. Price 3*s*. 6*d*.

The publishers believe that an accurate and readable translation of all the works of Virgil is perfectly in accordance with the object of the " Globe Library." A new prose-translation has therefore been made by two competent scholars, who have rendered the original faithfully into simple Bible-English, without paraphrase ; and at the same time endeavoured to maintain as far as possible the rhythm and majestic flow of the original. On this latter point the DAILY TELEGRAPH *says, " The endeavour to preserve in some degree a rhythm in the prose rendering is almost invariably successful and pleasing in its effect ;" and the* EDUCATIONAL TIMES, *that it " may be readily recommended as a model for young students for rendering the poet into English." The General Introduction will be found full of interesting information as to the life of Virgil, the history of opinion concerning his writings, the notions entertained of him during the Middle Ages, editions of his works, his influence on modern poets and on education. To each of his works is prefixed a critical and explanatory introduction, and important aid is afforded to the thorough comprehension of each production by the running Analysis. Appended is an Index of all the proper names and the most important subjects occurring throughout the poems and introductions. " A more complete edition of Virgil in English it is scarcely possible to conceive than the scholarly work before us."* —GLOBE.

R. CLAY, SONS, AND TAYLOR, PRINTERS, BREAD STREET HILL.

www.ingramcontent.com/pod-product-compliance
Lightning Source LLC
Chambersburg PA
CBHW032258280326
41932CB00009B/615